A
HISTORY OF THE ART
OF WRITING

THE MACMILLAN COMPANY
NEW YORK · BOSTON · CHICAGO · DALLAS
ATLANTA · SAN FRANCISCO

MACMILLAN & CO., LIMITED
LONDON · BOMBAY · CALCUTTA
MELBOURNE

THE MACMILLAN CO. OF CANADA, LTD.
TORONTO

A
HISTORY OF THE ART
OF WRITING

BY

WILLIAM A. MASON

WITH MANY ILLUSTRATIONS

New York
THE MACMILLAN COMPANY
1928

P
211
M3

12131

CONTENTS

CHAPTER   PAGE

I   EVIDENCES OF IDEOGRAPHY IN OUR WRITTEN LAN-
      GUAGE   1

II   PRIMITIVE PICTURE WRITING   18

III   PICTURE WRITING OF THE NORTH AMERICAN IN-
       DIANS   60

IV   PICTURE WRITING OF THE ANCIENT MEXICANS .   112

V   HIEROGLYPHIC WRITING OF THE SOUTH SEA IS-
      LANDERS   146

VI   CHINESE IDEOGRAPHIC WRITING   154

VII   HIEROGLYPHIC WRITING OF THE ANCIENT EGYP-
        TIANS   185

VIII   BABYLONIAN AND ASSYRIAN CUNEIFORM WRITING .   223

IX   THE HIEROGLYPHIC SYSTEM OF WRITING OF THE
       ANCIENT HITTITES   267

X   THE ALPHABETIC WRITING OF THE PHŒNICIANS .   286

XI   PRE-PHŒNICIAN SYLLABARIES AND MEDITERRA-
       NEAN SCRIPT   309

XII   THE GREEK ALPHABET   337

XIII   THE ROMAN ALPHABET   372

XIV   WRITING IN THE MIDDLE AGES   392

XV   EUROPEAN ALPHABETS DERIVED FROM THE GREEK .   443

XVI   THE AGE OF PRINTING   453

      BIBLIOGRAPHY   491

      INDEX   499

A HISTORY OF THE ART OF WRITING

CHAPTER I

EVIDENCES OF IDEOGRAPHY IN OUR WRITTEN LANGUAGE

EVERY one who has read a printed page of English, or any European writing, doubtless has wondered how the letters or words that he reads — or uses in writing to record his own thoughts — ever came to be used as the representations or symbols of spoken words. Our processes of thought in the ever-widening environment of these busy, modern days have become so automatic that we are apt to lose sight of the historical evidences of the long, constructive past written large over the pages of the voluminous present. That there is a whole volume of human history back of every one of the twenty-six alphabetic characters with which we write our thoughts may be a new idea to most readers of this book. Yet one will find as he investigates the subject that these simple symbols, apparently so arbitrary and meaningless to our latter-day eyes, are replete with the linguistic, even the domestic, history of countless generations of our remote ancestors. He will discover as he has unfolded to him their life-history that these characters have been designed, shaped and molded by many successive artists toiling under palm and pine; each one in his turn modifying, altering and simplifying them, using them for the day and generation of his own race to pass them on as a priceless inheritance to other nations.

Let any one for a moment scan the pages of a printed book — this one for instance — or any book in a European or Asiatic language, except the Chinese or its derived scripts, and he will discover what every intelligent person has known from childhood, that the intended thought of the writer is conveyed to the mind of the reader by means of printed characters of abstract form, which represent spoken words and which " spell out " the words phonetically, syllable for syllable, as they are pronounced. It is true that our own English language has many startling exceptions to this general rule, sufficient to make it the despair of all foreigners. Nevertheless, the principle holds true, with the most trivial exceptions, for the main body of the text of every book through all its pages from cover to cover. The printed words that we read, which are made up of the present, purely arbitrary characters which we know as alphabetic signs, convey to the mind through these abstract symbols word-pictures comparable to the primitive ideographs — idea-pictures — which were the ancient precursors and prototypes of these symbols. These printed or written words of the classical parchments, the medieval manuscripts and the modern books, it must be remembered, stand for the phonetic names of the intended things, representing them to the mind, but bearing no resemblance to them in form. By long association, however, these word-symbols, despite their apparently arbitrary character, call up in the mind of the reader the corporate things themselves; not alone their names, but their forms, qualities or attributes that the thousands of words in the language have come to represent. They are idea-pictures as well as sound-pictures. In fact they were idea-pictures first, ages before the primitive culture of advancing man arrived at the conception of using these pictures as signs to represent phonetic sounds.

So unconscious has this long association become, whereby tangible things and abstract qualities are recalled by arbitrary symbols, that it probably will be a matter of considerable surprise to many of our readers to learn that there ever was a time when writing was anything different. But it will be the purpose of this book to prove by incontestible evidence that practically all systems of writing can be traced back through successive stages of development to a primitive age, long anterior to the invention of letters, when all records were merely the pictures of the things or ideas expressed. We have only to look about us in the world to discover that we have had quite up to the present generation, in the records of the aborigines of our own land, in the writing of the Chinese and of other nations, the contemporaneous use by different peoples the world over, of almost every phase of this world-wide and age-long evolution of the wonderful art of writing. For national development in the matter of writing has been most unequal. Some nations for one cause or another — racial backwardness, isolation, servitude or other unhappy causes contributing to it — never to this day have evolved any system of written record; while other nations, some even contiguous through all the centuries to these laggards in civilization, invented and practiced the art of writing and enjoyed its beneficent results many millenniums ago. The African tribes, as is well known, though in contact with Egyptian civilization and its high culture over three thousand years before Christ, have failed up to the present day to develop any indigenous system of writing; while the history of Babylonian writing runs back to the fifth pre-Christian millennium. It is probable that the Homeric epics were chanted from memory during the early years of the second millennium before Christ, ere contact with the Phœnicians conferred upon the Greeks the art of perpetuating their heroics in visible, graphic form. The Romans, just before the birth of Christ, finding the Gothic barbarians of northern and western Europe illiterate and possessed of no other means of record than tallies of knotted cord and notched wood, taught them to write with the Roman letters. And the descendants of these same Europeans in the 16th and 17th centuries, coming in contact with the aborigines of this Western Continent, discovered them like children studying the primer of writing and drawing the pictures of the things and ideas that they desired to remember or to impart to others.

It doubtless will be a still greater surprise to the reader to be told that there are yet retained in our language not a few of the primitive pictures that antedate writing, altered and modified, to be sure, through ages of use, during which interval they have become greatly simplified and conventionalized. All written languages contain these silent witnesses of their pictorial origin, existing like the persistence of ancestral traits in individual tribes; or to be nearer our point, like the roots of their spoken words converging different dialects back to a common linguistic parent.

The reader will notice in the pages of this book, besides the alphabetic characters which we hope to be able to show later on probably are the corrupted forms of primitive pictures, other characters used as the representation of words that are not phonetic at all, but at a casual glance seem as arbitrary as the letters themselves, the component parts of printed words. They are in reality conventionalized pictures, in many cases retaining an indubitable resemblance to the things which they represent. After turning the title page the reader will come to the table of contents, and here at once he will find two kinds of characters, neither alphabetic nor phonetic. The chapters: one, two, three, etc., are represented by perfectly straight marks: I, II, III, etc. These, as all know, are the numerals used in the Roman system of notation. They do not " spell " the names of the numbers, but literally picture them. No mode of representation could be simpler or more elementary. The characters are nothing less than pictures of the fingers held up in counting; and they indeed are called "digits," from the Latin *digitus*, the finger. The numeral I represents one finger, II represents two fingers, and III represents three fingers. V, which represents five, is beyond question a highly conventionalized picture of the extended hand with its four fingers and the thumb. We shall endeavor to show throughout this book how pictorial characters and their lineal descendants, written symbols, have constantly undergone simplification from the original pictures through less and less complex forms until the final, simplest, abstract stage has been reached. To conclude the analysis, every school boy knows that IV is one less than V, and that VI, VII and VIII respectively are one, two and three digits more than V. X is a conventionalized picture of the two hands together, with the thumbs and fingers extended, somewhat resembling a mitten; while IX represents one digit less than X.

Opposite the chapter numbers in the table of contents will be seen the page numbers: 1, 2, 3, 4, 5, etc. Here again are characters wholly different from either the Roman numerals or the letters of the Roman alphabet — our classic inheritance. They are the Arabic system of notation. The characters have no phonetic value whatever.

They are devoid of any present, illustrative significance, as the Roman numerals. Their curving lines more closely resemble written script, being cursive in general character. They are to-day obviously pure symbols, but the last phase of a long development or transformation, possibly beginning in a picture of the idea in primitive days, and gradually simplified and conventionalized until finally reduced to the bare elements that we now see.[1] Their history and meaning are buried in the remote past of that mystical and romantic East that has left us so many other literary and scientific legacies and enigmas. The Arabs introduced them into Europe, but they probably obtained them from the Hindus. Herodotus informs us that they — the Arabs — borrowed them from India. We likewise are indebted to the peoples of the East: the Arabs, Egyptians, and it may be to peoples as remote as the ancient Chaldeans, for other arbitrary signs in common use as the symbols for ideas. It will be interesting before we begin to unravel the more complex mystery that surrounds the history of our alphabetic characters to refer to some of these symbols; for they are the survivals of a hoary antiquity long anterior to the age of writing, when pictures only were employed in " the short but simple annals " of the early races of remote antiquity. It will be of great interest to us in the prosecution of our quest to find that we still use for certain ideas pictures — corrupted it is true — that stand for these ideas not as printed words stand for the phonetic counterpart of spoken words, but as the pictorial repre-

---

[1] A more or less plausible explanation of the origin of the first three Arabic numerals is that they were derived from the representation of one, two and three horizontal strokes with a cursive glide line connecting them, owing to rapid sketching, thus:

sentation of the very things or ideas intended, and which they resemble in form or through analogy.

Let us turn to the dictionary for a few moments, for there we shall find a ready list of all the symbolic signs in use in our language. Probably no signs in any system of writing are more primitive than those which denote celestial and terrestrial feaures: — as the sun, moon, the planets, the arch of the sky, mountains, flowing water, trees, etc.; and it may be remarked here without digression to substantiate the fact by illustration — for that will be done later on — that there is a remarkable similarity in these signs in the many different world-systems of writing employed by peoples geographically isolated from one another and untouched or uninfluenced by each other's culture. The signs of the zodiac, given in most almanacs, are perhaps the oldest symbols that we have. Their origin is not yet definitely traced, but they are known greatly to antedate the classic period of Rome. There is a large zodiac painted on the walls of the Temple of Dendera in Egypt, dating back to the early days of imperial Rome, which has the identical objects: the ram, the bull, the twins, etc., pictured in much the same order in which we employ them to-day. They must have been in use possibly centuries prior to this period, descending from an ancient ancestry. In Indian art zodiacs are met with at a very early period; and in Babylonia as far back as the time of Nebuchadrezzar I (1130-1115 B. C.) boundary stones were carved with the representations of the heavenly bodies and stellar deities. We find the sun, moon, stars, and sometimes the archer, the scorpion, the goat, etc., carved at the top of these Assyrian boundary stones above the boundary descriptions, as a dedication or invocation to their heavenly deities. Fig. 1 is the illustration of a boundary stone of Nebuchadrezzar I, found in ancient Babylonia, reproduced from " A New Boundary Stone of Nebuchadrezzar I, from Nippur," by Wm. J. Hinke, Ph.D., University of Pennsylvania, 1907. Among the many signs shown in this particular example of invocation to the gods we distinguish the sun, moon, stars and the divinities indicated by the archer and the scorpion.

In the left-hand column of Fig. 2 the reader will find the zodiacal signs in their calendar order with the significant name of each given, so that he may judge for himself how far, even at the early period when we first meet with them, the signs had become modified from their original pictorial form to the highly conventionalized form shown.

Obviously No. 1 represents the horns of a ram; No. 2 the head and horns of a bull. No. 3 is a conventional representation of the ancient wooden statues of Castor and Pollux, even showing the top and bottom cross pieces of wood used to hold the uprights together. No. 4 represents the claws of a crab. No. 5 is a crude representation of a lion's tail. No. 6 probably is a literary abbreviation, being a corruption of the Greek word for " virgin,"— παρθενας. No. 7 is a crude representation of a balance. No. 8 is thought by some to be the legs and tail of a scorpion. No. 9 is the arrow of the Archer with a piece of the bow attached. No. 10 is difficult to analyze. It may be a literary corruption like No. 6, but Dr. Isaac Taylor [1] has pointed out that " it preserves the whole outline of Capricornus, the small circle being the head of the goat with the fore legs below and the body and tail extending to the left." Considering, however, how striking a characteristic a goat's beard is and how it sweeps back

[1] " The Alphabet. An Account of the Origin and Development of Letters." Isaac Taylor. 1883.

Fig. 1. Boundary stone of Nebuchadrezzar I, with signs of the heavenly bodies and celestial divinities.

from his chin, if this be a conventional picture of a goat, the long curving line on the right undoubtedly seems to represent the beard. It certainly has its characteristic swing and action. No. 11 is a true ideographic symbol like most of the others, really a conventional representation of the waves of water, a symbol almost universal in its usage, as will be explained and illustrated later on. No. 12 clearly is two fishes tied together.

In the astronomical signs used in almanacs for the sun, moon, planets, etc., we have illustrations of other pictorial or conventional symbols representing directly or metaphorically, by form or significance, the objects intended. The more prominent of these signs are illustrated in the right-hand column of Fig. 2. The signs for sun, moon, star and comet are obvious. They probably have been employed as ideographs since men first began to record annals and events, ages before syllabic or alphabetic writing was invented. We shall come across some of these several times in the signs employed for writing by different nations widely separated. (It is interesting to note in passing that " sun " in Chinese, which we shall soon show is a species of picture-writing, is the " face in the heavens.") Mercury is represented by his caduceus, which he carried in his hand in his flying embassies for the gods. Venus is metaphorically represented by her looking-glass. The earth is shown with its meridian and equator. Mars is symbolized by his shield and spear. The sign for Jupiter is a hieroglyphic representation of an eagle, Jove's sacred bird. The reader may note a resemblance in this symbol, more than fanciful, to the Babylonian sign for bird, shown in the third character in the second vertical row of signs in Fig. 80. Some authorities consider this peculiar sign a representation of Jupiter's thunder-bolt. The reader may note a distant resemblance between it and the sign that physicians mark on their prescriptions: ℞. This seems to be a custom which is believed to have prevailed from early Roman pagan days of invoking the help of Jupiter for the propitious operation of medicinal remedies.[1]

The planet Saturn is symbolized by a sickle, the sacred emblem of Saturn. The sign for Uranus records the name of its discoverer, Herschel, which for a long time was the proper name of the planet. This is a striking example

Aries, the Ram	Sun
Taurus, the Bull	Moon
Gemini, the Twins	Star
Cancer, the Crab	Comet
Leo, the Lion	Mercury
Virgo, the Virgin	Venus
Libra, the Scales	Earth
Scorpio, the Scorpion	Mars
Sagittarius, the Archer	Jupiter
Capricornus, the Goat	Saturn
Aquarius, the Water Carrier	Uranus
Pisces, the Fishes	Neptune

Fig. 2. Ideographic symbols used in astronomy. The signs of the zodiac and the heavenly bodies.

[1] Possibly a more reasonable explanation of this sign is that it is an abbreviation — Rx — for "Rex" (Jupiter Rex).

of the quite casual perpetuation of an historical fact, one in the course of ages quite apt to be forgotten, especially during troublous times; and it has been in consequence of the unhappy interruptions of cultural development from time to time, through desolating warfare, that so much has been irretrievably lost and forgotten that might have assisted us so materially in this history. It is highly probable that not a few written characters in the languages of the past have originated in a manner equally as novel as this sign for Uranus. Many modern Chinese characters appear to date back to an origin quite as fortuitous. Neptune is most appropriately symbolized by a trident, the emblem of the god of the sea.

There are other arbitrary signs in daily use, which, while not pictorial in their general character or origin, show the strong tendency in languages toward conventionalization and corruption of preëxisting forms. It is this tendency which doubtless has operated from the earliest times to transform our alphabetic characters from their historic, pictorial prototypes into their present meaningless, arbitrary forms. We will present a few of these arbitrary symbols yet lingering in our written language and in daily use by us. The dollar sign, $, probably is a modified figure 8, denoting a " piece of eight "— eight reals — a Spanish coin equivalent to our dollar. The character £, " pound sterling," is merely a capital L with a mark across it, and is an abbreviation of the Latin word *libra*. The character ℔, " pound weight," is formed from the first and third letters of the same Latin word, with a cross line to give it a distinctive character. The character ℘ is another form of P, the initial letter of the Latin word *per*, " by." The character ¶, denoting a paragraph in writing, is the exact reverse in form and color of the letter P. The section mark, §, is believed to be derived from the initial letters ∫∫ (old style) of the Latin words *signum sectionis,* " the sign of the section." The character & is a ligature combining the letters of the Latin word *et,* " and." The old style, *&,* distinctly shows the two letters, though in a somewhat involved and corrupted form. The sign @ is a graphic modification of the Latin word *ad,* " at " or " to." The interrogation mark ?, is described by Bilderdijk to be the representation of the first and last letters of the Latin word *quaestio,* " question," placed one over the other, as was quite common in writing abbreviations; thus: Q . The same authority also says that the exclamation mark ! is formed from the Latin word *io,* " joy," written vertically; thus: I . This may seem rather fanciful, but abundant examples of written characters made up in this figurative manner may be found in the archaic symbols of ancient languages and in phonetic characters in-the-making, like the Chinese, long since arrested in the development of its written characters at an early stage. Indeed, the figurative is the next stage of development after the employment of purely representative or ideographic signs.

There are many other symbols used in mathematics, music, chemistry, etc., as +, plus; —, minus; ×, times; $, a clef; and so on; which would be only a digression further to enumerate, but which retain in our written speech to-day the archaic principle of graphic representation. They represent the idea, not the word, and picture it to the mind often in a figurative form. It must be admitted, however, when all is told, considering the many thousands of words and characters in our written language, that there are comparatively few survivals to remind us of the former rich, graphic nature of the writing of those distant peoples of antiquity from whom our ancestors or precursors received their letters. Yet the sum of

all the evidence is quite too overwhelming to be doubted
that our present alphabetic signs are but the corruptions
of primitive pictures, each having lost through the attri-
tion of ages its peculiar pictorial character, having passed
through the transforming hands of many different na-
tionalities and races, each contributing its share of altera-
tion or modification, until they have become conventionalized and simplified into their present, latest arbitrary
form. We cannot say their last form, for future generations may yet mold and modify these alphabetic signs as
past generations of men have done; but we may confidently assert that no further radical change ever will or
can be effected. Within the last one hundred years the
old-style characters ſ , " s "; yᵉ, " the "; &, " and ";
have become obsolete; and it is already becoming the
vogue in certain types to omit the dot over the i. Possibly the cross to the t will before long be retired into
oblivion and other slight and unimportant modifications
at present undreamt may be made. Yet it may safely be
claimed that the final chapter is practically completed,
and that the long historic development of our written
characters forever is a closed book.

We also have a few words still lingering in our language, historic echoes from the past of our mother tongue,
that speak most eloquently of facts concerning whole
chapters of the early history of the materials and tools
with which our early precursors carried on the art of
writing. These words afford corroborative proof of and
establish in our imagination the ancient methods whereby
written records have been preserved in the various materials in which they have been inscribed and handed down
to us. A few examples of these words, freighted with
historic import, must suffice. " Paper " in its derivation
recalls the old Egyptian mode of writing on a material

made from layers of the pith of the papyrus reed. The classic name for it, *biblos,* has given us our word for bible. " Library " is derived from the Latin word *liber,* the bark of a tree used for paper. " Book " is from the Anglo-Saxon *boc,* " beech "; the bark of this tree having been employed by our immediate English ancestors for writing upon. " Tablet " comes from the Latin word *tabula,* " board," upon which writing was inscribed in the classic times by writing with a stylus through a coating of wax. We know that in Rome the laws were written on boards of oak which were displayed in the Forum.

There are other examples that could be instanced, but as they are apart from our main inquiry we will offer but a few concluding witnesses. " Pen " is derived from the Latin *penna,* a feather; " style " descends from the Latin *stylus,* the instrument with which the classic authors wrote upon their wax tablets; and " quill " comes from the old English word *quylle,* a reed. Perhaps no word more loudly proclaims its origin in the ancient usages of writing and book-making than our modern word " volume," which is derived from the Latin *volumen,* a roll. We know from classic sculptures and wall paintings, and have had it confirmed again and again by papyrus and parchment rolls preserved in the dry sands of Egypt, that the roll was the customary form of preserving written documents. The Egyptians themselves in their hieroglyphics employed the picture of a papyrus roll tied with a string to indicate documents, papyri and official writing generally.

Thus we find surviving in our language to-day words that tell the history of the old methods and processes of writing as regards the " tools of the trade." This record just as surely survives in this form and is as historically authentic as the same facts substantiated by ancient pictures and by the very books themselves that have come down to us from the ancient peoples who practiced the art of writing in the materials recorded by these surviving words. But in the matter of the evidences of a pictorial origin of our alphabetic letters, the very remoteness of the age, the fact that it was the earliest stage of the art of writing, and the impossibility of conceiving that men in this stage of development could so far analyze their own processes of growth as to be able to leave any record of it, precludes the possibility of ever finding anything written on the subject by those living in the formative days. It is the internal evidence alone that must suffice and convince us. We do not in fact need any further record of the origin of writing than that which we shall be able to read in the printed characters themselves when we shall have investigated the many diverse forms of the art of paleography as seen in the inscriptions of the different peoples of antiquity, of which authentic copies easily may be consulted in almost any library or museum. There are many missing links in the chain of development, and chapters in the story are wanting here and there; but in the main it is a well-connected story, and one that is full to the brim with living, human interest.

It will require no special appeal to the reader's imagination to foreshadow to him that this story of the evolution of writing deals with one of the most momentous agencies in the intellectual advancement of man. No other influence that man ever exerted has reacted so powerfully upon the development of his mental and spiritual nature as the invention of writing. Without the art of writing man would still be a savage as benighted as the unlettered heathen who still inhabit Darkest Africa. Without writing to conserve current ideas and ideals and transmit them to posterity, all advance in intellectual attainments, all uplift in spiritual thought that was not transmitted through the uncertain and errant instrumentality of memory would be lost. The acquisition of the art of writing above everything else distinguishes the civilized nations from the barbaric tribes; and whenever paleographic evidences are first met with in the life-history of any nation, we may confidently assert that the people practicing the art of writing, however crude the signs employed, were well advanced in the scale of civilization. It is this fact that makes any inquiry into the origin of writing a peculiarly interesting study, and the person who approaches the subject sympathetically will amply be rewarded, for he will see at every stage the noble struggle, pathetic at times, of man's emergence from his primitive barbarism and awakening to a conscious sense of his obligations to others, and of his ultimate high destiny.

CHAPTER II

PRIMITIVE PICTURE WRITING

PRIMITIVE men living in small, segregated communities, separated by mountain or water barriers from alien tribes for whom they entertained only feelings of hostile suspicion, had little need of the art of writing. Their lives were uneventful, and their annals, such as they had, were transmitted orally from father to son. For countless ages man must have existed without any means of written record. All that was preserved of his intellectual or moral advancement was attained solely through the medium of oral tradition. It has been said that necessity is the mother of invention. Until the necessity for writing arose, the very idea of any kind of record was unthought of and the means of carrying it out were still further from the conception of primitive man. The members of the aboriginal tribes when away on hunting or fishing excursions rarely ventured beyond the natural boundaries of their tribal lands, making verbal communication with each other always a matter of immediate possibility. Around the domestic hearth the daily events of the chase, affairs of the family, social and moral virtues and other concerns of the day, were discussed, and whatever knowledge of natural laws or of social well-being had been deduced from the affairs of their tribal life was transmitted verbally from parent to child and lived traditionally in the memories of successive generations. The historic and religious traditions of the various tribes, embodying their past history and their relations to the great universe about them and its mysterious cosmogony, as they viewed it, were chanted by the magicians and seers of the tribes at the times of their religious ceremonies.

These seers, shamans or medicine men, were men selected for their general intelligence, sagacity or strong personality; and were naturally endowed with unusual mnemonic ability. These were the early days before the memory had become weakened by its dependence upon written texts, when the full performance of its function was indispensable to the proper preservation of aboriginal knowledge. At these religious ceremonials the young men of the tribe were instructed concerning the mystic rituals, and were taught the great epics of the tribe to transmit them in their turn to others. Thus was knowledge conserved in the ages before writing or record making was understood or demanded.

History records that the ancient Sanscrit Vedas containing the religious dogmas and the moral and legal codes of the Ind were transmitted for ages, from generation to generation, through the unwritten epics of the priestly caste. The very name "veda," from *vid,* " to know "— of old applied to them — indicates that they were the vehicle of the transmission of knowledge. The oldest of these Vedas, the Rigveda and the Sâmaveda, are hymns, chants and tunes in metric composition, and are of marked archaism and simplicity as compared with the later prose Vedas. This affords infallible evidence of the fact that these earlier Vedas were chanted by the priests before writing was invented, the memory being assisted by the metrical composition. The Homeric epics, the Iliad and the Odyssey, have every evidence — historical and literary — of having been composed in the childhood of Greece. Homer was an itinerant minstrel, who gathered together in his incomparable poems all the knowledge of his day, reciting them before the youth of Greece to inspire them with virtue and valor. The poems became the chief authority in matters of history, religion and politics. They made a nation, a religion and a language. The minnesingers of Germany, who sang the verses of the Nibelungen Lied and the Gudrun, and the bards of Gaul, Briton, Ireland and Scotland, and those who chanted the skalds of Scandinavia, all had their part in disseminating knowledge before writing was known.

In the more primitive life, as man advanced in the scale of civilization and tribal life became more complex, and as tribes came into mutual contact with each other, enlarging their horizon of life and action, verbal speech proved inadequate as a means of communication. Also wars of self-protection or of conquest being waged between tribes speaking different languages, it became necessary to adopt codes of communication which could be mutually understood by various tribes. Since the combatants spoke in different tongues, what could be more natural at first than the adoption of a code of gesture signs? This is precisely what came about. An elaborate system of signs and gestures came into use whereby conferences were carried on and treaties enacted between the various alien tribes. This primary use of the hands in expressing emotions, actions and commands, through gestures of the sign-language, doubtless has been with many tribes and races the immediately antecedent stage — we may safely say the preparatory stage — of writing. It is more than an idle metaphor to liken this sign-language to actual writing in the air with the hands. We shall show later on that it was not so much the movements of the hands as the picture of the movements that prefigured in many cases the subsequent written signs of which they were the prototypes.

We have in our own American aborigines when they first came under the observation of Europeans ample corroboration of this precedent stage of sign-language before writing. Capt. W. P. Clark in his interesting book " The Indian Sign-Language " speaks of Iron Hawk, a Sioux Chief, who said to him: " The whites have had the power given them by the Great Spirit to read and write and convey information in this way. He gave us the power to talk with our hands and arms and to send information with the mirror, blanket and pony far away; and when we meet Indians who have a different spoken language from ours we can talk to them in signs." The character and extent of this primitive means of communication among the North American Indians cannot be realized by one unfamiliar with life on the Plains. Elaborate speeches by signs embracing every idea desired were carried on in this language. Ultimately, as the reader will see in the ensuing illustrations, many of these gestures reappeared in their pictographic records.

A single illustration of this sign-language must suffice. It is quoted from " Twenty Years Among Our Hostile Indians," by J. Lee Humfreville. The author says: " The sign language was very figurative. For instance, if an Indian desired to say that you were not truthful, he would touch his tongue with one finger and hold up two fingers towards you, signifying that you were double-tongued, that is, untruthful. If he wished to say that a given place was distant two, three, or more days' journey, he would twirl the fingers of both hands one over the other like a wheel rolling, inclining his head as if asleep and hold up as many fingers as there were ' sleeps,' meaning nights; thus indicating the number of days of travel necessary to reach the place in question. If he desired to refer to the past, he would extend the hand in front with the index finger pointed, drawing his arm back with a screw motion, meaning a long time back. If he intended to refer to the future, he would put his hand with the index finger at his back, pushing it forward with a screw motion, thus indicating a distant time in the future." There can be no doubt that sign-language is a more or less universal language, and probably has been the primitive medium of intercommunication in the intercourse of all early, uncivilized races. We learn that the original Chinese pictures that preceded writing were called *ku-wan,*— literally " gesture pictures," and that many of them were retained in the later picture-writing.

A very large number of the determinative signs that accompany so many of the hieroglyphic words on the Egyptian monuments are graphic pictures of human or animal forms or their parts, and are descriptive of the words which they depict. To illustrate a few of the many thousands of cases, in the following words, in addition to the proper, phonetic hieroglyphs which completely spell out the word, there is a pictorial index sign set beside it more fully to define its special meaning: — as " to dance," by a girl dancing; " he said," by a man pointing at his mouth; " to rest," by a recumbent figure; " to ascend," by a person walking up stairs; " to go," or " to turn," by figures walking in these different directions; " judgment," by an eye; " wonder," by a man with his hands upstretched; and so on, in hundreds of word-characters in the Egyptian hieroglyphics. How very human all this is! Though these sculptures are thousands of years old, they are as modern in spirit as though executed but yesterday. Human nature varies but little from age to age. We may instance one sign in primitive sign-language,— that of negation. It is well-nigh universal to express this meaning by extending the two hands at arm's length, implying " empty." From this gesture both the Egyptians and the Mayas, people of different continents, have obtained their ideographic signs for negation, as shown in the accompanying cuts. The first one is from the Egyptian hieroglyphics, the second one is from the Maya. The latter sign with the fingers of the hand represented will be seen again at the top of the combined sign for South in Fig. 46.

Another step in the development of writing was unconsciously taken by early man in the peculiar use of totem signs, so universally employed by many semi-civilized races. This was actually a definite system of record, — really a primitive genealogy. A totem is a character, generally pictorial, employed by savage peoples to indicate the clan, gens or family to which an individual belongs. The custom is almost universal among savage tribes to select the form of some animal, fish or bird, as a totem to distinguish between the different clans and families. These totems are frequently tattooed on the body in brilliant colors or painted upon the possessions of the family clan. The Haida Indians residing in British Columbia employ a wonderful variety of these signs which are tattooed upon the bodies of both men and women, or carved or painted on their implements or utensils. Fig. 3 is an illustration of the picturesque totem poles, elaborately carved with grotesque sculptures and bearing the clan and family totems of the Tsimshian Indians at Kitwankool, British Columbia. They very much resemble in their grotesqueness the stone sculptures of the Central American and Mexican Indians. The " tkis " which the New Zealanders erect before their huts are very similar to the totem poles of these British Columbia Indians, the designs being of quite the same order of grotesque sculpture.

The use of totems as autographs comes quite as near to real writing as any unlettered savage ever has approached.   Many examples are on record, some of them of the rarest historical importance in state and municipal archives, or in the libraries of historical societies of the Middle, Eastern and New England States of the United States, in documents involving the early settlers and the native Indians. The totem signature of Tammanen, here shown, one of the great chiefs of the Leni-Lenape Indians of Pennsylvania, to a deed conveying land to William Penn within a year after his arrival in America (1682) and now in the Pennsylvania State House, is one of the most treasured:

As this deed conveyed a considerable part of the land now covered by the city of Philadelphia, and throws an illuminating side light upon the shrewd bargaining of those early days even by the just Quakers, a digression is begged to give the deed in full: —

I, Tamanen, this 23d day of ye 4th month Called June, in ye Year according to ye English account 1683, for me and my heirs and assigns doe graunt and dispose of all my Lands Lying betwixt Pemmapecka and Nessaminehs Creeks, and all along Neshamineh's Creeks to Wm. Penn Proprietr & Gouvnr of Pennsylvania, &c: his heirs and Assigns for Ever, for ye Consideration of so much Wampum, so many Guns, Shoes, Stockings,

Fig. 3. Picturesque totem poles erected before the cabins of Tsimshian Indians at Kitwankool, British Columbia.

Looking-glasses, Blanketts and other goods as he ye sd
William Penn shall please to give unto me. In Witness whereof I have hereunto sett my hand and Seal ye
day and year first above written.

Tammanen's   X   mark.

Tammanen's totem was the serpent, so a serpent was
his autograph. Probably his individual way of drawing it,
which certainly is characteristic enough, differentiated it
sufficiently from the autographs of the other members
of his tribal and totemic family. Red Cloud's census, illustrated in Fig. 22, to be more fully described later on,
gives a most interesting list of autographic totems. Early
colonial archives in many of the Eastern and New England states contain quite a number of examples of the
totem signatures of the native Indian chiefs on documents
deeding their ancestral lands to the white people.

Fig. 4 shows the totem signatures of the " Kings and
Sachems of the Ancient Nations of the Susquehannah
and Savannah Indians " affixed to a memorial to the
" Great King of England and his Sachems " in praise of
William Penn, for his great kindness to them and because
" he has paid us for our Land, which no Governor ever
did before him." The document is in the Pennsylvania
Historical Society in Philadelphia, and is written by James
Logan, Penn's local agent, who attests to the signatures
of the Indians.

Another but somewhat adventitious influence in the development of writing, possibly trifling in its effect upon
the main stream of development, yet like the little rivulet
adding its quota to the volume of the current, was the
use of private ownership marks. From time immemorial
it doubtless was the custom to carve or mark upon implements of warfare, the chase and other personal posses-

sions, marks or signs indicating ownership. These signs
at first probably were only pictographs or geometric lines
in simple arrangements of parallel or parallel and crossed

Fig. 4. Totem signatures of the Susquehannah and Savannah Indians
to a memorial to King Charles II of England.

lines. Youths of to-day often make use of such signs
to proclaim their property, and many of us have seen
similar signs in use on farms and other places where
implements or tools are loaned about, to remind borrow-

ers of their ownership. To be sure it is far more common in this age of letters to use the owner's name or initials to indicate ownership; but before writing was in use or even picturing understood, mere geometrical lines, meaningless in their arrangement, probably were used. This obtains to-day among savage tribes having no written characters, and it probably was true of all times. We may call attention to a most interesting example of this primitive custom strangely preserved in the ancient Babylonian symbol for possession, represented in the fifth sign from the bottom in the last vertical row of signs in Fig. 80. The reader readily will recognize it to be an arrow or spear with four crossed lines cut on the shaft, indicative of ownership. We consequently have in this sign, which to the Babylonians first meant " possession," and then " name " (proper), a reminiscent picture of a most archaic custom.

Very early in the history of any people the want must have been felt for some definite means of record, some memory jog or tally, to record exchange or trading transactions, or various kinds of enumeration: — as of persons, things, time and space. Anecdotes recounted by many travelers agree in recording the universal awe and respect shown by savage people for the art of writing. Edward B. Tylor in his book " Anthropology " relates that John Williams, a South Sea Island missionary, when doing some carpentering work about the mission house, wrote a message with charcoal on a chip and sent it to his wife asking for his square. A native chief being amazed to find that the chip could " talk," for a long time afterward carried it about hung by a string around his neck.

The profound regard for the art of writing is further illustrated by the incident recorded by William Mariner

in his " Account of the Natives of the Tonga Islands."
Finow, the head chief, having intercepted a letter written
by Mr. Mariner to any captain who might touch at Tonga
to rescue him, " at length sent for Mr. Mariner and
desired him to write down something. The latter asked
what he would choose to have written; he replied: ' Put
down me.' He accordingly wrote ' Feenow ' (spelling it
according to the strict English orthography). The chief
then sent for another Englishman who had not been present and, commanding Mr. Mariner to turn his back and
look another way, he gave the man the paper and desired him to tell what that was. He accordingly pronounced aloud the name of the King; upon which Finow
snatched the paper from his hands and, with astonishment, looked at it, turned it around and examined it in
all directions. At length he exclaimed: ' This is neither
myself nor anybody else! Where are my legs? How do
you know it to be I ? ' and then without stopping for any
attempt at an explanation, he impatiently ordered Mr.
Mariner to write something else and thus employed him
for three or four hours in putting down the names of
different persons, places and things, and making the other
man read them. . . . Finow at length thought he had a
notion of it and explained to those about him that it was
very possible to put down a mark or sign of something
that had been seen both by the writer and reader, and
which would be mutually understood by them; but Mr.
Mariner immediately informed him that he could write
down anything that he had never seen. The king directly
whispered to him to put down Toogoo Ahoo (the king
of Tonga whom he and Toobo Nuha had assassinated
many years before Mr. Mariner arrived). This was accordingly done and the other read it, when Finow was
yet more astonished and declared it to be the most won-

derful thing he had ever heard of. He then desired him to write ' Tarky ' (the chief of the garrison of Bea, whom Mr. Mariner and his companions had not yet seen, the Chief being blind in one eye). When ' Tarky ' was read, Finow inquired whether he was blind or not. This was putting writing to an unfair test! Mr. Mariner told him that he had only written down the sign standing for the sound of his name and not for the description of his person. He was then ordered in a whisper to write: ' Tarky blind in his left eye '; which was done and read by the other man to the increased astonishment of everybody. Finow acknowledged this to be a noble invention, but added that it would not at all do for the Tonga Islands; that there would be nothing but disturbances and conspiracies, and he should not be sure of his life, perhaps another month. He said, however, jocosely, that he should like to know it himself, and for all the women to know it, that he might make love with less risk of discovery, and not so much chance of incurring the vengeance of their husbands! "

In primitive communities emerging from utter savagery, as tribal interests widen in their scope and embrace activities that extend to other tribes variously conditioned, the newer phases of the broadening life impose tasks upon the memory which are hard to meet and which require objective helps of some sort. We read in the early histories of most races traditions of the use of various kinds of mnemonic devices to support the memory in their varied transactions. With certain tribes notched sticks were used as aids to the memory; with others shells and beads strung on cords or thongs were used, much the same as the modern rosary or abacus; while others have used knotted cords ingeniously commingled and varied to recall to the mind the details of past events and to assist

in the record of enumerations, divisions and classifica-
tions; which the increasing complexity of an advancing
civilization made necessary. Marco Polo, the celebrated
Venetian traveler, writing in the 16th century, in speaking of the inhabitants of Zardandan — Yunnan, China —
says: "They have no letters, but make their contracts
and obligations by tallies of wood, one-half whereof one
keepeth, and the other which being afterwards paid, the
tally is destroyed."

The Algonquin Indians who formerly inhabited the
eastern parts of the United States, according to Dr.
Daniel G. Brinton, preserved their myths, chronicles and
the memory of important events, by means of marked
sticks, six inches long tied in bundles and painted with
marks and figures. As their art abilities advanced, in
place of single sticks, burnt, painted or notched wooden
tablets came into use, on which symbols were scratched
with flints or knives. The Walam Olum, illustrated on
page 93, is the highest example of this last stage of historical record of these Indians.

Dr. W. J. Hoffman states that he found in the collection of the Hon. A. F. Caronal of Los Angeles, California, a number of notched sticks which had been invented and used by the Indians at the Mission of San
Gabriel. The history of the sticks as given by Dr. Hoffman is as follows: "Immediately after the establishment
of the mission, the Franciscan father appointed major
domos, who had under their charge corporals or over-
seers of the several classes of laborers, herders, etc. The
chief herder was supplied with a stick of hard wood,
measuring about one inch in thickness each way, and from
twenty to twenty-four inches long. The corners were
beveled at the handle. Upon each of the facets were
marks to indicate the kinds of cattle herded; thus, one

cut or notch, a bull; two cuts, a cow; one cross, a heifer; and a > shaped character, an ox. Similar characters also were used for horses; respectively for a stallion, mare, colt and gelding. When only cattle were owned, no difference was made in the upper end of the stick; but when both kinds of animals were owned near the same localities or by the same settler, the stick referring to the cattle was notched V shaped at the head end and reversed or pointed to denote horns. Sticks also were marked to denote the several kinds of stock, and to record those which had been branded. In all of these sticks numbers were indicated by cutting notches into the corners, each tenth cut extending across the face of the stick. For instance, if the herder had thirteen oxen in charge, he selected that edge of the stick which bore upon the handle the > shape, and cut nine short notches, one long one, and then three more short ones."

Dr. Hoffman in "Beginnings of Writing" says in speaking of the Paloni Indians of California: "Each year the Paloni selected a certain member of the tribe to visit the settlement at San Gabriel to sell native blankets; every Indian sending goods providing the salesman with two cords made of twisted hair or wool, on one of which was tied a knot for every real received and on the other a knot for each blanket sold. When the sum reached eight reals, or one dollar, a double knot was made. Upon the return of the salesman, each person selected from his lot his own goods, by which he would quickly perceive the amount due and also the number of blankets for which the salesman was responsible. Among the Zuni a more highly developed method of knotting obtained. It appears possible that certain strands pertained to cult practices, others to war, etc.; knotted

fringes attached to the paraphernalia of members of cult
societies appear to be survivals of such practices."

These customs prevailing among the intelligent though
illiterate Indians of the past generation shed light upon
the early history of record making and bring to our
hands corroborative and authentic evidence in support of
the traditions concerning the primary stages in the art
of writing. Knotted cords are shown in the Egyptian
hieroglyphs, and the classic authors speak of the Scy-
thians and Germans using sticks for divination. We
read in Herodotus, Book III, Par. 98, the following
directions given to his soldiers and mercenaries by King
Darius: "The King took a leathern thong, and tying
sixty knots in it, called together the Ionian tyrants and
spoke thus to them:—' Men of Ionia, my former commands to you concerning the bridge are now withdrawn.
See, here is a thong; take it, and observe my bidding
with respect to it. From the time that I leave you to
march forward into Scythia, untie every day one of the
knots. If I do not return before the last day to which
the knots will hold out, then leave your station, and sail
to your several homes. Meanwhile, understand that my
resolve is changed, and that you are to guard the bridge
with all care, and watch over its safety and preservation.' " While this may not strictly be called a mnemonic
device in this particular instance, the tied thong stood in
lieu of a written record, Darius' subalterns being illiterate
and unable to record time. The Chinese have a well-
founded tradition that knotted cords were employed by
their ancestors as a means of recording ideas before writing was invented. In Tibet, Japan and other countries
the same custom prevailed.

It is a matter of authentic history that the Peruvians

about the time of the Conquest made use of the most
elaborate arrangement of cords known as quipus — quipu,
a knot — consisting of a principal cord of one color with
secondary and subsidiary cords of many different colors.
According to the particular use of the quipu, the several
colors represented certain ideas or things, while the knots
and loops combined in all possible ways indicated a great
many complex ideas. C. F. Keary in his " Dawn of History " describing Peruvian quipus says : " On the quipu
devoted to population, the colored strings on which the
number of men in each town and village was recorded
had depending from them little strings for the widowers,
and no doubt the widows and the old maids had their
little strings from the cord that denoted women. One
knot meant ten; a double knot, one hundred; two single
side by side, twenty; two doubles, two hundred; and the
position of the knots on their string and their form were
also of immense importance, each subject having its
proper place on the quipu and its proper form of knot."
As with every form of quipus, the Peruvian quipus when
returned to the place of registry required some means of
identification as to their contents. Some distinguishing
mark was needed to indicate the quipu for census, income,
war, etc. If such identifying marks were not agreed upon,
a messenger was necessary to convey the quipu who could
remember its subject matter. Apart from this the
adopted system of the quipus was so perfect and automatic
as a numerical system that they were self-explanatory.
The quipu illustrated in Fig. 5 is reproduced from " The
Ancient Quipu, a Peruvian Knot Record," by L. Leland
Locke (*American Anthropologist,* Vol. XIV, No. 2,
April–June, 1912). The original is one of a large collection of quipus in the American Museum of Natural
History, New York City. The Museum possesses a very

extensive collection of quipus, exhumed from Peruvian graves.

Knotted cords were used for records throughout the Eastern Archipelago and in Polynesia when the first trading ships arrived. One of the most famous examples of

Fig. 5. Quipu or Peruvian knot-record. The number of pendent cords (95) is indicated by knots on the ends of the main cord.

the rope device for a mnemonic record was the so-called " revenue-book " of Hawaii, which consisted of a rope four hundred fathoms long divided into sections corresponding to the various districts of the country. Each section of the rope was the complete record of a tax collector, who by means of loops, knots and tufts of different shapes and colors, kept a correct account of the personal property of the people. The weak point in the system was that each division collector had to " go along " with the record to explain and interpret it! This would to-day

be called a "junketing" scheme, and no doubt would be
very popular and much appreciated by the average public
office holder.

During the Middle Ages when learning was the exclusive posssession of those in the church and the court,
though not very prevalent with the latter, in certain parts
of England, notably in Staffordshire and the adjacent
counties, the country people living in the rural districts remote from churches made use of ingenious notched sticks
called "clogs" or "almanacs," to remind them of the
holy days of the church calendar. They were square
blocks of wood notched on the four edges with the days
of the week, the seventh notch being a long one. On one
side of each edge, which included three months, lines
from the notches bore dots or geometric marks indicating cycles of the moon. On the adjacent side, lines drawn
from notches corresponding to church festivals, fasts and
saints' days, bore characters symbolical of these holy days.
Dr. Plot, who wrote the "Natural History of Staffordshire" in 1686, speaking of these wooden tallies says:
"Canutus raigned sole king of England for 20 years;
during which time and the raigns of his two successors,
also Danish kings of England, many of their customs and
utensils, no doubt on't, obtained here, amongst which I
guess I may reckon an ancient sort of Almanacks they
call Cloggs, made upon square sticks, still (A. D. 1686)
in use here among the meaner sort of people, which I cannot but think must be some remains of the Danish government, finding the same with but little difference to have
been used also formerly both in Sweden and Denmark,
as plainly appears from Olaus Magnus, and Olus Worm-
ius; which being a sort of antiquity so little known, that
it hath scarce been yet heard of in the southern parts of
England, and understood now but by a few of the gentry

in the northern, I shall be the more particular in my
account of them. . . . They are here called *Cloggs,*
for what reason I could not learn, nor indeed imagine,
unless from the English log, a term we usually give to
any piece of wood, or from the likeness of some of the
greater sorts of them to the cloggs, where-
with we usually restrain the wild, extravagant, mischievous motions of some of our
dogs. . . . There are some few of brass,
. . . but the most of them are of wood, and
these chiefly of box; others there are of fir
and some of oak, but these not so frequent.
. . . As for the kind of them, some are perfect, containing the Dominical letters, as
well as the Prime and marks for the feasts,
engraven upon them, and such are our
Primestanes in the Museum at Oxford.
Others imperfect, having only the Prime and
immoveable feasts on them, and such are all
those I met with in Staffordshire; which yet
are of two kinds also, some publick, of a
larger size, which hang commonly here at
one end of the mantle tree of their chimneys,
for the use of the whole family; . . . and
others private, of a smaller size, which they
carry in their pockets.

Fig. 6. Clog
Almanac.
Bodleian Li-
brary, Ox-
ford, Eng-
land.

Two most interesting specimens of these
clog almanacs are preserved in the Bodleian
Library, in Oxford. One of them is in the
shape of a walking stick. The other (Fig.
6) is of boxwood, as Dr. Plot says, about
thirty inches long and three inches square.
The calendar begins at the top of the front edge on the
right hand face with New Year's Day, represented by the

Christian symbol of eternity, the " circle." Next in order comes the Feast of Epiphany, represented by a " star "; then follow on January 13, the birth of St. Hilary, indicated by a " cross "; on January 25, the Conversion of St. Paul, indicated by a " hatchet," St. Paul having been beheaded. The Purification of the Virgin, on February 2, is represented by a " heart "; St. Valentine's Day by a " true lover's knot "; St. Matthias by a " leg "— why, no one seems to know — St. David by a " harp "; St. Chad by a " branch "; St. Gregory by a " square," and the feast of the Annunciation of the Virgin, on March 25, by a " heart." [1]

In England, even well into the 17th century, tally-sticks were employed to record loans made to the government. They were notched to indicate the amounts in pounds, shillings and pence loaned; one-half of the tally being kept by the lender and the other half being deposited in the Exchequer; quite the same as described by Marco Polo. They were the indirect cause of the destruction of the Houses of Parliament by fire in 1834, owing to overheating in the burning of vast accumulations of these tally-sticks.

All of these primitive devices above described employed for mnemonic purposes were as far removed from true writing as the memory knot which people sometimes tie in their handkerchiefs, or the string tied around the finger to remind one of some thing or action. They were simply reminders to the persons who knew the facts. They did not — nor could they — impart information to anybody else not knowing the key. No one else could interpret them. They told nothing more than the knife

---

[1] A full description of this interesting clog almanac will be found in " The Calendar of the Prayer Book, Illustrated," published by James Parker & Co., Oxford, Eng.

placed in the wrong pocket, the tied up stocking or other
memory jogs we sometimes are accustomed to employ.
If the person — the Peruvians had a master of the quipus,
who had the custody of the records — forgot their significance, his own device failed to make any appeal to his
intelligence. It was somewhat different with devices like
the clog almanacs. The symbols standing for the different church days had a special significance that connected
them at once with the particular celebration of the day.
Nevertheless, the process was an appeal to the illiterate
mind. So long as men were limited to such unintelligent
and in some case unintelligible processes of record, as
knotted cords and tallies, we may be sure that no very
great advance could have been made in material or intellectual civilization. We do not find in the world to-day
a high state of civilization where there is illiteracy; rather
do we find barbarism and savagery. Letters, or a knowledge of them, always throughout the ages have been the
magic charm that ever has dispelled the gloom of ignorance and superstition; the lodestar that has guided men
upward to the higher intellectual and spiritual life. For
by writing, the thoughts of the foremost men of the times
have been widely disseminated among reading men, making intellectual growth in the community vastly more
rapid.

A curious note of distrust of the value of the art of
writing comes from the depths of Egyptian history. It
was Thot who invented writing. G. Maspero in the
" Dawn of Civilization " writes: " An old legend relates
that when the god (Thot) unfolded his discovery to King
Thamos, whose minister he was, the monarch immediately
raised an objection to it. Children and young people, who
had hitherto been forced to apply themselves diligently
to learn and retain whatever was taught them, would

cease to apply themselves and would neglect to exercise their memories!" Though King Thamos may have been slow to take up new ideas in the march of civilization, his educational theories were not so far astray for the fourth millennium B. C.

The development of writing has been an age-long evolution arising in the necessities of tribal and inter-tribal life, and demanded by the increasing complexities of society as savage man has advanced from his primitive state toward civilization and felt the need of recording his traditions and conserving his knowledge in some permanent and legible form. The first step in the direction of writing was taken when man early began to exhibit his in-born propensity for graphic expression, manifested in his attempts to imitate the shapes of the natural objects about him. Few races indeed in the history of the world have failed to exhibit evidences of this distinctly human talent. Many African and Polynesian races to-day seem to have developed nothing in the line of graphics beyond a rudimentary form of geometric decoration. Writing never has developed in this direction. Abstract and geometric though the alphabetic characters seem to be in their present form — no letters could be more so than the Roman capitals — yet if we are unable to convince the reader that each was the outgrowth of a specific, antecedent, pictorial form, we shall at least have proven to him that as far as history reaches, in every direction, the beginnings of writing seem to have been laid in pictorial art. It is the natural mode of graphic expression of the primitive races of mankind.

That the above statement is true, and that the desire to represent the varied objects of nature is a natural impulse in man, is illustrated and verified by the art of the oldest race of men known to have lived on the earth and to have left any record of their tenancy. Nothing in the history of art or archæology is more impregnated with the flavor of romance, or more eloquent of the story of human striving toward civilization than the remarkable drawings and paintings left by the cave dwellers of central Europe. It is one of the anomalies of art that the earliest known manifestation of pictorial art should be at the same time one of the truest and best. The early Greeks could hold nothing worthy up to the art of Paleolithic man — not even the proverbial candle, for it would have proven to be but a rush light — to compare with the rare fidelity to nature of the drawings which these rude men cut with flints or painted with colored earths or vegetable dyes upon the rocky walls of their caves, or carved upon their crude stone implements or with better skill etched with such delightful naïveté upon the bones of now extinct animals, ages before metals were used or even known. It is not our purpose to discuss here who these people were, whence their civilization, or in what way their art was transmitted, if at all, to later or descendent peoples. Their history is too indefinite as yet to enable us to state with any degree of certainty their true chronological and ethnological position. Geological and paleontological evidence sufficient to satisfy the highest scientific authorities places these people at the close of the last glacial period in Europe, contemporaneous with Arctic and semi-Arctic animals long since extinct: — as the mammoth (Elephas primigenius), the woolly-haired rhinoceros, wild ox or urus, aurochs (Bos bison), reindeer, cave lion, cave bear and other extinct animals whose portraits the Reindeer Man has so faithfully copied in outline on bone or slate, or painted in colors on the ceiling of his cave. Their drawings which are very numerous portray the mammoth, bison, ox, reindeer, hyena, cave bear and the horse, which with its erect mane and zebra-like characteristics gives further evidence, were it needed, of the vast prehistoric antiquity of their art. All of these drawings are replete with realism, and for spirit and dash are well-nigh unexcelled. Indeed, they uniformly dis-

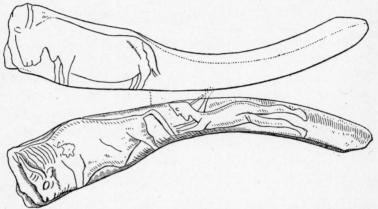

Fig. 7. Bison and man. Hunting scene. Obverse and reverse. From Laugerie Basse, Dordogne, France.

play a high degree of artistic excellence remarkable in the art of a primitive race. We will give a few reproductions of the drawings of the Cave Men, taken from " Prehistoric Art " by Thomas Wilson, published by the Smithsonian Institution, Washington, D. C. In one of these drawings (Fig. 7) etched on the antler of a reindeer found in a cave at Laugerie Basse, Dordogne, France, one sees the bison excellently well drawn with the hunter himself crawling up to him through the long grass, spear in hand. In another (Fig. 8), etched on a piece of slate stone found in the cave of La Madelaine, Dordogne, we have the mammoth as true to life as though sketched but yesterday in the Museum of St. Petersburg. But the reindeer was the favorite subject for the art of the Cave

Fig. 8. Mammoth. Etched on a fragment of his own tusk. From La Madelaine, Dordogne, France.

Men, and they depicted it in many characteristic attitudes. The remarkable drawing of the reindeer shown in Fig. 9 is reproduced from a picture carved on a piece of reindeer antler found in a cave near Thayngen, Switzerland.

Unfortunately, the world knows nothing more of the Cave Men and their unique and beautiful art than this

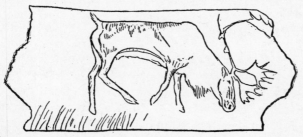

Fig. 9. Reindeer carved on a piece of antler. From a cave near Thayngen, Switzerland.

opening chapter. If their art developed into genuine picture writing, as most primitive art has done, there is not as yet sufficient evidence forthcoming to prove it. Dr. Arthur J. Evans frankly calls it picture-writing as it is, and looks upon it as a record of events, mainly of the chase, their principal occupation. Certainly no people ever made a better start, and it were a great misfortune

if their extraordinary and versatile talent failed of
fruition in this direction. Later on, in another chapter,
we shall refer to the similarity between the art of the
Reindeer Men and that of the American Eskimo.

Scattered over the wide world there may be found to-
day primitive or undeveloped races who have not yet
progressed in the scale of civilization to the high stage
of culture indicated by the practice of the art of writing, yet who exhibit a marked talent for or have attained a high degree of proficiency in the elemental art
of drawing. On the walls of caves in South Africa occasionally may be seen paintings of the primitive Bushmen,
the aborigines of the country, who occupied it before the
incursions of the Hottentots drove them into the il-
limitable forests or the mountain fastnesses. These rock-
paintings portray hunting scenes, many of them quite
elaborate, in which elephants, long-haired bovines, lions,
antelopes or other wild animals, together with human
figures, are depicted. While many of the drawings justly
may claim rather a high artistic rating, being very faithful reproductions of the natural forms, some even exhibiting the difficulties of perspective foreshortening, others
are wretched caricatures. Nevertheless, the drawings falling under this latter category and condemnation are no
worse than, and indeed very much resemble, the general
run of Phœnician animal and figure paintings so familiar
in Phœnician and pre-Hellenic pottery, found in the
Ægean Islands and on the Grecian littoral, where these
Semitic traders established their marts in the early centuries of the second millennium before Christ. The drawing of the animals is greatly superior to that of the early
Greeks and Phœnicians. It does not fall much below the
extraordinary talent of the Cave Men. But the drawing
of men is quite as weird and outlandish as that of the

heroes of Troy and Mycenæ and the ubiquitous traders of Tyre and Sidon, as exhibited in their decorated utensils and their hammered metal ware. The vagaries of racial development and historic progression in the continuous transmission of the elements that constitute civilization is sharply evidenced by the fact that it was these very Semitic traders, with their somewhat meager pictorial ability, who gave to the Greeks, as we shall show in the development of this story, their incomparable alphabet to hand down to the Romans and to ourselves. The poor Bushmen still remain the benighted denizens of the African jungle, as far from applying their graphic talent to any advanced stage of civilized development as they were millenniums ago.

That these Bushmen paintings are of more serious consequence than mere idle scribblings, and that they undoubtly were made as a record of actual events and to commemorate and celebrate unusual occurrences, is corroborated by the following incident given in " The Native Races of South Africa " by George W. Stow. A commando consisting of a combined force of Boers and Basutu, engaged in driving out the old savage inhabitants of the country, attacked and scattered a body of Bushmen lingering in the Boloko or Vecht Kop, near the southern border of Basutoland. Some time later, in a large cave in the vicinity where the Bushmen had secreted themselves, a recent painting in the well-known Bushmen style was discovered. It portrayed a hostile encounter in which several of the warriors were depicted with the guns of modern warfare. It evidently was a crude record of the battle with the Boers and Basutu.

Figure 10 is a portion of an extensive rock-painting by the Bushmen on the lower Imvani. It shows several elands beautifully painted and shaded in brown and white,

Fig. 10. Rock painting on the lower Imvani. By the Bushmen.

with lions attacking them shown in their characteristic coats of tan. The men are in black. Figure 11 is a characteristic illustration of Bushmen painting, representing buffalo, hunters and apes. It is easy to imagine that the creatures in the right hand upper corner playing "snap-the-whip" with such naïveté and abandon are the original "brownies"! A very much truer and more natural drawing is shown in Figure 12, in which both the animal — probably an antelope — and the hunters are drawn with considerable correctness as to form and perspective.

Pictures on rocks very much similar in spirit and exe-

Fig. 11. Painting by the Bushmen.

cution to the art of the Bushmen have been found in Algeria, and others much inferior are to be seen in Australia, the work of the aborigines of the austral continent, who seem to enjoy the distinction of being placed by common consent at the lowest rung of the ladder of civilization.

These drawings of primitive races while undoubtedly made for the purpose of record, the only kind known to these savages in their backward stage of progress toward

Fig. 12. Painting by the Bushmen.

civilization, are many removes from true writing. They illustrate in point of fact the very first step. It is the preliminary stage, separated by many intermediate stages from true writing. They have not progressed as far as and therefore lack the conventional character of the earliest Chinese picture characters, or the Sumerian and Akkadian linear symbols, the earliest known forms of the Babylonian and Assyrian writing, later to be described. There is not the slightest evidence in any of these cave pictures of the selection of any particular form agreed upon as the constant, conventional representative of any certain thing or idea. There is evident only the most elementary principle of graphics of representing things as they appear to the eye, drawing man and animals in their own likeness, and the other forms of nature in like manner; resorting to no symbol or convention, which is the result only of a wider and more universal intercourse than these simple and isolated communities had attained.

The selection of conventional figures — ideograms — to express or to stand for things or ideas was the result of generations of evolution growing out of a rich experience in pictography, when long familiar, characteristic forms, shorn of much of their pictorial details and accessories, had been adopted as conventions to symbolize, by some graphic resemblance or suggestion, objects or ideas. There is moreover in these paintings and drawings of the Cave Men, Bushmen, Australians and other aborigines, only the most puerile attempt to tell a connected, consecutive story, such as we shall see so successfully worked out by the North American Indians in their remarkable ritualistic and medicine songs. They attain their highest intellectual function only as pictures — pictographs — of natural objects, and of actions visible to the eye in " the living present." The representation of past or future action, or of any quality or attribute, never was attempted by these somewhat clever yet backward artists; for despite the fact that these pictographic records, excepting the drawings of the Cave Men, are but the work of yesterday, as time passes, they are the product of a civilization as yet in its earliest infancy.

The history and development of the art of writing the entire world over, among peoples of all races, whether occupying contiguous portions of the same continent separated from one another only by mountain barriers or developing their civilization in antipodal countries in far distant continents, seem to have progressed along lines of growth practically identical with each other. It has ever been the same universal development inherent in and concurrent with the slow unfolding of man's intelligence, evidenced in the annals of nearly every race and nation. We already have referred to the extraordinary inequality of relative development in the successive stages of writing and the comparative degree of skill shown in pictography between different races. This lack of uniformity in racial development, as has been pointed out, has been so great that it is probable that since the time when the ancient Egyptians or the Sumerian Babylonians first appeared upon the pages of history in the fifth millennium before Christ to the present time, all stages of the art of writing, from the rudest pictographs of the most savage Indian or benighted African to the true alphabetic writing practiced by the ancient Egyptians in their earliest known dynasty, have constantly been contemporaneous.

These successive stages in the evolution of writing can briefly be stated as follows: —

I. Pictographic or iconographic writing.
    (a) Mnemonic devices antecedent to pictography.
    (b) Disconnected and fragmentary pictures.
    (c) Connected stories, songs or epics.
II. Ideographic or hieroglyphic picture-writing.
III. Phonetic writing.
    (a) Syllabic symbols or signs.
    (b) Alphabetic characters.

In the first primitive stage of writing, in practically all systems, the things intended and indicated in the record, at first chiefly natural objects, then later human-made articles, were represented by crude pictures more or less true according to the artistic talent of the early scribes.

However they were employed, whether as memory jogs for the scribe himself or for the transmission of messages to a distant fellow tribesman, the pictures simply recalled the objects to the mind; the special and particular meaning of the record had to be divined through a series of mental experiences assisted by codes and conventions carried in the memory and entirely apart from the pictographic record. Without this *a priori* knowledge, these primitive records would indeed fulfill the definition of Bacon that "pictures are dumb histories." In the earliest stage, pictographic writing, it is entirely probable that there was no connection or at least only a loosely recognized one implied between the spoken word, the name used in the native vernacular to designate the object, and the picture representing the thing referred to. The picture recalled the thing itself to the mind, not the name of the thing, unless involuntarily called up by the reader. The employment of the ideograph to represent and recall the name of the thing as well as the corporate thing itself, or, later, abstract qualities and attributes derived from it, was a step arrived at only after the attainment of a high degree of civilization.

The second step in the history of writing was that of ideographic or hieroglyphic writing, in which a definite, significant picture, more or less conventional and simplified, selected by agreement or converging custom from among the many experimental pictures that formerly satisfied the artistic whims or ideals of the individual scribes, then became the fixed, pictorial correlative of its name. This was the starting point of institutional writing. The function of the ideograph still was only to recall the object to the mind, concretely not phonetically. Nevertheless, the name of the object became more and more closely and indissolubly identified with the picture of it, now that the ideograph became fixed and universal; especially since in the process of selection from among the then rich album of pictographs that had accumulated up to this stage, the one concise, irreplaceable picture which now represented any given thing in preference to all other pictures in the aborigines' album of forms, could have but the single reference. It is possible to trace in the tablet inscriptions of the linear Babylonian script, of which hundreds of examples are available from the third and fourth millenniums before Christ, the gradual modification and simplification of the large variety of pictures or signs employed in the archaic scripts to represent the same thing or idea, until eventually in the later inscriptions a common, unchangeable character became universally used for any given idea.

The highest function of the ideograph, now that the necessity was recognized for definite and fixed characters for all the objective things within the environment of our advancing nation, was that of expressing abstract ideas, qualities or metaphors. After the selection of a constant picture for the primary object, qualities, attributes, metaphors or other ideas associated with these objects, were represented by significant parts of the primary objects or by combinations of them: — as the hand for " power " or " authority ; " the arm for " strength "; the leg or foot for " fleetness; " the eye for " seeing "; the ear for " hearing "; the mouth to indicate " speech "; the sun and moon to represent " light "; the arch of the sky with a star to represent " night," or with the sign of water to represent " rain,"— as in the Egyptian hieroglyphs, the Chinese writing, and the Ojibwa Indian ideographs. Practically all written languages have passed through this ideographic stage of writing, sweeping over it and leaving only here and there a few mutilated mile stones by which it is possible for the paleologist to trace the highways backward. The Chinese, as we presently shall show, retain to this day in their written language many of their original ideographs, combining them in their unique, composite characters, with purely phonetic signs. They do not exist in their primitive forms, but as highly conventionalized variants, and are used just as they were thousands of years ago as pictures only, not to be read, but merely to catch the eye, the better to illustrate the phonetic meaning, and to distinguish between the scores of homophones with which the language abounds. In a precisely similar manner in the Egyptian hieroglyphs, the original ideographic picture, from time immemorial representing a word-idea, frequently stands beside the word in the line, picturing it to the eye and interpreting the phonetic signs which it accompanies, though the word is spelled out letter for letter in pictorial though alphabetical characters, to the complete satisfaction of any literate native. With the Egyptians this custom was partly due to the necessity of distinguishing between the many homophones, but also to their love of pictorial art, and the piquancy and variety that it gave to their hieroglyphic inscriptions. We already have referred to these ideographic determinative characters in describing the primitive sign-language, and shall still further describe them when we come to discuss the Chinese and Egyptian systems of writing.

The next and most important step in the development of writing was easily the most signal, intellectual achievement ever attained by man, and justifies Plato's remark that writing is " the divine art." It was an advance in culture pregnant with the profoundest benefit to posterity in all the countless ages to come. The substitution of ideographic pictures that represented natural objects in their visual forms and recalled them to the mind's eye, and, as culture increased, that pictured mental conceptions of their attributes and qualities by characters that represented only the phonetic values of their names, though it may appear to us of this age a very simple process, nevertheless must have been arrived at only after ages of primitive culture. But when the change was once fully effected, each nation or race as it evolved this significant transformation in the art of writing must rapidly have strode to the front rank of civilization of its day; for it had discovered the readiest and surest means of preserving and disseminating knowledge and experience. To put it more tersely, the change was one from a picture or symbol representing a thing to the symbol representing the name of the thing; in other words, the picture of a sound.

In oral speech, as is well known, things referred to are recalled to the mind of the hearer by name-words, from time immemorial applied to them, ages before picture-writing was conceived of and when the first human beings realized their precious birthright which so immeasurably differentiated them from the dumb beasts about them. Probably at first the specific words employed to designate natural objects were chosen through mimicry, and possessed some real or fancied similarity to the natural sounds of the objects indicated. This is not at all improbable. One may recall not a few words that seem to reproduce more or less phonetically the things of which they are the names, we may say the sound-pictures, — as the cries of animals and birds : — baa, moo, meow, peep, chirp, squeak, squark, etc.; sounds like tick, buzz, fizz, boom, puff, bang, and many others, not to mention the modern " honk " of the automobile horn. However, we must admit that languages never could have pro-

gressed very far on this basis of mimicry. Yet knowing
the natural instinct of primitive man for imitation, we may
be moderately certain that his vocabulary appreciably enlarged in the direction of the emotions aroused by natural stimuli, and that the name-words that he gave to
natural objects were to a limited extent expressive of
their qualities. For ages his wants in the matter of intercommunication with his fellow beings were satisfied
with his oral vocabulary, helped out with the sign-language and mnemonic aids; but when advancing civilization demanded a better system of communication and
record than cords and tallies, again his mind responded
along the line of imitation, and representative pictures
for generations served him for signs and symbols of the
things he wished to indicate.

To recapitulate then, hoping not to be tedious in this
analysis, we have seen how at first when early man felt
the promptings and experienced the desire to record his
ideas in written form, naturalistic pictures or pictographs
crudely drawn in imitation of natural objects were used
frankly and simply to portray ideas and actions connected with these objects. Next, specific, conventional
ideographs, selected and adapted by custom and still imitative in form and significant to the eye of the ideas conveyed, were employed in the various forms of tribal
transactions. This was the beginning of scientific writing. In the third and last stage, phonetic writing, all
pictorial or representative significance was dispensed with
as a necessity, as the sign or symbol was employed simply to express a word-sound. It is probable that in most
instances the primary ideographs, severely conventionalized and in time almost entirely stripped of their pictorial
significance, were continued as the phonetic symbols of the
vast number of nominatives in commission for all the nat-

ural and common objects visible to the eye. But the great change effected at this stage was that these pictures or symbols, at first used only to represent the implied objects or attributes of them, now were used not only to represent the objects themselves and their name-words, but these same sounds — or their initial sounds if these were polysyllabic — wherever they occurred as homophones or syllables in other words. This was syllabic writing. Some languages have stopped at this syllabic stage, notably the Babylonian; in which the characters represent either ideograms having no syllabic value and to be translated by the known name of the object, or phonograms having for their proper phonetic value syllables taken from the initial syllables of the words of which they were originally the ideograms. When the same character was used both as an ideogram and a phonogram — a syllabic character — its meaning in the ancient inscription can be judged only by the context. Several instances of this will be noted in the texts in Chapter VIII.

We do not claim that all written languages have passed through the complete genesis that we have just outlined. No such universal plan can be predicated of all languages. Probably very few nations have enjoyed such a period of continuous and undisturbed growth as to progress through all the stages of writing that we have indicated. Nations at certain stages of development in the " Art Preservative " have borrowed or adapted the system of writing of other nations, voluntarily or involuntarily, thereby modifying the progress of development of their own national systems. This interruption of natural development in most cases probably has been an acceleration rather than a retardation of progress, as the acquired system probably was the vehicle of expression of a more advanced nation. This will be found to be according to facts as we investigate in turn the various systems of writing of different nations.

It is evident that as a spoken language became rich in inflections, conjugations, and all the varied parts of speech of a living language, there would be legions of words in tenses, moods, cases and other grammatical forms, which could not be pictured in any way and which would tax to its furthest bounds any signary to supply characters for the ever increasing number and complexity of such words. These words, too, undoubtedly would be polysyllabic, making the task of finding suitable characters for them all the more difficult. All this complexity of procedure was remedied in the course of time — and it took time, ages — by the final simplification of the entire system; that of selecting a few symbols, conventionalized and reduced to their lowest terms, out of the thousands of hieroglyphs that lumbered the signary of the language, to represent the comparatively few fundamental, phonetic sounds in the spoken language, and with which all possible phonetic combinations could be made. This was alphabetic writing. When this final transformation was accomplished, all that preceded it forever was abandoned as so many rungs in the ladder of ascent, the summit having been attained. Scholarship only, especially that of the archæologist, has succeeded in retracing the steps and restoring this ladder so that we now may feel certain of the different stages leading up to the present almost universal system of alphabetic writing. Nothing is more significant than the slow development of the art of writing of the fact that in most ways men build on their past experiences like St. Augustine's ladder, gradually evolving new differentials of slight divergence out of what has gone before, only on the slow basis of associated ideas. Such a faculty as vision or genius seems to belong only to rare and gifted individuals, not to the race. So we find that the last step in the history of writing, the alphabetic stage, like all the earlier ones, was built upon the preceding stage. It was the natural, logical outgrowth of it, capping the apex of the literary structure like the final stage of Nebuchadrezzar's pyramid in Babylon.

In the final stage of this long historic development of the art of writing, the selection of the alphabetic characters needed to represent the comparatively few elemental sounds in the language naturally was made from among the many signs and symbols already in use in the ancient syllabary. It is not at all probable that new characters were invented, although they may have been borrowed from another, possibly a more advanced civilization, as the Japanese alphabetic characters were borrowed from the Chinese. At this late day the hieroglyphs employed in the syllabary had become considerably conventionalized and simplified, in some countries assuming a geometric character, in others a purely abstract form, while others like the Egyptian retained to the last a refined version of the early pictorial signs. In choosing the alphabetic characters, selection probably was made from among the most common syllabic signs in use of monosyllabic words, or words having initial sounds similar to the alphabetic sounds for which suitable characters were desired. That this method was the one generally pursued is the deduction which will be made from a critical study of the hieroglyphic writing of at least one great nation of antiquity, the Egyptian. On page 215 the reader will find a list of Egyptian words whose primitive, pictorial hieroglyphs supplied the signs for the alphabetic characters of sounds that were identical with the initial sounds of the native names of these objects.

This process of growth in written characters is according to the well-known principle of acrology, that is believed to have been the method of development and transformation of syllabic into alphabetic characters. It may not be universal. It may not be the manner in which our own alphabetic characters developed. Yet it seems reasonable, and we shall find historic examples in ancient languages to support the theory. It will be interesting to note a comparatively modern instance in our own language of this process of simplification by acrology, for it seems to suggest how the language, both spoken and written, may have developed under its application. The personal pronoun, I, has been in use in our spoken and written language for many centuries; but if one were to read very early English manuscripts he would come across the original Teutonic form of the word, *ich*. In the time of William the Conqueror the *h* had been dropped, as may be noted by reference to his charter of the City of London (Fig. 154), in which the king uses the form *ic*. Long since the *c* followed the *h* into desuetude and only the initial letter and sound of the early syllable have been retained, the rest of the word being suppressed. In very much the same way, probably, the alphabet makers proceeded with their devoted task through the centuries; simplifying, eliminating, refining, until the last finishing touches were added or disaster overtook their civilization before the complete evolution was effected.

We now will proceed to the investigation of the evolution toward writing of a primitive race uninfluenced by the culture of any former or neighboring civilization, but developing its graphic art through the necessities and demands of its own racial life and experience. Our researches under such conditions hardly can fail to indicate by parallel the natural lines of development of this art by the universal human family.

CHAPTER III

THE aboriginal inhabitants of North America when they first came under the observation of the white men, at the time of the European settlement of this country, already had a system of picture-writing, wide-spread in its use but of limited comprehensibility even among the members of the same tribe or family. No tribe had advanced further toward true writing than the most elementary stage, that of pictography,— drawing the picture of the thing intended, to recall it to the mind of the reader. The Dakota and Ojibwa Indians were about entering upon the second stage, that of ideographic writing, when the intrusion of European culture interrupted the natural development of their native, graphic systems.

When the white hunters or pioneers first traversed the vast forests of the New World they not infrequently observed pictorial notices or inscriptions, so-called, on the trunks of trees along the old Indian trails or portages. These inscriptions sometimes were cut on a blazed surface of a tree, or painted on birch bark or skin and attached to the trunk. They were inscriptions of warning, notices concerning game, direction, or ofttimes of challenge to the white man or to hostile Indians. Probably none of these inscriptions — drawings — is now extant, but copies of some of them sufficiently well authenticated have been preserved. A few of these will be considered later on. There is, however, another kind of inscription, the very nature of which has preserved it from loss or

serious deterioration,— inscription on rocks. These rock
inscriptions or petroglyphs of the Indians are to be found
in all parts of the United States from Maine to California, being more abundant in regions east of the Rocky
Mountains. In this area the various tribes speaking the
Algonquian dialects had their homes. The Algonquins
proper occupied the eastern littoral of this country, extending their boundaries far into the interior of the
continent. Over this entire region scattered petroglyphs
may be found, principally in Maine, Massachusetts, Pennsylvania and Ohio.   They also are somewhat plentiful in
Canada. They generally are to be found on smooth
boulders on the banks of streams or water courses, and
contain characteristic pictorial elements which indicate
a close relationship and distinguish them from the rock
inscriptions of other sections. The pictures in these inscriptions — as we shall call them for want of a better
word — with some notable exceptions are extremely
crude, as all the sculptured delineations of the Indians
are wherever found. Where the forms are recognizable
at all they generally are so faulty in draughtsmanship
that it is difficult either to conceal one's disappointment
or to withhold one's contempt at witnessing such weakness and puerility in pictorial expression.   The disappointment is the more keen when we learn of the beautiful imagery and metaphor of the spoken languages of
the Indians and their extreme picturesqueness of expression. The resources of these languages, especially the
Algonquian, are said to excel our own in picturesque color-
ings and poetic fancifulness, particularly as regards natural objects; enabling the Indian to express his innately
keen perception of nature in words replete with pictorial
meaning. It is the more difficult, therefore, to reconcile
the richness of his spoken language with the pitiable pov-

erty of his mode of graphic expression, at least in the rock inscriptions. It must be admitted, however, in extenuation of his limitations, that the intractable nature of rock sculpture had much to do with the backwardness of the Indians in this particular phase of their graphic arts. It must be remembered also that though first met with in North America in the 17th century, these Indians were only just emerging from the Stone Age. But we shall see later on that a very much higher degree of success in pictorial art was achieved by them in their drawing on leather and bark than in their petroglyphs.

The most noted Indian petroglyph is the well-known Dighton Rock inscription, cut on a boulder in the Assonet River, a tributary to the Taunton River, in Dighton, Massachusetts. As the inscription antedates the arrival of the Pilgrims, its age is unknown, but no very early historic period is attributed to it; for the pictorial elements are those current with the Algonquins of the early colonial days, whose work it undoubtedly is. Much has been written about this celebrated petroglyph, and for some time it was erroneously believed by many scholars to be the work of the Northmen, who under Lief Ericsson were known to have temporarily sojourned in New England in the 10th century. It is perhaps the only Indian petroglyph that rises to the dignity of an inscription. The vast majority of them seem to be only rude sketches, mere peckings or scribblings,— meaningless graffiti. Some of them consist largely of totemic marks, as those at Oakley Springs, Arizona, which were cut by the Hopi Indians to commemorate visits paid to that locality. It might seem that these graffiti offer to certain members of the present generation of Americans a refuge behind this aboriginal custom and an excuse for similar modern offenses.

Other rock carvings, like those in the Pipe Stone Quarry, Minnesota, and scattered quarries and ledges elsewhere, where pipe stone was cut, exhibit the totems of families or tribes indicating proprietary rights in the quarry or portions of it. But the Dighton Rock inscription, as the reader will see by consulting a reproduction of it (Fig. 13) is of a much higher order of rock sculpture. Since 1680, when Dr. Danforth made the first copy of this inscription, many other drawings have been made of it. Cotton Mather, whose pen and tongue won him such unenviable renown in his persecution and prosecution of the so-called witches of Salem, tried his pencil on this inscription, but failed to show any resemblance either to Dr. Danforth's drawing or to the average of those that followed. It must be explained that the rock is in the bed of the river, partly covered at high tide and has been subjected for several hundred years to the natural erosion of water and fluvial débris. The inscription consequently has become increasingly more and more obliterated as recurring spring freshets have washed over and eroded the rock. Successive drawings of it have been made by Dr. Greenwood in 1730; Mr. Stephen Sewell, a well-known antiquarian, in 1768; another in 1788 by Mr. James Winthrop, and since then by a number of antiquaries; but nearly all differ more or less in their details, especially those mentioned. The cut herewith shown is a copy of a drawing made by Dr. Baylies and Mr. Goodwin in 1790, and is generally conceded to be one of the most authentic of the many drawings made of the inscription. As will readily be observed the ideas of form are very rudimentary and the draughtsmanship is extremely crude. Schoolcraft in his "Archives of Aboriginal Knowledge" tells of his taking a copy of the inscription to a well-known Indian seer or Meda of the

Algonquin tribe. He seemed to experience little difficulty in interpreting to his own satisfaction (!) the meaning of the drawings; yet the extreme limitations of this mode of expression and the correspondingly wide latitude in interpretation obviously showed that the pictures conveyed nothing but suggestions to the mind of the reader. This is true of every form of pictorial inscription of the North American Indians. The key to the interpretation of all these inscriptions, on any material whatsoever, is to be found not so much in the characters themselves as in the imagination and responsiveness of the reader. The ideographs — if the so-called inscrip-

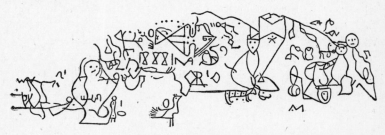

Fig. 13. Rock inscription by the Algonquin Indians. " Dighton Rock," near Taunton, Massachusetts.

tions ever rise to this level, though they rarely do — are suggestive, not specific. Briefly, a part of this Indian seer's description of the many pictures and characters in the inscription ran about as follows: — The large drawing on the left is an ancient prophet or war chief. His wife is beside him. The large triangular object above is the lodge of the seer or prophet. The semi-circle of dots above it signifies six moons,— the number of months for the preparation or consummation of the exploit recorded. The spotted animal in the lower part of the picture is the totem of the principal war chief of the expedition. The three characters looking like hour glasses are headless bodies, recording the number of victims killed. The figures on the right are the enemy.

The reader will need no further admonition that he must not look to these so-called inscriptions for any evidence of writing as such, nor should he waste his time in a futile search among the scrappy marks in this particular Indian inscription, or any other, for any trace of written characters. They do not exist in any Indian picture-writing of any sort. Certain pictorial elements of universal currency, as will be explained later on, were on the point of becoming conventional ideograms ready for later generations of Indian culture to be further simplified into abstract, alphabetic characters. One of these characters cut on the Dighton Rock passed with the Algonquins everywhere as the conventional representation of a man. It became highly differentiated, and in the four forms shown in Fig. 36 represented respectively a man, a woman, a dead male victim, and a dead female victim.

Another extensive petroglyph is the one at " Indian God Rock," cut on a boulder on the bank of the Allegheny River near Franklin, Pa. It is at the present time in a bad state of preservation and for the most part is almost undecipherable. Other important examples are the carvings on rocks in the Susquehanna River near Conowingo, Maryland, at Hamilton Farms and in numerous localities along the Kanawha River, West Virginia. At Millsboro, Pennsylvania, and at Cunningham's Island, Lake Erie, are some very elaborate rock carvings. The sculptures consist of many figures closely crowded together, among them being men, animals, birds, footprints of animals and other objects. The character of the drawing, as shown in the illustrations, Fig. 14 and Fig. 15, is very similar to the petroglyphs already illustrated, being the work of the same great family of Indians, the Algon-

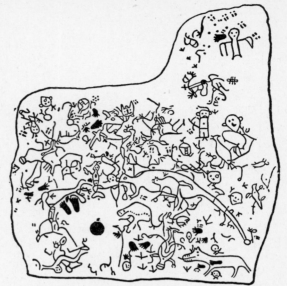

Fig. 14. Petroglyphs at Millsboro, Pennsylvania.

Fig. 15 Algonquian petroglyphs.   Cunningham Island, Lake Erie.

quins. At Safe Harbor, Pa., where there are rock carvings, the inscriptions undoubtedly refer to hunting, as

Fig. 16. Indian petroglyphs in Nebraska.

there are footprints of animals and birds depicted, as
well as the outlines of men and birds. They probably indicate the prevalence of game. It is somewhat remarkable, however, that the outlines of fish occur so very infrequently in these petroglyphs. Occasional petroglyphs

are to be found throughout the region of the Allegheny Mountains and quite abundantly in Ohio. There also are many petroglyphs on cliffs and on walls of the cañons of the Colorado River. Rock inscriptions also abound in great numbers on rocks along the banks of the Walker River in Nevada, in Nebraska, and others of our Western States. Fig. 16, the reproduction of a photograph of petroglyphs in Nebraska, is typical of these rock sculptures of the aborigines of the United States. From coast

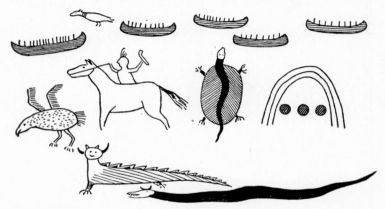

Fig. 17. Myeengun's inscription. Inscription Rock, near Pictured Rocks, Lake Superior.

to coast and from the Great Lakes to Arizona and New Mexico the same general characteristics of pictography prevail, indicative of the same low stage of human culture and crudity of art expression that characterizes the petroglyphs of the far eastern tribes.

In the " Archives of Aboriginal Knowledge," Schoolcraft gives an account of an inscription painted on a cliff known as Inscription Rock on the banks of the Carp River near the Pictured Rocks on Lake Superior, Canada. It is reproduced in Fig. 17. It was copied on birch bark by the Indian chief Chingwaük, a man well versed in the *kekeéwin,* or pictographic method of communicating ideas. He was a member of the Wabeno or Medicine Society, and understood the Midéwiwin ceremonial of the aboriginal religion. The inscription portrays the exploits of a chief, one Myeengun, literally "merman-totem." This briefly is the explanation of the inscription given by the Indian : — The lake was crossed near a small bay in five canoes. There were sixteen braves in the first canoe, nine in the second, ten in the third, eight in the fourth, and eight in the fifth also. The first canoe was commanded by Kishkemunasee, the Kingfisher, whose totem is drawn above the canoes. The expedition took three days, as is indicated by the three suns under the arching sky. The man on horseback is the Meda or magic-maker who is supposed to assist the expedition. The bird is Migazee, the eagle, the symbol of courage. The tortoise is Mikenock, the land tortoise, quite uniformly in Indian inscriptions symbolizing reaching land, the objective. The fabulous creatures below are animal spirits that have been invoked to aid in the exploit.

One hardly can look upon or contemplate these rude attempts of the North American Indians to record their thoughts or deeds without feelings of unconcealed pity for the artistic meagerness and almost total failure of purpose of their symbols through the inadequacy of their system. Some rude form of graphic art leading up to a definite system of writing, some rude record of the activities of tribal or family life ever has been the unconscious aim of almost every race of mankind. "Till men could leave behind them a record of acquired knowledge, the sum of their acquisitions must have remained stationary." Without this instrumentality culture becomes impossible or its transmission slow and precarious. The nations that early have developed an intelligible and practicable system of writing, like the ancient Babylonians and Egyptians, have been the ones to lead the van in the march of civilization; transferring the torch of learning unquenched from generation to generation, as the sacred fires of their altars were conserved. It is therefore with no little pathos in contemplating these crude records of the American Indians that we recall the lines of Freneau in referring to them:

> " Here still a lofty rock remains
>   On which the curious eye may trace
> Now wasted half by wearing rains
>   The fancies of a ruder race."

It will be a decided relief to turn to another species of record in which, owing to the favorableness of the materials, a much greater degree of success in graphic art was attained by the Indians than in their rock sculptures. In the earlier Colonial days of this country records made by the Iroquois, Leni-Lenape and other Indian tribes, on birch bark, leather, wood and other materials, were quite common. Birch bark in particular was largely in vogue, being used extensively in recording treaties, contracts and tribal " counts " or histories. It may be considered the Indian's paper. Only a limited number of examples of this kind of record will be presented here, because a more extended exposition of Indian pictography would be out of place and unwarranted; moreover, it would be an unnecessary interruption of the prosecution of our inquiry, as the records are quite similar in their general pictorial characteristics. A sufficient number only will be given to illustrate by their general character the manner and mode in which an unlettered race enters upon the primary stages of record making in their long and tedious evolution toward true writing. As mankind seems to have been much the same the world over, at the several different stages of civilization, the pages that we shall have revealed to us of the life-history of the aborigines of the New World doubtless will prove to be similar to the opening chapter of the same historic evolution that began in the primitive pictures of the Turanian inhabitants of the Old World, and passing through the re-

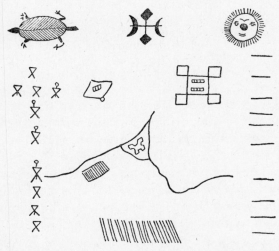

Fig. 18. Wingenund's inscription on birch bark. Muskingum River, Ohio.

fining agencies of the Semitic races finally developed into the alphabetic writing of the Aryan Greeks.

One of the most romantic inscriptions that has come down to us is the one illustrated in Fig. 18, taken from Schoolcraft's " Archives of Aboriginal Knowledge." It was found in 1780 cut on a tree trunk on the bank of the Muskingum River in Ohio. It was drawn with charcoal and bear's grease. It may be remembered that after the conquest of Canada in 1758–59 the Indians headed by Pontiac formed a plan simultaneously to attack the military posts of the British west of the Alleghenies. Nine

out of twelve stockades were taken. Only Fort Pitt and
Fort Detroit successfully resisted. The inscription relates the exploit of Wingenund, chief of the Delawares of
the Muskingum. The tortoise is the totemic symbol of
the main branch of the Delawares. The geometric device
is the totem or armorial badge of Wingenund. The ten
lines under the sun probably denote two expeditions of
six and four days respectively. The oblique lines at the
bottom represent twenty-three warriors. The ten pictographic men on the left represent the vanquished enemies,
six dead and four captive. Some of them are male and
some are female. The small fort is one on Lake Erie
taken in 1762; the square-bastioned fort is Fort Pitt at the
confluence of the Allegheny and Monongahela rivers, the
present site of the city of Pittsburgh. The cross-hatch
lines represent the town.

The posting of this sketch doubtless was an act of
bravado, or one of exultation. That this was not infrequently done may be inferred from an occurrence
experienced and related by Schoolcraft himself. In the
summer of 1820 he was a member of the United States
exploring expedition to the sources of the Mississippi
near Fond du Lac, Minnesota. The party consisted of sixteen persons with two Indian guides. Schoolcraft relates:
" One morning as we prepared to leave the camp, a
small strip of birch bark containing devices (Fig. 19)
was observed elevated on top of a split sapling some
eight or ten feet high. One end of this pole was thrust
firmly into the ground, leaning in the direction we were
to go. . . . It was a symbolic record of the circumstances
of our crossing the summit and of the night's encamp-
ment at this spot." Schoolcraft goes on to explain that
the drawing depicted the commanding officer with his
sword, the mineralogist, interpreter and three other offi-

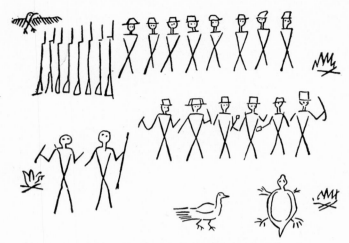

Fig. 19. Birch bark inscription. Fond du Lac, Minnesota.

cials. Also the eight soldiers with their guns. All of these were drawn with hats on,— the distinguishing mark of the white man. The two Indian guides were drawn hatless. Three camp fires were shown, indicating the number of days spent in camp. The object of this record was a notification and warning to other Indians of the presence of this party of white men.

The Dakota and Sioux Indians about a century ago kept tribal " diaries," or calendric counts, now spoken of as " Winter Counts," wherein was recorded the principal event of each winter. They were painted on skins, sometimes on a tent set apart for this purpose. Each picture or ideograph stood for one winter and chronicled the most important occurrence of that year. There were several of these counts. The most noted of them was one kept by the Dakota nation and painted on a buffalo robe (Fig. 20). It was begun in 1800–'01 by Lone Dog, and was maintained for a period of seventy-one years. There were other similar counts of the Da-

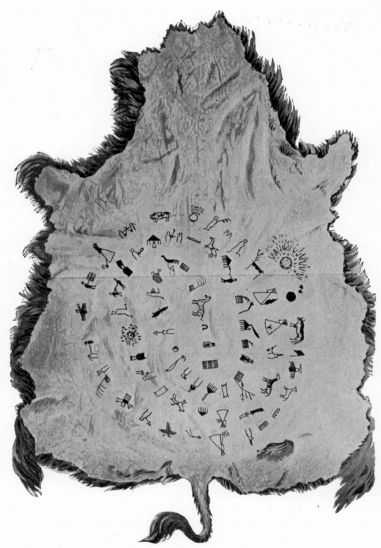

Fig. 20. Winter Count on a buffalo robe. Kept by the Dakota Indians, 1800–1870.

kotas. One was begun in 1775–'76 and maintained until 1878–'79. Still another was begun in 1786–'87 and extended to 1876–'77. What is reputed to be one of the original robes is now (1920) in the Museum of the American Indian, Heye Foundation, New York City. The meaning of the pictures in Lone Dog's count was ascertained by Lieut. Reed at Fort Sully, Dakota, in November, 1876, and by Garrick Mallery at Ft. Rice. It is safe to say that this record is unique among savage or uncivilized peoples. The chronicle begins in the middle of the robe, as the reader will note, and progresses spirally outward, each year being individualized by a single pictograph. The first one,— that for the year 1800–'01, seen in the lower middle part of the robe, symbolizes: " Thirty Dakotas killed by Crow Indians." Among the many winters illustrated are: " Many-crows-died-winter "; " First-flag-winter " (when the first United States flag was seen) ; " Small-pox-used-them-all-up-again-winter "; " Horse-shoe-winter " (when the first shod horse was seen). One of the most interesting of the pictographs is the one designed to record the winter of 1833–'34. It depicts the moon with stars darting across it, and records beyond a doubt the great meteoric shower over the United States which occurred on the evening of November 12, 1833. White-Cow Killer in his count portrays it in a very similar manner, but explained it as " Plenty-stars-winter." The pictograph drawn to symbolize the year 1855, an Indian taking the hand of a white man, records the treaty of peace made in that year by Gen. Harvey with certain tribes of the Dakotas. The year 1869–'70 is represented in these counts by a black sun with stars around it,— a most graphic portrayal and record of the total eclipse of the sun, which occurred August 7, 1869. The next and last pictograph depicts a battle between the Crows and the Uncpapas; the latter losing fourteen but killing twenty-nine out of thirty of the former. The central object is the stockade, the fourteen dead lying around it. Without the explanation of the unhappy Lone Dog the Indians themselves must have interpreted this pictograph to be an explosion of gunpowder! The drawings in all these " counts " of the Dakotas though rather faulty are very spirited, and generally — but not always — are readily intelligible; being a marked advance in artistic treatment over the earlier rock pictographs of the Algonquins of the East. But this is the natural progress of the art of graphic expression as it develops in skill and perfection through the practice of a century or two.

The Pima Indians, of the Gila River reservation in southern Arizona, kept calendric counts very similar to those of the Dakotas. Frank Russell gives a very interesting account of them in the 26th Annual Report of the Bureau of American Ethnology, 1904–'05. Russell enumerates four chronological records of the North American Indians: (1) The Walam Olum of the Delawares, to be described in this chapter, the definitive account of which was published by Dr. Daniel G. Brinton (1885); (2) The Lone Dog winter count, just described; (3) The series of Kiowa calendars, somewhat similar to the winter counts of the Dakotas, a description of which by James Mooney appears in the 17th Annual Report of the Bureau of American Ethnology; (4) The Records of the Pimas.

During his sojourn among the Pima Indians Mr. Russell recovered five notched calendar sticks. Two of the sticks were " told " him by the possessor. The record covers a period of seventy years, dating from the season immediately preceding the great meteoric shower of

November 12, 1833, as do the oldest of the calendric counts among the Kiowa. There are traditions of older sticks that have been lost or buried with their keepers. Juan Thomas, of the village of Blackwater, had lost his stick in some inexplicable manner, but he was continuing the history with pencil and paper. "It is noteworthy," says Mr. Russell, " that the change from stick to paper introduced a tendency to use pictorial symbols rather than merely mnemonic characters, such as are most easily incised on the surface of a stick having clearly marked grain."

The Pima year begins with the saguaro harvest, about June. It is the season for feasting and rejoicing. As there is no winter, there are no " winter counts," but the years are recorded by harvests. There are but two seasons in the Gila valley, the season of torrid heat and that of ideal weather. " The onset of the former coincides with the harvest season, and the new year is therefore adapted, albeit unwittingly, to seasonal change. The year mark is invariably a deep notch across the stick. . . . The records of the early years are memorized and there are few minor notches to aid in recalling them. The year notches are exactly alike, yet in asking a narrator to go back and repeat the story for a certain year, the writer found that he never made a mistake."

Most of the symbols on these sticks are geometric or conventional; yet some are pictographic if not ideographic. Only one symbol had come arbitrarily to designate a single event. This was the T-shaped character which was used to record the " tizwin drunks," or festivals at which saguaro or agave liquor was brewed and freely imbibed. A very good idea of the symbols and pictographs carved on these calendar sticks may be gained by examining those selected for illustration in Fig. 21.

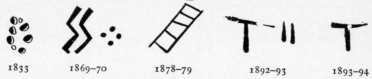

1833   1869–70   1878–79   1892–93   1893–94

Fig. 21. Pictographs selected from the Calendric Counts of the Pima Indians, Gila River Reservation, Arizona.

The pictograph for 1833 very much resembles that for the same year, the " plenty-stars-winter," of the Dakotas. The pictograph for 1869–'70 records an unusually heavy winter rain which gullied the hills deeply. The zig-zag lines constitute a definite ideogram for water, almost universally employed the world over. The pictograph used as a symbol for the year 1878–'79 illustrates the principal event of the year, which was the building of the Southern Pacific railroad along the southern border of the Gila River reservation. The symbol for the year 1892–'93 records that " a dance at Salt River occurred in which two men drunk with whisky killed each other." The same symbol — really an ideogram —employed to designate the year 1893–'94, is laconically read as follows: " the village of Hiamtam and the Gila Maricopas had a dance together, *but no one was killed*"!

We will now give a few illustrations of the manner in which the illiterate Indians of the Great Plains responded to the new requirements of a civilization foreign to them and their primitive culture in matters of official records, petitions to their governors or commissioners, letters, etc. Fig. 22 is a reproduction of a part of a census roll taken by Red Cloud, chief of a tribe of the Dakotas at the Pine Ridge Agency, Dakota, comprising Red Shirt's band. " Owing to some disagreement, the agent refused to acknowledge that chief as head of the Indians at the agency and named another as the official chief. The In-

Fig. 22. Red-Cloud's Census — Red-Shirt's Band.

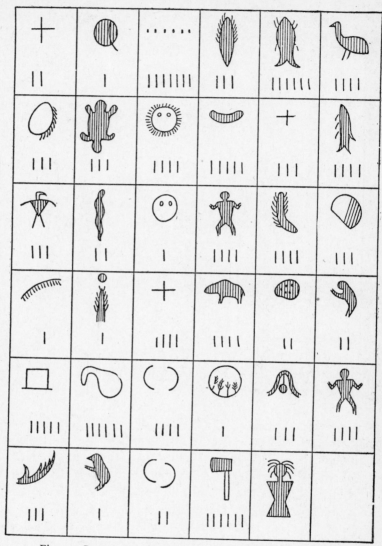

Fig. 23. Census roll of Indian band at Mille Lac, Minnesota.

dians under Red Cloud exhibited their allegiance to him by attaching or having their names attached to seven sheets of ordinary manila paper, which were sent to Washington." (Garrick Mallery in Annual Report, Smithsionian Institution, 1882–'83.) The family names of the nineteen Indian braves in this band, designated by their totems drawn in the customary manner as proceeding from their heads, in order are: Leafing, Horned Horse,

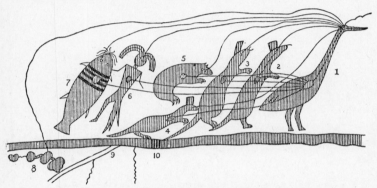

Fig. 24. Petition of Chippewa Indians from Lake Superior to the U. S. Government at Washington.

White Whirlwind, Wolf Ear, Afraid-of-Elk, Feathers, Tall Man, Elk Head, Ring Owl, Standing Bear, Small Ring, Charging Hawk, Afraid-of-Bull, Medicine Horse, Two Eagles, Red Shirt, Bear Nostrils, Spotted Horse, and Afraid-of-Bear. Fig. 23, the census roll of an Indian band at Mille Lac, Minnesota, is a more complete document than the above. It was drawn and given to the agent by Nago-Nabe, a Chippewa Indian, during the progress of the annuity payments in 1849. It designates by pictographic characters — totems — each family of the band and the number of individuals in the family. This number is recorded by the several vertical lines below the totem signs.

The tangled turnout of animals shown in Fig. 24, which more nearly resembles a hunter's catch, is in reality a dignified and important petition presented to the United States government in January, 1849, by a delegation of Chippewa Indians from Lake Superior. The party was not accredited by their local agent, so in lieu of the official credentials they presented a pictographic petition consisting of five sheets of white birch bark on which were drawn the totems of the different members of the band of Indians. The illustration shown is the first sheet, the petition itself. The chief (1) is represented as the leader of the delegation. He is of the Crane clan. Following him are three representatives of the Marten clan (2, 3 and 4). The other three members of the party were sent as representatives of the Bear, Man Fish and Cat Fish clans, respectively, and were designated in the petition, the same as their companions, by their painted totems (5, 6 and 7). The lines drawn from the eye and heart of the Crane to the eyes and hearts of his fellow petitioners indicate respectively: " union of views " and " unity of feeling and purpose," that actuated every member of the delegation. The line drawn from the eye of the chief forward denotes the course of the journey; the one leading backward to the small lakes (8) indicates the desired grant which constitutes the object of the journey. The long parallel lines across the sheet at 10 represent Lake Superior, and the short parallel lines (9) a path leading from some central point on its southern shore to the villages and interior lakes at 8, at which place the Indians desired to settle and pursue the arts of peace and civilization.

In the Annual Report of the Smithsonian Institution for 1882–'83 Garrick Mallery gives a description of a letter sent by a Cheyenne Indian named Truth-following-

his-Wife, to his son, Little-Man, at the Pine Ridge
Agency, Dakota, asking him to return home, and notify-
ing him of his sending him fifty-three dollars for this
purpose. The whole episode is so interesting and the
" letter " so entertaining and characteristic of Indian

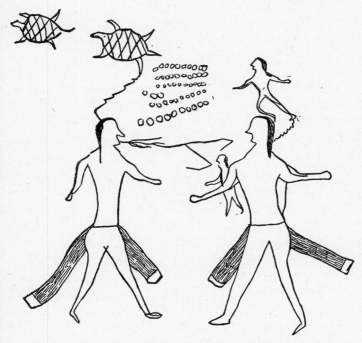

Fig. 25. Letter to Little-Man from his father, a Cheyenne Indian.

" writing " that we reproduce the cut in Fig. 25 and quote
the following from Mr. Mallery's account: " The letter
was evidently understood by Little-Man, as he immediately called upon Dr. V. T. McGillycuddy, Indian agent
at the Pine Ridge Agency, and was aware that the sum of
$53 had been placed at his credit for the purpose of en-
abling him to pay his expenses in going the long journey

to his father's home in the Indian Territory. Dr. McGillycuddy had, by the same mail, received a letter from
Agent Dyer, enclosing $53, and explaining the reason for
its being sent, which enabled him also to understand the
pictographic letter. With the above explanation it very
clearly shows, over the head of the figure to the left, the
turtle following the turtle's wife, united with the head of
the figure by a line, and over the head of the other figure,
also united by a line to it, is a little man. Also over the
right arm of the last mentioned figure is another little man
in the act of springing or advancing toward Truth-fol-
lowing-his-Wife, from whose mouth proceed two lines,
curved or hooked at the end, as if drawing the little
figure towards him. It is suggested that the last mentioned part of the pictograph is the substance of the communication, i.e., ' come to me,' the larger figures with the
name totems being the persons addressed and addressing.
Between and above the larger figures are fifty-three round
objects, intended for dollars."

In the religious rites and ceremonies of the American
Indians, notably the Ojibwas and Dakotas, extensive use
was made of charts or scrolls of birch bark or skin from
which were sung the Medas or Medicine-songs. These
Medas were the traditional songs of the tribes, and related to their religion, their bodily and spiritual salvation,
and whatever of aspiration or endeavor actuated them in
life. Among the Ojibwa Indians, a branch of the great
Algonquian linguistic family, there is a religious society,
known as the Midéwiwin or Great Medicine Society.
The Midé or Wabeno who presides over this society is
supposed to possess the powers of prophecy and the art of
healing. He is the Medicine Man of the tribe, and the
seer or pow-wow who leads by his incantations the peculiar
traditional ceremonies which make up the religious rites

incident to the periodic invocations to the Great Spirit who preserves human life, or guarantees spiritual life to the members of the tribe. The invocations are chiefly prayers for health, healing medicines, future happiness, rain and a plentiful harvest. The Midé chants the songs from a chart or scroll of bark or leather upon which are painted pictorial, mnemonic symbols suggesting the ideas in the song either directly, by metaphor or by symbol.

While we may not be able to look upon these ceremonial observances as anything other than sorcery, we must

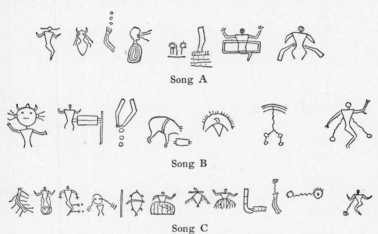

Song A

Song B

Song C

Fig. 26. Mnemonic ceremonial songs of the Ojibwa Indians.

credit the Indians, if with credulity and fanaticism, yet with fervent religious sincerity. It is with this spirit that we should read their " songs." The first two songs in Fig. 26 are from the Midéwiwin Society of the Ojibwa, and are reproduced from the Report of the Smithsonian Institution for 1885–'86. The following description is from the article by W. J. Hoffman. The songs are invocations to Kitshi Manido, the Great Spirit, to grant life and happiness, and to give knowledge of healing medicines and remedies. Each of the phrases is repeated before advancing to the next, as often as the singer desires, and in proportion to the amount of reverence and awe with which he wishes to impress his hearers. There is usually a brief interval between each of the phrases, and a longer one at the appearance of a vertical line, denoting a rest or pause. One song may occupy, therefore, from fifteen minutes to one-half an hour.

Song A is interpreted as follows:

(1) When I am out of hearing, where am I? (The lines extending from the ears denote hearing; the arms denote toward the right and left, being the gestures of negation, usually made by throwing them outward and away from the front of the body.)

(2) In my house, I see.   (Light indicated by lines extending from the eyes; the horns denote superiority of the singer.)

(3) When I rise it gives me life, and I take it. (The arm reaches into the sky to receive gifts which are handed down by the Good Spirit. The short transverse line across the forearm indicates the arch of the sky; this line being an abbreviation of the curve usually employed to designate the same.)

(4) The reason why I am happy. (Asking the Spirit for life, which is granted. The singer's body is filled with the heart enlarged, i.e., fullness of heart, the lines from the mouth denoting abundance of voice or grateful utterance,— singing.)

(5) The spirit says there is plenty of medicine in the Midé wigwam. (Two superior spirits, Kitshi Manido and Dzhe Manido, whose bodies are surrounded by lines of sacredness, tell the Midé where the mysterious remedies are to be found. The vertical waving lines are the lines indicating

these communications; the horizontal line at the bottom is the earth's surface.)

(6) The Spirit placed medicine in the ground, let us take **it.** (The arm of Kitchi Manido put into the ground sacred plants, indicated by the spots at different horizons on the earth. The short vertical and waving lines denote sacredness of the objects.)

(7) I am holding this that I bring to you. (The singer sits in the Midéwiwin and offers the privilege of entrance by initiation to the hearer.)

(8) I have good favor in the eyes of my Midé friends. (The Good Spirit has put life into the body of the singer, as indicated by the two mysterious arms reaching toward his body; i.e., the heart, the seat of life.)

Song B runs along in quite the same line of thought, as follows:

(1) I hear the spirit speaking to me.

(2) I am going into the medicine lodge.

(3) I am gathering medicine to make me live.

(4) I give you medicine, and a lodge, also.

(5) I am flying into my lodge.

(6) The spirit has dropped medicine from the sky where we can get it.

(7) I have the medicine in my heart.

Song C is reproduced from the Report of the Bureau of American Ethnology for 1888–'89. It is interpreted as follows:

(1) My arm is almost pulled out with digging medicine. It is full of medicine.

(2) Almost crying because the medicine is lost.

(3) Yes, there is much medicine. You may cry for it.

(4) Yes, I see there is plenty of it.

(Rest. Dancing begins.)

(5) When I come out the sky becomes clear.

(6) The spirit has given me power to see.

(7) I brought the medicine to bring life. (The Thunder Bird who brings rain. A common ideograph among the Indians.)

(8) I, too, see how much there is.

(9) I am going to the medicine lodge.

(10) I take life from the sky.

(11) Let us talk to one another.

(12) The spirit is in my body, my friend.

W. J. Hoffman in referring to these songs says: " The mnemonic songs of the Ojibwas present the most interesting pictographs, and evince the highest degree of graphic skill attained by the Ojibwas. Almost every form of simple or complex ideograms is here portrayed; presenting types of simple delineation as well as abstract ideas and various attributes thought to be almost beyond the range of portrayal without the aid of a more advanced method of writing." These ceremonial songs will afford the reader ample opportunity to observe the probable mode by which in the development of writing pictographic signs have developed into constant, ideographic symbols of recognized currency. Also the way in which by pictorial synecdoche a part of a body or thing, by its action, attribute or function, came to represent an idea connected with the thing itself,— as the eye for seeing; the ear for hearing; the mouth for speaking; the uplifted hand for reaching; etc. In the same way, if the Indians could have been allowed to develop their own ideography, the hat — which was their distinguishing symbol for the white man — in the course of time probably would have become the phonogram for their spoken word for white man, and eventually in a highly conventionalized and simplified form possibly become the alphabetic character for the initial sound of this same word. Such considerations make the pictography of our American Indians, more particularly that of the Ojibwa, of unusual interest, for we see in it writing in the first stage of its genesis. Unfortunately for science — possibly for the Indians, who can tell? — the chapter closed at this stage, and a new and better system of writing was adopted.

As in the historic East, mortuary inscriptions in tombs, on stele and in other forms, have preserved more of ancient writing than any other agency, we naturally look for evidences of this form of inscription among the Indians. Nor are we disappointed, for pictorial epitaphs on Indian grave-posts were quite common in the early days of the New World. But being painted on wood, most of them have perished. Longfellow in his " Song of Hiawatha " thus alludes to this custom:

" And they painted on the grave-posts,
     On the graves yet unforgotten,
     Each his own ancestral Totem,
     Each the symbol of his household;
     Figures of the Bear and Reindeer,
     Of the Turtle, Crane and Beaver,
     Each inverted as a token
     That the owner was departed,
     That the Chief who bore the symbol
     Lay beneath in dust and ashes."

Three of these grave-posts, or " adjedatigs," are illustrated in Fig. 27. They are reproduced from Schoolcraft's " Archives of Aboriginal Knowledge." The first one is the grave-post of Shingabawassin,—" Image-Stone," a noted chief of the St. Mary's band of Indians who inhabited the regions about Lake Superior. His

totem, the crane, is depicted reversed, which is the significant mode of representing totems on Indian grave-posts.
The Australian aborigines have a similar custom of invert-
ing the totem. Indeed, in medieval times the leopards on
the escutcheons of the English kings were reversed to in-

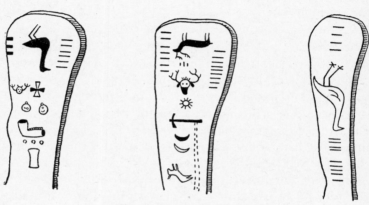

Fig. 27. Indian grave posts.

dicate the decease of the king. We may recall here the
inverted torch which denoted death in the classic sculptures. The six marks on the right indicate the number of
important enterprises, probably battles, in which the chief
had been engaged. The three different marks on the left
record the number of treaties of peace which he had at-
tended. The other symbols are not all so easily understood. The calumet is of course the symbol of peace, and
the hatchet below it that of war. The cross is probably a
totemic sign of insignia. The deer's head may only refer
to the deceased's chief occupation of the chase. The other
signs appear undecipherable.

The second illustration shows the adjedatig of Wabo-
jug, a celebrated war chief who died near Lake Superior
in 1793. The family totem, the reindeer, is represented

reversed as customary. The horizontal marks on either side of the totem sign indicate the number of important enterprises in which he had been engaged, probably battles, expeditions or treaties of peace. The three vertical lines beneath the totem indicate the number of wounds received in battles. The moose's head refers to a desperate encounter with this animal. The hatchet symbolizes war. The significance of the remaining signs is not clear. The crescents may be bows and refer to the chase, or they may refer to some moonlight expedition. The third adjedatig is that of another chief of the crane clan, inverted like the others, with lines of credit for courage in battles.

We will close this interesting, but what plainly threatens to be digressing, phase of Indian pictography by one more ritualistic song, the most noble of any on record; one that rises to the level and dignity of an epic. Among the many manuscripts left at the time of his death by Samuel Rafinsque-Schmaltz, a learned scholar residing in Philadelphia, was a copy of a cycle of records written in pictographic or ideographic characters by the Leni-Lenape Indians. E. G. Squire, the literary executor of Rafinsque, says in his " Historical and Mythological Traditions of the Algonquins ": " Among these manuscripts was one entitled the Walam Olum (literally, ' painted sticks '), or painted and engraved traditions of the Leni-Lenape, comprising five divisions; the first two embodying the traditions referring to the creation and a general flood, and the rest comprising a record of various migrations, with a list of 97 chiefs, in the order of their succession, coming down to the period of the Discovery. This manuscript also embraces 184 compound mnemonic symbols, accompanied by a sentence or verse in the original language, of which a literal translation is given in English. The only explanation which we have concerning it is contained in a footnote in the hand of Rafinsque in which he states that the manuscript and wooden originals were obtained in Indiana in 1822, and that they were for a long time inexplicable, until with a deep study of the Delaware and the aid of Zeisberger's Manuscript Dictionary in the library of the Philosophical Society, in Philadelphia, a translation was effected. This translation, it may here be remarked, so far as I have been able to test it, is a faithful one, and there is slight doubt that the original is what it professes to be, a genuine Indian record. The evidence that it is so is, however, rather internal and collateral than direct. . . . As already observed, it has strong internal evidence of being what it purports to be, evidence sufficiently strong in my estimation to settle its authenticity. I may however add, that, with a view of leaving no means unemployed to ascertain its true value, I submitted it without explanation to an educated Indian chief, Kahgegagah-bowh, George Copway, who unhesitatingly pronounced it authentic, in respect not only to the original signs and accompanying explanations in the Delaware dialect, but also in the general ideas and conceptions which it embodies. He also bore testimony to the fidelity of the translation."

This is Rafinsque's Walam Olum of the Leni-Lenape Indians, which, if authentic,[1] is one of the most remarkable documents ever inscribed by an uncivilized race. It is the first of the three songs constituting the Walam Olum, and describes the creation and cosmogony of the world from the Indian's point of view:

[1] The text and drawings which follow have been taken from no less an authority than the eminent Americanist, Daniel G. Brinton, published in this author's "Library of Aboriginal American Literature," 1885.

At first, in that place, at all times, above the earth,

 On the earth (was) an extended fog, and there the great Manito was.

 At first, forever, lost in space, everywhere, the great Manito was.

 He made the extended land and the sky,

 He made the sun, the moon and the stars.

 He made them all to move evenly.

 Then the wind blew violently, and it cleared, and the water flowed off far and strong.

 And groups of islands grew newly, and then remained.

 Anew spoke the great Manito, a manito to manitos.

 To beings, mortals, souls and all.

 And ever after he was a manito to men, and their grandfather.

 He gave the first mother, the mother of beings.

He gave the fish, he gave the turtles, he gave the beasts, he gave the birds.

 But an evil Manito made evil beings only, monsters.

 He made the flies, he made the gnats.

 All beings were then friendly.

 Truly the manitos were active and kindly

 To those very first men, and to those first mothers; fetched them wishes,

 And fetched them food as they desired it.

 And all had cheerful knowledge, all had leisure, all thought in gladness.

 But very secretly an evil being, a mighty magician came on earth.

 And with him brought badness, quarreling, unhappiness.

 Brought bad weather, brought sickness, brought death.

 All this took place of old on the earth, beyond the great tidewater, at the first.

A few examples of the graphic art of the Lenape Indians are extant, and give corroboration of the reputed artistic skill of this tribe of American aborigines. One of them (Fig. 28) is a slate gorget or charm, which these Indians were sometimes wont to bury with the dead, on which has been etched a remarkable hunting scene. It was found near Doylestown, Bucks Co., Pennsylvania, by Bernard Hansell, in 1872. It is now in the possession of Col. H. D. Paxson, of Philadelphia, and its authenticity is vouched for by Henry C. Mercer, late curator of the Museum of American and Prehistoric Archæology in the

Fig. 28. Slate gorget of the Lenape Indians found near
Doylestown, Pennsylvania.

University of Pennsylvania. The etching which is reproduced from an article on " Prehistoric Art " by Thomas Wilson, in the Smithsonian Institution Report for 1896, depicts a traditional combat between the Indians and the mammoth, which is known to have inhabited North America at the close of the glacial epoch and possibly to have tarried long thereafter.[1] Its wonderful similarity to the art of the Cave Men of the Reindeer Period is most startling, as will instantly be noted by the reader. But there is

[1] Candor compels us to state that few archæologists believe that life in America dates back to so remote a period. While some, like Aleš Hrdlička, Curator of the Division of Physical Anthropology, U. S. National Museum, Washington, D. C., do not believe in an antiquity above 10,000 years, others double this period and yet are far this side of the glacial epoch.

no known ethnological reason for this similarity, nor any archæological reason other than the very early age of primitive art development common to both.

Among the various tribes of the North American Indians, more especially those dwelling east of the Mississippi River, perforated shell beads were extensively employed both as articles of personal adornment, as necklaces, bracelets and other ornaments of dress, as well as the basis of exchange of goods and property. It being their most prized and valuable possession, it passed as currency among them. Under the name of "wampum," it was in general use throughout the eastern part of the country and was the medium of exchange in trading and bartering. Land was sold by the Indians to the white men for wampum, sometimes made by the shrewd white man himself for this most profitable market. From the weaving of wampum beads into collars and belts originally intended and worn as articles of bodily adornment, it seemed but a natural step to utilize these, their most precious possessions, in sealing compacts, treaties and land exchanges. It thus came about that wampum in the form of belts was used as a mnemonic record of important events. It actually became a material for writing, as much so as papyrus, parchment or birch bark. This use of wampum by the unlettered savages of the new continent forms a romantic chapter in their history and development toward civilization.

Wampum belts were extensively used by the Indians in ratifying treaties between tribes and in recording events of unusual importance and significance, and as such they were held in the most sacred reverence. The particular record took the form of the principal idea in the event memorialized, portraying it objectively or by attribute or metaphor. If the subject matter were not capable of pictorial illustration, any conventional form or pattern agreed upon was selected as the " memory jog." These pictures, forms or patterns, woven into these ornamental belts, served as a record of history, a primitive registry of deeds. One of the sachems of the tribe, a man noted for his robust memory, was appointed " Keeper of the Wampum," just the same as the Peruvians appointed the keeper of the quipus, and, as we shall see later on, with the Babylonians also; except that the records of the latter could be read, whereas the shell records of the Indians, like the quipus records of the Peruvians, first had to be learned by rote and memorized under the suggestion of the pictures or pattern on the belt. To quote from W. H. Holmes, former Chief of the Bureau of Ethnology, Washington, D. C.: " At a certain season each year the belts were taken from the treasure house and exposed to the whole tribe, while the history and import of each were publicly recited." Loskiel, in his " Missions of the United Brethren," in referring to wampum belts somewhat similarly records: " They (the Indians) refer to them as public records, carefully preserving them in a chest made for that purpose. At certain seasons they meet to study their meaning and to review the idea of which they were an emblem or confirmation. On such occasions they sit down around the chest, take out one string after the other, handing it about to every person present; and that they may all comprehend its meaning, repeat the words pronounced on its delivery in their whole convention."

The uncertainty and fallibility of this most inadequate method of record is too obvious to call for comment. It is not surprising to learn, through their history, of the pitiful misunderstandings between contracting parties in regard to the true interpretation of certain compacts over which wampum belts had mutually been exchanged, and which eventually led to war with all its concomitant evils. Captain de Lamothe Cadillac in 1703 tells of an Indian chief whose nation had received through the hands of the Ottawas a wampum collar from the Iroquois. They had had it some time, the chief pathetically said, and " the old men had forgotten what the collar said! "

One of the most noted and successful attempts at pictography with wampum is the famous Penn Treaty belt shown in Fig. 29, now in the possession of the Pennsylvania Historical Society in Philadelphia. It is claimed to be the original belt given by the Leni-Lenape sachems to William Penn at the time of the famous treaty at Shackamaxon on the Delaware in 1682. The belt is of white wampum with two figures in the middle in dark colored beads representing respectively an Indian and a white man clasping hands in a bond of friendship. A compact, by the way, that was never broken. The white man is depicted in the manner common with most Indian scribes, with a hat. The authenticity of the belt is guaranteed by the facts of its transfer to the Pennsylvania Historical Society. In 1857 Granville John Penn, a great-grandson of William Penn, presented the belt to the Society. At the time of its transfer Mr. Penn said in guaranteeing the reliability of the belt: " In the first place, its dimensions are greater than those used on more ordinary occasions, . . . being composed of eighteen strings of wampum, which is a proof that it was the record of some very important negotiation. In the next place, in the center of the beads, in a rude but graphic style, are two figures,— that of one evidently intended to be represented in the European costume, wearing a hat; which can only be interpreted as having reference to the treaty of peace and friendship which was concluded between William Penn and the Indians and recorded by them in their own simple but descriptive mode of expressing their meaning, by the employment of hieroglyphics."

It is known that large numbers of wampum belts were in the possession of the Wyandotts, Hurons, Iroquois and other tribes of Indians inhabiting the tract of coun-

Fig. 29. The Penn Treaty Belt. Given by the Indians to William Penn. In the Pennsylvania Historical Society, Philadelphia, Pennsylvania.

try now covered by the states of New York, Ohio and Pennsylvania. They had in most cases a significant ideograph, representative of the event memorialized by the belt,— the calumet or peace pipe, a totemic pictograph of the contracting nation, or later Christian crosses, worked into the groundwork of the beads. A very few other wampum belts are in existence. In the agency building of the Onondagas in Onondaga County, New York, is one of the most perfect specimens of wampum belts in existence. One of the chiefs of the Onondagas declares that there is a tradition that it commemorates a covenant between the Indians and the government of the United States. Fig. 30 is a picture of this belt. In the center is a house which appears to have three principal divisions. (It is more than likely that the Indian who wove the pattern had been to Washington with the commissioners and had seen the Capitol with its central rotunda and dome and the flanking wings.) On either side of the house are two men " who appear to stand beneath protecting arms which pass over their heads, connect with the house and grasp the hands of the first personages immediately on the right and left." Any one familiar

with the imaginative mind of the Indians will at once
recognize this sketch as their mode of objectifying in
metaphorical form the protection afforded by the government from its official center, the Capital of the nation.
There are in all no less than fifteen figures of men who
stand clasping hands left and right around the belt. There
can be little doubt that this commemorated an important
treaty. The nature of the pictographic design, as well
as the fact of its unusual size, proclaims this.   There are
fifteen rows of wampum, with 650 beads in each row,
making a total of 9,750 beads.

Fig. 30. Wampum belt belonging to the Onondaga Indians.

Fig. 31 is a beautiful wampum belt eleven and one-
half inches long made of six strands of blue beads with
a white cross in the middle. It belongs to the class known
as " Missionary Belts," and is similar to the Jesuit missionary belts of the Hurons. Dr. Daniel G. Brinton suggests that the two pyramids on either side of the cross
are symbolical representations of church steeples. The
belt probably commemorates some friendly alliance between two Christian communities of converted Indians.

The Eskimos, or Innuit, residing on the Pacific Coast
in Alaska have developed a remarkable talent for pictographic record. As these Indians are very generally un-

lettered, this graphic mode of record is their chief means
of communication when absent in person, and they make
extensive use of it. As their art is contemporaneous, specimens are easily procurable, and most museums contain
excellent specimens of it. The National Museum in
Washington is particularly rich in specimens, and contains
a large number of fine examples. The drawing in most
of these carvings, which are generally etched on bone,
ivory or wood, is very truthful, and evidences a high
degree of technical skill and considerable attainment in
art. We are indebted for the greater part of the follow-

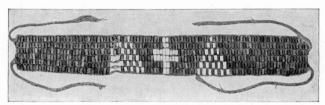

Fig. 31. Wampum Missionary belt.

ing brief account of the art of the Eskimos to Walter J.
Hoffman, M. D., from whose admirable work " The
Graphic Art of the Eskimos," published by the Smithson-
ian Institution in 1895, we have freely borrowed.

Fig. 32 (A) is the record of a hunt, and is similar
to many other such records made by the natives residing
on the coasts of the Bering Sea and the Pacific, in Alaska,
to inform their visitors or friends of their departure for
a designated purpose. They are depicted upon pieces
of wood, which are placed in conspicuous places near the
doors of their habitations. The following is Dr. Hoffman's explanation of the characters:

" No. 1, the speaker, with the right hand indicating
himself and with the left pointing in the direction taken;
No. 2, holding a boat paddle, ' going by boat '; No. 3,

the speaker holding the right hand to the side of the head, to denote ' sleep,' and the left elevated with one finger erect to signify ' one night '; No. 4, a circle with two marks in the middle, signifying an island with huts upon it; No. 5, same as No. 1; No. 6, a circle to denote another ' island ' where they touched; No. 7, similar to No. 3, with an additional finger elevated to signify ' two nights ' or ' sleeps '; No. 8, the speaker with his harpoon, the weapon with which he sometimes hunted, and with the left making the gesture sign to denote ' sea lion.' The hand is held edge-wise, with the thumb elevated, then pushed outward from the body in a slightly downward curve. No. 9 represents a ' sea lion,' which the hunter, No. 10, secured by shooting with bow and arrow. No. 11 is the boat with two persons in it, the paddles projecting downward beneath it. No. 12 is the winter habitation of the speaker." The story may be told somewhat as follows: " I am going on a canoe trip and shall stay over night in one of the huts on the island. From there I shall go to the next island, where I shall remain two nights. I shall hunt for sea lions while there, and shall return home by canoe, bringing my friend with me."

A

B

Fig. 32. Pictographic notices of the Eskimos of Alaska.
A. Record of a hunt.
B. Record of departure.

Fig. 32 (B) is another example of the graphic records of the Innuit. Dr. Hoffman describes it as follows:

"Nos. 1, 3, 5 and 7 represent the person spoken to. No arms are indicated, as no response is supposed to be made by him. No. 2 indicates the speaker with his right hand to his side or breast, indicating ' self,' the left hand pointing in the direction in which he is going. No. 4, both hands of the speaker are elevated, with fingers and thumbs extended, signifying ' many.' When the hands are thus held up, in sign language, it signifies ' ten,' but when they are brought forward and backward from one to another, many. (Among the " Plains Indians " of the Indian Territory, when both hands are thus held up for ' ten,' and then thrown downward to the left, it signifies ten times ' ten ' or ' one hundred.' The latter practice of indicating any number multiplied by ' ten,' by thus throwing to the left both hands, has not been found to obtain among the Alaskan natives.) No. 6, the right hand is placed to the side of the head to denote ' sleep ' or ' night '; in this instance denoting ' many sleeps '; or, in other words, ' many nights and days '; and the left hand points downward to denote ' at that place.' No. 8, the right hand is directed toward the starting point, while the left is brought upward toward the head —' to go home,' or ' whence he came.' " This simple narrative may briefly be stated thus: " I am going on a journey to a distant place. I shall remain there many days (or nights) ; but I shall return home again."

The most characteristic art of the Innuit is manifested in the carved records of hunting and fishing expeditions etched on bone and ivory, upon their implements, household utensils and other articles. Their drawing of animals in its truthfulness to nature and its spirited action is strongly reminiscent of the Cave Men. So striking is this similarity that W. Boyd Dawkins in his " Early Man in Britain," 1880, p. 233, says: " On passing in review the manners and customs of all the savage tribes known to modern ethnology, there is only one people with whom the Cave Men are intimately connected in their manners and customs, in their art, and in their implements and weapons. . . . The most astonishing bond of union between the Cave Men and the Eskimos is the art of representing animals. Just as the former engraved bisons, horses, mammoths and other creatures familiar to them, so do the latter represent the animals upon which they depend for food. On the implements of the one you see the hunting of the urus and the horse depicted in the same way as the killing of the reindeer and walrus on the implements of the other." Mr. Dawkins believes that they belong to the same race, having been driven northward by sturdier peoples. Arthur J. Evans in his lecture: " The European Diffusion of Pictography and its Bearings on the Origin of Script," delivered before the University of Oxford, also alludes to the apparent racial affinities between the existing far northern races and the Cave-Men. He says: "It is interesting to observe that it is in the extreme north of Europe, where the conditions most approach those of the Reindeer Period, that purely pictographic methods have remained the longest." In regard to the art work of the Lapps, Prof. Evans says: " The Lapp troll drums (Fig. 33), used as a means of divination by the native shamans, show a variety of linear figures and symbols which had a traditional interpretation. The variety of gestures displayed, somewhat rudely it is true, by the various figures on this drum, illustrate the intimate and ever recurring connection between pictography and gesture language."

The strong similarity between these Lapp pictographic records, as shown in the drum illustrated and those of the Eskimos, is so striking as to suggest an artistic inheritance

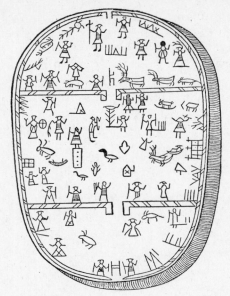

Fig. 33. Lapp troll drum. (From A. J. Evans.)

descended from some common, ancient, ancestral source. It is a remarkable fact, if this connection between the Eskimo and the Reindeer Man of antiquity can be established, that they have conserved their art so many centuries, losing nothing, yet on the other hand gaining so little. But before we accept such a theory, we should bear in mind the probable historic migrations of these different peoples. The Eskimos of America, in common with all the aboriginal inhabitants of the country, north or south, are believed to have descended from Mongol tribes emigrating from Mongolia, and entering the extreme northwest of the country, over the Aleutian Islands. The Lapps, somewhat akin to the northern Mongolians, and speaking a language of the Mongol type, are believed to have been forced northward in Europe into their present semi-arctic home by the more southern races. We certainly shall need much more knowledge concerning these races than we have at command to-day before we can be certain of the racial affinities that seem to lie on the surface.

It would seem as though the rigors of an extreme northern climate to which the Eskimos have been so long inured had checked the further development of their art, arresting it in its earliest stage. This is no more surprising than the arrest in a later stage of its development of the written language of the Chinese, a people enjoying a salubrious and temperate climate. In any event, we witness in these Eskimo inscriptions writing in its making, and they are interesting to this extent that they offer us perhaps the very best examples of graphic record that the world has to offer, if it is primitive. They are frank to a fault. Their message is mainly that of the sign-language, and the pictographs consist almost wholly of pictures of objective things and of man's reaction in his relations to them. Their records are almost wholly devoid of any subjective thought; the subtle metaphor, figure and synecdoche that permeate the pictography of the American Indians are quite absent.

Two more examples of Eskimo graphic art will be given; the first, Fig. 34, being a carving made of walrus ivory, now in the office of the Alaska Commercial Company, San Francisco, California. The following interpretation of the pictographs was verified by Vladimir Naomoff, a Kadiak half-breed, to Dr. Hoffman: " No. 1 is a native whose left hand is resting against the house, while the right is directed toward the ground. The character to his right represents a ' shaman stick ' surmounted by the emblem of a bird — a ' good spirit '— in memory of some departed member of the household. It was suggested that the grave stick had been erected to the memory of his wife. No. 2 represents a reindeer. No. 3 signifies that one man, the designer, shot and killed another with an arrow. No. 4 denotes that the narrator has made trading expeditions with a dog sledge. No. 5 is a sailboat, although the elevated paddle signifies that that was the manner in which the voyage was last made. No. 6 represents a dog sled, with the animal hitched up for a journey. No. 7 is a sacred or ceremonial structure. The four figures at the outer corners of the square represent the young men placed on guard, armed with bows and arrows to keep away those not members of the band, who are depicted as holding a dance. The small square in the center of the inclosure represents a fireplace. The angular lines extending from the right side of the structure to the vertical partition line show in outline the subterranean entrance to the structure or lodge. No. 8 is a pine tree, upon which a porcupine is crawling upward. No. 9 is a similar species of tree from the bark of which a bird (a woodpecker) is extracting larvæ for food. No. 10 is a bear. No. 11 represents the owner of the record in his boat holding aloft his double-bladed paddle to call for help to drive fish into a net. No. 12 is an assistant fisherman, one who has responded to the call, and is observed driving fish by beating the water with a stick. No. 13 represents the net which, as is customary among many

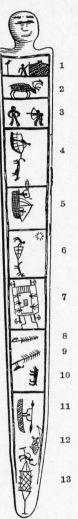

Fig. 34. Carving on walrus ivory, in possession of the Alaska Company.

of the tribes of the Great Lakes, is usually set in moderately shallow water. The figure over the preceding characters denotes a whale, with line and harpoon attached, which was caught by the fisherman during one of his fishing trips."

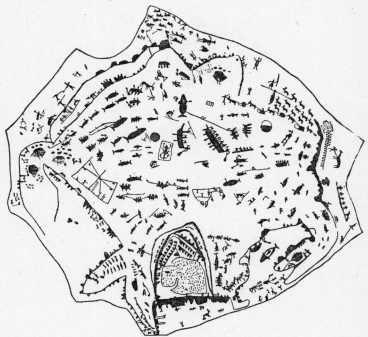

Fig. 35. History of a year of the Chukchi.

In Fig. 35 is reproduced a "History of a Year of the Chukchi." The original was drawn on walrus skin and records the life and activities of the tribe through one year. This cycle is indicated by the two suns, the dark or winter sun near the center of the skin and the summer sun appearing just above the northern horizon, shown to the right. Around the outer margin may be seen the shore line, while upon the space within are depicted rather indiscriminately ships, boats, whales, habitations and scenes of hunting and adventure. The well-known Eskimo hut with its tunneled approach is represented, as are also other smaller habitations with boat scaffolds. The well-filled umiaks between the two suns and others in the various groups are particularly well drawn. The greater part of the pictographs illustrate fishing exploits in which whales are being harpooned and pursued by fleets of hunters in their umiaks. In one drawing the whale is represented as " blowing." In other scenes are shown sledges drawn by long strings of dogs or reindeer; encounters with bears, seals and walruses; and many other activities of Arctic life. The general similarity of this winter record to the buffalo robe " count " of the Dakota Indians is truly remarkable. But for versatility and naïveté the Chukchi greatly excel the Dakotas.

In concluding this rather lengthy but we trust not uninteresting description of the graphic art of the North American Indians, as employed by them to record events and for purposes of communication, in short writing in its widest significance, we will refer the reader to Fig. 36, where we have assembled in one chart pictographic characters selected from Indian inscriptions, ceremonial songs and other sources. Many of these pictographs or symbols by their wide currency among scattered tribes assume the importance and arrive at the stage of development of ideograms. They are highly simplified, conventional characters, which in most cases hardly could be reduced to simpler, graphic elements. It will be of interest to the reader to compare them with the earliest symbols of the pre-Babylonian script out of which the cuneiform writing of the Babylonians, Assyrians and Persians developed. He will find in Fig. 80 and Fig. 81

characters no less pictorial in form than these Indian ideograms. There is this important difference, however: the
linear Babylonian inscriptions are actual, phonetic writing; the characters, though originally only pictures, as
those of the Indians, are definite, phonetic signs for syllabic sounds.   The inscriptions can be read and interpreted
by those who know the ancient Sumerian vocabulary. On
the other hand, as we already have remarked, Indian picture-writing is not writing at all. The pictures or symbols
do not always convey to the mind fixed ideas. Often the
subject pictured is not intended at all, but instead some
attribute of it or a metaphorical allusion which must be
surmised by the context. A cursory glance at Fig. 36 will
reveal quite a few of these metaphorical symbols.

It is a pitiful commentary on the stage of culture
of the North American Indians that they had no more
reliable mode of recording their tribal history than one
that could not be read after the heat of the events which
it fatuously presumed to record had cooled down. But
we should not in our inherited self-sufficiency be unchari-
table toward these otherwise intelligent and in many
ways noble-minded Children of the Plains. They were the
victims of their age-long isolation from all sources of
civilized culture. We do not have it on record in any
museum in the world that our illiterate ancestors of
Northern and Western Europe even possessed the knowledge or skill of picture-writing when Cæsar's armies introduced the Roman alphabet among them about the
beginning of the 1st Century A. D. There is no tradition
of any form of record practiced by the Britons prior to
the Romans, unless it be the use of cord tallies and
notched sticks.

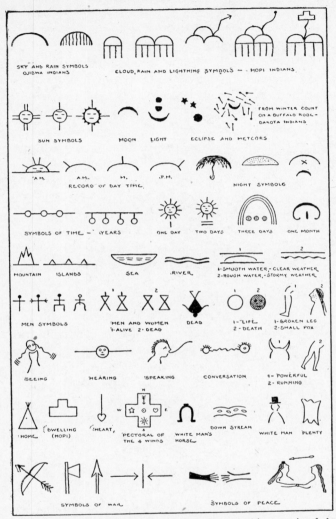

Fig. 36. Graphic symbols selected from pictographic records of the North American Indians.

CHAPTER IV

PICTURE WRITING OF THE ANCIENT MEXICANS

At the time of the Spanish Conquest in the 16th century there existed contemporaneously in Mexico two centers of civilization, the Maya in the peninsula of Yucatan and the Aztec in the broad table-land of central Mexico where the present City of Mexico stands. Judged by the very scant remains of the arts of architecture, sculpture and writing saved from the ruins of these two Indian nations, their civilization and culture were quite the same, though the Maya was somewhat further advanced than the Aztec. But the conquest of the country was so complete and thoroughgoing, that when these Europeans had finished with their preliminaries, there was hardly ·a vestige of native culture left for rehabilitation. The Spaniards under Cortes entered Mexico April 21, 1519. On August 13, 1521, the Aztec nation around the present City of Mexico was practically annihilated, even the majority of the inhabitants sharing the almost total destruction of the temples and almost every local evidence of native art and culture. Though the Aztecs were inexpressibly cruel in their customs, they had advanced to a comparatively high plane of civilization. It is true that they practiced horrible barbarities in the human sacrifices made in their temples by the priests, under a religion reeking with primitive belief in bloody atonement and sacrificial offerings of human souls for the propitiation of their avenging gods. But it always has been a question for individual judgment whether the followers of Cortes, carrying on their flags the motto: "Friends, let us follow the Cross, and under this sign, having faith, we shall conquer," were any less cruel than the poor Aztecs whose institutions they all but utterly destroyed, when they could have spared and built upon them.

Cortes had no regard for any form of religion that was not based on orthodox Christianity. He was a religious bigot, so common in that age. Witnessing, therefore, religious ceremonies cruel in themselves and repugnant to his inherited beliefs, he ordered the destruction of every record that might perpetuate this native religion. Obeying his harsh orders to the letter, his equally ruthless and ignorant followers set out upon the systematic destruction of the thousands of books, manuscripts and documents which this really highly advanced civilization had accumulated up to that time. Zumarraga, first bishop of Mexico, burned the precious manuscripts by the "mountain heap," five cities alone yielding up 16,000 books to the relentless Spanish governor, who destroyed every leaf. In Yucatan a similar fate overwhelmed the Maya civilization. The Spanish priests destroyed all books and manuscripts wherever they were found. Diego de Landa, second bishop of Yucatan, wrote: "We find great numbers of these books, but as they contain nothing that did not savor of superstition and of the devil, we burnt them all; at which the natives grieved most keenly and were greatly pained." Out of the tens of thousands of these sacred ceremonial books used by the Maya priests in their temples, and possibly other forms of native literature of a secular character, only a paltry few fragments are known to have been saved from this heartless and bigoted destruction. Of these manuscripts, or "codices," as they are called, only four have been published. They are the Codex Troanus and the

Codex Cortesianus in Madrid, probably being the two
halves of the same codex; the Codex Peresianus in Paris;
and the Codex Dresdensis in Dresden.

Of the Aztec writing there are nine principal codices
scattered over Europe or in private libraries: two in the
Vatican Library, one in Vienna, one in Boulogne, one in
the British Museum, one in the Bodleian Library, Ox-

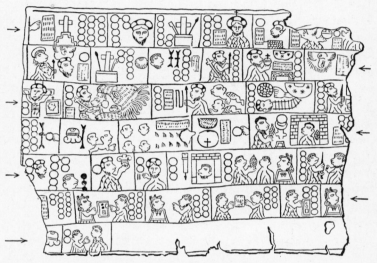

Fig. 37. Mexican picture writing. Roman catechism subsequent to the Conquest. The arrow heads indicate the direction of the reading.

ford, one in Liverpool, and two privately owned. There
are many other codices which are post-Columbian. There
are in addition sixteen small fragments collected in Mexico in 1803 by the famous scientist Alexander von Humboldt. These are all the important manuscripts known to
be in existence. The Humboldt fragments are now in the
Royal Library of Berlin. They are written — drawn —
on paper made from the Agave Americana, some being
painted in black outline, others in colors used symbolically

to represent various meanings. Some of these codices are quite long, being made of short pieces of paper carefully pieced into one long strip and then folded up. One of them measures fourteen feet in length. At least one of these fragments (Fig. 37), a Roman catechism, was written immediately subsequent to the Conquest; but as it is in the mode of picture-writing practiced by the native Aztecs and familiar to them, we will employ it as an introduction to the native manuscripts, concerning which we are forced to confess that after four hundred years of persistent study they are only a little more intelligible to scholars to-day than when first studied by them.

The pictures in this catechism read boustrophedon, the first, third, fifth and seventh lines reading from left to right; while the second, fourth and sixth lines read reverse, from right to left, as is indicated by the profiles in the majority of cases facing one as he reads. In this latter respect it conforms to what appears to be the universal custom in all picture and hieroglyphic writing of every nation. Its striking similarity in arrangement to the early stages of Babylonian writing is most remarkable when we consider the separation in time and space of these two civilizations. In order that the reader, probably unfamiliar with the primitive appeal of pictures to the mind, may get from this manuscript the knowledge which it imparted to the unlettered Indian, we will very briefly explain the ideograms and hieroglyphs.

The catechism begins in the first section of line 1 at the left and runs:

Section I. "There are 14 articles of faith." The hieroglyphs here are the tablet indicating article and the cross suggestive of faith.

Section II. "Seven appertain to the Deity."

Section III. "And the other seven to the holy humanity of our Lord, Jesus Christ." The hieroglyphs here are the cross, spear and sponge; implying the passion of the Lord.

Section IV. "Those (seven) which appertain to the Deity are these:"

Section V. "The first (article) to believe in one omnipotent God."

Section VI. "The second, to believe that He is God, the Father." The imperial globe and scepter are mutilated in the manuscript.

Section VII. "The third, to believe that He is God, the Son."

The second line begins on the right as follows:

Section I. "The fourth, to believe that He is God, the Holy Ghost." The Holy Ghost is depicted as a winged bird.

Section II. "The fifth, to believe that He is the Creator." Above are the starry heavens, below a house of bones, indicating the lower regions.

Section III. "The sixth, to believe that He is the Savior."

Section IV. "The seventh, to believe that He is the Glorified." The two black symbols may mean "commandments." They seem to be so employed later on. They very much resemble crudely pictured scrolls tied up with cord. The Egyptians used a somewhat similar hieroglyph which meant a book or document.

Section V. "Those (articles) which appertain to the holy humanity of our Lord Jesus Christ are the (seven) following":

Section VI. "The first, to believe that our Lord Jesus Christ in so far as He was a man, was conceived of the Holy Ghost."

This ends the second line, and at this point the poor

scribe went astray. He should have introduced another section with the two circles in it or placed the two circles together with the one circle in Section VI at the end of the second line instead of placing them in the first section of line 3; for the catechism reads: " The second, to believe that He was born of the Holy Virgin Mary, she being a virgin before and after his birth."

The third line begins on the left and runs:

Section I. " The third, to believe that He suffered and died to save sinners." The hieroglyph is a corpse in a grave. The numbering from here on evidently is at fault, as we have just explained.

Section II. " The fourth, to believe that He descended into Hell and brought out the souls of the holy fathers who were abiding there in hope of His blessed coming." Besides the picture of God and the devouring Hell, we may note three definite hieroglyphs frequently occurring in other Mexican manuscripts and in the codices; — namely, the tablet, the short path with the foot tracks and the symbol for the heart, here inverted, within the yawning jaws.

Section III. " The fifth, to believe that He arose again from the dead on the third day." The hieroglyph for " arising " is represented by a line going up, down, and then up again.

Section IV. " The sixth, to believe that He ascended into Heaven, where He sitteth at the right hand of God, the omnipotent Father." The ascent into heaven, judging by the hieroglyph, looks very much as though the scribe believed it to have been effected by a ladder. It will be noted that the hieroglyph for heaven is rather a fixed character, as shown in the two examples in this catechism. In the following figure it is rendered very differently, yet both are conventional representations of the sky and the stars. The Ojibwas and Egyptians also employed very similar signs, differing only in the character of conventionalization.

Section V. " The seventh, to believe that He shall come to judge the quick and the dead."

The fourth line is not quite so easy of interpretation as the rest of this most unique manuscript. It begins on the right. Section I reads according to the catechism: " The good should know, to give them glory, because they kept His holy commandments." The seven circles belong to the previous section. The import of this first section seems to be the portrayal of a good man. The conferring of honor is represented in the same way as in the fourth commandment in the next line. The next three sections illustrate the passage in the catechism: " And to the wicked eternal punishment, because they kept them not. Amen." We see flames, the heads of the damned and an inverted heart.

The part of the manuscript relating to the Ten Commandments begins at the end of the fourth line in the extreme left-hand section. The catechism reads: " The commandments of God's law are ten."

Sections I and II of the fifth line on the extreme left are drawn as one, without any vertical dividing line. The catechism reads: " The first three appertain to the honor of God," and then: " And the other seven to the advantage of the neighbor." The commandments proper begin in the next section, the second apparent section in the fifth line marked with one circle and representing God holding up a heart, and end on the sixth line directly under this section, marked with ten circles. The catechism reads: 1. " Thou shalt love God above all things." 2. " Thou shalt not take the name of God in vain." 3. "Thou shalt keep holy the feasts." 4. "Thou shalt honor thy father and mother." 5. "Thou shalt not murder." (Sixth line) 6. "Thou shalt not commit adultery." 7. "Thou shalt not steal." 8. "Thou shalt not bear false witness or lie." 9. "Thou shalt not covet thy neighbor's wife." 10. "Thou shalt not covet thy neighbor's goods."

The three remaining sections, the one at the left of the sixth line and the two on the seventh line, interpret the three concluding paragraphs in the catechism: "These ten commandments may be comprised in two: (1) "To serve and love God above all other things," (2) "And thy neighbor as thyself." (See Romans XIII, 9.)

This unique and naïve example of picture-writing admirably illustrates the manner in which the Spanish priests disseminated knowledge of the scriptures among the Mexican people. They resorted to the mode of employing pictures, ideograms and symbols, with which the more intelligent of the populace already were familiar. Beyond a doubt pictures had been from the very earliest times with the Mexican people the only means of communication, when, in the absence of oral authority graphic records had to be resorted to. At the time we are writing about the native priesthood appeared to have had a written code understood by themselves, as we shall proceed to show; a highly conventionalized form of hieroglyphics probably relating only to religious ceremonials; but to the great mass of the people pictures were still the only mode of appeal.

In the Mendoza collection of Mexican manuscripts are five sheets of picture-writing relating to the birth, education, adoption of a profession and marriage of Mexican

Fig. 38. Education of Mexican children, eleven to fourteen years.

boys and girls. Fig. 38 [1] is a reproduction of the sheet
relating to the education of children between eleven and
fourteen years of age. The four sections respectively correspond to the ages eleven, twelve, thirteen and fourteen
years. In the left-hand column are represented the father
and his son. In the right-hand column we see the mother
and her daughter. The "education" at eleven and twelve
appears to be chiefly corrective and repressive. The
father is represented punishing his son by compelling
him to inhale the noxious smoke of the aji plant, or leaving him tied naked on the ground until obedience is secured. The girl of eleven is punished in the same way
as the boy, but at twelve her punishment is made salutary
and productive. The scribe illustrates her working " over
time " at night, sweeping up the house. Night is represented by a hieroglyph showing the vault of the heavens
with both stars and darkness indicated. The other
hieroglyphs in the pictures are the circles to indicate the
age of the children; the protruding tongue, always employed in Mexican pictures to indicate speech, advice and
authority; and the full and half oval patterns to indicate
the ration of one and one-half rolls a day as the reasonable bounds of good breeding in eating, beyond which
would be gluttony. The remaining pictures illustrate the
occupations of boys and girls of thirteen and fourteen
years. The boys carry faggots on their backs, row canoes
laden with produce, or fish with the net; while the girls
make bread or cakes, cook in utensils, or weave on the
hand loom. The allowance of food becomes more liberal,
being two loaves daily.

These two manuscripts give an excellent idea of the
general nature of the native Mexican picture-writing.
The message or record desired to be expressed is con-

[1] From the Tenth Annual Report of the Bureau of American Ethnology.

veyed to the mind of the reader primarily through pictures that vary in detail and rendering according to the nature and development of the story; also by definite ideograms or hieroglyphs, more or less constant, generally
pictorial but often symbolic, that have come to represent an object or an idea,— as the tablet, the Holy Ghost
and the heart, in the Mexican catechism just described;
and the protruding tongue in the manuscript illustrating
the education of Mexican children. In this mode of picturing ideas the Mexicans proceeded along lines similar
to the Ojibwa Indians of North America in their ceremonial songs, only their drawing was infinitely truer to
nature and far more artistic than the Ojibwa. In the
catechism there seems to be nothing more than a
mnemonic aid to the one who scans the record and who
already knows the general content and meaning of the
pictures. In the series of four pictures just described,
which are in every way similar to the remaining sheets in
the collection, the story is told in a way so fresh and
naïve that "he who runs may read" the meaning. So
far Mexican picture-writing advances beyond the North
American Indians only in artistic technique, in which it
vastly excels the latter.

But the Mexicans progressed a long step beyond the
ideographic stage of writing. While they had not reached
at the time of the Conquest the point where each sound
was indicated by a sign or a hieroglyph, they had arrived
at a transition stage between the purely ideographic and
the phonetic stage of writing. According to Dr. Daniel
G. Brinton, the well-known Americanist: "the native
genius had not arrived at a complete analysis of the
phonetic elements of language, but it was distinctly progressing in that direction."

Many instances can be given to show that in their pic-

ture-writing the Mexicans resorted to the rebus or " ikonomatic " form of indicating a word phonetically. Instead of picturing the thing itself, an attempt was made
to indicate its name; and this form of sound-writing was
carried out by them in the almost universal way of choosing or substituting for the symbol expressing the idea the
picture or symbol of another idea the word name of
which — often only the initial sound of the word — was
the same or quite similar. For example, in Maya *kayab,* a
" month," is represented by a turtle head, *ak* or *ac,* and
a footprint, *be* (*beil* in Maya) ; *chikin,* " west," is represented by a hand, *chi* and the sun, *kin.* The name of
one of the Mexican chiefs was Itzcoatl, meaning " Knife-
Snake." In the manuscript known as Le Tellier Codex,
the name is represented in pure picture-writing by a
serpent, *coatl,* with stone knives, *itzli,* on its back. A
line connects this ideographic picture with the conventional representation of a man, in the same manner as in
the Dakota census rolls. In the Vergara Codex the
king's name is rendered in rebus form. *Itz* is represented
by a weapon with blades of obsidian, *itzt* (*tli*) ; an earthen
pot, *co* (*mitl*), and above it the sign of water, *a* (*tl*).
In other words, phonetically: Itz-co-atl.

In the Maya inscriptions, written or sculptured, it is
evident that there were employed together with the ideographic pictures other elements, known as glyphs or cal-
culi from their resemblance to pebbles, which symbolized
syllabic sounds. Bishop Landa, already quoted, quaintly
wrote of them nearly three hundred years ago: " This
people (the Maya) also used certain characters or letters, with which they wrote in their books their ancient
matters and their sciences, and with them and figures
and some signs in the figures, they understood their matters and could explain them and teach them." After

the zealous bishop had destroyed or ordered destroyed every native book he could lay his hands on, he undertook to study their written language and actually made out an alphabet or syllabary giving to each hieroglyph its alphabetic, phonetic equivalent in the Spanish tongue. If the devout bishop had looked before he leaped, and had been more of a student than a religious fanatic, his belated researches might have been more reliable. It is not believed to-day that the Maya writing is alphabetic. It probably is partially syllabic to the extent that we have just shown. But the reader must not expect even at this late date any very complete or elaborate statement concerning the principles of this syllabary, if syllabary it may prove to be. What is really known about it is more suggestive and collateral than direct. E. Förstemann, who has made an exhaustive study of the Mexican inscriptions, says that " in their decipherment we are as yet only at the very beginning." Nevertheless, such satisfactory progress in their interpretation has been made of late that there is good reason to hope that before long the mystery of their complete meaning, thus far so baffling to scholars, will be solved.

We will now give a few illustrations of the rebus plan adopted and pursued by the Mexicans in their picture-writing. Dr. Brinton in his " Essays of an Americanist " refers to the writing of the name of the town " Tamoc." A Mexican tribe speaking a different language from the Aztecs, had a town named " Tamuch," meaning in their language " near the scorpions." Of course the word had no such meaning, nor any meaning, in the Aztec language; consequently they could not picture it in its true meaning and retain the native sound. They called it " Tamuoc " and proceeded to find objects by which to picture it that had names approaching in sound the native name. Fig.

39 shows the naïve result. It is the picture of a man holding a measuring stick. Now in Nahuatl the verb to measure is *tamachiua;* the measuring stick is *octocatl.* It was decidedly fortuitous that these allied words were available from which they were able to take the initial syllable for the foreign word " Tamoc." Then they did exactly what the Egyptians often did, as we soon shall see. To make the meaning clearer or the hieroglyph more understandable, they added the footprints on the measuring stick, in Nahuatl, *xoctli;* just to emphasize more strongly the sound of the final syllable.

Fig. 39. Mexican picture-writing of the name of the town " Tamoc."

In the ethnological collection of the American Museum of Natural History, in New York City, there is an ancient Mexican map drawn on coarse native cloth, measuring five feet by six feet, from the southwestern part of the state of Oaxaca. The roads are indicated by foot tracks, the same as in the codices and other examples of Mexican picture-writing. It is known to be a map of the town called by the Aztecs " Yolotepec " and by the Mixtecs, of whose culture this is an unique example, " Yucuini." This seems to be a case in which the Aztecs instead of retaining the native name took the meaning of the word and translated it into their own tongue. In both languages the meaning is the " Hill of the Heart." In the Mixtec hill is *yucu,* and heart is *ini.* In the Aztec hill is *tepetl,* and heart is *yollotl.* But how has the native scribe indicated the name " Yucuini " on his map? By drawing

Fig. 40. Title on a map of the town " Yolotepec," Mexico. Original in the Museum of Natural History, New York City.

in an unoccupied part of it the beautiful title-piece reproduced in Fig. 40. It is nothing else than the picture of a heart on a hill, both very highly conventionalized and ornamented. The reader already is familiar with the hieroglyph of the heart, as the poor Aztecs were with the real thing; for had they not many opportunities of seeing it offered up from the breasts of thousands of living victims to their insatiable war god whose emblem was a necklace of six human hearts!

There are many other examples of rebus-writing by the ancient Mexicans, particularly the Aztecs. One is the representation of the well-known name Chapultepec,

meaning " Grasshopper Hill." The name was indicated
by the picture of a grasshopper on the conventionalized
representation of a hill, as in the former example. From
a few precious fragments of Aztec codices we will select
the pictured names of the two Mexican towns following.
One is the town of " Toltitlan," which means in Aztec
" near the place of the rushes." Now *tollin* means " place
of the rushes," so *tol* is illustrated by a picture of rushes.
The word *tetlan* means " near something," and its second syllable, *tlan* is found in the word *tlantli,* meaning
" teeth." So in the picture a set of teeth are drawn right
among the rushes. Again, the town " Acatzinco " means
" the little reed grass." Reed grass was called *acatl,* and
this was illustrated by a picture of the reed grass. So
far so good. But some ideograph must be selected to
indicate the remaining sounds in the word. The lower
part of the body in Aztec was *tzinco;* so the hieroglyph
was finished by drawing the reeds growing out of the
hips of the body! Dr. Brinton calls this method of writing " ikonomatic writing." The reader who would like
further to pursue this matter of rebus-writing as carried
out by the ancient Mexicans will find in Antonio Penafiel's " Nombres Geográficos de México " over 450
facsimile illustrations in color of geographical names of
places in Mexico.

One of the fragments collected in Mexico by Alexander von Humboldt is a unique manuscript which closely
corresponds to the Domesday book, in idea, not in form.
Parcels of land bounded by a main road and a cross road,
indicated by footprints between the lines, and running
back to a water course, appear divided into parallel
strips. Proprietorship in the lots is indicated at the right
on the lot frontage on the main road in every case by
the head of a man drawn conventionally and expression-

less. From these several heads which indicate generically
" man "— women are represented either with a coiffure
or with two marks across the face — short lines are
drawn to the accompanying name hieroglyphs precisely
as in the census rolls of the Indians of North America.
Fortunately, some European scribe, probably soon after
the Conquest, has very neatly written the interpreted
name of each person beside his hieroglyph. They appear
to be, most of them, the names of the Aztec kings or
chiefs, as shown by the royal headband, or of prominent
chiefs ruling or living at the time of the Conquest; making
this a most important archæological document. It obviously is a survey or inventory of the royal demesne, possibly a portion of the record of the division of the " crown
land " among the nobility. King Motecuhzoma (Montezuma) is represented at the bottom, which seems to be
as in other native Mexican manuscripts the beginning of
the record. He was the ninth king of the Mexicans,
reigning at the time of the Conquest, and was known as
Xocoyotzin, " the young "; not the elder Motecuhzoma,
the fifth king, otherwise known as Ilhuicamina, " he who
shoots at the heavens." Motecuhzoma means in the native language " the angry lord." This could hardly be
expressed in picture-writing. If the attempt had been
made to depict it in his face, we fear the native scribes
would have been so successful that their king could not
have been distinguished from the gods, who are almost
always represented with the most grotesquely horrible expression of countenance. Ilhuicamina, however, was
hieroglyphically represented in the codices by an arrow
piercing the symbol of the heavens. In another manuscript the name Montezuma — which probably was pronounced by the natives Moquauhzoma — is pictured in
the most novel and unique manner, significant of the pecu-

liar acrologic method of phonetic writing employed by the
Mexicans. The pictures chosen are a "mouse-trap,"
montli; the head of an "eagle," *quauhtli;* a "lancet," *zo;*
and the "hand," *maitl.* The initial syllables of the pictured words making up the name of the King. In the
seventh division from the bottom in this map is the name
of the prince Cuauhtemoc, who defended the City of
Mexico against the soldiers of Cortes for ninety days
after the death of Montezuma. His name literally means
"Swooping Eagle," and the hieroglyph represents the
head of an eagle with footprints directed downward.

Among the other twenty-five names, pictured in the
several parcels of land allotted to the proprietors or
their heirs, in this map, are the two represented in Fig.
41. The lower one, the seventeenth in the manuscript,
is the hieroglyph of the name Imexayacatzin, which the
Spanish scribe has written beside the picture. It exactly
interprets the meaning of the name, which is "the face
made of her thigh"; literally *imex-xayacatl,* from
xayacatl, "face," and *metz-tli,* "thigh." It refers to a
horrible festival of the Mexicans in which a woman
victim was sacrificed, flayed, and a priest dressed in her
skin wore a mask made of her thigh! The upper one, the
eighteenth in the manuscript, is the hieroglyph of the
name Xipanoctzin, literally *Xip-panoc-tzin;* being derived
from *xiutl,* "turquoise," and *panoc,* "he who crosses a
river." The turquoise is represented by its recognized
symbol, which consists of concentric circles surrounded
by sparkling lights, placed in a boat.

These examples will serve to illustrate the manner in
which the Mexicans represented polysyllabic words by
combining the pictures of words whose initial syllables
corresponded in sound to the syllables of the word to be
pictured. It is the principle of acrology or the rebus.

No positive evidence has yet been adduced to show that the Mexicans advanced much beyond this stage. The Egyptians, ages before them, proceeded in precisely the same way; but they carried out the evolution of writing to its ultimate conclusion, and in the last stage of development dropped the syllabic sound, retaining only the initial

Fig. 41. Mexican rebus-writing of two proper names,— Xipanoctzin and Imexayacatzin. From a native map.

sound, consonant or vowel, using the picture of the original word or syllable to represent this elemental, alphabetic sound with which they built up words phonetically, just as we do to-day.

Sylvanus G. Morley, who has published the latest monograph on the Maya inscriptions, writes:[1] " Al-

---

[1] " An Introduction to the Study of the Maya Hieroglyphs," by Sylvanus Griswold Morley. Smithsonian Institution. Bureau of American Ethnology, Bulletin 57, 1915.

though there are undeniable traces of phoneticism among the Maya glyphs, all attempts to reduce them to a phonetic system or alphabet which will interpret the writing, have signally failed." Continuing he says: "Unfortunately, it must be admitted that but little advance has been made toward the solution of this problem . . . as each glyph is in itself a finished picture, dependent on no other for its meaning, and consequently the various elements entering into it undergo very considerable modifications in order that the resulting composite character may not only be a balanced and harmonious design, but also may exactly fill its allotted space. All such modifications probably in no way affected the meaning of the element thus mutilated. . . . Great license was permitted in the treatment of accessory elements so long as the essential element or elements of a glyph could readily be recognized as such." There are many pitfalls for the student who essays to interpret the Maya glyphs. Not only are any two glyphs meaning the same thing rarely alike, but often they are utterly dissimilar. This is the more unfortunate, as such signal success has been achieved in the interpretation of the very complicated numerical and calendric signs, which constitute the great bulk of all the Mexican and Yucatan hieroglyphic writing. Prof. Ernst Förstemann, of the Royal Library, Dresden, in an extended study of the Dresden Codex, was the first to work out the intricate vigesimal system of numeration used by the Maya. Since this, practically the entire body of numerical and calendric signs, with their many cycles, has been interpreted.

Let us now examine the codices. As we have said, but four of the Maya and only a few fragments of the Aztec writing on paper exist. All the rest went up in burnt offerings to the triune God of the Spaniards because they detected in them the worship of polytheism, so abhorrent to the intolerant Christians of that age. No thought of native history, archæology or culture stood before this consuming bigotry; and in the name of perverted Christianity the abundant written literature of every nation and people in Central America all but utterly perished from the face of the earth. From the few specimens of writing that have survived this holocaust scholars are slowly and laboriously unraveling the mysteries of the hieroglyphs. Very little progress has been made up to the present time, and, outside of the numerical signs, only a comparatively few symbols are definitely known.

The codices, as will be seen by consulting Fig. 42, consist of pictorial drawings with hieroglyphs generally placed above and to the left of them. The pictures are drawn in outline and filled in with colors used conventionally. The illustration is a reproduction of Plate XXIX of the Codex Troano. It is a characteristic example of all the codices. The pictures in every instance are most grotesque and outlandish. Why this is so it is difficult to imagine. The technical skill employed often is unquestionably of a high order. One is almost forced to the conclusion that their mode of portraiture was controlled by the hierarchy of the priests who may have prescribed the style of drawing for each individual god. If this were not so, it is inconceivable that such monstrosities ever could have been invented, much less perpetuated. We know that a somewhat similar state of affairs existed in ancient Egypt. The Egyptians were capable of rising to the highest levels of art expression; but for ages the Egyptian artist was fettered by the narrow conventions prescribed for him by the traditions of the priesthood. But any one who does not see in the beautiful paintings and sculptures of the Egyptian tombs and temples the

Fig. 42. Reproduction of Plate XXIX, Codex Troano.

loftiest examples of dignified restraint and artistic imagination fails to view them with sympathy and understanding. But the art of the Mexican codices, on the other hand, while ingenious and interesting, is more apt to inspire in our minds repugnance and disgust for their gross distortion and hideous ugliness. If they were meant to inspire fear of the gods, and nearly all of the pictures are representations of the gods, they certainly could not have planned much better than they did.

The hieroglyphs on the Maya codices are of two kinds:

Fig. 43. Variations of the hieroglyph employed for the numeral twenty.

first, the numerals. These are the dashes and dots seen just above the pictures. Dots were used up to four, then a dash indicated five. Dots above this dash were used up to nine, then two dashes indicated ten. Again dots above the two dashes were used up to fourteen, then three dashes indicated fifteen. Sixteen, seventeen, eighteen and nineteen were similarly represented by one, two, three and four dots over the three lines representing fifteen. This is as far as this system was continued. It was not carried over twenty. The hieroglyph for twenty had many varieties in the different codices, all distinguished by the jaw with two, sometimes more, teeth; as will be seen illustrated in the upper row in Fig. 43. In the sculptured inscriptions several variations of another type were used to represent this important number; shown in the lower row in this same figure. The latter appear open on the right, as they were attached to the left of the hieroglyphs.

The second class of hieroglyphs in the codices are those just above the numerals and constitute the inscription proper. Of these so-called inscriptions Cyrus Thomas, who has made a thorough study of the codices, says: " The general purport of the inscriptions has not been ascertained with certainty, yet the fact that half of them are numeral symbols, calendar symbols, etc., leads to the conclusion that they contain little of anything relating to the history of the tribes by whom they were made." The Dresden Codex appears to consist wholly of numeral series. It has come to be accepted as a general belief that the subject matter of all the codices as well as of the sculptured glyphs in the inscriptions on the monuments chiefly if not wholly relates to calendric counts, year series or astronomical references. Being so frequenly associated with the pictures of the gods and the day signs known to typify them, the import of the inscriptions probably was to keep the run of the feast days and ritual observances sacred to each particular god.

The Mexicans computed time in so-called " months," the years consisting of eighteen months of twenty days each. The extra five days though intercalated were not recognized. They were " superfluous " or " evil " days. Bishop Landa says: " The entire year had eighteen of these (20-day periods) and besides five days and six hours." It is evident that the Maya knew the exact length of the year; but there is no evidence in their inscriptions that they corrected their calendar to allow for the accumulation of these six hours, as we do. Every four years they discovered that they had an extra day in their year, and every eighty years an extra month on their hands; but they probably did not know how to extricate themselves from the dilemma, for they had planned their impossible calendar 3930 years ahead, as has been deciphered from one of the sculptured stelæ (Stela N) at Copan.[1] It is not known to this day what year the series was begun, and if it were, probably all the labor spent on the giant masses of sculptured blocks at Copan, Quirigua, Palenque and other places were futile on account of the false reckoning. Yet it is easy to misjudge a people, and it is obviously unfair to criticize a nation that has been so grievously interrupted in the progress of its development. The Mexicans discovered that their calendar was wrong and doubtless long discussed its rectification. Who shall say that some Mexican Julius

[1] The highest recorded period of time figured out by the Maya is in the Dresden Codex, and consists of 12,466,942 days, or 34,156 years. The Maya were exceptionally good mathematicians. In computing the revolution of the moon they varied but .02 from the correct result in seventeen revolutions. One of their periods, worked out in the Dresden Codex, shows a remarkable ability in figuring out abstruse mathematical problems, as the least common multiple of several difficult cycles. The period contains 113,880 days or: —

    312 Solar years of 365 days each
    195 Venus years of 584 days each
    146 Mars years of 780 days each
     39 Venus-Solar periods of 2,920 days each
    438 Tonalamatls of 260 days each
      6 Calendar Rounds of 18,980 days each

The Calendar Round of 18,980 days or 52 years itself indicates the solution of a highly abstruse mathematical problem which involved every possible combination of the 260-day period (a tonalamatl) with the 365 positions of the year, and enabled the Maya to know in advance with what name-days the successive years would begin, when the twenty name-days repeated each other in an endless and invariable sequence. The mathematics of the problem are too involved to be explained here, as it concerns difficult operations in the permutation and combination of combined series. If one wishes to know more about this matter, he will find it in Mr. Morley's excellent monograph.

Cæsar, Augustus or Pope Gregory in time may not have found a way to correct it? We have not yet extricated ourselves from the astronomical muddle we are in concerning the precession of the equinoxes through the ancient and honorable signs of the zodiac; and we continue in our astronomical statements to locate the sun in signs over 30° east of its true position in the heavens. Of course we know better and realize the error, but we perpetuate it month after month and year after year. If some cataclysm should befall our civilization and a future antiquary should come across this erroneous record of time, he probably would not have a very high opinion of our scientific attainments.

Another singular time count used more frequently by the Mexicans throughout Central America as a ceremonial or religious period than the secular year of 365 days was the cycle of 260 days, in 20 intervals of 13 days each. This sacred period was divided into four parts of 65 days each, assigned to a particular planet, star or cardinal point, with attendant divinities. Then again each " month " was divided into four periods of five days each, each day having its own divinity. All these divisions of time with their divinities, stars and other occult relationships, made up a multiplicity of signs the majority of which are now recognized in the hieroglyphs and properly interpreted; but the key is missing. No one knows when these periods started or where they connect with the Gregorian calendar. We are in the same dilemma in regard to the native table of measures. One Vicente Pineda in his " Gramatica de la Lengua Tzal-tal " (1887), defines the system as follows:

20 units = 1 net-ful
20 net-fulls = 1 bundle of bacs
20 bundles of bacs = 1 grandfather

20 grandfathers = 1 grandmother
20 grandmothers = 1 great-grandfather!

Fig. 44 [1] contains the symbols of the twenty days of each month with their names. Each is supposed to be the picture of some object. It probably was originally, but they have progressed so far in the process of conventionalization that in the majority of cases the original object cannot always be detected. We will venture to give the meaning of some of these symbols, as given by Dr. Brinton in " A Primer of Mayan Hieroglyphics." Ik means air, wind, breath, spirit, soul or life. The character within the cartouches is that of the four winds. Akbal probably is derived from *akab,* " night." Other examples of this symbol distinctly show it to be a mouth with teeth, perhaps suggesting the thought of annihilation. The symbol for Kan is believed to represent a shell pendant or bead, *kan,* which was used for money, quite the same as wampum with the North American Indians. Chicchan probably is derived from *chich kuch,* " twisted threads." They are suggested in the criss-cross lines. The symbol for Manik is a hand grasping, and probably is a corruption of *mach,* " to grasp." The character representing Chuen is the picture of a " mouth " with fangs, *chi,* shown very clearly in other examples having cuspid and fanged teeth. Sometimes a calabash, *chu,* also is drawn within the circle to suggest the name sound more clearly. Ix very probably is derived from *xiix,* " scattered grain husks," which the symbol seems to indicate. In the symbol for the month Caban we see very obviously delineated a woman's " cork-screw curl," *cab.* The symbol for the month, Ezanab, is the picture of the " sacrificial knife "

[1] Reproduced from " Central American Hieroglyphic Writing," by Cyrus Thomas, Annual Report (1903), Smithsonian Institution, Washington, D. C.

of flint or obsidian of corresponding name. The symbol
for the month, Ahau, generally is believed to be a conventionalized representation of a " face." The name is

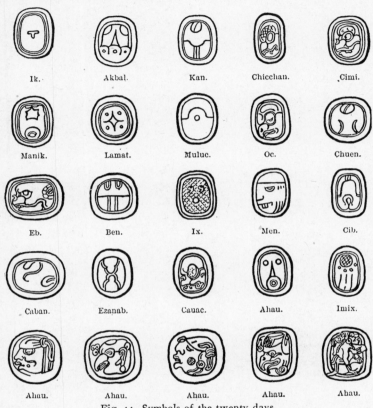

Fig. 44. Symbols of the twenty days.

taken from two different sources, *ah,* " lord " or " king ";
and *ah,* " to rise." Five other examples of this important
day sign are given in the last row, chiefly taken from
the sculptured glyphs of the monumental inscriptions.

It must not be supposed that the meaning of the
hieroglyphs, that is, the things themselves, represented by

the pictures, primarily had any significance in the choice of the hieroglyphs for the months. In some cases this may have been true. But it is probable, as is exemplified in the general character of Mexican hieroglyphs, that the desired symbol chosen as the hieroglyph for the month was that of some thing the name of which closely corresponded with the name of the month. It is highly probable, however, that the early Mexican scribes in looking about for their corresponding word-symbols preferably selected, whenever possible, the names of objects or things that had some correspondence of idea as well as of sound to the things whose hieroglyphs were desired. We already have given instances of this fact, and many more have been noted.

Fig. 45, also taken from Cyrus Thomas, illustrates the symbols employed by the Mexicans for the eighteen months and the supplemental " month " of five days. The word Pop means a " mat." It probably is suggested in the cross-hatch lines. It is doubtful what the character for Uo illustrates. The Mexican scribes had their own doubts about it and sometimes appended a highly conventionalized representation of the tongue, indicating " speech," probably to indicate the meaning *uooh,* a " written character," as Dr. Brinton points out. Zip pictures the sun below a flint knife, indicating the " slain " or " departed sun "; a play on the phrase *zipik kin,* the " sunset." That this is the meaning intended, is indicated by the occasional use of a determinative sign, *mac,* signifying " to extinguish." The word Zotz means a " bat," and the sign illustrates one. Xul probably is derived from *xulub,* " horns." The deer, if not his horns, obviously is in evidence. Yaxkin means " new sun " or " strong sun." It is represented in true rebus manner by the yax sign above and that of the sun, *kin.*

In the case of the month Ceh, we have an excellent example of ellipsis. The meaning *ceh* is "deer," but it is suggested by the flint knife used in sacrifices of this animal. The lower part of this symbol, as in the symbol for Yax and Zac, is the day sign, *cauac*. The month called Mac probably was dedicated to the Bat God. Above is the mac sign, the extended hands, generally in-

Fig. 45. Symbols of the months.

dicating "nothing." Kankin means "the yellow sun," and the symbol expresses it in true rebus manner, as it combines the symbol for the sun, *kin,* and that for yellow. Pax is the picture of a "drum," *pax che.*

It may be of interest to show the way in which the Mexicans represented the cardinal points. They paid great respect to them, and they frequently occur throughout the inscriptions. They are shown in Fig. 46.

The sign for north, Xaman, has the picture of the

North Star god and the lunar prefix. That for south, Nohil, has the extended hand, *mac,* and what appear to be flames surrounding the *yax* sign. The sign for east, Likin, consists of the sun symbol, *kin,* surmounted by the twentieth day sign, Ahau. Edward Seler points out that this probably comes from *ahal kin,* " the sun rises." The sign for west, Chikin, represents the hand above the sun

| Xaman | Nohil | Likin | Chikin |

Fig. 46. Hieroglyphs of the four cardinal points, North, South, East and West.

sign. Dr. Seler explains it to indicate the hand in the position of eating, and refers to the fact that in Maya " to eat " is *chi.*

The most extensive Mexican remains bearing inscriptions are to be found at Palenque. Here flourished, probably from the 2nd century to the 6th century, A. D., the ancient Maya civilization in its " Golden Age." There were three principal centers of this early Maya civilization: Palenque in southern Mexico, Quirigua in Guatemala, and Copan in Honduras. During this period sculpture reached its highest level of excellence. The best examples are to be found at Palenque and Copan. Many of the sculptured figures on the stelæ at Copan have much of the beauty and grace of Grecian sculpture at its best. This is especially true of Stelæ D and H and other stelæ and altars at Copan. There is much that is grotesque, as everywhere in Maya and Aztec sculpture, but the finest examples are as praiseworthy as any sculpture in existence.

There was a sudden termination of this civilization in

the south, and when it reappeared in northern Yucatan at Uxmal, Chichen Itza, Mayapan and other centers, between 800 and 1000 A. D., the art of the period manifested itself in a remarkable development of architecture, with only very scant sculptured inscriptions. For two hundred years prior to the Discovery great internecine strife was threatening the entire Maya civilization; the total extinction of which was hastened and finally consummated by the Spanish conquerors only a few years after their arrival in America.

In Palenque are the massive ruins of several great temples. Here are the two Temples of the Cross, the Temple of the Sun and another structure known as the Temple of Inscriptions. All of these buildings are profusely covered with sculptures and inscriptions. Fig. 47 is a reproduction of the left-hand slab of the Tablet of the Cross from the Temple of the Sun. To the right of the central slab, which shows an elaborately foliated cross on a sacrificial altar, is a third slab very similar to the first. On each of the outer slabs, at the back of the priests, are six vertical rows of glyphs, in seventeen horizontal lines, as will be seen in the left-hand slab in the illustration. The glyphs on the left-hand slab, at least for several horizontal rows down, are combined with the heads of the gods who presided over the special days that they represent. The glyphs are to be read downward in pairs, beginning at the left. Dr. Förstemann interprets the entire inscription to be a series of cycles of the thirteen- and twenty-day periods, carried out over an interval of nearly 400 years; the object probably being to fix the dates of the recurrence of certain feast or fast days in the calendar. The illustration gives an excellent idea of the general character of the many inscriptions at Palenque, Copan, Quirigua and other places in Mexico and Guatemala.

The sculptured glyphs are in very strong relief, and the excellent state of preservation of the giant blocks is such that the glyphs are very easily distinguishable, and in point of fact all have been translated and known to consist of numerical and calendric signs.

Fig. 47. A portion of the Tablet of the Cross from the Temple of the Sun, Palenque.

CHAPTER V

In the middle of the Pacific Ocean, 2000 miles west of
South America and hundreds of miles east of any other
island in Polynesia, lies the lonely speck of land known as
Easter Island, a small volcanic island, but fifteen miles
across at its widest diameter. Here lived at one time a
superior race of people in an advanced state of civilization. The coast of this island, with some interruptions, is
surrounded by a wall or terrace, built of large stone slabs,
seven to eight feet long. Some of the terraces thus formed
are three hundred feet long, and contain vaults in which
the dead were laid, wrapped in native matting. On these
terraces were placed enormous monolithic statues of
super-men with long straight noses and unusually pendu-
lous ears, such as are produced by distending them by
heavy ear rings. Many of these statues are from twelve
to twenty feet high, the tallest being as much as thirty
feet in height. Many scores of these statues are to be seen
in all parts of the island, most of them fallen, while many
others evidently lie where they were being transported
from the quarries. In the quarries, which are of volcanic
rock, are scores of figures in every stage of completion,
some over sixty feet long. Besides these stone figures
there are to be seen in the island many wooden figures
carved in the form of bird-like men, the shape being that
of the frigate-bird. This bird is rarely if ever seen in this
distant land, and the bird-cult which formed the basis of

important rites of the natives now centers about the native tern, a very different kind of bird. This seems to point to an exotic origin of this bird-cult. Many other evidences of the comparatively high state of civilization of the former inhabitants of the island seem to indicate a culture not indigenous to the island, but coming from without.

Easter Island was first visited, as far as definite records show, in 1863. In that year Peruvian slavetraders landed on the island and captured a large number of the inhabitants, including among those kidnapped all of the native chiefs and persons of authority. It has been reported that at the time of the discovery of the island the inhabitants were cannibals. This seems quite incompatible with the fact that they were in possession of a system of hieroglyphic writing or mnemonics, that appears to have been well understood among the initiated. The writing was executed on broad, flat boards, some of them as much as six feet long, covered on both sides with finely engraved hieroglyphic symbols. Many of these boards have been discovered on the island, and these with fragments of other boards now repose in various museums. After the kidnapping of the leading men, the meaning of the symbols seems to have been lost to the inhabitants. Besides, Catholic missionaries, who followed the visit of the Peruvians, did not look with much favor upon this pagan writing, which to them seemed to savor of the evil one, and ordered that the boards should be burned; which was very generally done.

We shall follow very closely in our brief description of this peculiar system of hieroglyphic writing the article published in the Smithsonian Institution Report for 1889, by Wm. J. Thomson, U. S. N. The writer says: " The native traditions in regard to the incised tablets simply assert that Hotu-Matu, the first king, possessed the knowledge of the written language, and brought with him to the island sixty-seven tablets containing allegories, traditions, genealogical tables and proverbs relating to the land from which he had emigrated. A knowledge of the written characters was confined to the royal family, the chiefs and to certain priests or teachers. But the people were assembled at Anekena Bay once each year to hear all of the tablets read." The cruel disaster that overtook these people terminated this period of their civilization, and the traditions of the tribe were all but forgotten.

Mr. Thomson's report continues: " A man called Ure Vaeiko, one of the patriarchs of the island, professed to have been under instruction in the art of hieroglyphic reading at the time of the Peruvian visit, and claimed to understand most of the characters. Negotiations were opened with him for a translation of the tablets, but he declined to furnish any information on the ground that it had been prohibited by the priests. Finally the old fellow, to avoid temptation, took to the hills with the determination to remain in hiding until after the return of the *Mohican* (the U. S. S. *Mohican* under Lieut. F. M. Symonds). As a compromise it was proposed that he should relate some of the ancient traditions. This was readily acceded to, because the opportunity of relating the legends to an interested audience did not often occur, and the positive pleasure to be derived from such an occasion could not be neglected. . . . At an auspicious moment photographs of the tablets owned by the bishop of the island were produced for inspection. Old Ure Vaeiko had never seen photographs before, and was surprised to find how faithfully they reproduced the tablets which he had known in his young days. A tablet would have met with opposition, but no objection could be made against the photograph, especially something possessed by the good bishop. The photographs were recognized immediately and the appropriate legend related with fluency and without hesitation from beginning to end. The story of all the tablets of which we had any knowledge were finally obtained, the words of the native language being written down (by Mr. Salmon) as they were uttered, and afterward translated into English."

The beauty of expression of the following lamentation, the translation of the tablet shown in Fig. 48, must be admitted by every one:

> The sail of my daughter,
> Never broken by the force of foreign clans,
> The sail of my daughter,
> Unbroken by the conspiracy of Honiti!
> Ever victorious in all her fights.
> She could not be enticed to drink poison waters
> In the cup of obsidian glass.
> Can my sorrow ever be appeased

Fig. 48. Hieroglyphic inscription carved on wood. From Easter Island. Obverse.

While we are divided by the mighty seas?
Oh my daughter, oh my daughter!
It is a vast and watery road
Over which I look toward the horizon;
My daughter, oh my daughter!

Mr. Thomson points out that a casual glance at the
Easter Island tablets is sufficient to note the fact that they
differ materially from other kyriologic writings. The pictorial symbols are engraved in regular lines on depressed
channels, separated by slight ridges intended to protect
the hieroglyphics from injury by rubbing. In some cases
the characters are smaller and the tablets contain a
greater number of lines, but in all cases the hieroglyphs
are inscribed on and cover both sides as well as the beveled edges and hollows of the board upon which they are
engraved. The symbols on each line are alternately reversed; those on the first line stand upright, and those on
the next line are upside down, and so on by regular alter-
nation. This unique plan makes it necessary for the
reader to turn the tablet over and change its position at
the end of every line; the characters being found to follow in regular progression. The reading should com-
mence at the lower left-hand corner, on the particular side
that will bring the figures erect, and follow as the characters face in the procession, turning the tablet at the end
of each line, as indicated. Arriving at the top of the first
face, the reading is continued over the edge, to the nearest line at the top of the other side, and the descent continued in the same manner until the end of the inscription is
reached. This boustrophedon method is supposed to have
been adopted in order to avoid the possibility of missing
a line of the hieroglyphics in reading.

Ure Vaeiko's fluent interpretation of the tablet was not

interrupted, though it became evident that he was not
actually reading the characters. It was noticed that the
shifting of position did not accord with the number of
symbols in the line; and afterward where the photograph
of another tablet was substituted, the same story was continued without the change being discovered. The old fellow was quite discomposed when charged with the fraud
at the close of an all-night session, and at first maintained
that the characters were all understood; but he could not
give the significance of hieroglyphs copied indiscriminately from tablets already read by him. He explained at
great length that the actual value and significance of the
symbols had been forgotten; but the tablets were recognized by unmistakable features and the interpretation of
them was beyond question; just as a person might recognize a book in a foreign language and be perfectly sure
of the meaning without being able actually to read it.

The writing — drawing of course — on these tablets is
composed of pictorial symbols carrying the signification
of the images they represent or attributes of them. The
execution would be a creditable production with the assist-
ance of the best etching tools; and it is a truly wonderful
result of patience and industry, to have been accomplished
by means of obsidian points, or possibly shark's teeth.
The more so as the minute size of the hieroglyphs made
it well-nigh impossible to convey anything more than the
general appearance of the objects delineated.

A critical study of the hieroglyphics of Easter Island is
being made with the hope that valuable information may
be secured in regard to the origin and history of these
people.

In the island of Oleai, or Uleai, one of the most west-
erly of the Caroline Islands, there has recently been discovered a new native script which has been most interest-

ingly described by J. Macmillan Brown.[1] The script is unlike any other known script. It is partly ideographic, partly geometric, and throughout is highly conventionalized and simplified. The syllabary consists of fifty-one characters, which in their entirety seem to make a very consistent series, evidently acquired through many generations of native culture. Mr. Brown reproduces in his article the entire syllabary, as written down for him by the chief, Egilimar, who signs the document, spelling out his name in the native characters, with the English spelling in parallel beside them.

Mr. Brown says: " This Oleai script is manifestly the product of long ages, for the use of the organizers of a highly-organized community of considerable size. In other words, it must have belonged to the ruling class of an empire of some extent, that needed constant record of the facts of intercourse and organization." According to Mr. Brown's account, there are many signs in this archipelago of a former civilization of considerable antiquity and extent. In the fringing reef of Ponape, there are vast ruins of great houses with walls six to fifteen feet thick, consisting of enormous basalt columns brought from twenty miles away. The buildings and quays cover eleven miles.

These two hieroglyphic scripts, coming unexpectedly out of the Pacific Ocean, give us an altogether new conception of the inhabitants of the islands of the South Sea. The Caroline Islands are hundreds of miles east of the Philippine Islands, visited only infrequently by sailing or steam ships; while Easter Island is thousands of miles further seaward, and is rarely visited by any packet ship

[1] " A New Pacific Ocean Script," by J. Macmillan Brown. Article No. 43 in " Man, A Monthly Record of Anthropological Science," Vol. XIV, 1914.

throughout the entire year. We may well inquire how these totally different systems of writing developed in these remote islands, and what their origin was. Scholars are studying the question and we may hope that before long we may be able to trace the sources of origin and the lines of development of these two mysterious systems of writing.

CHAPTER VI

CHINESE IDEOGRAPHIC WRITING

IT is to the Flowery Kingdom, the land of quaint customs and queer ways, in which the past lives in the present, that we must turn to find a modern language in which the primitive pictures of a by-gone past still linger in the written script of the living generation. In the written language of the Chinese we find in every day use characters which, if not recognizably pictorial in their modern form, exhibit elements which indubitably betray their descent directly from the original pictures used in the primitive days before writing was employed. Not a few of these characters in constant use to-day by the Chinese are but slightly modified by the process of conventionalization from their ancient prototypes. Even where no trace of their obvious source of derivation is manifest, and this doubtless is true of the great majority of all the Chinese characters — the effacement due to ages of conventionalization being so nearly complete — there is yet in the construction of most of the written characters ample testimony of the original pictorial basis of the script.

The most cursory investigation into the nature of these characters will reveal the radical difference between Occidental writing and that of the far Orient. This difference is to be found not only in the shapes of the characters — these differ in most languages — but in the fundamental construction of the written script. Chinese writing is not phonetic in the sense that European writing is. In the latter, as already has been explained, every constituent

154

syllable in every word is represented by a character — an alphabetic sign — which is the constant symbol of this phonetic element wherever it occurs. With the exception of a very few arbitrary signs and symbols used in arithmetical notation and mathematical operations, music, weights and measures, a few of which earlier were illustrated, there are no other written signs employed than these few alphabetic characters. In Chinese writing, on the other hand, the six hundred fundamental characters or ideographs which form the basis of the written language, and of which two hundred and fourteen, the so-called " radicals " or " classifiers," enter into almost every written word in the language, are not phonetic at all. They are ideograms; now very much conventionalized, but originally representative of the things intended. The characters and the sounds for which they stand have no logical correspondence whatever. In the last analysis perhaps this also may be said of our own alphabetic signs and of their proper sounds; but not so of the written words which they spell, for they are phonetic. The Chinese characters are strictly word-pictures, or more truly idea-pictures,— ideograms. In most cases the symbols are arbitrarily chosen; in other cases — a very few — they reveal themselves as very highly conventionalized pictures of the things intended. Each character is the symbol of a simple, elementary sound, a monosyllable, whether the symbol consists of one or of twenty or more brush strokes, of one or of many fundamental characters in one combined character. It is true that thousands of Chinese words of the Kia-shing classification have a phonetic element. Most of the combined characters have a symbol to picture the monosyllable, the sound-word, together with one or more ideographs to picture its particular meaning; as there are hundreds of homophones in the language.

Together they make up the written character for the monosyllable.

The Chinese written language has no alphabet, for it has no spelling. It likewise has no visible parts of speech. The same character without change of form may be used as a noun, verb or adjective; all grammatical relations being indicated by position in the sentence. It is a language of roots and has no grammatical terminations to denote number, case, tense, person or other grammatical modifications. There are no inflections, the language being devoid of conjugation, declension and every form of grammatical construction. There are devices employed for indicating parts of speech, but they do not affect the drawing of the characters, which are made up of an odd assortment of ideograms, phonograms and arbitrary symbols, often combined in the most illogical and whimsical manner. How can such characters be conjugated, declined or indicate tense and mood?

It follows from this very brief description of Chinese writing that every distinct idea must have its own proper sign, and any and every new idea must require a new symbol different from every other sign in the language. No matter how involved an idea may be, a single character, simple or complex, the correlative of a monosyllabic sound, will be its symbol. As the growing syllabary increased in complexity and the language in descriptive phrases, special characters had to be invented to illustrate ideas like the following: " a bay horse with a white belly "; " a horse with a white spot on his forehead "; " a dark horse with a yellow stripe along its back "; " the last pig in a litter "; " to look at a notice on a gate "; " to lift up the dress when going up stairs "; " the noise made by the grinding of the teeth "; " reading the records of the family in the hall of ancestors "; " an untimely death under nineteen years "; or " to announce the death of a parent or relative by the nearest mourners on the seventh day." Here is the character for the last definition: 訃   The left hand character in the compound is the sign " to speak "; the right hand one is that for " to divine." The square-shaped figure in the first character is the picture of the mouth and is its written symbol. The four lines above it represent " words." All three signs are among the 214 radicals which form the basis of the written language. The spoken word that stands for all this circumlocution is simply " *fu*." The character for the same word, *fu,* meaning " father," is a hand with two marks over it; being an illustration of the world-wide ethics of domestic responsibility! The reader will discover at the outset that we now are dealing with a peculiar system of writing. It is not exactly ideographic nor is it purely phonetic. Many words are wholly ideographic and few are exclusively phonetic. It appears to be a system based on ideography advancing into phoneticism but arrested at this stage before it reached the alphabetic stage.

The result of this strange and arbitrary method of writing is that with only a few hundred phonetic sounds in the language to deal with, there are innumerable homophones, signifying hundreds of different meanings, each requiring a specific character. In the spoken language the context and the very comprehensive system of intonation and gestures elaborated by the Chinese amply suffice to explain the meaning; but in the written language the Chinese do precisely what the ancient Egyptians did: set the picture of the specific idea or thing intended — the ideograph — beside the phonogram to illustrate the particular meaning and to differentiate it from the many other homophones.

The Chinese written characters may be classified as follows: 1. *Hsiang hsing,* pictograms or hieroglyphs. They include all the characters which represent the conventionalized rendering of the primitive pictures that composed the bulk of the ancient written language. There are about 600 or more of these characters. Of these signs 214 have been selected as keys or determinatives, the so-called radicals, which enter into the compound characters making up the great bulk of all the words in the language. They include signs and symbols of natural and celestial objects, man, animals, habitations, utensils and numerous other artificial objects. 2. *Chih shih,* suggestive signs. Representing ideas to the mind by the relative positions of the component parts of the sign: — as the ideograph of the sun above a line — the horizon — to suggest the idea of " morning "; the sun beneath a line or behind a tree to suggest " sunset "; two doors with several marks beneath them to indicate " a crowd in a doorway," as here shown: 閧 or a piece of wood between two doors to indicate " an obstruction "; two lines criss-cross forming a cross and the symbol of the hand indicating " to lay cross-wise "; the ideograph of a mouth with a line in the middle — something in the mouth — to suggest the idea of " to talk " or " sweet "; or a man within a square meaning " a prisoner," or the same hieroglyph with the sign of water beside it meaning " to swim," as in a pool. There are about 107 of these characters. 3. *Hui i,* combined ideograms. Characters made up of two or more primitive signs so associated as to convey the meaning of the idea to the mind through the eye: — as the sun and moon to indicate " light "; a mouth and a bird to indicate " singing "; a dog and a mouth, " to bark "; an ax and a tree, " cutting "; a man and a whip, " driv-

ing "; a man on a cliff, " danger "; a hand and a woman,
" safe "; a mouth at a door, " asking," or an ear at a
door, " listening." An ear and a knife picture the meaning " to cut off the ears "; two hands joined, " cordial-
ity "; a man and a child, " to carry "; a man and two
concentric squares, " to pace back and forth "; and many
similar, fanciful characters. The character for " divi-
dend ": 份 is a characteristic example of scores of Chinese symbols. The left-hand symbol is the sign for man,
the upper one that for the number eight (which can be divided!) and the lower one is the sign for knife, which
symbolizes division. As is the case in hundreds of other
Chinese characters there is no phonetic element. It is interesting in this place to note that the compound character
composed of the sign for man and that for hand stands
for " gesture language," communicating at a distance; a
procedure ages ago fallen into desuetude. The persistence of this sign in the written signary is sufficient evidence of the existence of gesture language in the youth of
civilization before writing was evolved. There are about
740 of these combined ideographic signs in the language.
4. *Chuan chu,* inverted signs. Signs in which the meaning
is conveyed by the inversion of the character or a significant change in position of its component parts: — as the
hands pointing to the right or the left to indicate these
directions, or characters above or below a line to indicate
these positions. There are about 372 of these signs. 5.
Chia chieh, metaphorical or " borrowed " signs; compound signs that suggest a fanciful meaning borrowed
from the association of signs in the character: — as
" beautiful " represented by a woman and a bird; " love "
by a woman and a child; " forgetfulness " by a heart and
death; " time " by the sun, the earth and the sign for

measure; and hundreds of similar metaphorical symbols, for there are over 600 such signs in the language. 6. *Hsieh sheng,* phonograms. These constitute the great mass of the written characters in the language, 20,000 to 30,000 or more signs. They are composed of different, specific, phonetic signs, combined with one or more ideographic determinatives or " radicals," to give the particular meaning and to distinguish between homophones. Thus it will be seen that there are over 2400 characters in the Chinese written language that, if not actually pictorial, are representative in one way or another of the idea intended; either as simple ideographs or by the way in which the parts of the characters are associated or arranged.

In the earliest stages of writing the Chinese scribe doubtless represented the objects intended by rude outlines of them; then as the necessity for representing finer shades of meaning manifested itself, qualities, attributes and metaphorical deductions referring to objects already recorded by ideograms became represented by modified or associated forms of these objects or parts of them. This may be called the process of trope or metonymy, by which a part of an object suggests the whole, or some quality of it. It is precisely what all primitive people have done at this stage of development. The ancient Babylonians employed the arm to denote " strength"; the hand, " authority "; the foot, " walking." The Egyptians employed the legs to denote " walking "; the eye to indicate " judgment," an " overseer "; the feather to denote " equality," as the feathers of a bird were assumed to be equal; and wings to denote " protection." The Dakota Indians, as we have seen, used parts of the body to denote derived significances in much the same way as those just mentioned.

The primitive pictures have now become almost entirely obliterated in the modern Chinese script; lingering only as an indistinct echo of their remote archetypes. In certain archaic inscriptions, or in manuscripts that seem to have escaped the edict of Emperor Tsin-Chi-Hoang-Ti, who in the 3d century B. C. ordered that all books should be burned, and in the earliest antique bronzes yet extant, we may still see their earliest conventionalized forms. But it is the internal as well as the outward evidence that confirms by silent witnesses on every hand the theory of the descent of the Chinese characters from early pictographic originals. As in other matters in the Celestial Kingdom, the written language presents the spectacle of arrested growth; for the system lies intermediate between primitive picture-writing and modern alphabetic writing. It contains the run-down, almost indistinguishable elements of the former, and the undeveloped elements of the latter. The Japanese, long since in adapting the Chinese written characters to their spoken language, simply picked out a sufficient number of symbols to form an alphabet of some forty-seven characters corresponding to the simple, phonetic elements of their spoken language: — *i, ro, fa,* etc. They gave the name " irofa " to their alphabet, just as the Greeks formed their word, the basis of ours, from the first two sounds in their alphabet,— " alpha beta." With these alphabetic characters the Japanese spell out their word sounds very much the same as we do.

In attempting to seek the original pictures in the present Chinese script we shall be doomed to disappointment except in a trifling number of instances. In Egypt the entire process is set as a feast before our eyes; the original pictures, the alphabetic signs and the cursive script all attest to the long historic development of their system of

writing. Egyptian writing began with pictures, the hieroglyphs. So did the Chinese. It is not conceivable, however, that the latter ever approached even in the remot-
est degree to the naturalness and beauty of the Egyptian
hieroglyphs. Everything that has been preserved of the
earliest stages of Chinese writing points to the most grotesque method of drawing. It never can be known how
many centuries these pictures were employed before the
conventionalizing process began to modify them, nor
through how many centuries this process extended. But
the same human influences that operated to transform the
early Sumerian pictorial characters into the Babylonian
linear and later cuneiform, and that transformed the
Egyptian hieroglyphs into the hieratic and demotic forms
of writing, doubtless operated to modify and transform
the primitive picture-writing of the Chinese into the individual elements of the odd-shaped forms that they employ
to-day.

What are judged to be the earliest examples of Chinese
writing occur on some bone carvings recently discovered,
one of which is reproduced in Fig. 49. We can best describe these inscribed carvings by quoting the following
excerpt from a letter of Dr. Berthold Laufer, of the Field
Museum of Natural History, Chicago, Illinois. " In
1899 several thousands of bone fragments and bone carvings inscribed in a very archaic style of character were
exhumed in the Province of Ho-nan. Most of these objects apparently served for purposes of divination, and
contained oracles accompanied by the replies of the shamans. Much work has been spent on the decipherment of
these inscriptions, and a good many characters can easily
be identified; but a complete and in every respect satisfactory result has not yet been attained. The date of
these bones also is still controversial, some assigning

them to the Shang dynasty (1766–1154 B. C.); others, to
the Chou dynasty (1122–255 B. C.). The former period,
however, is more probable. The objects of bone are
usually miniatures made in imitation of larger objects of
bronze or jade. Thus, there are reproductions in bone
of all sorts of weapons, like swords, arrowheads, spear-
heads; further, bells, dragons, alligators, disks and so on.
Jade disks and rings play a prominent part in the earliest
period of China and at various functions. The disks symbolize the Deity of Heaven, the rings were badges of rank
or emblems bestowed by emperors upon deserving of-
ficials. What the purpose of the rings in bone was is not
yet known. The characters in these bone inscriptions represent the earliest form of Chinese writing thus far
known."

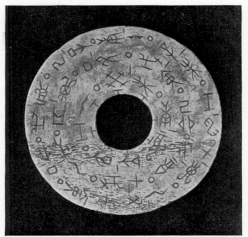

Fig. 49. Inscribed bone ring. Earliest form of Chinese writing.

Fig. 50, reproduced from the *Journal Asiatique* (April
and May, 1868), shows two examples of very ancient
Chinese inscriptions. No. 1 was engraved on a lance. It
dates from the dynasty of Hia, 2150 B. C. It reads in the
ordinary Chinese fashion down the columns and from
right to left. The first character is the modern 壬

meaning " master " or " king." The second and third are doubtful. The fourth, fifth and sixth are the proto-types of the modern 作玨㫓戈 , *tsŏh tiâo kô,* " to carve a lance." The second inscription is from the dy-nasty of Chang (1783–1402 B. C.) and reads in modern Chinese: 忄隹正月王春吉日丁

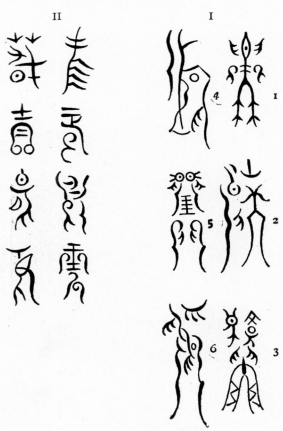

Fig. 50. Chinese inscriptions from lances. No. 1, Dynasty of Hia, 2150 B. C. No. 2, Dynasty of Chang, 1783–1402 B. C.

wêí tchíng yonĕh wâng tchûn kĭh jĭh tîng.

" It was only the day Ting of the cycle, in the first moon of Autumn, that the king fixed upon as favorable, or of good augury."

It is perfectly possible by consulting certain Chinese dictionaries or by tracing back the characters as they occur in antique bronzes and coins, to establish a similar genesis of many if not most of the Hsiang-hsing characters. The radicals, called *tse-pu,* selected from these characters, and used as determinatives in the great majority of words in the language, are the symbols or ideographs principally of the material objects of nature that early would appeal to man and with which his first needs in record making naturally would be concerned. They may be classified about as follows:

1. Natural objects and phenomena; — sun, moon, hill, valley, cliff, cave, desert, field, rain, wind, fire, evening, time, etc.

2. Botanical and mineralogical objects; — wheat, rice, bamboo, wood, grain, wine, salt, metal, stone, gems, earth, etc.

3. Zoological objects; — man, including parts of the body,— head, hair, whiskers, face, eye, mouth, teeth, etc.; father, woman, child, horse, dog, sheep, ox, hog, tiger, deer, tortoise, dragon, etc.

4. Utensils; — knife, spoon, chest, net, plow, vase, boat, etc.

5. Actions; — to see, to eat, to touch, to walk slowly, to speak, to kill, to enter, to stride, to fly, etc.

6. Qualities; — large, small, high, low, slender, square, black, white, yellow, azure, perverse, base, etc.

These are a few of the many ideas pictured by the two hundred and fourteen radical signs that serve as interpreters for almost every compound in the language, introducing and explaining it to the reader. They are not to be read in the compound character. They simply are indicative.

Fig. 51 illustrates a few of these radicals. One cannot escape the significance of most of those shown. Nevertheless, it must be admitted that the great majority of all the radicals have lost all trace of their former graphic nature if not their pictorial significance, and remain purely arbitrary symbols. The two characters for " man " are obvious in their significance. Both are in common use in everyday writing. Almost every compound character relating to man or ideas connected with him will have this as an index sign. The characters for: " a man walking," " the leg," and " to walk " (not shown in the figure), all have the outstretched legs. The Sumerian scribes employed a somewhat similar sign for walking: ㄥ. The Egyptians used the two legs: ∧ as the Chinese do; and we have seen that the North American Indians also used the same graphic device (see Fig. 36). The sign for " shelter " and " to cover," implying shelter or protection, are used with this obviously graphic significance in many compounds for words conveying this meaning or for metaphorical ideas closely related to it. The character for " roof " is quite reminiscent of the familiar pictures of the heavy roofs with their cumbrous cornices that cap the Chinese temples. In most compound characters having the idea of a protecting roof, either actual or metaphorical,— as " house," " palace," " sky," " night," " grouping," " a place," etc., this sign surmounts the compound; as in the following:

| House | Porch | Palace | Tank | Cave | To contain, as the earth does. |

We will digress for a moment to analyze a few of these characters, for they add their testimony to the present inquiry. The character under the " roof " in the third sign is a " spine." The middle character in the symbol for " tank " is the radical sign for " streams "; the upper one pictures the overhanging sky, the lower one being the tank. The symbol for " cave " consists of the signs " roof " and " to enter." Again the legs. The last symbol is compounded of the graphic idea of the roof or sky and the radical character meaning " fields."

The series of archaic pictures for " roof," from which the modern sign has descended, shown in the accompanying cut taken from ancient bronze inscriptions, illustrates conclusively the lineal descent of this symbol. The decidedly tent-like form of the first pictorial character is as graphic a record of the early life of the Chinese or Mongolian tribes as a chapter of written history. It is the picture of a man under a tent. The reader will note the progressive stages of simplification and conventionalization:

The significance of the characters for " receptacle," " mountain," " hair " and " claws," in the selections from the radicals, all are too apparent to require comment. The circles in the signs for " sun," " mouth," " moon," or any other round object, always are " squared " in the Chinese characters. The character " to speak " is a mouth with something in it! The divided fields of the rice meadows are well illustrated in the character for " field." " To see " is a compound radical consisting of that for " one's self "— the upper part — and a man walking; literally, " to go and see " or " find out." In the character for " rain " we may detect the falling drops, while the long horizontal line above undoubtedly indicates the sky or clouds. The characters for " feathers," " wings " and " whiskers," while clumsy and ridiculous as pictures, nevertheless are recognizable or understandable, graphic symbols of these objects. In many Chinese characters where there are a number of small things to record, as feathers, hair, rain (drops), salt, a mesh, the heart (blood), or things in bulk or division, we are quite apt to find many lines or marks in the characters. The character for " door," a double-folding door apparently,— by the way, almost exactly the same as the Babylonian character,— is one of the most common symbols in the language, being used in scores of words where the actual idea of a " door " or " opening " is implied; of going in or out; of bolting with a bolt, or " bolting " through like a horse: 闖, or in all shades of metaphorical meanings of related significance; as well as in scores of cases where its use is apparently indefensible except as an arbitrary sign. So whimsical and unscientific is the written language of the Chinese. Doubtless they can with reason fling at the vagaries of our English writing and its pronunciation; but at least we enjoy a consistent, alphabetic basis to our words if we occasionally do stray away from it in phoneticism. The crosses on the characters for " net " and " salt " illustrate the naïve way, just referred to, that the Chinese have of indicating a collection of many things, or bulk. Their position within the net or hamper in which salt was carried evidences the simpleminded ingenuousness of the early scribe when casting about for pictures of these commodities. The character for " wagon " is the geometric top view of this object, and is one of the very few pictures that has successfully resisted the conventionalizing processes so fatal to the continuity of original types. Archaic forms of this sym-

perpendicular	to see
curved	bow
hooked	
man	sign from heaven
a man walking	rain
to cover	wings, feathers
a shelter	whiskers
roof	teeth
receptacle	door
mountain	
streams	net, caught
field	wagon
sun	
mouth	grain for wine
to speak	vase (tripod)
ear	salt lands
hair	bird
nails, claws	
heart	deer
leg, foot	horse
broken leg	tadpole
head	tortoise

Fig. 51. Selections from the 214 Chinese radicals, with their significance.

bol in which the wheels are shown round, despite the views, are illustrated in Fig. 53. The "tadpole" was fearfully and wonderfully devised by the clever Chinese scribe. Likewise the "tortoise"!

When it comes to expressing implied meanings, occult ideas, and all the flowery, fanciful ellipsis in which the Chinese love to exercise their minds and indulge their vocabulary and in which they are such adepts, they exhibit the most marked ingenuity in the combination of symbols to express their particular thought. The analysis of a limited number of these symbols will suffice to explain to us the general character of the majority of them and the fanciful way in which they combine significant characters to produce symbols pregnant with meaning. A Chinese writer says: "A character is not sterile; once bound to another it gives birth to a son, and if joined to another a grandson, and so on." The characters which combined to make up the symbol and convey the intended idea of the word to the mind are for: house, "cover" and "to conceal"; song, "bird" and "mouth"; profit, "grain" and a "knife"; errand boy, "man" and "to assist"; to nourish, "roof" and "son"; to preserve, "son" and "man" under a line, denoting "protection"; twins, two "son" signs; brilliant, three "suns"; whisperings in another's ear (scandal), three "ears"; the rumbling of carriages, three "wagon" signs; map, "field" and "pencil"; sty, "swine" within a square; furniture, "man" and "fire" (it would be surprising if the Chinese have any saying comparable to our proverb "three removes are as good as a fire"); ashes, "fire" and "hand"; mankind, "man" and "two"; cross-roads, "hill" and "to divide"; rain pattering, "rain" and "words"; winter, "ice" and the obscured "sun"; to scratch, "hand" and "claws"; to follow, "three men tandem"; to carry pig back, a " child " and " one's self " walking; storm, the sign for " rain " surmounted by the sign for a " broom "; conspicuous, a " mountain " under a line denoting the " sky "; to curse, " two mouths " and a " man walking " (men seem to have the same unenviable reputation the world over!) ; to love, " woman " and " son "; beautiful, " woman " and " bird "; intelligence, " head " and " movement." " Sincerity " is represented by a man standing beside his " word "; and " tear " by an " eye " and the symbol for " water." A married woman is represented by the signs for a " woman," a " hand " and a " broom." A mare is represented by the sign for " horse " with the " woman " sign beside it. But the same sign also means a " nurse "! These are but a passing few of the many hundreds of compound symbols for words obtained by combining significant signs. They are characteristic of the system in its totality.

We will now undertake to trace back a few of the common symbols to their origin, or at least to the earliest known archaic form; that the reader may judge for himself in his examination of these signs of the correctness of the theory of the development of writing from primitive pictures, and of the practical universality of the process. The reader should be warned, however, that the Chinese pride themselves,— perhaps unduly,— on the facts of this process in their writing, and are wont to see strange parallels between their characters and the shapes of objects. Nevertheless, there are so many patent and undisputed correspondences that the evidence is overwhelmingly in favor of their theory and of the practically universal one of primitive picture-writing. It would be idle, as well as foolishly skeptical, to doubt the authenticity of the sequence of development of individual symbols shown in the long series of pictures in their own dic-

tionaries by which the Chinese trace the historic development of so many of their individual characters, step by
step, from their earliest to their latest forms. These
forms have been obtained by the Chinese antiquarians
from many authentic sources: — ancient bronzes, coins
and sculptured inscriptions in other imperishable materials.

Fig. 52 illustrates a few characters selected mainly
from the two hundred and fourteen radicals, giving their
archaic prototypes as obtained from ancient dictionaries,
manuscripts and from antique bronzes and sculptures. It
will be noted how crude the original pictures were and
how far the later scribes departed from them. The sun
in the second character, " morning," is shown on the horizon. The primitive character for " source " is symbolic,
but is altogether intelligible. The Egyptians employed a
sign almost identical with this one to indicate " light."
The character for " rain " shows the drops beneath the
line of the sky, which is arched in the ancient drawing. In
the sign for " thunder " we have represented the sky
above with clouds and the thunder beneath them. The
character for a " sign in the heavens " is most interesting.
The ancient sign shows the sky line, two stars and the
oracle in the shape of a mouth with something of import
in it. The modern character is a very exact counterpart
of the ancient sign. The primitive sign for " fire " is decidedly representative, and the modern one follows it
rather closely. The modern signs for " eye," " mouth,"
" nose," " ear," " teeth " and " claws " are rather close
copies of the ancient signs, and exhibit no little resemblance to the real things. The circles and curves have
been " squared," but this was the fate of all 'he archaic
Chinese hieroglyphs in their transformation into the
modern brush characters. The modern character for

"heart" does not represent it objectively as the ancient sign did, but suggests it functionally, by indicating the drops of blood. In the sign "to steal and secrete" we have a picture of the hand within a box. "Sincere conversation" is represented by the picture of a man, a mouth and streams flowing from it. The ancient signs for a "place of rest" and a "hermit" are most suggestive. In both the human figure is most expressive. The sign for "written documents" may need explanation. In the earliest times writing was executed on split bamboo splints which were subsequently tied together. Both signs in their drawing illustrate this and record the fact. We already have commented in a previous chapter on the use of this sign by other nations. The arrow beside the bird sign in the character for "pheasant" records a tale in regard to the sport-loving peasantry of China. The modern character for "tadpole" is quite a fair reproduction of the early drawing, and is much more successful as a picture than the symbols for animals in general. They mostly are very complicated, and generally have four strokes at the bottom, denoting legs, as shown in the character for "horse" in Fig. 51, with other strokes for ears or horns. The wretched "dragon" could not have been worse caricatured than by the early scribe, so the poor medieval imitator saved himself further trouble by attempting to follow the original!

There are many cases of drollery and humor among the Chinese characters, some probably being accidental but others beyond a doubt exhibiting the native sense of humor of the early scribes. The character for "dangerous": 始 is indicated by a woman, a mouth and the sign for deflected, or crooked; that for "arbitrary": 徹 by a man, a woman and the sign for crooked;

I	II		I	II	
⊙	日	sun		中	to hit the center
	旦	morning		図	to steal and secrete
	泉	source		字	to protect / a written character
	小	constellation		問	to ask
	明	light		偲	sincere conversation
	雨	rain		室	a place of rest
	霝	thunder		仙	a hermit or recluse
	曆	sign in the heaven		佃	to till the ground
	火	fire		瞿	watchful
	人	man		鬯	a fragrant plant
	了	child (son)		弓	bow
	目	eye		矢	arrow
	口	mouth		戚	hatchet
	鼻	nose		冊	written documents
	耳	ear		舟	boat
	小	heart		魚	fish
	齒	teeth		雜	pheasant
	爪	claws		黽	tadpole
	泪	tears		象	elephant
	立	to stand erect		龍	dragon

Fig. 52. Evolution of modern Chinese characters from ancient ideographs. Column I, the ancient ideographs. Column II, the modern characters.

that for " surfeited ": 俗 by a man, a woman and a mouth; while for " talkative ": 俵 just a man and a woman are employed,— this time the man coming first! " Tyrant ": 伯 is indicated by a man and the sign for one's self; " quarreling ": 咯 by a woman and two mouths. " Intrigue " is represented by three woman signs; and " fate " or " good luck " by a man and a spoon.

The character for wife: 婦 consists of the sign for woman, the first sign, and that for broom, the upper part of the right hand sign. So far the character is romantic and inoffensive; but it assumes an ominous aspect when we discover that the combined sign on the right is that for " a storm "!   (One may see the streams descending from the sky.)

There is a unique domestic sequence, the significance of which must be left to the reader's consideration, be he man or woman. " Peace ": 安 is represented by a woman under a roof; " home ": 家 by a pig under a roof; " to marry a husband ": 嫁 by a woman and a pig under a roof! To be unfortunate is represented thus:

凶 Is it not to be in a box? A mulberry tree is the picture of a tree with three hands in the branches,— a very poetical representation. The character for " slander ": 訕 is at once ideographic and fanciful. In it we find the three radical signs for words, mouth and mountain. It has no phonetic element. It literally means in English: " making a mountain out of a mole hill."

This character will serve to illustrate the artistic way in which most of the signs in compound characters are changed in proportion and so arranged as to balance and " square up " the symbol; giving it, as in the majority of Chinese signs, a definite, decorative character.

In Fig. 53 will be found a few further selections of modern Chinese characters with several examples — as far as we now can judge in progressive order of development — of the archaic pictures that served for written characters in the ages before conventional writing had developed. They have been taken from the earliest known manuscripts and inscriptions on stone, gems, ivory and bronzes,— weapons, utensils, bells and art objects. It would be difficult for the most skeptical critic — and there are such — of the theory of the descent of written characters from primitive pictures to deny this origin of the Chinese characters, at least many of them. One notes in the characters illustrated a consistent relation between the following symbols in the series, not lost throughout, though the final character may bear but a slight resemblance to the earliest one. The modern character is given on the right, at the end of the series.

The sign for " heaven " originally was very suggestive, but seems early to have degenerated into a purely abstract symbol of no graphic significance whatever. The curving line of rolling cloud masses persists throughout the early ideographs for " cloud." Evidently it represents the contour of a cloud, and is suggested in a strange inversion of position in the modern character by the bottom sign which is that for " crooked." As in many instances in the Chinese characters, the original pictorial symbol has been abandoned and the idea which it represented is expressed in a purely literary form. The dual signs employed to picture the idea of " light," the sun and moon, seem to have been used from time immemorial. The symbols for "mountain" have varied throughout their transformations only in the matter of proportion. The several archaic characters for "child" all represent most graphically the open sutures of the bones of the head, so peculiar to very young children. They are indicated in the modern character by the broken horizontal line in the middle of the square. The progressive transformation of the characters for "ear" is most interesting. The convolutions are well expressed in two of the signs, and the idea is retained in the modern symbol as a reminiscence by the two horizontal lines in the middle of the character. Little change of any significance is to be noted in the compound symbols representing "singing"; the modern sign being a conventional but strict interpretation of the earlier forms. The "horse" becomes progressively and regularly conventionalized as time advances; the four dashes indicating the four legs being the only representative features persisting in the modern character. The characters for "wagon," as previously commented upon, are decidedly representative throughout, being quite as suggestive in the modern rendering and even truer in diagram than in any of the earlier symbols. The different drawings of the "incense vase," though differing greatly in detail, show common features recorded in the final, modern character.

From what we have shown it appears that the modern Chinese system of writing, though practiced in the 20th century of the Christian era, really is a semi-primitive system. It is not pictorial. It is not strictly ideographic. It certainly is not alphabetic. There probably does not exist another written script similar to it. Its development seems to have been arrested at the critical point where other ideographic and hieroglyphic systems have been

heaven

cloud

light

mountain

child

ear

singing

horse

wagon

incense vase

Fig. 53. Successive stages of development of Chinese ideographic symbols
from the most archaic signs to the modern characters.

purged of their overburdened signary, first to a limited
number of syllabic signs, then to a mere handful of alpha-

betic characters derived from this reduced signary. The Chinese written system has not undergone this selective, phonetic process; but retains its lumbering signary, adding to it day by day specific signs for new words entering into the vocabulary. Its vast complexity must be the despair of the youthful Celestial and the limit of endurance of the patient printer, who must know the exact location in his printery of the fonts of every one of the thousands of characters required in the printing of modern books. Such a thing as a typewriter, a linotype or a monotype machine in China is inconceivable.[1]

Before we proceed to the analysis of another system of writing we will describe the picture-writing of a tribe living in one of the border states of China, but long since under the influence of Chinese civilization. A remarkable pictorial script has somewhat recently been discovered in the prefectures of Li-Kiang and Ho-King in the Chinese province of Yunnan (N. W. Yunnan), just south of Tibet. Here live the Mo-so, considered by the Chinese as one of the aboriginal tribes occupying the country before the intrusion of the Chinese. They speak a Tibetan dialect, not Chinese; and the few among them who can write use either Tibetan or Chinese characters, according to the latitude of the region. In early times the Mo-so were ignorant of writing and used notched sticks, as Chinese tradition asserts, and as recorded of them by Marco Polo and referred to by us in the first chapter of this book. The hieroglyphic writings discovered exist in a few rare books which have found their way into Europe, England

[1] As this book goes to press we read of a new simplified, national phonetic writing in China, the *Chu Yin Tzu-Mu,* authorized by the government and being officially introduced by it into the country. It consists of thirty-nine symbols,— twenty-four initials, twelve finals and three medials or connecting sounds. With these phonetic symbols every word in the language may be expressed.

and this country. They do not seem to belong to any historical line of native paleographical development, and they are still less the current writing of the tribe. Nevertheless, Prof. Lacouperie [1] believes that " this sacred writing embodies survivals of the pictorial stage of notation independent of synchronical dates and progresses elsewhere, which seems (within their limited area of self-progress) to be proper to all races of mankind, the white race with exceptions."

These Mo-so manuscripts are the work of the native priests, the so-called Tong-pas, who are shamanistic sorcerers, " representing the aboriginal form of religion that obtained in times prior to the introduction of Buddhism among the Mo-so people of Tibet." The hieroglyphic signs are arbitrary and symbolical, " known only to a small number of initiates, who transmit their knowledge to the oldest son and successor in their profession as sorcerers."

One of these rare manuscripts lately was presented to the American Geographical Society by Francis H. Nichols, author of " Through Hidden Shensi." The author describes the manuscript, which he brought with him on his return from Tibet, as " a book in the Tong-ke, the original language of the Mo-so tribe, who now speak and write Tibetan." " Books like this," says Mr. Nichols, " are exceedingly rare and difficult to obtain. I consider myself fortunate in having secured this manuscript. Part of it I have been able to translate." Unfortunately, this part of Mr. Nichols' papers never has been found, so the manuscript remains untranslated up to the present.

[1] " Beginnings of Writing in and around Tibet," by Terrien de Lacouperie, *Journal of the Royal Asiatic Society*, Vol. XVII. 1885. London. In this article the author treats of the development of writing in many different countries among primitive peoples, and gives many reproductions in outline of Mo-so pictorial manuscripts.

However, the manuscript has been made the subject of a monograph: " The Nichols Mo-so Manuscript," by Berthold Laufer, Ph. D., Field Museum of Natural History, Chicago, Ill., and we are highly privileged to quote from and use the material of this monograph.

The manuscript consists of four folios of two pages each of heavy native paper sewed together on the left-hand margin by means of treble, yellow silk threads. We reproduce in Fig. 54 one of the four pages from this manuscript, which are illustrated in fac-simile in Mr. Laufer's pamphlet. The characters appear to be hieroglyphic, each one being an ideograph directly picturing the object for which it is intended. There are also here and there a very few apparently phonetic characters. The writing is in black Chinese ink executed with a pointed wooden stylus, as at present used by all Tibetan tribes. The disposition of the writing between the long horizontal lines, and the division of the space into sections by the short vertical lines, is very similar to the Mexican catechism and to the Babylonian tablet writing, which we are soon to examine. It really is remarkable that there should be this similarity in arrangement in systems of writing so widely separated in point of time and geographical location.

Mr. Laufer in describing the symbols says: " The second folio (the one shown in our illustration) opens with a design of waves, common to the art of the East in general. It fulfills a purely ornamental function; likewise the following spiral pattern, which is very frequently found in the beginning of Tibetan books. The first symbols are the sun and moon, or month. The striking characteristic of Mo-so writing is the naïve and refreshing realism manifested by the representations of animal pictures. We see many birds on the wing, well outlined heads of mam-

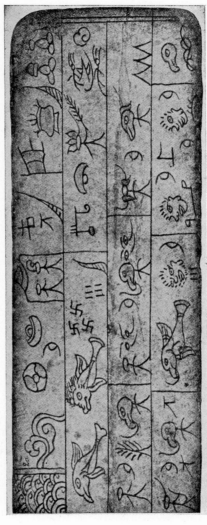

Fig. 54. Second folio of the Nichols Mo-so manuscript. From "The Nichols Mo-so Manuscript." By Berthold Laufer, Ph.D. Reprinted from *The Geographical Review*, April, 1916, Vol. I.

mals, and even complete beasts like a horse, a stag and a tiger. . . . In the human face we find the front as well as the profile represented in the Nichols manuscript. As a rule, the human figure is strongly abridged, characterized by a circle to which lines are attached, marking arms and feet. In the first line (of our illustration) we observe the outlines of a house, in the interior of which are standing two persons, the second being distinguished by a headdress. This design is many times repeated in our text. . . . It is an expression of the idea of the family, man and wife in their house. . . . Headgear, presumably a helmet, is met also in connection with warriors brandishing a weapon, a symbol meaning ' to fight.' "

There is another primitive, ideographic system of writing in China, that of the Lo-lo, a tribe showing strong ethnic and linguistic affinities with the Mo-so. They speak a language somewhat similar to the latter and to the Tibetan. Mr. Laufer speaking of this system of writing says: " In the writing of the Lo-lo the pictographic characteristics, if they ever existed, have disappeared; and the symbols are composed of decidedly geometric elements. They are preëminently ideographic, while Mo-so has a pictographic substratum, with a tendency to strive for simplification. There is no similarity or coincidence between Lo-lo and Mo-so characters." (A Lo-lo manuscript of twenty folios recently has been reproduced in fac-simile by Prof. F. Starr, of the Chicago University.)

In closing this chapter we again will refer to Lacouperie's article in the *Journal of the Royal Asiatic Society*. The author is strong in the belief that the Chinese characters came from the early Babylonian signs and symbols. He says: " The few thousand written words which formed the whole material of the ancient Chinese books rest on a basis of some five hundred different signs (tradition says 540) ; the oldest forms of the half of these have been preserved. Compared with the few hundred characters which, in the same way, form the basis of the ancient writing of Babylon, they display the most remarkable likeness. Taking into account the allowance to be made for the difference of material used for writing — which has caused the wedge to vanish — their identity is indisputable. This identity goes beyond the mere shapes, sounds and meanings, as many other peculiarities are common to the two writings; the Chinese presenting an imitation, somewhat imperfect, of the other. Comparative researches on a scientific footing show, beyond any doubt, that the elements of the early civilization of the Chinese, and the basis of their knowledge and institutions, were borrowed from a region or people connected with the old culture fostered in Babylon." Others have pointed out the general similarity between the Chinese characters and those of the linear Babylonian writing; but no one, we believe, has carried the comparisons quite so far as has Lacouperie. The reader, himself, will note the similarity between the symbols engraved on the bone ring, Fig. 49, one of the oldest known Chinese writings, and the most ancient forms of the linear Babylonian writing shown in Fig. 80.

CHAPTER VII

OF all the systems of hieroglyphic writing that the people of any age have devised for recording or transmitting thought that of the ancient Egyptians stands preëminent, and looms in the popular imagination as the hieroglyphic system par excellence. It is the one that has given its own and the classic name to all such systems of writing. It maintains this unique position not alone on account of its historic and romantic associations, but for the artistic perfection, variety and clever ingenuity of its wonderfully fascinating symbols. Nothing in the way of writing ever has equaled the Egyptian hieroglyphic writing for its quaint picturesqueness, its extreme human interest, or for its beautifully decorative effect, whether sculptured on stone, painted on tombs or written on papyri. Entirely apart from their literary content, the arrangement of the hieroglyphic characters on the temple façades, friezes, columns, and over the broad wall spaces, added ornamental effectiveness to the architectural construction and enlivened its severe monumental dignity with their picturesqueness and variety of detail.

The exact period of time when the Egyptian hieroglyphs were evolved is utterly lost in the impenetrable depths of ancient history. Herodotus saw them in the 6th century B. C., and writes that the Egyptian interpreter translated them for him. He calls them by their own Egyptian name which he translated into Greek,— ἱερογλυφικός, or " sacred writings "; from ἱερός, " sacred,"

and γλύφειν, " to carve." The earliest Greeks who ever
went down into Egypt, and there is authentic historic evidence of their having been there as early as the 8th century B. C., looked upon the perfected hieroglyphic inscriptions at Memphis and other important centers of Egyptian culture, at that time many centuries above a thousand
years old. Joseph no doubt learned to read them with
ease, and when Moses floated in his tiny ark among the
bulrushes of the Nile the neighboring temples that cast
their reflections in the swift current of the sacred river,
and the subterranean tombs slumbering beneath the warm
sands in their vicinity, bore inscriptions that had been read
by successive generations of Egyptians for untold centuries. Indeed, before the Greeks had emerged from barbarism or Abraham had founded Judea or the pyramids
were, the hieroglyphs had been invented and were in use
as a national writing in lower Egypt for many centuries.

Civilization developed early and rapidly in the Nile
valley, and the " dawn of history " broke upon the early
culture of this fertile valley ages before its first faint glim-
merings penciled the rougher lands of Europe. Writing
in an advanced stage of development, we may say in its
final stage, antedated the pyramids, those early mile
stones of history, by many centuries of advanced culture.
Amelia B. Edwards, in " A Thousand Miles up the Nile,"
says: " The Egyptians invented their alphabet so incon-
ceivably long ago that they were in the full possession of
vowels and consonants and the art of spelling words by
means of letters instead of syllables, when they carved
the oldest inscriptions in existence." Champollion, the
younger, son of the renowed French savant who discovered the key and first translated the hieroglyphs, says:
" One seeks in vain in all Egypt for traces of the infancy
of writing. The greater part of existing edifices upon the

ancient soil appear to be not first essays, but a renaissance
of the art of a civilization that had been interrupted by an
invasion of barbarians anterior to the year 2000 before
the Christian era. The inscriptions which decorate these
monuments show us, in effect, the hieroglyphic writing
already as complete in form as the last sculptured writings
of the Egyptians of the second and third centuries after
Christ."

It is no mere flight of fancy to say that in her buried
tombs and porphyry sarcophagi, in her ruined temples
with their gigantic statues, Egypt renews her youth and
breathes again her ancient life in every mummy exhumed
from her pregnant sands; a living death, a deathless life,
strangely and prophetically substantiating her ancient
belief in the resurrection of the soul after 3,000 years of
transmigration. Rameses the Great, lying — or rather
standing — in the Boulak Museum in Cairo, eloquent of
the history of the sesqui-millennium before Christ, mutely
communes with the moderns of the closing years of the
sesqui-millennium after Christ. His grandiloquent inscriptions on the temples with which he covered Egypt
can be read to-day with as much ease as the writing of
any existing nation. But for long ages up to the opening
years of the last century these hieroglyphic inscriptions
were as a sealed book. They were not only undecipherable, but the fact that they were inscriptions at all seriously was questioned.

In Rome there had stood since the time of the Cæsars
as many as twelve Egyptian obelisks brought from Egypt
by the early emperors to adorn the temples of the Eternal
City. The import of their hieroglyphic inscriptions was
not even guessed for over eighteen hundred years. It
was not until Napoleon's spectacular invasion of Egypt
offered the opportunity, that the decipherment of the

Egyptian hieroglyphs was finally attempted and consummated. Every student is familiar with the story, now an historic romance, how Boussard, a young French artillery officer, discovered in the year 1799 near Rosetta, a few miles from Alexandria, the now famous Rosetta Stone (Fig. 55), a slab of slate containing a tri-lingual inscription in hieroglyphic, demotic and Greek writing. The Greek inscription of course could be read; but the hieroglyphic, the sacred writing of the Egyptian monuments, and the demotic, the writing of the educated Egyptian people, were undecipherable, being in the unknown characters of an unknown tongue. The world long had awaited the genius of French initiative and scholarship to unlock the mysteries of Egyptian epigraphy and was immediately to be enlightened. Jean François Champollion, a noted French scholar, turned his attention to the inscriptions and applied his scholarship to their translation with the most memorable success. He detected and rightly guessed that the name of Ptolemy, plainly read in the Greek inscription, was contained within the cartouches or ovals, several times repeated throughout the hieroglyphic inscription. It is now known that the royal names always were so written within these cartouches. Champollion previously had seen on the island of Philæ, before the Temple of Isis, an obelisk, since removed to Corfe Castle, England, with a single vertical line of hieroglyphs down the middle of each face consisting mainly of cartouches similar to those in the Rosetta inscription. Fortunately, at the base of this obelisk were two inscriptions in Greek, a petition to Ptolemy Euergetes II, consort of Queen Cleopatra, by the priests of the Temple of Isis, and the reply of the king. The inscriptions are so historically interesting that we cannot quite resist this appeal from the depths of

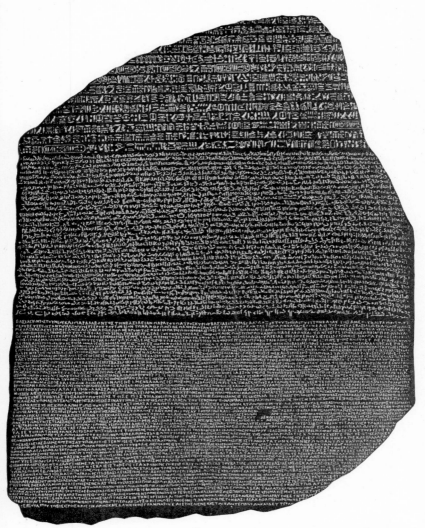

Fig. 55. The Rosetta Stone. Original in the British Museum, London.

time, feeling sure that we shall not lose the interest of the
reader if we venture to reproduce them here; they are
so very human in their implications, even if the social
amenities existing between traveler and entertainer were
so completely reversed from our sordid modern days!
The petition of the priests is as follows:

" To King Ptolemy and Queen Cleopatra his sister
and Queen Cleopatra his wife, gods Euergetae, welfare:
We, the priests of Isis the very great goddess (worshiped) in Abaton and Philae, seeing that those who
visit Philae,— generals, chiefs, governors of districts in
the Thebaid, royal scribes, chiefs of police, and all other
functionaries, as well as their soldiers and other attend-
ants, oblige us to provide for them during their stay, the
consequence of which is that the temple is impoverished
and we run the risk of not having enough for the customary sacrifices and oblations offered for you and for
your children, do therefore pray you, O great gods, if
it seem right to you, to order Numenius, your cousin
and secretary, to write to Lochus, your cousin and governor of the Thebaid, not to disturb us in this manner,
and not to allow any other person to do so, and to give
us authority to this effect, that we may put up a stele
with an inscription commemorating your beneficence toward us on this occasion, so that your gracious favor
may be recorded forever; which being done, we and the
Temple of Isis, shall be indebted to you for this among
other favors. Hail."

Here follows the King's order:

" King Ptolemy and Queen Cleopatra the sister and
Queen Cleopatra the wife, to Lochus our brother, greet-
ing: Of the petition addressed to us by the priests of
Isis in Abaton and Philae, we place a copy below, and
you will do well to order that on no account they be

molested in those matters which they have declared to us. Hail."

Little did these very clever priests of Isis dream that this stele, erected through such a transparent but successful palaver to the august Ptolemy, ultimately would become a potent factor in the decipherment of the hieroglyphs in which the inscription was written; far transcending in importance the trivial cause of its dedication and erection. Champollion in his investigations noted the similarity of the cartouches of Ptolemy in the Rosetta stone and on the obelisk of Philae and subsequently identified the cartouches of Cleopatra in the latter inscription. By the help of common letters in the two names he soon was able to assign phonetic values to the twelve different hieroglyphic characters in these three cartouches.

The reader will find the cartouche of Ptolemy in the bottom line of our reproduction of Line XIV of the Rosetta Stone (Fig. 57) and in the central cartouche of the three cartouches given in Fig. 56, reproduced from " Dictionnaire E'gyptien en E'criture Hieroglyphique " by Champollion the Younger, who completed in 1841 the great work begun by his illustrious father. The name Ptolemy (Ptolmais) is spelled the same way in both cartouches, as follows: the " square " (a shutter or door), P; the " semicircle " (a cap or stone polisher), T; the " knotted cord," O; the " lion," L; the " tongs," M; the two " reeds," AI; and the " crochet " or " yoke," S. The remaining signs in the cartouche, as translated in Line XIV of the Rosetta Stone, read: " ever-living, beloved of Ptah." The two cartouches of Cleopatra (Fig. 56), read downward, the same as all vertical cartouches on the Egyptian monuments; but the horizontal reading where there are two hieroglyphs side by side differs in the two carto ches. As indicated by the facing of the

pictures as one reads — as far as we know a universal
custom in all hieroglyphic writings — the left-hand cartouche reads from right to left, the general custom
throughout all Oriental writing, while the right-hand one
reads from left to right. Many instances of this counter
direction in reading is found in the Egyptian hieroglyphs.
The name Cleopatra (Kleopatra) is spelled as follows
in the cartouches: the " quadrant," K; the " lion," L;
the " reed," I (English E); the " knotted cord," O;
the " shutter," P; the " eagle," A; the " hand," T; the
" mouth," R; and the " eagle," A. The remaining hier-
oglphs are determinative signs, used precisely as the
Chinese employ their radical signs, to indicate the particular meaning and to avoid misconception through
similarity of sound. The egg indicates the feminine gen-
der, and the image that the one intended is a deified
person.

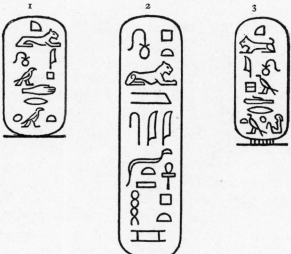

Fig. 56. Cartouches of Egyptian monarchs. 1 and 3, Cartouches of
Cleopatra. 2, Cartouche of Ptolemy.

This was the clue, rather a slight one, it must be admitted, upon which Champollion had to work. But slender as was the thread and extensive as was the tangled tapestry of concealed thought that he had to unravel, after many years of painstaking and tireless effort, aided by rare scholarship and assisted by a knowledge of the Coptic language, the language of the modern fellaheen, which proves to be quite the same as the ancient Egyptian, Champollion, assisted largely by his son, eventually translated the entire inscription on the Rosetta Stone and restored the ancient language of the hieroglyphs. No more superb example of scholarship ever was consummated, and the entire world of letters to-day acknowledges its deep indebtedness to these brilliant French scholars.[1]

The Rosetta inscription, as will be seen, consists of fourteen lines of hieroglyphic, thirty-two lines of demotic and fifty-four lines of Greek writing. It turned out to be a decree of apotheosis of another Ptolemy, Ptolemy Epiphanes, King of Egypt (204–180). To give the reader a better idea of this memorable inscription we have reproduced from William Osbourn's " The Monumental History of Egypt," line XIV, the concluding line of the inscription (Fig. 57). It is reversed from the original, as the reader will see by comparing it with the reproduction of the stone itself, in order to read with the Greek and English from left to right. The inscription at once reveals to us the peculiar nature of Egyptian hieroglyphic writing. The characters are largely pictorial, and one sees images, parts of the human body, an owl, a bee, a snail, plants, implements, as well as con-

[1] It is recorded that Dr. Thomas Young, the noted English scientist and scholar, as early as 1818 assigned the proper phonetic value to six of the Egyptian hieroglyphs.

Fig. 57. Line XIV of the Rosetta Stone, with phonetic and Greek transliterations.

ventional geometric figures. By the accompanying translation, given in parallel, it will be noted that the characters are largely phonetic signs, but that purely ideographic signs also are employed. For instance, the word for " writing," *schai,* in the opening word of the line, is spelled phonetically, but with the added figure of a man in the attitude of writing. The next time the word occurs it is not spelled out at all, but is represented ideographically by a picture of a split reed used for writing attached to a cord from which is suspended the hanging ink bottle carried by the scribes. That is, the word is suggested by the picture of the writing materials. This hieroglyph occurs twice in the second line. The word " tablet," *koi,* is first spelled phonetically, then the picture of a tablet immediately follows for more perfect identification, precisely as the Chinese do. The words for " image " and " king " are not spelled out phonetically but are represented, the one ideographically by the picture of a man, the other symbolically as a metaphor. The character for " name," in the phrase: " in the king's name," is represented symbolically by a blank cartouche.

Before entering upon our brief analysis of the Egyptian hieroglyphic system of writing we will give one or two characteristic specimens of the inscriptions. Fig. 58 is a reproduction of the celebrated obelisk in Central Park, New York City, popularly known as " Cleopatra's Needle." It is one of the few obelisks outside of Egypt. There is one in London on the Thames Embankment, removed there in 1877. Another is in Paris, removed there in 1843 from the Temple of Luxor, where Rameses II — Rameses the Great — erected it sometime in the 16th century, B. C. There is another in Constantinople bearing the cartouche of Thothmes III, set up by the Emperor Theodosius in 399 A. D.; besides several in Rome, as we already have mentioned.

The Central Park Obelisk and its companion on the Thames Embankment, also called by our English cousins

Fig. 58. Egyptian Obelisk in Central Park, New York City.

" Cleopatra's Needle," stood together for hundreds of years in Alexandria, Egypt. The Romans had removed them from the ruins of the Temple of On, Heliopolis, where they were erected by Thothmes III in the 16th century B. C., to adorn the Temple of Cæsar in the year 22 B. C. The New York obelisk was presented to that city by the generous Ismaïl, Khedive of Egypt, and transported to this country in 1880. The view shown in the illustration is the east face, which, like the north one, is entirely uninjured except at the extreme bottom; the hieroglyphs being wonderfully preserved by reason of their strong *intaglio relievo*. As will be noted, there are three vertical rows of hieroglyphs in each face. The hieroglyphs in the central row in each face relate to Thothmes III and probably were cut by his directions; spaces being left for his successors, whether intentionally or not it is hard to say. The hieroglyphic inscriptions on the outside lines relate to Rameses II, and doubtless were cut by his orders; the spaces on the obelisk being appropriated by this spacious and spectacular monarch for his glorification. And amply has he taken advantage of the opportunity — as was his custom — to resort to grandiloquent language. Since the hieroglyphic characters are so clear in the illustration, we will give a full translation of the inscription, based on the interpretation of the two scholarly Egyptologists, Brugsch and Chaba.

Left-Hand Line

Horus: the Strong Bull
Son of the Sun-God Kheper.
The King of Upper and Lower Egypt
(Ra-user-ma-Sotep-en-Ra),
The Chosen One of the Sun,
The Golden Horus.

Rich in years; Grand in victories.
Son of the Sun,
(Ramessu Meriamun).
He issued from the loins
To receive the crowns from the
    Sun God Ra,
Who created him to be the
    Sole Monarch,
Lord of the two Worlds.
(Ra-user-ma-Sotep-en-Ra).
    Son of the Sun.
(Ramessu Meriamun)
  The Splendor of Osiris
    Like the Sun.

CENTER LINE

Horus: the Strong Bull
Crowned in Thebes
The Lord of Diadems
His Kingdom is as lasting as the
Sun in the Heavens.
(Beloved of Tum, Lord of On (He-
liopolis), Son of his loins
Thoth created him Thothmes).
They created him in the Grand Hall
From the perfection of their own limbs,
Being conscious of the Great Deeds
    he was to accomplish.
He whose Kingdom should be of
    long duration.
The King of Upper and Lower Egypt
(Ra-men-Kheper),
Beloved of Tum, the Great God,
    and of
The Circle of his Divinities.
He who gives all Life, Stability
    and Happiness.

RIGHT-HAND LINE

Horus: the Strong Bull,
Beloved of the Sun-God Ra,
King of Upper and Lower Egypt
(Ra-User-ma-Sotep-en-Ra)
The Chosen One of the Sun
Possessor of the Two Worlds.
Son of the Sun,
(Ramessu Meriamun).
A handsome and Kind Hearted Youth:
Resplendent as the Solar Orb on the Horizon.
Lord of the Two Worlds
(Ra-user-ma-Sotep-en-Ra).
The Chosen One of the Sun
Son of the Sun
(Ramessu Meriamun).
The Reflected Splendor of
The God Tum
Who gives Life.

Possibly the reader may be able to make some sense out of the hieroglyphic inscriptions on this obelisk, the characters are so largely ideographic. If he will examine with a reading glass the right-hand vertical column of hieroglyphs, he may, after a fashion, be able to follow the translation. Above the upper cartouche — indicated by brackets in the printed translation — is a bee, the character employed for " king " and selected on account of the bee's wonderful faculty for organization. Below the cartouche " the chosen one of the sun " is represented in person seated beside the sun, which is shown as a circle. Above the middle cartouche the " son of the sun " is represented by a goose and the circle of the sun. The goose being especially delectable to the Egyptians, its picture was used by them to indicate a child, more particularly a son. Below the third cartouche is the same character with the corresponding significance. The phrase " resplendent as the solar orb on the horizon " is represented ideographically by rays radiating from the orb of the sun, while the horizon is represented by the sun just above a curved line, almost precisely as the Ojibwa and Chinese represented it.

Not alone have the sculptured monuments of Egypt supplied us with specimens of the beautiful writing of these talented Orientals of antiquity. They are the most conspicuous examples of the art, and challenge our attention and admiration from almost every standing ruin or fallen architrave throughout the land. They are for the greater part the proud glorifications of the kings and of their mighty achievements over their enemies extending over a score of centuries from the time of the great pyramids — which by the way are notably silent, being probably the work of alien conquerors, about 3000 B. C.— to the Ptolemies in the 3rd century before Christ. It is from the tombs of Egypt, brilliant with their frescoed inscriptions on walls and ceilings recounting the daily life, the moral and religious aspirations of the deceased kings, priests, courtiers and civilians, that we obtain some of the most valued and intimate records of the past of this truly wonderful people. It is from the tombs also, where they have been preserved from injury through the ages of political vicissitudes, that there have come the priceles papyri, examples of which are scattered through the museums of Europe.

Many of these papyri are transcriptions of the very ancient " Book of the Dead," a work corresponding in its moral and spiritual thought to the Hebrew scriptures. There are many versions of it extant, all characterized by lofty and inspiring religious

ideals and aspirations. They are variously entitled:
" Chapters of the Coming Forth by Day," " Chapters
of Making Strong the Beatified Spirit," etc.; but the
most common name for these books of the sacred literature of the Egyptians is the one first given, the " Book
of the Dead." Many of the passages in these papyri are
as noble in thought, broad in humanity and devout in true
religious spirit as anything ever penned by the Hebrew
prophets. This is said with no discredit to the lofty
thought of the Old Testament, but as the highest eulog-
ium of the Egyptian sacred writings. The papyri consist
of sheets of beautiful, fine paper made from the papyrus
plant neatly glued together in long strips and subsequently rolled up and tied with a cord. A picture of one
of these papyrus rolls with the cord tied about it may be
seen in the third character beneath the horizontal line
in the first word in the inscription given in Fig. 60. Some
of these papyri are very long. The Papyrus of Ani is 78
feet long. That of Nebseni from Thebes, 1600 B. C., is
77 feet long. The Papyrus of Nu, one of the oldest, is
65 feet long.

One of the most perfect of the Egyptian papyri is that
of Hu-nefer, Hu the Good, found at Thebes. It is 18
feet long and of superb artistic execution, being drawn in
color with illuminated chapter, rubrics and important
words in red. Hu-nefer was the overseer of the palace,
inspector of cattle and scribe to his august majesty Seti I,
King of Egypt, about 1370 B. C. We give in Fig. 59 [1]
a reproduction of the beginning of the Papyrus Hu-nefer.
It is one of the many versions of the " Book of the
Dead." The inscription opens with a hymn to Ra and
Osiris.   It begins in the left-hand upper corner and reads

[1] From " The Book of the Dead." E. A. Wallis Budge, Keeper of the
Egyptian and Assyrian Antiquities, British Museum.

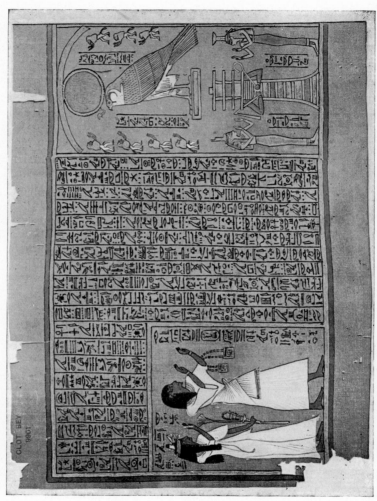

Fig. 59. Portion of the Papyrus Hu-nefer. The Book of the Dead.

downward and to the right in the nine vertical columns over the beautiful vignette of Hu-nefer and his wife, then continuing in the long vertical columns from left to right, interrupted by pictures and vignettes throughout its entire length. Though the progression of the writing in the hieroglyphs is downward in the vertical columns and from left to right as the columns run, in each long horizontal line where there is more than one hieroglyph the reading is from right to left. In this connection a remark by Herodotus concerning the Egyptians is interesting. He says: " When they write or calculate, instead of going like the Greeks from left to right, they move their hand from right to left; and they insist, notwithstanding, that it is they who go to the right and the Greeks who go to the left " (Herodotus, Book II, Chapter 36). Herodotus probably did not know that his ancestors in Greece only a few hundred years before his time wrote like the Egyptians and Orientals from right to left.

In Fig. 60 we give Budge's transliteration and translation in Egyptian and English of the nine vertical columns of hieroglyphs over the vignette of Hu-nefer and his wife, ending with the first character at the top of the tenth column, the first long column of hieroglyphs. As in the translation of the Rosetta Stone, the characters are reversed to read with the English from left to right. As the characters are larger and clearer than in our reproduction of the original papyrus, an analysis of them is more practicable. Again we find, as in the inscription on the Rosetta Stone, numerous pictures, recognizable in most cases, of birds, animals, men and utensils; including the chicken, owl, beetle, crane, snail, serpent, images, men and parts of men,— head, foot, arm, leg, hand, eye and mouth; also a lute, bowl, tongs, vases, and other objects;

as well as representations of the sun, stars, heaven, the horizon and many other symbols.

The word Hu-nefer in the second line is spelled alphabetically throughout. The square " scroll " is *h*, the " chicken " is *u*, the " lute " is *n* (in some cases *nefer*), the " snail " is *f*, and the " mouth " *r*. The statue is an indicative character and informs us that this is the name of a man. Ancient Oriental languages always had a strange aversion for vowels. Some were indicated while others had to be supplied by the reader. In the Phœnician writing there were no true vowels, as we shall discover later on. In the first line the word *keft* is spelled phonetically. The " shaded circle " is *k*, the " snail " is *f*, and the " semicircle " is *t*. Again, *uben-f*, " he riseth," also is spelled phonetically. The " chick " is *u*, the " leg " is *b*, the " zigzag " line, which primarily represents water, is *n*, and the " snail " is *f*. Again *e* is suppressed and must be supplied. Lest this word might be confounded with a homophone of a different meaning, the sun is shown with its scintillating rays of light, to indicate the particular meaning in the text. The first word in the second line, *pet*, is spelled alphabetically; the " square " being *p*, and the " semicircle " *t;* then the ideograph of the sky, quite the same as the Ojibwa and Chinese, is added for identification. When the word occurs again in the fifth line, it is represented only ideographically.

Thus it will be seen that the Egyptian hieroglyphs consist of alphabetic, syllabic and ideographic signs used side by side often in the same word. It was not always necessary. The alphabetic signs after they were evolved out of the original ideographs were all-sufficient; but the Egyptians were notably conservative. They loved the beauty and variety of their written characters, as well they

1. *tua* ᚱ*Rā* *xeſt* *uben - f* *em* *xut* *ȧbtet* *ent*
Adoration of Rā   when   he riseth   in   the horizon   eastern   of

pet *ȧn* *Ausar* *Hu-neſer* *maȧxeru* *t'eṭ - f* *ȧnet' - hrȧ - k*
heaven. Behold Osiris Hu-nefer,   triumphant, he saith; Homage to thee,

Rā *em* *uben - f* *Temu* *em* *ḥetep - f* *uben - k*
Rā   in   his rising.   Temu   in   his setting.   Thou risest

sep sen *peṣt - k* *sep sen* *xāȧ - θ* *em sutenet* *neteru* *entek*
(twice), thou shinest (twice), diademed as king of the gods.   Thou art

neb *pet* *neb* *ta* *ȧri* *ḥeru*
lord   of heaven,   lord   of earth,   maker   of the beings of heaven

xeru *neter uā* *xeper* *em sep* *ṭep*
and of the beings of earth, God One, who came into being in time primeval,

ȧri *taiu* *qema* *rexit* *ȧri* *Nu* *qema*
maker of the world, creator   of mankind,   maker of the god Nu,   creator of

Ḥāpi *ȧri* *net* *se-ȧnx* *ȧm*
Hāpi,   creator   of the watery abyss, making to live   what is therein,

se-θes *ṭuu* *se-xeper* *reθ*
binding fast the mountains, making to come into existence men and women.

Fig. 60. Transliteration of the first nine columns of hieroglyphs of the
Papyrus Hu-nefer

might, and were loath to lose any of them from their signary. In consequence, although having an extensive alphabet of characters sufficient for every possible elemental sound in their vocabulary, and many duplicate characters of the same letter, for varying meanings and references, they used also the syllabic characters employed in the older signary, and the representative pictures used before either syllabic or alphabetic hieroglyphs were invented. It is true that the ideographic, interpretative pictures, met with so frequently in later Egyptian writing, are comparatively rare in the most ancient writing. Probably as the homophones in the language multiplied it became increasingly necessary, or was the custom, to employ these ideographs more extensively as determinative signs.

The reader by this time must be eager to see and refer to the Egyptian alphabet, that he may himself be able to spell out the hieroglyphic words; for the majority of the characters are alphabetic, though there are many ideographs and syllabic signs that make the reading of the Egyptian hieroglyphs somewhat difficult. Possibly he already has learned to recognize many of these characters, for in the cartouches examined and in the inscription on the Rosetta Stone and in the perusal of the inscription of Hu-nefer he has met with a large majority of the common alphabetic signs employed by the Egyptians. We say common, for the Egyptians employed a large number of different hieroglyphic signs for the same alphabetic sound, choosing them according to the sentiment, implication, and in some cases the delicacy of the context. For example, in the case of the letter L, if it occurred in the name of man, the " lion " was used; in the name of a queen, the " lotus " was employed. There were twenty different A's to choose from, thirty H's, and

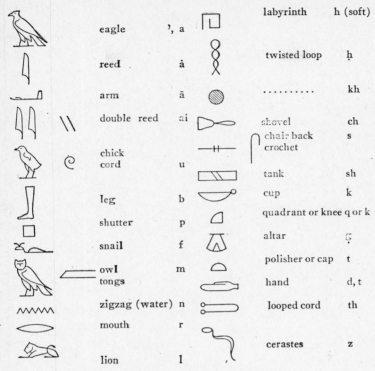

eagle	', a		labyrinth	h (soft)
reed	à		twisted loop	ḥ
arm	ā		....	kh
double reed	ai		shovel	ch
			chair back crochet	s
chick cord	u		tank	sh
leg	b		cup	k
shutter	p		quadrant or knee	q or k
snail	f		altar	ç
owl tongs	m		polisher or cap	t
zigzag (water)	n		hand	d, t
mouth	r		looped cord	th
lion	l		cerastes	z

Fig. 61. The common Egyptian alphabet.

many different duplicates of nearly every letter in their alphabet.

In Fig. 61 we give a table of the Egyptian alphabetic characters with their names and phonetic values. It is not arranged historically, as it contains signs used in the earliest period together with a few evolved in later times. The alphabet employed in the Old Kingdom consisted of 23 characters, chiefly consonants. The vowels came first, but they mostly were disguised sounds. The first one, the "eagle," was hardly *a,* but a mere breathing. So also was the "arm." The "chick" represented a sound

something like our w. The two " reeds " and the alternative parallel lines, *ai;* the alternative characters for *u*
and for *m;* the " lion," *l;* and the alternative characters
for *s* are not included in the ancient alphabet, although
they were employed by the Egyptians in their hieroglyphic
writing for many centuries. The hieroglyph of the
" mouth " originally was used alike for the two consonants *l* and *r,* the context alone indicating the one intended. Later when the need of differentiating and expressing both consonants became necessary or desirable,
the " mouth " was retained as the symbol for *r,* and the
" lion " was chosen to indicate *l.* The selection of the
lion to represent the consonant *l* was made on the principle of acrology, already explained and further to be
illustrated in connection with the evolution of the Egyptian alphabet. The native name of the lion, *labo,* began
with *l,* as in our English name; consequently the lion was
chosen from among other words beginning with *l* on account of its appropriateness as a symbol, or possibly its
claim upon the popular imagination.

By far the greater number of the alphabetic signs as
well as most of the hieroglyphs used by the Egyptians
were pictorial. There are very few conventional or
geometric symbols. Champollion has classified the
hieroglyphic characters as follows: — heavenly bodies,
the human figure and its parts, domestic and wild animals, birds, reptiles, fishes, insects, plants, fruits, flowers,
clothing, furniture, armor, utensils, instruments, buildings, geometric forms and grotesque images. In the alphabet given one finds the eagle, reed, extended arm,
chicken, leg, shutter, snail, owl, flowing water, mouth,
lion, twisted cord, shovel, tank, bowl, altar, cap, hand,
tongs and the serpent. These signs were the ones most
commonly used, and constitute what may be considered

the Egyptian alphabet proper. But the Egyptians used a very much more extensive palette in their word painting, having as we have said many duplicate signs and a great number of syllabic symbols. We give in Figure 62 a few additional alphabetic and syllabic signs in frequent use in the inscriptions through hundreds of years. Among the symbols we recognize a crane, battlement, hoe, stylus, lute, knotted cord, headdress, throwing stick, plants, feather, lasso, whip and the plan of a house. This list practically constitutes a secondary alphabet. Yet we could add to it many more symbols that the Egyptians frequently used for the sake of variety, as we use different words of the same meaning to avoid repetition and redundancy.

Let us consider now how the Egyptians came by their

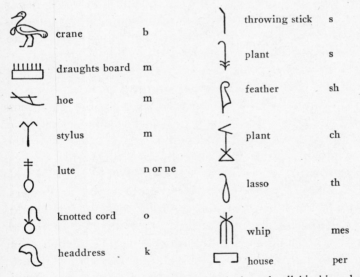

crane	b		throwing stick	s
draughts board	m		plant	s
hoe	m		feather	sh
stylus	m		plant	ch
lute	n or ne		lasso	th
knotted cord	o		whip	mes
headdress	k		house	per

Fig. 62. Selections from supplemental alphabetic and syllabic hieroglyphs employed by the Egyptians, with their names and phonetic equivalents.

unique alphabetic signs. We find them in the full flower of mature development even in the very earliest inscriptions extant; and there was but little material change in their form in the hundreds of centuries during which they served this wonderful nation with the elements of their written language. The fully developed system of hieroglyphic writing with phonetic alphabetic characters was in use in the time of Menes, the first king of the First Dynasty, which date is fixed by Dr. Flinders Petrie at 4777 B. C. It is a remarkable triumph of archæology and a veritable romance of history that the mummy of this king, who but yesterday was supposed to be purely mythical, discovered at Thebes in 1897, now reposes in the Gizeh Museum in Constantinople. In the great pyramid of Cheops (4th dynasty, 3700 B. C.) there have been found one or two hieroglyphic inscriptions, probably quarrymen's or inspectors' brush-painted memoranda, being cartouches of King Suphis or Chufu, pronounced by the Egyptians " Kufu," but wrongly interpreted by the ear of the Greek Herodotus as " Cheops." Here is one of the cartouches taken from Prisse D'Avennes " Histoire de L'Art Égyptien ":

It is written with rare facility by one practicing a fully developed system of writing. Reading from right to left the first character is *k,* the chick is *u,* the snail is *f,* and the chick again is *u.*

One of the oldest Egyptian inscriptions known is that of King Sent (2d dynasty) written to his grandson, Shera, before 4000 B. C. King Sent's cartouches are rather frequently met with. The spelling is alphabetic, as will be seen in the accompanying cut, and the characters are the same as those used by the Ptolemies of the second century B. C.:

In the absence of any earlier record the antecedent stages of development of the Egyptian hieroglyphs must be purely conjectural and based on analogy. Some eminent authorities dispute the claim that the hieroglyphs have developed out of original pictures, but that at some brilliant epoch in the early Egyptian hierarchy they were invented by fiat, as it were. They point out that in many cases the ancient names of the characters became obsolete so early that no explanation for their phonetic value is discoverable even in the earliest inscriptions. But the general argument is far from convincing, nor is it natural. It is inconceivable that a people at any stage of civilization could, out of hand, from no inherited material, have invented such a wonderful alphabet. It is quite too superhuman an effort to believe of any people, no matter how advanced in culture. The overwhelming evidence of the hieroglyphs themselves, the analogy of the growth of other written languages, as well as the consensus of opinion of the majority of Egyptologists, favor the belief that the alphabetic signs have descended from primitive pictures many of which are still retained in the signary. Fig. 63 illustrates a few of these primitive ideograms taken from the inscriptions. They are wonderfully like the Ojibwa and Chinese symbols, and give every evidence of having come down from the most remote era of antiquity. They were used with almost no modification as long as the hieroglyphs lasted into the Greek and Roman classic period.

Fig. 63. Selections from primitive Egyptian ideographs.

It requires no stretch of the imagination to believe, for the nature of the hieroglyphs incontestably points to the fact, that the early Egyptians in their first attempts at written record drew the pictures of the things referred to in their records the same as the American Indians, both of the Plains and of Mexico, the primitive Chinese, and the people about whom we are yet to speak. The facts seem to prove that in the evolution of their art of writing the Egyptians progressed along these three stages of development: — I. Representative or imitative signs. In this archaic stage the Egyptian scribe simply drew or painted representations of the sun, moon, stars, mountains, plants, animals, weapons, utensils, etc., as necessity required in communicating or recording facts. These in time became somewhat conventionalized and laid the foundation for the determinative ideograms used in later times. II. Symbolic signs. When it became necessary to portray actions, motives and sentiments, the scribes resorted to: (1) Synecdoche,— using a significant part instead of the whole of the figure of representation; — as the legs drawn forward or backward to indicate " going " or " coming," or bent to indicate " jumping "; the eye with drops to indicate " crying " or " grief," or two eyes to indicate " seeing "; the ear to indicate " hearing "; the tongue " speaking "; the hand holding a vase to indicate " offering "; two arms holding a paddle meaning " to convey," or an arm holding a shield meaning " combat "; and many similar symbols. (2) Metonymy. Portraying cause for effect and vice versa; employing the instrument to represent the effect produced; — as the sun to represent day or time; the moon to represent a month; the pictures of the various implements used in writing to indicate the act of writing, as we already have learned; and many like examples. (3) Metaphor. Representing an idea by a resemblance real or fancied to the properties of some object; — as a book to represent " knowledge "; a lute, " goodness "; an eye, " judgment "; a crocodile, " evil "; a bee, " king "; or the head of a lion to indicate " superiority." III. Phonetic signs. In this last period of development of the Egyptian hieroglyphic writing there probably were two stages: syllabic and alphabetic phoneticism. This can only be surmised, as we have no record of priority of the one over the other. We find syllabic and alphabetic signs used side by side from the very earliest historic times.

The inadequacy of ideographic writing to minister to the needs of the rapidly advancing nation must very early have manifested itself in an effort to invent a more flexible and responsive medium of communication, that more closely would coördinate with the native speech, and be its ready and legible means of written expression. Undoubtedly the Egyptians at a very early period must have conceived the desirability of selecting symbols to represent the elemental phonetic sounds in their spoken words instead of contenting themselves with different individual symbols for every object and idea, as in the Chinese system of writing. Our very first acquaintance with the hieroglyphs is at this advanced stage. The alphabetic characters already had been chosen and the scribes were in possession of an extensive alphabet, syllabary and ideographic album of signs capable of expressing by writing every shade of meaning that the mind could conceive and the tongue express. Our next inquiry then is: how was the selection of these syllabic and alphabetic signs effected?

It is probable that for a long period prior to the final invention of alphabetic signs a very large number of syllabic symbols had been in use to express the phonetic values of monosyllabic words and syllables. These syllabic signs probably had been selected from among the simplest or commonest ideograms of monosyllabic or polysyllabic words and used thereafter in writing as the phonograms of the initial syllables in these words. The difference in use then was that the symbol which formerly was employed to indicate the name of an object or idea was later used as the sign for the sound of the first syllable of this name wherever it occurred in writing any polysyllabic word whatever. As an illustration of this we again will refer to the sign *pet*, occurring several times in the inscription of Hu-nefer. Originally it was the ideogram for " heaven," *pet*. Subsequently it was employed as the sign for the syllable *pet* in any other word wherever it occurred. Scores of similar instances might be cited. Finally a finer analysis and differentiation of the syllabic sounds into their simplest phonetic elements being desired, the alphabetic signs were evolved as a consequence of this cultural advance of the Egyptian scribes. The presumptive evidence is almost overwhelming that the Egyptians in the great majority of cases chose for these alphabetic characters signs already popular of syllabic or monosyllabic words whose initial, elementary sound corresponded to the alphabetic sound for which a sign was sought. This was carried out on the principle of acrophony or acrology, as already explained.

No inconsiderable proportion of the common hieroglyphs betray by their native names the source of their derivation, and substantiate the generally accepted theory in regard to the manner of selection of these signs. Running over the characters in the common Egyptian alphabet (Fig. 61), we may note a number of these instances. The native name for " eagle " is *ahom;* for " reed," *ake;* for the " arm," *āa;* for the " leg," or rather " to walk," *bu;* for " shutter," *pu;* for " snail," *fent;* for " owl," *moulak;* for " water," *nu;* for mouth," *ro;* for " lion," *labo;* for the " fret " or " labyrinth," meaning " to enter," *ha;* for the " twisted loop," *hake;* for the " tank," *she;* for the " hand," *tot;* for the " looped cord," *thethet;* and for the " serpent," *zst.* Following Fig. 62 we find that the native name for " crane " is *bak;* for the " lute," *nefer;* for the " headdress," *klaft;* for the " throwing stick," *hu;* and for the " feather," *shu.* The author is not certain that every one of these names is entirely authentic. They have been taken from the lists of various eminent Egyptologists, who do not always agree with one another. It may be in some cases that the names as given are not those in vogue in ancient times when the hieroglyphs were being evolved. It has not been

possible to verify this and probably it never will be. We
believe, however, that no further facts are necessary to
prove the origin of the Egyptian alphabetic characters.
That we cannot find any transitional stage of pictography
or ideography antecedent to the alphabetic stage is no
valid argument against the development of the latter
signs out of the former; but rather an evidence of the
immense age of Egyptian civilization, through the farthest stretches of which much doubtless has been lost.

When the complete alphabet was once selected, a new
difficulty must have confronted the scribes, which they
solved in a most unique and picturesque way. The language abounded in homophones; some sounds having as
many as twenty or forty different meanings. To indicate
the particular meaning in the text, after the word had
been phonetically spelled out, a pictorial, interpretative
ideograph of the thing intended was added for more complete identification. For example, there were forty different meanings for the monosyllable *ha,* twenty for *ab,*
twenty for *apt,* fifteen for *aft* and for *ant,* eleven for *ah,*
and so on. When *ab* was used to mean " dancing," the picture of a girl dancing was drawn after the phonetic characters, a reed and a leg. When *ab* was used to indicate the
meaning " thirst," three determinative ideograms were
appended; first a dog jumping up, then the symbol for water, and then a man pointing to his mouth, as here shown:

When *apt* was used to mean " judgment," it was followed by the picture of an eye; when used to mean a
" duck," the picture of a duck was added; when used to
mean a " measure," the picture of a wooden measure was
drawn. If *aft* was used to signify " four," four marks

were added. If used to indicate "jumping," the word was first spelled out phonetically,— a reed, a snail and a hand, and then legs were added, as shown in the sketch: —

When the word was used to mean "rest," a man was drawn in a reclining attitude. *Ant* meaning "time of day" had a picture of the sun. When it meant "to destroy" it was followed by the picture of a bird of prey. The word *taben* had several meanings. One of them meant "to move around." The syllable was spelled with a hand, a leg and the character for *n;* then a spiral and a pair of legs were added as here shown: —

Sef, meaning "yesterday," was followed by the sun, the day sign. When it meant a "baby," it was indicated by a child sucking its thumb! There were several meanings to the word *seseft.* One of them was "disgusting." This was indicated by the ideograph of a nose and the representation of a man holding his nose, thus: —

There is abundant evidence of the fact that the Egyptians at times resorted to the rebus form of writing, the same as the Mexicans. An example of this — possibly intentionally humorous — comes from an inscription of Ptolemy XV at Edfu. The name lapis lazuli, which in Egyptian is *khesteb,* appears. Instead of writing the word phonetically in alphabetic characters, the scribe has whimsically borrowed the meanings " to stop," *khesf,* and " a pig," *teb,* and thus illustrated the word by a picture of a man holding a pig by the tail!

We will close this description of the hieroglyphic writing of the ancient Egyptians by giving examples of their " hieratic " and " demotic " writing. The characters used in the hieratic style of writing were a highly conventionalized and cursive rendering of the hieroglyphs. Inscriptions in hieratic characters date from the very earliest dynasties, and so far as we know seem to be contemporaneous with the earliest hieroglyphic inscriptions. Fig. 64 is a fragment of the Papyrus Prisse, now in the Bibleotheque Nationale, in Paris. It is a copy made about 2500 B. C. of the Precepts of Ptah-hotep, written to his son, instructing him how to behave in the various conditions of life. The original was composed during the

reign of Assa, eighth king of the fifth dynasty

(about 3350 B. C.). It is replete with the most beautiful homilies, as trite to-day as when penned over five millenniums ago. The sage father enjoins his son as follows: —

"If thou hast become great after thou hast been lowly, and if thou hast amassed riches, after poverty, so that thou hast become, because of this, the first in thy city; and if the people know thee on account of thy wealth, and thou art become a mighty lord, let not thy heart be lighted up because of thy riches, for the author of them is God. Despise not thy neighbor who is as thou wast, but treat him as thine equal."

The third line in the fragment reads:

" Who shall make me to speak noble words? How shall I tell him (my son) the words of those who have heard the wise counsels of olden times, the counsels which have been heard from the gods? "

These moral precepts were written over five thousand years ago; yet the father refers in these early years of human history to the wisdom of the men of old and desires his son to follow their example.

Fig. 64. Egyptian hieratic writing. A page from the Papyrus Prisse. About 2500 B. C.

It will be interesting to compare the development of the Egyptian hieratic characters from the parent hieroglyphs with the somewhat similar evolution of the Chinese script from their primitive pictures. While the ultimate symbols, except in a few individual cases, are wholly dissimilar in the two systems of writing, the character of the transformation is quite the same in both. In both systems, as a rule, the resulting characters bear little positive resemblance to the parent pictures. In Fig. 65, adapted from Champollion, we have selected seven objects, and show the transformation of their respective written characters from the early hieroglyphs to the final conventionalized symbol. The objects in their order are: bird, fish, vase, son, gate, star and ax. The first two horizontal lines are Chinese, the lower two are Egyptian. Throughout, the Egyptian hieratic signs are very much simpler and less complex than the Chinese. The whole process affords us an illustration of the general evolution of writing from the primitive pictures employed in archaic times to the simplified symbols used in the later stages of civilization. Historical and archæological facts substantiate the belief that this evolution is practically universal. Although carried out in symbols and signs greatly varying from each other, every great original system of national writing seems to have progressed along the same lines of development.

I. CHINESE WRITING

II. EGYPTIAN WRITING

Fig. 65. Comparative development of Chinese and Egyptian hieroglyphic characters from the earliest archaic symbols to the later conventional signs. (The signs in the last row are the Egyptian hieratic characters.)

The Egyptians carried the process of simplification of their hieroglyphic writing to a yet more advanced stage, developing a third system of writing, the demotic, already familiar to us in the Rosetta Stone. It was virtually a shorthand rendering of the hieratic characters, only still further simplified. They were used by the educated Egyptian people in the ordinary affairs of life, in legal and business documents, letters and in civil and domestic affairs, in general. We will give one example of demotic writing, Fig. 66. It is from a parchment found in Egypt and dates from the eighth year of the reign of Ptolemy Epiphanes (196 B. C.). It is the protocol of a judicial contract, naming the contracting parties, and begins as follows:

> "The year 8 of (the month of) Choïak, the 4th of King Ptolemy, son of Ptolemy and Arsinoe, gods Philopatores, and of the priests of Alexander, and of the gods Adelphes," etc.

The writing is in a beautiful hand, and is legible and elegant. Calligraphic skill could hardly be carried to a higher degree of perfection.

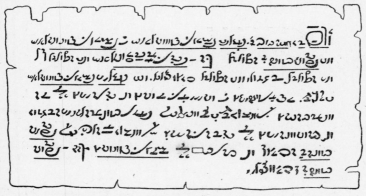

Fig. 66. Egyptian demotic writing. Parchment from the reign of Ptolemy Epiphanes.

Surely the art of Egypt as shown in her sculptured monuments, in her painted tombs and in her wonderful hieroglyphs and written papyri reveals to us a nation advanced to the very highest levels of civilization. Truly the men of old received their inspiration from the gods, as Pliny has said. In no other way has knowledge and the experience of civilization with its moral and religious reactions more surely descended from generation to generation than through the art of writing.

CHAPTER VIII

BABYLONIAN AND ASSYRIAN CUNEIFORM WRITING

EVERYBODY is familiar with Talleyrand's facetious remark that " language is intended for the concealment of thought." We remember too that Trench speaks of words as " fossil history." How true these statements are of many lost languages which have concealed for ages the thoughts of their scribes, yielding up their buried secrets only after generations of devoted archæologists and philologists had earnestly labored toward their decipherment. Some of these lost languages only recently have been recovered after having remained undeciphered for countless centuries; while others, the languages of great and powerful nations of antiquity, still await the scholar who shall discover the key to unlock their hidden mysteries. Fortunately, keys lately have been tried upon those mystic writings hitherto unlocked, the Hittite and Maya; and the hieroglyphs of Hamath and Carchemish, as well as those of ancient Yucatan and Mexico, are slowly unfolding like shrouded mummies, soon, let us hope, to reveal the content of their meaning.

It is entirely inconceivable to us of the present age that knowledge of our language ever could become lost to the world, or that the language of any existing nation could utterly disappear from the face of the earth and knowledge of its very existence be forgotten. Such an event probably never again could happen under the present improved conditions of international comity. Yet in the past this fate has happened as a matter of course, and has been the Nemesis that has overtaken some of the greatest nations of antiquity. Disaster in war generally meant national annihilation. The cities of the conquered people were destroyed, their entire country was devastated, and those of the inhabitants who escaped the sword were carried away into captivity. Their language was blotted out of existence and remained dead to the world, as in the case of Babylonia and Assyria, until the genius of the last century revived its spirit and recovered its ancient message to men. Herodotus referring to the fate of Babylon says: " Darius having become master of the place destroyed the wall and tore down the gates; for Cyrus had done neither the one nor the other when he took Babylon. He then chose out near three thousand of the leading citizens and caused them to be crucified." In Joshua VI, we read concerning his capture of Jericho: " And they utterly destroyed all that was in the city, both man and woman, young and old, and ox, and sheep, and ass, with the edge of the sword "; and in Joshua XII, of the capture of Hazor: " And they smote all the souls that were therein with the edge of the sword, utterly destroying them; there was not any left to breathe; and he burnt Hazor with fire." In II Kings XXV, we read in turn of the capture of Jerusalem by Nebuchadrezzar and the captivity of the Jews: " And he carried away all Jerusalem, and all the princes, and all the mighty men of valor, even ten thousand."

So it has ever befallen the great nations of antiquity, who have developed their racial characteristics and their languages through ages of peaceful isolation, until becoming a numerous and powerful people, they have entered upon an era of conquest over their less powerful neighbors; only in turn to be ruthlessly vanquished by other nations more powerful than themselves. As annihilation was the fate that almost invariably overtook any nation that was overcome in the vicissitudes of war — and the mightier the defense and the more heroic the struggle the heavier were the vengeance and retribution visited upon the vanquished armies by the conquering nation — it is little wonder that so much in the way of record has been lost. On the contrary, it is a marvel that so much has been recovered, and that we are able almost entirely to restore the chain of the development of culture with only a few missing links here and there.

Fortunately, the Hebrew race, while suffering as much as, if not more than, any other nation through war and conquest, has by its tremendous conservatism and individuality preserved its literature through disaster, captivity and expulsion. But of their conquerors and all other nations that preceded them,— Babylonian, Ninevite, Hittite, Persian, excepting only the Egyptian, almost every vestige of the art and literature, their palaces and populous cities, became lost and forgotten for thousands of years. Xenophon only 300 years after the fall of Nineveh passed over the ruins of the city without knowing it. So soon after her glories burned out in that terrible holocaust when the victorious Medes captured and destroyed the city in 606 B. C. was the prophecy fulfilled that we read in Nahum III: "And it shall come to pass that all they that look upon thee shall flee from thee, and say: Nineveh is laid waste; who will bemoan her? Whence shall I seek comfort for thee?" So also in turn was the might and pride of Babylon humbled and her cities and palaces destroyed, until the prophecy of Isaiah was fulfilled: "And Babylon, the glory of Kingdoms, the beauty of the Chaldee's excellency, shall be as when God overthrew Sodom and Gomorrah. It shall never be inhabited,

neither shall it be dwelt in from generation to generation.
. . . But wild beasts of the desert shall lie there; and
their houses shall be full of doleful creatures."

It will be irrelevant further to remind the student of
history of any succeeding national cataclysm beyond the
destruction of the powerful Persian monarchy and the
overthrow of Cyrus and the destruction of Persepolis by
Alexander the Great in 333 B. C. In these succeeding,
annihilating waves of struggle for national supremacy
we witness, when we include the fall of Carchemish, the
Hittite capital, in 717 B. C., ending that great monarchy,
the successive blotting out of the Babylonian and Assyrian cuneiform writing, the Hittite hieroglyphic writing, and finally of the Persian cuneiform writing; all of
which as far as the intelligibility of their message to men
was concerned remained lost to the world down to the
last century.

The story of the recovery of the lost languages of
Babylon and Assyria is a profoundly fascinating tale,
one of the absorbing romances of history. It is not without its pathetic side, for it is shot through and through
with the long historic development of man as he slowly
has risen in the scale of civilization, gradually perfecting
the means whereby he has conserved the sum of knowledge acquired from his ancestors and transmitted it with
all its added human experiences to posterity. For ages
the story remained a sealed book, whose secret was long
locked up in the desert sands of Mesopotamia far beneath
the arid, wind-swept surface, whereon here and there
through the long centuries past have been picked up an
occasional tablet containing inscriptions in a script and
language unknown to men.

But these occasional *relica antiqua,* found on the un-
suspected sites of Babylonian and Assyrian cities and

distributed among the museums of the world to excite the wonder or encourage the scholarship of investigators, were not the only witnesses of the departed literature of the past. For centuries the remarkable cuneiform inscription on the great rock façade at Behistun (Fig. 67) had been the wonder and mystery of generations of men. For over two thousand years men came and went, gazed up at this mighty cliff rearing its crown over sixteen hundred feet above the plain, wondered and speculated over the unknown characters and went their way no wiser than the rest of mankind before them. So thoroughly was the thought of their author concealed in the strange and inscrutable vehicle of its expression. All sorts of wild and unreasonable conjectures were made concerning the inscription even by scholars; but no progress toward its decipherment was made until the German scholar, Dr. Georg Friedrich Grotefend, in 1821 suspected the presence of the name of Darius in the lines of the inscription. Detecting the regular recurrence of a sequence of certain characters and reasoning by analogy he assumed the correspondence between the inscription and the translations of Persian literature in the classic authors. Many of these translated phrases began with the reiterated formula: " I —— King of Kings, son of —— King of Kings," etc. He thus was able to locate the name of the king and to suspect the characters that composed the word. However, no further progress was made until Sir Henry Rawlinson in 1851, after years of persistent and scholarly investigation combired with rare erudition, discovered the key to the decipherment of the cuneiform characters, wrested from the almost inaccessible heights of the Rock its historic secret, and translated the entire inscription. This feat of scholarship was perhaps the most brilliant single effort ever accomplished in archæology, and redounds with everlasting credit to the memory of this talented English scholar.

Fig. 67. Cuneiform inscription of King Darius. Rock of Behistun.

The Behistun inscription proved to be a proclamation by no less important a personage than Darius the Great. The inscription is trilingual, being in Persian, Medic and Babylonian, as Grotefend correctly suspected. The Persian, being in the mother language of the modern Persian, having first been deciphered, it was not so difficult a task to decipher the other parallel inscriptions, the Medic and the Babylonian, and to restore the old languages. This of course was not done all at once, but the thousands of inscriptions translated since Rawlinson's day constantly have added to the known vocabulary of these ancient languages.

Before entering upon an analysis of the cuneiform

mode of writing, we will briefly recall the history of the
ancient peoples who have inhabited the valleys between
the Persian Gulf and the Caucasus Mountains, that the
reader may the better be able to attach a human interest
to these inscriptions and their archaic prototypes. In the
long, narrow valley between the Tigris and the Euphrates
rivers, known in classical times and to-day as Mesopotamia —" between the rivers "— civilization dawned at
a period far more remote than is known of any other
country, Egypt itself not excepted, though but yesterday
the latter country was believed to be the older. From the
very earliest times the valley where now are situated
Mosul and Bagdad was teeming with the activities of a
race of people who have left us much evidence of their
civilization. We have authentic documents of theirs that
carry us back to 4500 B. C., while there are noted scholars
who bespeak for them a civilization dating to the seventh
and eighth pre-Christian millenniums. At the later period,
when their historic traditions begin, we find in the valley
a Turanian people, a Mongol race, who probably came
from Media and the regions about Mt. Ararat and the
Caspian Sea. This was at a time that long antedated the
migrations of either the Semitic or Aryan races from
their Caucasan homes, if this really be the point of their
origin. From their own records, inscribed on terra cotta
tablets or engraved on stone, we learn that this Mongol
race superseded an earlier " dark-faced people " who lived
in the valley before them. Who this earlier race was history fails to inform us, as they do not seem to have left
any record of themselves. They probably were a savage
people, or at least uncivilized. We may remember in this
connection the invasion of the Peloponnesus by the Dorians, who conquered a primitive Pelasgian race, who, scholars are convinced, were of the early Turanian family.

One branch of this Mongol race in Mesopotamia inhabited the northern part of the valley, called by them Akkad, "the mountains," giving the name Akkadian to their language. Another branch inhabited the southern part of the valley, which they called Sumer (or Sumir), "the river valley," and which has given the name Sumerian to their language. The two languages are in reality only dialects of one language, decidedly Turanian in its structure. Sumer extended from the site of Babylon to Kaldu, the biblical Chaldea, in the extreme southern end of the delta of the Tigris and Euphrates. The city in Chaldea best known to us through its mention in the Bible was Ur, the southernmost city on the Euphrates, almost at its confluence with the Tigris. Far to the north of these people lived the Semites, yet to emerge from barbarism and overrun the Mesopotamian valley; under whom in the many succeeding centuries the cuneiform writing was fully to be developed. A proper conception of the early date about which we are writing may be gained by recalling that Abraham, the father of the Hebrew race, emigrated from this city of Ur — "Ur of the Chaldees" — probably in the reign of Hammurabi, *circa* 2200 B. C., to establish the Hebrew nation.

So much for the history of these early peoples. We now can understand that we are dealing with the civilization of a people, the earliest known who have left us any record of their existence in this region, which for four millenniums formed the background of the historical drama of European civilization and culture. Here if anywhere we should find the sources of writing. Nor are we entirely disappointed; for we come as near to the spring as we probably ever shall come. Nor is it any surprise, but a beautiful confirmation of the quite universal rule, to find the writing of the Sumerians and Akkadians, the so-called linear Babylonian script, almost purely pictorial; really not writing at all, but drawing. But we are getting a little ahead of our story to describe this unique text just at this moment.

Before Rawlinson had deciphered the Assyrian cuneiform writing, bricks of Nebuchadrezzar, the great Babylonian king, written in the cuneiform text, were familiar in Europe. No small part of the immense débris forming the outer conformation of the great mound of Nippur as well as that of Birs-Nimrud in Babylon was made up of these large bricks of Nebuchadrezzar's restoration of the

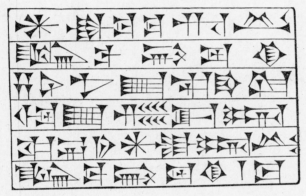

Fig. 68. Brick with cuneiform inscription of Nebuchadrezzar.

temple of Baal (Bel). Many of the bricks bear the cuneiform inscription shown in Fig. 68, which is a facsimile of one of the originals.

The inscription refers to Nebuchadrezzar's restoration of this temple, the temple of Baal, the Babel of the Bible, and is to be translated as follows: " Nebuchadrezzar, eldest son of Nabopolassar, King of Babylon, restorer of the tower and of the pyramid, I." The reading in the position of the tablet on the page is from left to right, corresponding to the European custom. Specimens of these bricks may be seen in almost any museum or collection of archæology. This is the script known as " cuneiform," and was employed by the Babylonians and Assyrians for many centuries down to about the third century before Christ. It is so called on account of the wedge-like character of the strokes of the writing. By far the greater

Fig. 69. Tablet with cuneiform inscription from Warika.

number of all inscriptions thus far found have been written — incised — on soft clay subsequently baked, with a blunt pointed instrument or stylus, probably the three-sided stem of a rush, which produced these wedge-like marks. Many inscriptions also have been found carved on slate, marble, alabaster or other stones; but the wedges which were natural and incident to inscriptions in soft clay were copied in the stone and became the standard forms in the written syllabary however and wherever used.

It perhaps will easily be noted in the inscription illustrated that the wedges are arranged in certain well-defined groupings separated from one another. These groups constitute the different syllables of the words. The script is not alphabetic but syllabic; each character being the representation, the picture we may say, of a syllable, the successive groups making up the words. The reader hardly can fail to see the general pictorial or outline character of these signs. Indeed it was early discovered that the cuneiform characters, apparently so abstract and conventional in their form, were but the survivals of an extremely archaic script, linear and pictorial in its character, of which they were the direct lineal descendants.

In excavating among the ruins of Warika, the ancient Huruk or Erech, Henry Rawlinson discovered a tablet in the common cuneiform characters (Fig. 69) which he translated as follows: " Beltis, his lady, has caused Urukh, the pious chief, King of Hur, and King of the land of the Akkad, to build a temple to her." The lines are to be read from left to right and downward in each section or column as the marginal numbers indicate. In the same locality Rawlinson subsequently found another tablet (Fig. 70) bearing what appeared most obviously to be the same inscription without a trace of cuneiform marks; but each cluster of lines, apparently so arbitrary in the cuneiform inscription, assuming a pictographic character, with geometric outlines. The assumption was made then, and every subsequent discovery amply has corroborated it, that the cuneiform characters of the Babylonians and Assyrians are the conventional rendering, after successive generations of modified usage, of the archaic, hieroglyphic characters of the system of writing employed by their immediate predecessors, the Akkadians and Sumerians. They were the last echoes of their original, pictorial prototypes, repeated through the centuries by successive generations of scribes, becoming diminishingly a more and more feeble imitation of their historic originals as time went on. In the course of time, through conventionalization and simplification, the characters became so modified

Fig. 70. Tablet from Warika in early linear Babylonian characters.

that they bore little resemblance to their originals; so much so that it is probable that the origin of their written language became completely lost to the later Assyrians and Persians.

The full story of the origin of the cuneiform writing only lately has been fully demonstrated through the excavations conducted by the University of Pennsylvania at Nippur, by De Sarzec at Telloh, and other excavations in ancient Mesopotamia. In the higher strata of the débris

of the ruined cities of Mesopotamia, containing the remains of the civilization of the middle and later kingdoms
of Babylonia and Assyria, are found tablets containing
inscriptions in the later cuneiform already referred to;
but as lower and lower strata are reached, carrying us
down to the remains of earlier cities, we find the characters gradually changing their forms from age to age,
looking more like representations of actual things; until
finally we come upon inscriptions in which the wedges
have altogether disappeared, and each sign is drawn in
lines,— no longer writing as we know it, but veritable
outline drawing. Thus may each puzzling cluster of
wedges, which for a score of centuries served a great nation for the characters of its written language, a language
exceptionally expressive and complete in its inflections, be
traced back to its pictorial prototype. This early pictorial
script, now known as the linear Babylonian, is distinctly
representative, as we would naturally expect the archaic
writing of a primitive people to be. In this respect it affords a confirmation of the theory of the almost universal
pictorial origin of written speech. When all the missing
links in the chain of development are supplied, it probably
may appear that this early pictorial script was the parent
from which have descended through the Hittite and Phœnician some of the letters of the Greco-Latin alphabet. It
is yet too early to speak dogmatically in the matter, as so
many transitional factors in the development are missing;
but the weight of evidence seems to favor the far East as
the source of some of our alphabetic characters. But we
are anticipating our story.

The linear Babylonian script in its very earliest discovered form already had progressed as far as the third
stage of writing: that of phonetic, syllabic writing. It had
passed the pictographic and ideographic stage, leaving no

record of its use. Being prior to the civilization that demanded monumental and civil records in permanent material, the earliest pictographic records on bark, skin or whatever material may have been used in the primitive stage of civilization, altogether have perished. But many original ideograms having no syllabic values were carried over from the earlier pictography and employed in the tablet inscriptions, as well as many characters which were used both as ideograms and as phonograms. Many, perhaps most, of the characters were well advanced toward simplification, being conventionalized and highly geometric. Nevertheless, there are enough of the pictographic characters reminiscent in the early syllabary, significant in pictorial form of the ideas conveyed in their meaning, to point indubitably to a much earlier period, more remote than we dare predicate, before syllabic signs were employed in writing, when pictures of the things intended were drawn and which stood for the objects themselves in the record.

That this is the case is amply attested by even a casual comparison of the characters in tablet inscriptions of the linear Babylonian style of different epochs. It is possible to trace the same character back through earlier and earlier stages, noting its increasingly pictorial aspect with its age; or, per contra, its marked simplification and abstract quality as later inscriptions are examined. The earliest known inscriptions are largely ideographic, almost pictographic in many characters; the later inscriptions containing fewer ideograms and more phonetic characters. Nevertheless, we must admit, that even in the earliest and most archaic inscriptions discovered, it is not always easy to recognize the original objects. Owing to the limitations of primitive culture, the inexperience of the scribes, and the lack of artistic ability, each scribe drew the characters in his own crude, faulty way, often incorrectly; so that it is quite impossible always definitely to distinguish the character and identify it with the object intended. But with each succeeding age the characters become more conventionalized, standardized and simplified; losing in the process their pictorial character until in the later cuneiform it is almost totally obscured.

There have been discovered four remarkable preBabylonian inscriptions belonging to the very earliest archaic period of this system of writing that we are now describing. They are among the very oldest inscriptions in the world. It is difficult to classify them as to priority of age, they all are of such extreme archaism. This is attested by the crudeness of the art, the variability of given characters even in the same tablet, but particularly by the evident experimentation in the manner in which the characters succeed each other in the line or column of reading. In the earliest stages of primitive writing — pictographic writing— the pictures or hieroglyphs, whether read from right to left, left to right, or downward in the column, must certainly have been drawn upright. The tablet already shown (Fig. 70) indicates that even at an early date in this pre-Babylonian script a radical change was made in the position of the signs, whereby they appear upright only when viewed from the right hand side of the tablet. It is reasonable to assume that those inscriptions are the oldest in which the characters are drawn upright as they are read, and which most nearly approach our idea of primitive pictography. On this assumption we refer the reader to Fig. 71, possibly the earliest of these pre-Babylonian inscriptions, if not the very oldest inscription at present in existence; one that in the present stage of archæological discovery carries us further back toward the beginnings of human writing than anything yet re-

vealed to us. It is known as the Father Schiel tablet from
its discoverer. The characters are highly archaic, carrying us back almost to the primitive pictures before conventionalization had at all seriously set in to modify their
outlines. They are drawn upright in vertical columns —
technically called " registers " when separated by incised
lines as later was the custom — and are to be read downward and from right to left according to Oriental usage,
as indicated by the marginal numbers at the top of the
tablet. One can be quite sure of the identity of a number
of these signs; that is of their former ideographic significance, whatever their syllabic meaning may be in the text.
We can distinguish a star, a jar, a foot, trees, a chair or
throne, and possibly a gate. But as Dr. George A. Barton
says: " Of such a brief inscription in characters so archaic, any translation in the present state of our knowledge is most uncertain." A more or less satisfactory
translation, mainly Dr. Barton's, is the following:

1. Gar-du-en-gub
2. 600 bur of a field in the land of ——?
3. a libation he pours out. May the God, lord
   of Eridu bless.

Fig. 71. Tablet with archaic hieroglyphs, discovered by Father Schiel.

The proper name Garduengub, occupying the first column on the right, is apparently spelled out with phonetic, syllabic characters. There could be no other way of accomplishing it. Proper names are for the most part arbitrary and cannot be pictured. To be sure we already have seen how primitive people, ignorant of the art of writing with signs or symbols, drew their totems to indicate personal possessions. We have referred to the private marks in sections of the pipe-stone quarries of the American Indians, property marks on weapons, utensils and implements, and more particularly to the totemic signatures of proper names drawn on treaties and deeds. It is significant of the advanced stage of civilization of these old Sumerians of six millenniums ago that they had passed the pictographic, the ideographic, and had reached the syllabic stage of writing, and were able to spell out a name like Garduengub, if this is the proper transliteration, with phonetic characters. Nevertheless, we shall see further on that while Enshagkushana, a known king and the first known king, wrote his name in the conventional characters of the written language, he used the pictures that described his kingly qualities as set forth in his name, quite the same as Standing Bear drew his totem on Red Cloud's census (Fig. 22). The characters in Garduengub's name really are pictures, or at least ideographs. The first one appears to be an early form of the symbol for " night," and closely resembles the Chinese, Egyptian and Ojibwa symbols for night: The second character probably represents a covered pot; the third a throne; and the fourth obviously a human foot. The remainder of the inscription is written in characters probably largely ideographic.

Fig. 72 and Fig. 73 are respectively the obverse and reverse of two of the most interesting of all Babylonian tablets. They are known by their French name, the " Monuments Blau," from their discoverer, Dr. A. Blau. They belong like the preceding to the most archaic class of hieroglyphic inscriptions. The writing, which is engraved on stone, is in characters just emerging from the ideographic stage, and the inscription quaintly combines written characters and pictorial drawings. In Fig. 72 the characters are engraved in six vertical registers in two horizontal rows or lines, technically called " columns," arranged on either side of the figure drawings.[1] Between the figures the inscription is carried in three rows or lines of one register each. Fortunately, the upright position of the two figures indicates the reading position of the tablet. The characters are drawn upright in the vertical registers, and are to be read downward and from right to left across the tablet, as indicated by the marginal numbers. The direction of the writing exactly corresponds to the Chinese writing. The second tablet is to be re..d in the same direction and manner. Among the hieroglyphic characters in these two unique inscriptions — and there is hardly one that does not seem to be the picture of some object — may be recognized the human head and hand, a bird, a fish, a reed, jars, vases and other forms.

A translation of these extremely archaic inscriptions is most difficult on account of the fact that the age is so remote that the hieroglyphs have not become standardized, and it is a matter of great difficulty to identify them with the more constant and highly conventionalized characters of the later syllabary. Attempts have been made by scholars to translate them, but the results have been so experimental and divergent, that we will not consider

[1] The application of these two terms, registers and columns, more properly applied to monumental inscriptions, is uncertain in these early experiments in writing. The terms are more or less interchangeable until we reach the fully developed linear-Babylonian writing.

Fig. 72 and Fig. 73. The Monuments Blau. Early Babylonian (Sumerian) hieroglyphic writing. Showing obverse and reverse of each tablet.

them here.[1] The inscriptions, doubtless like the previous example, are votive tablets, inventories of gifts to a temple, as the amounts indicated by the circles at the top of the several columns would seem to indicate.

Another extremely archaic tablet, quite as unique as the foregoing ones and probably belonging to the same early age, is that known as the Hoffman tablet, in the collection of the late E. A. Hoffman in the General Theological Seminary in New York City (Fig. 74). It is engraved on a beautifully prepared piece of black stone, about four inches square. The characters appear ideographic — almost pictographic — like the preceding inscriptions. One can make out utensils, vases, jars, a deer's or ass's head, trees, a star and other objects. While some signs evidently are ideographic, others are syllabic signs based on ideographic prototypes. There also are quite a number of purely geometric or abstract, syllabic signs. Oriental scholars have essayed to translate this inscription, but again it must be admitted that on account of the uncertainty of the symbols the translations leave very much to be desired.[2] The reading as in the three archaic inscriptions just examined is from right to left in the three horizontal lines or columns; the words or sentences, which are read downward, being separated by vertical lines and grouped into registers, three in the first line, two in the second, and four in the third. The tablet, probably like the foregoing, is a votive tablet or inventory accompanying and recording gifts to a temple of Shamash. But the reader must not imagine that the characters are pictures

[1] The reader is referred to the translation of Thureau-Dangin in "Revue Semétique," 1896; also to that of George A. Barton in the *Journal of the American Oriental Society,* Vol. XXII, 1901.

[2] The reader will find an elaborate translation of this remarkable tablet by Dr. Barton in the *Journal of the American Oriental Society,* Vol. XIII, 1902.

of the gifts. Possibly none of them is. They probably are largely syllabic. The amounts given in this inventory, probably in this case certain measures of land, are indicated by circles which have been neatly and accurately drilled into the stone at the right of or the beginning of the registers, as in the preceding inscription. A tablet of

Fig. 74. Tablet with early Babylonian hieroglyphic writing. From the Hoffman collection, General Theological Seminary, New York City.

almost identical workmanship with the Hoffman tablet is in the collection of Babylonian tablets in the Museum of the University of Pennsylvania, Philadelphia (Fig. 75). The size, shape and finish of the two stones are practically the same, to the slightly convex curving edge lines, and the drill holes used for numerical purposes. The characters are somewhat more carefully drawn in the second tablet; but the reading arrangement is the same in both, and the drawing of the symbols indicates the same early age of pictorial writing.

The writing in these two archaic Babylonian tablets plainly shows it to belong to the early experimental stage, when the scribes had not yet found themselves. This is evidenced by one character which occurs three times in the two tablets, each time being drawn somewhat differently.

Fig. 75. Early Babylonian tablet in the museum of the University of
Pennsylvania, Philadelphia, Pa.

It is the character next to the last on the right in the top
and bottom horizontal lines in the University of Pennsylvania tablet, and the last character on the right in the
middle section of the top line in the Hoffman tablet. The
same character also occurs in the Schiel tablet (Fig. 71)
in the left upper corner. The characters in these tablets
seem to be somewhat differently arranged than those in
the preceding tablets. It may be an earlier experiment
or it may be a later transitional style. It is difficult to
judge. If the tablets are correctly placed as shown in the
cuts, then we have a document corresponding in general
arrangement with the Monuments Blau, except that the
characters are not placed above each other nor in vertical
registers, but are disposed for the most part horizontally,
reading from right to left along the horizontal lines
rather than downward; thus requiring three horizontal
rows of signs instead of two.

The striving for a fixed, constant method in the arrangement of the signs in these early tablet inscriptions is
illustrated in the very archaic inscription on a brick from
a temple built by Our-Nina, who is known to have ruled

in Shirpoula some time between 4500 and 4000 B. C.
The characters in this inscription (Fig. 76) have so far
advanced toward the conventional standard of the final
syllabary that there is no difficulty in identifying them.
The inscription reads downward in the three vertical
rows, strictly speaking registers, beginning at the right
and running according to the marginal figures as follows:

1. Our-Nina
2. King of Shirpoula
3. Son of Nini-hal-shin
4. The abode of Ghirson
5. He has constructed.

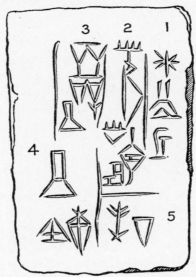

Fig. 76. Babylonian brick of Our-Nina. About 4000 B. C.

After the experimental stage of this earliest form of
the linear Babylonian writing, as practiced by the Akkadians and Sumerians, a permanent change already referred
to was effected in the position of the hieroglyphic signs.

For some reason or other, possibly on account of ease in handling and inscribing the tablet while held in the hand, the characters subsequently were drawn on their sides in horizontal rows, or registers; being upright in these registers, as they always were in the more archaic inscriptions, only when viewed from the right. This change resulted in the reading being from left to right in horizontal lines according to the method of the Occident. In monumental inscriptions the older method obtained through many centuries, even after the cuneiform had displaced the linear method. One of the finest illustrations of the monumental style of writing is the superb statue of Gudea, Priest-King (Patesi), who ruled in Lagash (Shirpoula) in southern Babylonia, about 2700 B. C. The statue illustrated in Fig. 77, which represents Gudea as Architect of the Temple, is one of three very similar statues now in the Louvre, each having elaborate inscriptions carried across the dress or over the backs of the figures. The characters are in the transitional stage, being mainly linear, and retain the old hieroglyphic shapes in a highly conventionalized and geometric form with only a slight trace of the already adopted cuneiform. The inscriptions are read from right to left along the horizontal rows and downward in each vertical register.

Illustrations of the later phase of the early pre-Babylonian inscriptions, referred to above, in which the characters are drawn " on their sides " are given in Fig. 78 and Fig. 79. They show the final conventionalized hieroglyphic characters known as the linear Babylonian signary, out of which the cuneiform of the Sargonic period (about 3800 B. C.), the first Semitic period, was developed. Fig. 78 is a fragment of baked clay made in the reign of King Enshagkushanna, who reigned in Nippur prior to 4500 B. C. The characters are quite regular and

Fig. 77. Gudea, Priest-King of Lagash, as Architect. About 2700 B. C.

follow the typical, conventional standard of the developed syllabary. The lines of writing are horizontal, but the characters are on their sides, as already stated, showing it to be a comparatively late inscription. Yet there is no trace of the cuneiform. The characters are purely linear, but so far developed that the translation is certain. Listen now to the message of this ancient of kings, the earliest known king in the world, in the language which he spoke:

1. En-lil
2. Lugal kur kur ra
3. En-sag-kush-an-na
4. En ki-en-gi
5. Lugal . . .

Translated this reads:

1. To Enlil
2. King of the lands . . .
3. Enshagkushanna
4. Lord of Kengi
5. King of . . .

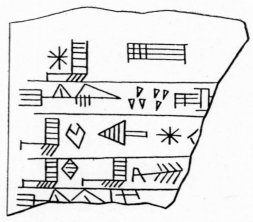

Fig. 78. Linear Babylonian inscription of Enshagkushanna. 4500 B. C.

We will now enter upon a brief analysis of the graphic characters in this inscription, for it will throw much light upon the stages by which a written language has sprung from and developed out of primitive picture-writing. To the most casual observer the individual signs must appear to be, what they really are, drawings. Probably with but few exceptions they are but slightly modified pictures of the things defined in the words or syllables for which they stand. They are the conventionalized descendants of pictographic or ideographic drawings of things intended, in records made by the illiterate precursors of the Sumerian inhabitants before syllabic writing was invented. Let us see how they came into use as written characters. The first character, a " star," in common with many of the archaic Babylonian signs, is variously used either as an ideogram or the sign for a syllable. This is the common progressive development. As an ideogram, the sense in which it is used in the first line of this text, as well as in the first line in the inscription of Our-Nina, it symbolizes deity; in which context it is not pronounced, being merely a determinative sign denoting deity or kingship. It is used precisely in the same way as the determinative signs that we already are familiar with in the Chinese and Egyptian hieroglyphics. As a syllabic sign it loses all of its ideographic value and has no other significance than the representation of the syllable *an*. It has this syllabic value and no other when it occurs in the third line. This sign illustrates the metaphorical development of many of these archaic characters. Primarily it was the picture of a "star," *ana,* in the Sumerian language, and had this single significance; but as gods and kings, equally in the heroic ages, were endowed with superhuman attributes, the celestial bodies were used to typify or represent them also. Consequently in time this character became employed to represent variously a star, a god or a king. Finally when civilization advanced to the stage of syllabic writing, the sign was arbitrarily chosen to stand for the sound *an,* the initial sound in the word *ana,* as well as to represent ideo-

graphically a " star," a " god " or a " king." This is the
history of many of these primitive characters; and it has
its parallel probably in the historic development of most
of the world's great languages. The second character in
the inscription is an ideogram like the first, and is the representation of a " throne." As an ideogram, probably the
sense in which it is used in the first line, it is *Belu, Bel;*
and stands for lord. As a syllable, in which sense it occurs
in the third line, it has the value *en.* It is probable that
this syllabic value became attached to it when phonetic
writing was employed by reason of its being the first syllable of Enlil, the chief god of the Sumerians. In an entirely similar way, doubtless in most languages, the primitive picture of some important word was chosen as the
character to represent the phonetic value of the initial
syllable of this word. The reader already is familiar with
this process of acrophony in the Egyptian hieroglyphics.
The Babylonian syllabary abounds in it. In the fourth
line where the " throne " sign occurs twice its two meanings are well differentiated; the first one having the ideographic meaning " lord " while the second has no ideographic significance whatever, but is simply the symbol for
the syllable *en* in Ki-en-gi, the ancient name of Babylon.
The third sign in the first line also is probably an ideogram and represents a country intersected by canals.
Babylon — Kengi — was sometimes represented thus in

the archaic inscriptions: ⊞⊟⇒⫤⟩. This is a conven-

tional picture of a flat country of canals and reeds, characteristic of all Mesopotamia. The right hand character in
this compound is the same as the last sign in the fourth
line,— *gi;* originally meaning a " reed," of which it is the
picture, but subsequently used only for the phonetic value

gi wherever occurring. It does not need any stretch of
the imagination in viewing this character from the right
of the page, the viewpoint of all the symbols in inscriptions of this order, to discern its resemblance to the reed.
In other inscriptions of about this same age the likeness is
yet more marked; as in the drawing of the reed in the
second register of the second Monument Blau, which will
be recognized as a purely naturalistic picture of the reed.

Continuing our analysis, we may take up the strange
character *lugal* at the beginning of the second line. This
is a compound of *lu,* the lower, or right hand part, and
gal, the upper, or left hand part, and means " king." The
character *lu* is a crude representation of a man with angular head and body. In earlier inscriptions the drawing is
cruder but much more realistic. The *gal* sign signifies
" great," and is the picture of a raised hand, often represented with four fingers and a thumb, as shown in Fig. 80,
and as such symbolizes power and authority. The reader
will find the character *lugal* at the top of the second column of Our-Nina's inscription and at the beginning, the
left, of the second and of the last line in the brick of Nebuchadrezzar. The name in the meantime had changed
from the Sumerian *lugal* to the Semitic *sar* (shar). It is,
however, still to be translated as " king." The next character, the group of three small signs repeated, symbolizes
the idea of land. In other inscriptions it is drawn much
more naturally, as illustrated in Fig. 80, appearing decidedly like mountains, and often to be so translated. The
second and third characters in the name Enshagkushanna,
although here used phonetically, were originally the ideograms respectively for " heart " and " protector," or
" guardian." How suggestive of the qualities of a king!
The heart, except for the accidental prolongation of the

lines at the top, really is a very good drawing of the object. As in all later Sumerian and Babylonian characters there are no curved lines.

We will give the translation of the seven lines in the left hand column in Fig. 79, from a clay tablet of Entemena, governor of Shirpoula (Lagash), about 4500 B. C.:

1. (En) te-me-na,
2. (Pa) te-si
3. of Shirpoula;
4. to whom power was given
5. by En-lil,
6. who was nourished by the milk of life
7. by Nin-ha-sag.

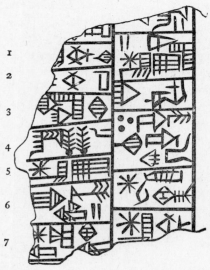

Fig. 79. Fragment of a tablet of Entemena, about 4500 B. C.

The inscription is a mixture of ideographic and syllabic writing. The fourth line is wholly ideographic, as is also the sixth. In the fourth line "power" is represented by

an arm and the five fingers of the hand. It is believed that
the parallel angular lines represent tattooing. The two
onions are the characters commonly used for " giving."
In the sixth line the idea of " nourishing by the milk of
life " is expressed by the ideograph for " mouth " with
the cup of milk beside it, which is the ideogram for
" nourish "; also by the other vase-like character which is
the ideogram for " milk " and the reed-like sign which is
the ideogram for " life." Again we will remind the
reader that all characters should be viewed from the right
of the inscription to see them in their objective aspect. It
is customary to place the inscriptions in the position
shown, as the reading then proceeds like our English and
European reading from left to right.

In the four columns of graphic characters in Fig. 80
we give over seventy symbols selected from the very extensive syllabary of the ancient linear Babylonian system
of writing, which was the progenitor of the cuneiform
system and which formed its basis. They have been taken
from early tablet inscriptions found chiefly at Telloh,
Lagash, Nippur and other places in ancient Babylonia.
The characters are in the reading position, and should be
viewed from the right of the page to observe their pictorial significance. In every case the ideograph, which the
reader will note is a picture represented as an outline
drawing, illustrates or interprets the meaning of the word
in the syllabary. Most of the symbols are recognizable,
though all are more or less conventionalized. The symbol
for " constellation " is so remarkably like the Chinese as
almost to suggest an historic association between the two
nations at some remote epoch. It is not by any means the
only instance of similarity in the written characters of
these two nations. The character for " night " is very
similar to the symbols employed by the North American

Indians and the Egyptians. It is almost identical with the Chinese character for rain, which pictures the rain falling from the sky, as the Babylonian symbol seems to represent the night as descending from the sky. The character for " month " is an example of metaphor. The sun, drawn square instead of round, is used to represent a day, and the three angular lines within the character indicate thirty. As a whole the symbol means thirty days. This is precisely the way but not exactly the form in which the American Indians represented days. The character for " ox " represents the face and horns of an ox, *alpu* in Babylonian. It is believed, but with no certain substantiation, that this symbol has been perpetuated as a written character in name and form through all the ages down to the present day in the shape of the initial letter of our alphabet. In Phœnician it was *aleph* (Fig. 101), and in early Greek *alpha* (Fig. 131). The character for " fish " never became much conventionalized. We find it in the second example of the Monuments Blau represented very naturally. The character for " destiny " obviously is a variant of the symbol for " birds." Until the characters began to assume a fixed form in this early stage of Babylonian writing we find many variations of bird forms. One will be found in the second register of the upper line in the obverse of the first Monument Blau. This character, however, with the several double angular lines, was particularly used to indicate the meaning " destiny." At first this seems anomalous until we remember the custom in primitive days of divination by the flight of birds. We already have explained the symbols for " man " and " king." The character for " child " or " son," also shown at the top of line 3 in the brick of Our-Nina, is an instance of the selection of a sign by metaphorical suggestion. The characters by which " seeing " and " hearing " are portrayed are almost as direct as the pictography of the Dakota Indians; the sensations being objectified by the out-going lines. " To take oath " is to swear by the stars in heaven. The character " to throw " undoubtedly portrays the boomerang or throwing stick. The authenticity of the sign for " door " with its pivoted post is amply confirmed by the many stone door sockets that have been recovered from Babylonia and Assyria. It was cus-

Fig. 80. Babylonian ideographic symbols.

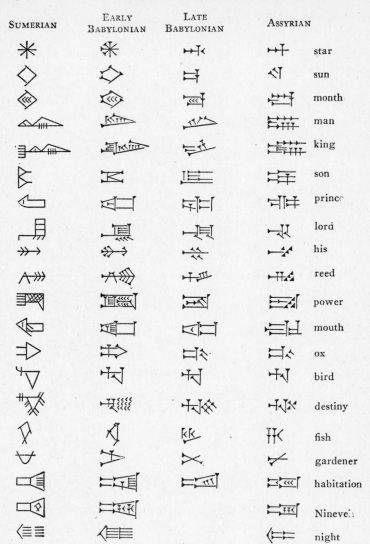

Fig. 81. Successive stages of development of the cuneiform characters from the early Sumerian form of the linear Babylonian to the Assyrian.

tomary to engrave these door sockets with inscriptions, and some of the finest specimens of Babylonian inscriptions have come from this source. The beautiful inscription of Sargon I, to be described later on, is from a door socket of one of the temples of this king in Nippur. In an earlier chapter we explained the evolution of the cross-barred arrow from a proprietary sign to the general character indicating the personal pronoun " his." The harp, though fragmentary, suggests this instrument in a most graphic manner.

We shall have to admit that there are not a very large number of these linear Babylonian symbols that seem to picture the meaning of the signs. As we have said, our first acquaintance with the script reveals it well advanced in conventionalization toward the purely geometric or abstract stage. Under Babylonian influence the evolution was carried a stage further. The characters became more simplified, many lines were eliminated, and the cuneiform line was substituted for the simple line. In Fig. 81 we have selected twenty characters of the early linear Babylonian syllabary and have traced them through three successive stages of historical development, extending over two or three millenniums to the perfected Assyrian just prior to the classic period. One can trace the progressive elimination of superfluous lines and note the ultimate tendency toward horizontal and vertical lines. The primitive sign for " gardener " appears to have been a plow or hoe. Nineveh was a fishermen's town on the Euphrates, and was represented by a fish drawn within a house.

We will now give two examples of Babylonian writing, both in the transitional stage, between the early linear and the late cuneiform style. Fig. 82 is an inscription on a door socket of Sargon I, who reigned in Nippur, Babylon, about 3800 B. C. The primitive characters are not in the least disguised, but still show the original pictures, though highly conventionalized. The inscription begins at the first line in the left-hand vertical column and reads from left to right and downward in the column to the bottom, then proceeding similarly down the right-hand column. The characters are largely ideographic. The inscription translated reads as follows:

" Shargani-shar-ali (Sargon), son of Itti-Bel, the mighty King of Accad and the dominion of Bel, the builder of Ekur, the Temple of Bel in Nippur. Who-

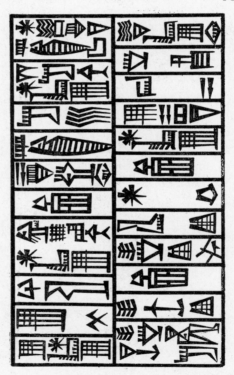

Fig. 82. Inscription of Sargon I, on a door socket from Nippur. Museum of the University of Pennsylvania.

ever removes this inscribed stone, may Bel and Shamash tear out his foundation and exterminate his posterity." [1]

The date of Sargon's reign is established by Nabu-naid (Nabonidas), the last king of Babylon who reigned 555–539 B. C. He undertook the restoration of the temple of Ebarra in Sippar, rebuilt by Nebuchadrezzar. One of Nabu-naid's tablets describing the temple and how Nebuchadrezzar had hunted for the foundation stone relates: ". . . 18 cubits of ground I removed and the foundation stone of Na-rim-Sin, son of Sargena, which during 3,200 years no king that went before me had found, Shamash showed me."

One of the most notable of the early Babylonian inscriptions of the period following the linear Babylonian and Sargonic types is the famous Code of Hammurabi, King of Babylon about 2250 B. C. It was found in 1901, not in Babylon, but in the acropolis of Susa, whither it had been carried as a trophy of war some time around 1100 B. C. by one Sutruk Nahunte, the Elamite king. It is a tall cylindrical block of diorite eight feet high, almost completely covered with the very finest inscriptions. Five columns have been chiseled off probably by the Elamites on account of their offensive character. Hammurabi doubtless was the Amraphel of Genesis xiv, 1. " He codified the existing laws that the strong might not oppress the weak, that they should give justice to the orphans and widows, and for the righting of wrong." The laws of Hammurabi are in many cases almost identical with those of the Old Testament, and their pervading spirit is Jewish throughout. This is not surprising when we know that Abraham is supposed to have gone out of Ur in Chaldea

[1] " Light on the Old Testament." Albert T. Clay.

during the reign of Hammurabi. He doubtless took with him the genius of the prevailing Babylonian common law.

It is not our intention to give here more than the most cursory glance at this remarkable monument, to quote a line or two from its forty columns of fine writing, to attest to its quaint barbaric justice, and to give in parallel one of the laws. After a grandiloquent prologue in which the king is praised to the skies, as only these Orientals know how to do, Hammurabi's laws begin: " If a man bring an accusation against a man and charge him with a (capital) crime, but cannot prove it, he, the accuser, shall be put to death." This is quite in line with some of the passages in the harsh Mosaic code. Another capital offense, which if followed by our modern city rulers might lead to more honesty and less danger in building construction, was punished under the terms of the following law: " If a builder build a house for a man and do not make its construction firm, that builder shall be put to death." But the following law is an evidence that the modern single-tax propaganda is just about four thousand years old: " If a man rent a field for cultivation and do not produce any grain in the field, they shall call him to account, because he has not performed the work required on the field; and he shall give to the owner of the field grain on the basis of the adjacent fields."

The laws of Hammurabi made a very fine and proper distinction between voluntary and involuntary injury. One of the laws reads: " If a physician open an abscess (in another's eye) with a bronze lancet and destroy his eye, he shall pay silver to the extent of one-half of his price." In the case of voluntary injury, we find among these laws the prototype of the Mosaic " eye-for-an-eye " edict. We give in Fig. 83 a reproduction of this law in the beautiful cuneiform characters of the original. In Baby-

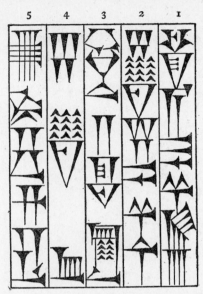

Fig. 83. Part of the extensive inscription of the Laws of Hammurabi. About
    2250 B. C. " If a man destroy the eye of another man, they shall destroy
    his eye."

lonian it reads: (1) *Sum-ma a-wi-lum* (2) *i-in-mâr a-wi-
lim* (3) *uh-tab-bi-it* (4) *i-in-sŭ* (5) *u-ha-ap-po-du*.
Translated into English it reads: " If a man destroy the
eye of another man, they shall destroy his eye." Being a
monumental inscription, the signs are drawn upright in
vertical registers, the reading being downward and from
right to left, as indicated by the marginal numbers.

It may be said in passing that not only many of these
laws of Hammurabi but many of the epic traditions recorded in the early tablet inscriptions are signally like the
Hebrew traditions. We find among them the story of the
creation, of the flood,— the latter almost identical with
the Hebrew version — and other traditions so startlingly
like those that we read in the Old Testament as to compel

us to seek a common source for them. As regards the tradition of the flood, the reader is reminded that almost all nations in their annals record a universal flood. Sargon, whose door socket inscription we have just read, was the Moses of his day; having been abandoned in an ark of bulrushes smeared over with pitch, and thrown into the Euphrates, to be found and subsequently to become the ruler of the people.

Finally let us return after our wide wanderings in the historic valley of Mesopotamia to the great rock of Behistun in Persia. We have since our first view of the inscription on this remarkable rock traced the development of the cuneiform system of writing to its primitive sources in ancient Akkad and Sumer, the higher and lower plains of this extensive valley which has nourished for so many centuries the childhood civilization of the races of Western Asia. We have studied the pictorial script of these pre-Semitic races who inhabited the valley so many millenniums ago, taking us back so far toward the beginnings of writing that we were only one remove from the primitive pictographic stage of their uncivilized forebears, from whom they took their ideographic pictures and incorporated them into their later syllabary. Their earliest attempts, as we have seen, were pictorial in appearance, partly ideographic and partly syllabic in significance. We also have studied the later linear script, the pre-Sargonic syllabary in vogue during the fifth millennium before Christ, when the ideographs were developing into settled, conventional syllabic signs. In many instances the pictorial prototypes of the later written characters easily were recognizable in these archaic signs, every one of which, with hardly an exception, was an outline drawing. There was no trace yet of the cuneiform. This was first encountered in the reign of the first great Semitic king, Sargon I, about the end of the fourth millennium. His inscriptions, by the way, were in the Semitic language, but with characters chiefly Sumerian. Before his time, the prevailing language was Turanian. In Sargon's time the transformation from the linear to the cuneiform system of writing was only half effected. The pictures were still plainly recognizable and remained so for many hundreds of years to come. But gradually the lines began to show the cuneiform mark, sometimes on one stroke, again on another, like the serifs on the Roman letters.

By the time of Hammurabi, at about the third pre-Christian millennium, conventionalization had so far advanced that the resemblance of the cuneiform characters, then fully established, to their linear prototypes was apparent only to the practiced eye. But the grouping of the cuneiform characters into forms reminiscent of the original ideographs was still apparent. These groupings of cuneiform marks which remained as the successors of the original ideographs had lost in the intervening centuries many of the lines of the old pictures; but the process of simplification had been progressive, if slow, and it was possible to trace any particular cuneiform sign of the latest period, however conventionalized, through its successive stages of simplification back to its primitive prototype of four millenniums of antiquity.

We have now traced the development of the cuneiform characters down to the end of the Babylonian dynasty in the 7th century B. C. There probably was no further change in the system in Babylonia. For Darius the Persian destroyed Babylon in 666 B. C. This practically terminated the use of the cuneiform in Babylon after being in vogue over three thousand years. Persia now took up the torch of learning and kept it burning. The Medic tribes who borrowed the Assyro-Babylonian system of cuneiform writing with its "cumbersome homophones, polyphones, ideographs and determinatives," greatly simplified it. They discarded the idea of a syllabary, which with the Assyrians amounted to almost 300 characters, and very largely assigned elemental phonetic values to the few characters that they adopted. With the twenty consonants, which they recognized, they added four vowel sounds and certain modifications of them, making in all some thirty-six or thirty-seven alphabetic and syllabic signs. This near-alphabet is the distinct contribution of the Aryans to the progress of the art of writing. " The ordinary Persian writing was identical with that of the Medic. A cuneiform alphabet, consisting of some thirty-six or thirty-seven forms, expressive of twenty-three distinct sounds, sufficed for the wants of the people, whose language was simple and devoid of phonetic luxuriance. Writing was from left to right, as with the Aryan nations generally. Words were separated from one another by an oblique wedge; and were divided at any point at which the writer happened to reach the end of the line." (" The Seven Great Monarchies of the Ancient Eastern World," George Rawlinson, M. A.)

On the great rock of Behistun Darius has written his history in the Persian cuneiform of his day. He begins: " I am Darius the great king, the king of kings; the king of Persia, the king of the provinces, the son of Hystaspes. . . . From antiquity we are descended; from antiquity hath our race been kings. Thus saith Darius the king: Eight of my race were kings before me. I am the ninth." He then enumerates the twenty-three provinces over which he rules and goes on to relate how he overthrew the revolting kings of Babylon, Media and other rebellious countries.

Fig. 84 is a reproduction of Column II of the Behistun

inscription, showing the highly conventionalized cuneiform character in use in Persia at that time. Translated it reads: "Thus saith Darius the king: Then did Nidintu-Bel flee with a few horsemen into Babylon. Thereupon I marched to Babylon. By the grace of Aurmazda I took Babylon, and I captured that Nidintu-Bel. Then I slew that Nidintu-Bel in Babylon." The unfortunate general is the third one from the left in the group of bas reliefs from the rock, shown in Fig. 67. There are nine rebel princes in all standing before the "King of Kings," chained together, neck to neck, with their names inscribed overhead. Above Gaumates one reads: "This is Gaumates, the Magian; he lied; he said, I am Smerdis, son of Cyrus." And so over each captive in turn occurs the reiterated statement: "This is . . . ; he lied; he said he was king of . . ." Farther along in the inscription, in defending his own integrity with inimitable naïveté, Darius says: "Oh, thou that shalt be king hereafter, see that thou art not guilty of deceit. . . . Thou that readest upon this stone my deeds, think not that thou hast been deceived, neither be thou slow to believe them. . . . Aurmazda be my witness that I have not spoken these things with lying lips." The great inscription concludes as follows: "Says Darius the King: By the grace of Aurmazda that which has besides been done by me, which is much, I have not inscribed on this tablet. On that account I have not inscribed it, lest he who hereafter might peruse this tablet, to him the many deeds that have been done by me elswhere might seem to be falsely recorded." Finally the inscription ends, somewhat like Shakespeare's curse: "Says Darius the King: Thou who mayest hereafter behold this Tablet which I have engraved, and these figures, beware lest thou injure them. As long as thou livest, as long preserve them."

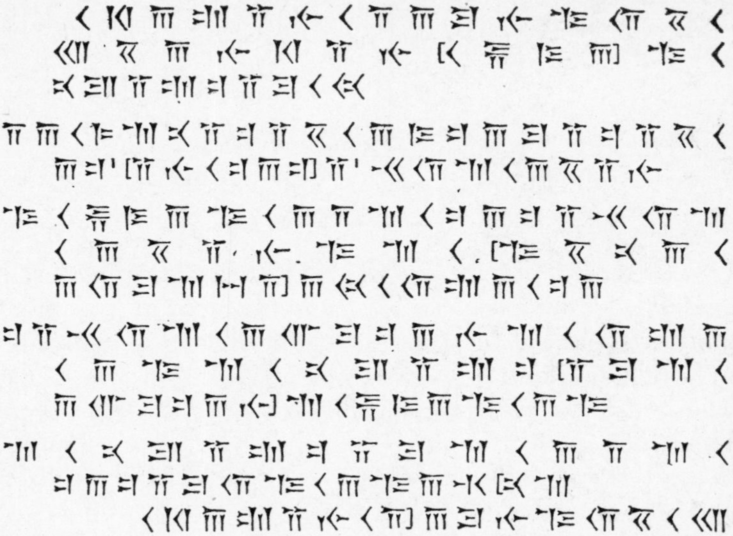

Fig. 84. Part of the cuneiform inscription of King Darius on the Rock of Behistun.

Sir Henry Rawlinson's extraordinary decipherment of the inscription on the Rock of Behistun, besides being a milestone in the history of archæology and the open gate to Babylonian and Assyrian literature, has proved by the many correspondences of names and events the historical accuracy of many passages in Herodotus and Xenophon, as well as the accuracy of Darius' extensive chronicle of events with its profuse asseverations of personal honesty. The entire inscription may be found in " The History of Herodotus," by George Rawlinson and Sir Henry Rawlinson, a work of surpassing scholarship, abounding in critical notes and essays on the historical writings of Herodotus.

CHAPTER IX

THE HIEROGLYPHIC SYSTEM OF WRITING OF THE ANCIENT HITTITES

UNTIL the early part of the 19th century Europe was unaware of the existence of another system of hieroglyphic writing, one of great antiquity and geographically of wider distribution in the cities where it was used and where inscriptions in this paleographic system have been found than almost any of the ancient systems of writing that preceded or followed it. In the year 1812, probably thirty centuries after the clever sculptor had cut the mystic characters upon its face, the traveler-scientist Burkhardt discovered at Hamah, a small town in Syria about twenty miles down the river Orontes from the site of Kadesh, the ancient Hittite capital, a remarkable stone imbedded in the wall of a native house, covered with a carved inscription in quaint and peculiar hieroglyphics in a style hitherto unknown. Since the discovery of this first inscription stone other specimens have been found in Hamah — the ancient Hamath of the scriptures, referred to in II Kings, XVII, 24, and in other biblical passages — until five stones in all have been recovered from this locality containing inscriptions in hieroglyphics, the complete decipherment of which in the immediate future may possibly prove the system to be one of the missing links in the chain of historic development of our English alphabet.

It is significant of the irreparable damage and widespread wanton destruction of the many priceless relics of antiquity, to read in William Wright's " The Empire of the Hittites " of the extraordinary vigilance bestowed and the ruses resorted to to restrain the religiously fanatical and jealous Arabs from destroying these precious inscriptions. Wright took no chances with such barbarian iconoclasts, who, as soon as ever they suspected that such relics had any value to Christian unbelievers, were bent on their immediate destruction. This fate already had befallen the Hittite inscriptions of Aleppo; the Moabite stone with its priceless Phœnician inscription, fortunately restored in part after it had been willfully broken into pieces; and the many other inestimable relics of antiquity which have been burned by the ton for lime, broken up into building stones, or in one way or another have become irretrievably lost to archæology. Being unable to remove the stones, plaster casts were promptly made of the inscriptions, and after untold vicissitudes they were forwarded to London where they now repose in the British Museum, that great repository of the art and archæology of the world. Another fragment from Hamah, larger and with a more extensive inscription than the first one, is reproduced in Fig. 85. The hieroglyphs show that the system had become a fixed, definite one — probably a syllabary — with constant characters that had reached a high degree of pictorial conventionalization. In each of the two inscriptions the reading is leftward in the first and odd rows and rightward in the even rows, the animate objects facing one as he reads the line.

Since the initial discovery at Hamah, inscriptions in this system of hieroglyphic writing have been found scattered over a wider area than the remains, either paleographic or architectural, of any other nation anterior to the classic period. From Southern Palestine to the Black

Sea and from the Levant to Hallah (Babylon) on the Euphrates and Nineveh on the Tigris, these carved inscriptions have been rescued from the dust of ages. Who were the people who carved these inscriptions so widely distributed, what was the nation that held sway over so

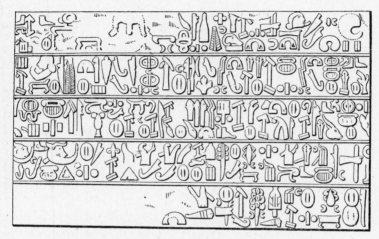

Fig. 85. Hittite inscription from Hamah.

broad a dominion, and what is the significance of their system of writing in its relation to the other world systems being considered by us? A brief answer to these inquiries will enable us the better to understand the historic connection between the stages of writing of the peoples involved, as the recurrent tide of years carried this culture westward toward Europe.

In regard to the first two inquiries we can offer fairly definite information based on credible, historic evidence, satisfactory now to all students of history and archæology. Concerning the inscriptions, while they cast a glow of illuminating light over the entire horizon of hieroglyphic writing, shining with the promise of early dawn

over the birth of the alphabetic characters, it is as yet
a little too early in the day completely and definitely to
trace the specific influence of this system, intermediate as
it appears to be between the oldest Babylonian (Sumerian) picture-writing and the Phœnician letter characters,
upon the latter. We are, however, on the very border-
land where the Phœnician and Hebrew systems of writing
originated after the decadence of the old Babylonian
picture-writing and the passing of the hieroglyphic system
under discussion. We have, then, if we may be allowed
the simile, almost literally reached the land of Canaan,
the land of promise and expectancy in our culture quest.
One more stage and we shall have reached the shores
of the Mediterranean whereon lived the versatile Phœnicians, who gave to the Greeks and the Hebrews the prototype of our alphabet. But we must proceed *festina
lente*. It is our purpose now briefly to locate and connect this extensive and obviously important civilization
with the other centers of ancient culture, to establish its
proper historic influence, and then at once to pass to a
consideration of the hieroglyphs themselves.

From the localities in which their sculptures have been
found we know that these peoples, the Hittites of the
Bible, were the immediate northern and eastern neighbors of the Phœnicians, the somewhat unimportant
Amorites probably intervening on the northern seaboard.
We have then this extensive civilization with its advanced
art of writing touching the Phœnician, contemporaneous
with it and allied with it at times for defensive purposes.
It is not altogether unreasonable to believe that its system of writing must have had some influence over that
of the latter.

For centuries the Hittites occupied the broad, partly
debatable ground north of the great Syrian Desert, con-

tended for alternately by the Assyrian and Egyptian
kings, the one in the immediate east the other in the far
southwest. It is probable that they were diverse but
cognate tribes, descended from a common stock and fed-
erated together for defensive purposes. In the beginning of this civilization, in the middle of the third pre-
Christian millennium, even before Babylon had become
a royal city, they first appear on the historical map as a
people probably closely allied in racial affinity with the
Akkadians, the early settlers of Babylonia — whom we
recognize as the authors of the early linear Babylonian
script — and other primitive Mongol races, as the Kas-
sites and Minni of Media. Successive waves of emigration flooded them over the fertile valleys from their ancestral home on the southern foothills of the Caucasus. One
of these waves early overwhelmed Northern Syria and
Northern Mesopotamia. These were the Mitani of the
cuneiform inscriptions who occupied the country during
the 18th and 17th centuries B. C. The rising Assyrian
power was able partly to overthrow this Mitani Kingdom and to take possession of Mesopotamia. About contemporaneous with this these same races, designated in
the cuneiform inscriptions as the Khatte, invaded Syria
about 1500 B. C., from their native country, Cappadocia.
Other tribes, as the Lukki, from whom Lykia (Lycia)
takes its name, occupied the central regions. Through
the weakness of the Egyptian and Assyrian powers in the
15th and 14th centuries B. C., this great civilization extended itself over all Syria to Mt. Hermon in Palestine.
They had maintained for centuries a vacillating diplo-
matic attitude toward both the Assyrian monarchy on
the east and the Egyptian monarchy on the southwest.
Whenever the foreign armies were in evidence, tribute
was forthcoming; but when they retired or when from

any internal or other cause the power of the dominating empire was weakened, the tribute was withheld.

We shall the better be able to judge of the historic position of the Hittites in their relation to the Assyrians and to learn of the international ethics of the age if we consult for just a moment a few quotations from the court records of the times concerning the amenities existing between these two nations. It is a one-sided statement, for the records of the latter nation only are available. These can be read. The Hittite cannot. Moreover, the Assyrians possessed in the vast clay deposits of their valleys unlimited and inviting resources for writing; while the Hittites had only hard and discouraging stone as the material for their records.

Tiglath-Pileser I, 1130 B. C., first refers to the Hittites in commencing a struggle that lasted 400 years between the two monarchies. Assur-Nasir-Pal (883–858 B. C.) says in the great inscription at Nimrud: " To Carchemish in Syria I directed my steps. The tribute due from the son of Bakhiani I received; — swift chariots, horses, silver, etc." . . . " The chariots and warlike engines from Carchemish I laid up in my magazines. The kings of all those lands who had come out against me received my yoke." . . . " From Carchemish I withdrew. To Gaza, the town of Lubarna of the Hittites, I advanced: gold and vestments of linen I received." . . . " In those days I occupied the environs of Lebanon. To the great sea of Phœnicia I went up. Up to the great sea, my arms I carried. I took tribute of Tyre, Sidon, Gebal, Maacah, . . . Phœnicia and Arvad " (" Records of the Past," iii, 73). Shalmaneser, son of the former, says in his Black Obelisk of Nimrud: " In my eleventh year, for the ninth time, the Euphrates I crossed; cities to a countless number I captured. To the cities of the Hittites of the land of the Hamathites I went down. Eighty-nine cities I took, Rimmon-Idri (Benhadad) of Damascus, and twelve kings of the Hittites." Finally Sargon II (722–705) ended the long and stubborn war by the final overthrow of Carchemish the eastern capital of the Hittites. We will quote from Oppert's translation of Sargon's famous inscription: " In the fifth year of my reign Pisiri of Carchemish sinned against the great gods. . . . I lifted up my hands to Assur, my Lord. I made him leave the town. I made them throw him into chains of iron. I took away the gold and silver and the treasures of his palace. The Carchemish rebels who were with him and their properties I transplanted to Assyria. I took among them 50 cars, 200 riders, 3,000 men on foot, and I augmented the part of my kingdom. I made Assyrians to dwell in Carchemish, and I placed them (the Hittites) under the domination of Assur, my Lord." At least, transportation and colonization were more merciful and reasonable than wholesale crucifixion and destruction.

These stubborn and protracted campaigns, lasting through centuries, only show what a mighty empire was that of the Hittites. On the west, over five hundred years before we hear of the Hittites in the cuneiform inscriptions, Thothmes I of Egypt, about the middle of the 17th century B. C., determining " to wash his heart," as the hieroglyphics say, by wreaking vengeance against the Asiatics who had dared to encroach on his territories, began expeditions against the " Khatte," which were continued intermittently for nearly 500 years. In the great inscription of Thothmes III at Thebes he recounts his attacks against Carchemish on the Euphrates and Kadesh on the Orontes in his nine separate campaigns against the " Kheta." Rameses II, so-called " The Great," met them in the famous historical battle of Kadesh, and an extremely interesting entente followed. We will quote a few lines from the heroic poem of " Pentaur," written in Egyptian hieroglyphs, 1316 B. C.: " The miserable king of the Hittites had assembled together the people of the two rivers, the Dardanians from the shores of the Ægean Sea, the islanders from Arvad, the hardy mountaineers from Moesius, the people of Aleppo and Carchemish. . . . From the remote parts of Asia Minor the mighty host converged on Kadesh on the Orontes. They left no people on the road whom they did not bring along with them. They covered mountains and valleys like grasshoppers without number. No such multitude ever before had been seen. They swept all the wealth of the country before them, so that they left neither silver nor gold behind them." After this extravagant account of the magnitude of the enemy's resources, the poem goes on in its inimitable Oriental naïveté of expression to say how the king turned the tide of battle after being deserted by all his warriors: " Not one of my princes, not one of my captains, not one of my knights was there. My warriors and my charioteers had abandoned me; not one of them was there to take part in the battle." Under these circumstances and knowing the prowess of Rameses II (from his own records!) we are not surprised in continuing this fulsome poem to read that " the king returned in victory and strength; with his own hand he had smitten hundreds of thousands to the earth " (" Records of the Past "). In the great Temple of Luxor at Karnak which Rameses has covered with his inscriptions may be seen this warrior-king, immense in stature, alone as the poem records, with the slaughtered Kheta lying about him. On the walls of the great temple at Ipsambul on the upper Nile may be seen another bas relief of the battle of Kadesh. The sculpture is nineteen yards long, eight yards high, and contains 1100 figures.

Nevertheless, in spite of the fulsome and vainglorious account of the bravery of Rameses and of the " famous victory " of the Egyptian king, it is significant to read that at the conclusion of the battle Rameses seemed to have felt that it was for the best interests of the Egyptians to effect a treaty of peace with Kheta-Sira, the king of the Hittites. And further to show his good faith — it may have been for other reasons as well — Rameses married the daughter of the " miserable " Kheta-Sira!

On the walls of the great Temple of Karnak may be read to-day as legibly as when carved thirty-seven centuries ago this treaty of peace between Rameses II and Kheta-Sira. The inscription is a copy of the original treaty engraved on a silver tablet and borne into Egypt by the emissaries of the Hittite king, as the hieroglyphs themselves say. This famous treaty of peace, the first offensive and defensive alliance on record, may yet become of commanding importance in the decipherment of the Hittite hieroglyphics when a copy of the original tablet is found. Fig. 86 is a reproduction of a sketch of the inscription made by the late Dr. W. Max Müller [1] from the original hieroglyphs. We will claim indulgence for giving in this place a partial translation of the treaty, on account of its extraordinary historical importance, and the prospect of its future help in unlocking the mysteries of the Hittite hieroglyphics. After a lengthy preamble in true Oriental style the inscription reads — leftward from the right-hand end of the third line from the top, where Kheta-Sira himself is pictured: —

(Line 1) " The Grand-duke of Kheta, Kheta-Sira,

[1] " Der Bundnisvertrag Ramses II und des Chetiter Königs," in " Mitteilungen der Vorderasiatischer Gesellschaft." Dr. W. Max Müller.

bringing to Pharaoh life, welfare, health, implores peace from the Majesty of Osymandyas, of the Son of the Sun. (Line 2) Rameses Meiamun, the giver of life, ever and eternally, like his Father, the God of the Sun, daily. A copy of the silver tablet of (Line 3) the Grand-duke of

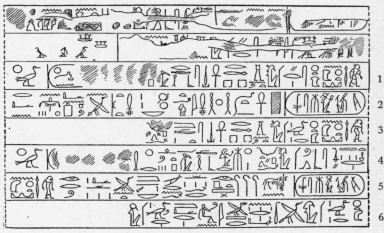

Fig. 86. Inscription in Egyptian hieroglyphics on the walls of the Temple of Karnak, containing a copy of the treaty of peace between Rameses II and Kheta-Sira, the king of the Hittites.

Kheta, Kheta-Sira, bringing to Pharaoh life, welfare, and health, through his ambassador. . . . (Line 4) Tara-tiisobu and his ambassador Ramose, soliciting peace from the majesty of Osymandyas, the Son of God, (Line 5) Rameses Meiamun, Courtier of the Bulls, who sets his frontiers as he wills in every land. The agreement which was made with the Grand-duke of Kheta, (Line 6) Kheta Sira, the powerful, the son of Maü-ra-si-ra." After more lengthy and involved asseverations as to the greatness of the contracting parties the treaty of peace proper begins in the frankest possible manner: " Behold this it is: Kheta-Sira, the Grand-Duke of Kheta, covenants with Ra-user-ma, approved by the Sun, the great ruler of Egypt, from this day forth, that good peace and good brotherhood shall be between us forever. He shall fraternize with me, he shall be at peace with me, I will be at peace with him forever. . . . The Grand-Duke of Kheta shall not invade the land of Egypt forever, to carry away anything from it; nor shall Ramesu-Meriamen, the great ruler of Egypt, invade the land of Kheta forever, to carry away anything from it forever." (The peace turned out to be only an armistice, for the Hittites revolted under Rameses III.)

Archæological research is close on the trail of the original of this important treaty of peace. In 1907 Dr. Hugo Winkler discovered at Boghaz-Keui a clay tablet containing in Assyrian characters a copy of the original treaty. It will probably not be long before a copy is found in the original Hittite hieroglyphs, which will extend the knowledge already acquired of them; for a beginning has been made and scholars are on the high road to success.

The first scholar to attempt a translation of the hieroglyphs was no less a personage than the entertaining but often unreliable historian Herodotus, who in traveling in Syria in the 4th century B. C. was shown the great bas relief in the Pass of Karabel, on the road from Smyrna to Sardis, twenty-four miles from the latter city. Herodotus promptly classed it, along with some genuine Egyptian sculptures in the neighborhood, as a monument of the great King Sesostris, his name for Rameses II. He says the inscription is in the sacred characters of Egypt and reads: " With my shoulders did I win this land " (Book II, Chap. 106). Fig. 87 is a reproduction of this sculpture and shows, very imperfectly, the hieroglyphic characters that Herodotus took for Egyptian.

Herodotus easily can be forgiven for his mistake. While the individual characters are wholly different from the Egyptian, they both are pictorial in nature, though the Hittite contains a larger number of conventional

Fig. 87. Hittite sculpture with inscription in the Pass of Karabel.

signs. This will be detected at once by a glance at the inscription from Hamah. Only a few of the signs appeal to the eye as recognizable objects. The greater number have lost their primitive ideographic forms and have become conventionalized to a high degree of geometric regularity. However, taking them altogether, there are quite a number of ideographic characters in the Hittite hieroglyphs. We find human and animal heads, hares, birds, arms, hands, feet, vases, utensils, weapons and many objects as yet undetermined. Invariably the inscriptions read boustrophedon, toward the faces and action of the ideographs, the whole series of hieroglyphs being alternately reversed in the succeeding

Fig. 88. Hittite sculpture found near Malatya in 1894.

lines. This is corroborated by the ending of the last line which falls short of the others on the left. In the earliest inscriptions the forms of the characters are more pictorial, in the latter ones they become quite cursive. In the Hittite bowl found in Babylon (Fig. 92), the

Fig. 89. Hittite sculpture and inscription. The Lion of Marash.

characters are so cursive as to have lost nearly all pictorial significance. All that we are certain of are a foot and a vase; all the other forms are highly conventionalized.

We will show two typical examples of Hittite sculpture and writing. One is a bas relief, a Hunting Scene, found near Malatya in 1894 (Fig. 88). The other is the well-known Hittite Lion found at Marash (Fig. 89). Both are remarkably like the Assyrian sculptures. In the first example the writing corresponds to the Egyptian method of placing all inscriptions upon the background. The second follows the general mode of almost all Hittite, as well as Assyrian sculptures, of carrying the inscription without interruption across the background and the figures; a method much less effective than that of the more methodical and artistic Egyptians. Both examples, if we are correct in our interpretation, appear to contain many ideographs. If this is so, they must belong to the early age of Hittite writing, to which age most authorities also attribute the Hamah inscriptions. What this date may be is at present wholly conjectural. That their system of writing greatly antedates the time of Thothmes I, must be conceded. A nation that could hold its own for 500 years against the cultured Egyptians must have been equally advanced in the arts of civilization. Mariette, the noted Egyptologist, advances the daring proposition that one of the dynasties of the foreign domination in Egypt known as the Hyksos dynasty, under which the great pyramids were built, was Hittite (*circa* 2130–1700 B.C.). Col. Conder, in "The Hittites and Their Language," dates the Hittite hieroglyphs from the opening centuries of the third preChristian millennium, contemporary with the first Kassite dynasty of Babylon.

A very interesting example of Hittite art is the bas relief of a man in the Metropolitan Museum, New York City (Fig. 90). He is represented with a staff, a full beard and the knitted cap so characteristic of Hittite

Fig. 90. Hittite bas relief in the Metropolitan Museum, New York City.

work. If the feet had not been broken off, we probably would see the up-turned shoes, also peculiar to the people of this country. The writing covers the background and crosses over the figure, covering all parts except the head. As in most Hittite inscriptions, the characters are in horizontal rows separated in this instance by dividing lines quite the same as we are familiar with in the Babylonian inscriptions. The characters seem to be very much more conventional and geometric than any of the preceding inscriptions, indicating a later period. However, the relic has aged so considerably that it is difficult to identify the individual symbols. The signs that are conspicuous are strikingly like the linear Babylonian signary.

Fig. 91. Bowl with Hittite inscription. Found in Babylon.

The Hittite bowl from Babylon, illustrated in Fig. 91, is a rather remarkable relic of this early Oriental civilization. The original is of black basalt, about thirteen inches in diameter and nine inches high. The sketch was made from a cast in the Semitic Museum, Harvard University, Cambridge, Mass. The original is in England. The inscription is deeply incised in the stone and although considerably time-worn is perfectly legible for the greater part. Prof. Sayce has remarked upon the hieratic character of the signs. They do not actually resemble the Egyptian hieratic characters; but doubtless being of a later age of Hittite writing the symbols have undergone a marked modification in conventionalization. They are distinctly cursive. In Fig. 92 we give a diagram of the inscription, which appears to be written for the greater part in three horizontal rows without any separating lines. The reading is from right to left; but whether

Fig. 92. Hittite inscription on the Bowl from Babylon.

the lines are to be read around the bowl in succession, or the signs are to be read downward in the more or less vertical rows is not yet known. We can only guess where the reading begins. The bowl is altogether a unique relic of a bygone day, and doubtless some day will

Fig. 93. The bos of Tarkondemos. Bi-lingual inscription in Babylonian cuneiform and Hittite hieroglyphics.

play its part in enlightening us concerning the civilization of the Hittite nation.

At least one bi-lingual inscription in Hittite and Assyrian characters has been discovered. It is the silver bos of Tarkondemos, a plaster cast of which is in the British Museum, happily discreetly taken when it was originally offered for sale. It has since become lost. It will be seen in the cut (Fig. 93), that there are several hieroglyphs disposed about the figure of the royal personage, while encircling the whole is an unbroken band of Assyrian cuneiform characters. Of course the latter can be read, although scholars still differ concerning a few of the signs. Prof. Sayce gives the following translation of the circular cuneiform inscription: —

Tar — rik — Tim-me, Sár mat Er — me — e
" Tarrick-timme, King of the country of Erme."

Dr. Hilprecht, however, gives the following translation: " Tarkudimmie, King of the country of the Metani." The Royal name, Tarku (or Tarrick) timme (or dimme) represented by the goat's head and the character under it, is given twice, either side of the head, beginning the inscription which is in complete duplicate in front of and to the rear of the royal personage. Thus were established the values of some six Hittite characters. This number has slowly been increased by philological research and comparison with the early Babylonian linear script, which it somewhat resembles, and from which it undoubtedly sprung, until several scores of signs have been assigned more or less fixed values. William Wright (" The Empire of the Hittites ") has assigned phonetic values to some thirty symbols. Col. Conder has been much more ambitious, and has ventured tentative values for almost every symbol in the signary, over 160 signs (" The Hittites and Their Language," Col. C. R. Conder). Despite this array of " guesses," outside of the bi-lingual inscription of Tarkondemos, no Hittite inscription yet has been satisfactorily translated. The system appears to be syllabic, not alphabetic. It has not developed to the latter advanced stage. In this respect and in other ways it resembles the linear Babylonian. In execution there was a slight difference between the two. The symbols in the latter were linear and almost always incised, while the Hittite symbols were in heavy bas relief. Both systems of writing were the mode of expression of contemporary Mongol races before the complete emergence of the Semitic races. Prof. Sayce comments on the fact that the Hittite hieroglyphics are a modification of the early Babylonian before the rise of Assyria; and Col. Conder points out that of the 160 Hittite signs only about 40 cannot be identified with the linear Babylonian.

CHAPTER X

THE ALPHABETIC WRITING OF THE PHŒNICIANS

IN our historical pilgrimage to the land of the alphabet we now have reached the conclusion of the first stage of our journey. We have proceeded from the once fertile valley of Mesopotamia through the highlands of Asia Minor, along the immemorial caravan routes that connected the East with the West and on which were conveyed the wealth, the arts and the civilization of the ancient world, to the very shores of the Mediterranean Sea. In the tableland of Akkad and the valley of Sumer we discovered in our archæological investigations the oldest writing in existence; written — literally drawn — on stone or on clay tablets by a primitive Asian race, in outline ideographs, just as much drawing as any diagram that ever was drafted. The world hardly can hope ever to come nearer to the original sources of writing than the primitive picture-writing of the proto-Babylonians. Crossing the wide valley of the Tigris and the Euphrates we found here and there in chronological sequence tablets and inscriptions in the Semitic language, written in the Babylonian and Assyrian conventional cuneiform characters in use for three millenniums until classic times. We next crossed the vast empire of the Hittites, contemporaneous with that of Assyria, stretching from the Euphrates quite to the Mediterranean Sea. Scattered here and there in far-flung cities and provinces we observed and examined inscriptions in the peculiar Hittite hieroglyphics. In many cases the hieroglyphs closely resembled the older

286

Sumerian and linear Babylonian ideographs; being pictorial in general character, and bearing not the least resemblance to the cuneiform writing with which they probably were contemporaneous.

Here on the shore of the Mediterranean, where the ancient world came in contact with the confines of the western civilizations, we become acquainted for the first time with the true alphabetic writing of the smallest nation of antiquity that has left any footprints along the great highways of world culture, or made any lasting impression upon the material agencies of civilization. Here we encounter a nation of very limited geographical extent but powerful in the influence it exerted over other nations with which it came in contact. The Phœnicians were not a numerous people, but they possessed that high degree of intelligence, energy, skill and craftsmanship that made the products of their civilization desired by many other nations. For over one thousand years, from about 1500 B. C. to 500 B. C., the Phœnicians maintained more or less undisturbed a small, compact, but powerful monarchy; whose temporal boundaries were barely more than two hundred miles in length along the eastern shore of the Mediterranean Sea and but thirty-five miles in greatest width to the lofty mountains of Lebanon on the east. The present city of Beirut is on the ancient soil of Phœnicia.

Beyond the ranges of Lebanon lived the Israelites, closely allied by racial affinity with the Phœnicians, and in the time of David and Solomon bound to them by national ties and the sympathies of an almost equally advanced civilization. Both nations originally had emigrated from lower Mesopotamia early in the third millennium B. C. Abraham, according to biblical account (Genesis xi, 31), led the Hebrew race out of " Ur of the Chaldees " to the land of Canaan; and we have it on the authority of He-

rodotus that the Phœnicians themselves record that their
ancestors originally came from the Erythræan or Southern Sea, that is the Persian Gulf. This is believed to have
been about 2200 B. C. North of Phœnicia extended the
mighty empire of the Hittites from Lydia and Dardania
on the west to the Euphrates on the east, where it touched
the equally puissant civilization of the great Assyrian
monarchy in Mesopotamia. Far to the south of Phœnicia
and Palestine lay the sunny land of Egypt from which
the Israelites had journeyed to the land of Canaan some
time in the 14th century B. C.

In comparison with the powerful monarchies of the
east and south, whose influence affected them in many
ways, the civilization of the Phœnicians at their principal
cities of Tyre and Sidon, situated only twenty miles apart
on the Mediterranean sea coast, may seem from a political standpoint insignificant indeed. Yet these two Semitic
nations, the Phœnicians and the Israelites, have influenced
more profoundly the western civilization and the culture
and refinement of Europe than all the civilizations that
had preceded them. The one, through the incomparable
literature of the Hebrew Scriptures, has established the
underlying basis of all the religions of Europe, while the
other has given the basic forms for the written languages
of all the nations of Europe and central Asia.

The Phœnicians undoubtedly were the cleverest people
of their age, and their fame, like their markets, was world-
wide. Long before the time of Homer they bore the reputation of being the world's artificers; excelling in the
weaving and dyeing of fine textiles, as skillful carpenters
and masons, and adepts in the fabrication of articles of
iron, copper and precious metals. Theirs was the first
merchant marine of history. Their ships rode every sea
and visited every coast and mart from the Euxine to the

Atlantic. The shores of Cornwall, where they mined min-
erals, were almost as familiar to them as the Isles of
Greece and Italy, the Delta of the Nile, or other Mediterranean ports where they distributed their wares. In I
Kings v, we read that Solomon contracted with Hiram,
king of Tyre, to assist him in the building of the Temple,
as " there is not among us any that can skill to hew timber
like unto the Sidonians." Also in II Chronicles ii, 14, we
read: " The son of a woman of the daughters of Dan,
and his father was a man of Tyre, skillful to work in
gold, and in silver, in brass, in iron, in stone, and in timber, in purple, in blue, and in fine linen, and in crimson;
also to grave any manner of graving, and to find out every
device which shall be put to him, with thy cunning men,
and with the cunning men of my lord David, thy father."
Considering the confidence placed in the superiority of the
handiwork of the Phœnicians by the people of Israel and
their dependence upon them in many ways, it is not surprising that the Hebrews eventually should have adopted
from the Phœnicians their alphabet, which early Hebrew
coins show to be but slightly modified from the original,
though they did so far depart from it in their later script.
It is a commentary on the forceful influence of these Orientals that the Greeks, with whom the Phœnicians traded,
and who probably were illiterate when these clever traders first visited them, also should have adopted their
alphabet, as we shall learn in a succeeding chapter.

There are two important and rather well-defined types
of the Phœnician alphabet. The Moabite or Tyrian, the
older, dates from about the 9th century B. C. It developed at Tyre and was used during the ascendancy of that
city. It later was employed chiefly by the inland Semitic
tribes in Moab and Syria, and was used by the Jews down
to the time of the Captivity. The Greek alphabet, as we

shall show later on, came from this type, early traders having introduced it into Greece shortly after the time of the Trojan war. The other type, known as the Sidonian, dates from the 6th century B. C., and was in use at Sidon and the principal cities in Phœnicia and at Carthage in Africa immediately subsequent to the conquest of Phœnicia by Nebuchadrezzar. The two varieties of alphabets were used side by side in different sections of Phœnicia, Judea and Syria for centuries. It would appear that the earlier Phœnician traders used the Moabite form. The Israelites and Jews both continued to use this variety of the Phœnician alphabet, but the Phœnicians themselves, after the destruction of Tyre by Nebuchadrezzar, used the Sidonian script.

The oldest Phœnician inscription to which a definite date can be assigned is the remarkable inscription of Mesha, king of Moab, on the monument known as the Moabite Stone, now in the Louvre at Paris. It was discovered in 1868 in the vicinity of the Dead Sea, on the site of Dibon, the ancient capital of Moab, by Mr. Klein, a missionary. Unfortunately as soon as the neighboring Arabs surmised that it had any value to Christians they fell into a quarrel over its possession, and the precious monument which had withstood the ravages of time and the violation of man for over 2700 years was broken by them into forty odd pieces, by being heated and having water poured over it. However, it has been partially restored to its original condition, and the lost lines, of which squeezes fortunately had been taken before its destruction, have been supplied by plaster facsimiles. In the reproduction of a photograph of the monument shown in Fig. 94, the more legible lines are those which have been restored.

In II Kings iii, we read of the rebellion of Mesha

Fig. 94. The Moabite Stone.

against Jehoram, king of Israel, when the Israelites " rose
up and smote the Moabites, so that they fled before them;
but they went forward smiting the Moabites, even in
their own country. And they beat down the cities, and on
every good piece of land cast every man his stone and

filled it; and they stopped all the wells of water, and felled all the good trees; only in Kir-haraseth left they the stones thereof; howbeit the slingers went about it and smote it." The rebellion was not altogether to be unexpected, as we read earlier in Chapter iii: " And Mesha, king of Moab, was a sheepmaster, and rendered unto the king of Israel an 100,000 lambs, and an 100,000 rams, with the wool." The Moabites chafed under this yoke and its heavy tribute, as well they might, and rebelled against Israel, as the Bible and Mesha himself both inform us. The rebellion, it seems, was not entirely without success, for Mesha shut himself securely in the fortress of Harosheth, near Arnon, sacrificing his eldest son, while the Israelites consoled themselves as " the slingers went about the fortress and smote it " and returned to their own land. Mesha, however, escaped and lived to erect this remarkable monument of victory!

In the inscription Mesha gives us his version of the rebellion which clears up the omissions in the biblical account. He tells us that he slew seven thousand men and women and damsels, and that " he took the . . . of Yahweh and dragged them before Kemosh "; and that " he took Yahas and added it to Daibon." He finishes his inscription by informing us that he rebuilt the citadel and royal palaces and the destroyed cities of Moab. It is known that Jehoram reigned from 896 to 884 B. C. We have, therefore, a very exact date for this unique monument.

There are thirty-four lines in this Phœnician inscription, the words being separated by dots, and the sentences by short vertical lines. The original, now in its third millennium, necessarily is very illegible. The reader hardly may be able to make out any of the characters, they are so

Fig. 95. Inscription on the Moabite Stone. Restored by Mark Lidzbarski.

obliterated with the recurring erosion and incrustation of
the ages. He will find, however, in Fig. 95 a most careful and scholarly reconstruction of the original inscrip-

tion reproduced from the "Handbuch der Nordsemitisch" by Mark Lidzbarski. It represents the Phœnician
characters quite as they must have appeared when first
chiseled. The reading is from right to left in the time-
honored Oriental manner, from which the East hardly
has deviated to this day. We give below an enlarged copy
of the first and second lines of the inscription, with a part
of the third line to the short vertical line that ends the
sentence. Following this is given the phonetic equivalents
of the letters, with the vowels — that are almost wholly
omitted in Phœnician inscriptions — in brackets. An English translation also is given. It may be quite possible for
the reader with the help of the phonetic transliteration to
follow the original inscription, as most of the characters
resemble not a little the corresponding letters in our own
alphabet. Indeed, if he will consult the alphabet as shown
in the first column of characters in Fig. 101 he will be able
to detect in them a strong family likeness to the corresponding letters of our own alphabet; as one might trace
family features in the lineaments of portraits of his ancestors.

1. 'AN(O)K(I). M(E)Sh'(A). B(E)N. K(A)M(O)ShM(A)LD. M(E)-
L(E)K. M(O)'AB. HED—
2. IB(O)NI | 'ABI. M(A)L(A)K. 'AL. M(O)'AB. ShL(I)Sh(I)N.
Sh(A)T. V'AN(O)K(I). M(A)L(A)K—
3. TI. 'ACh(A)R. 'ABI |

1. I am Mesha, son of Kamoshmald, king of Moab, the
D-
2. ibonite | My father reigned over Moab thirty years,
and I reign-
3. ed after my father |

The reader will note that the writing in this inscription is true alphabetic writing in the final stage; a development in the art of writing hitherto unknown in the East, where we have found only ideographic and syllabic writing, with the undeveloped alphabetic writing of the Persians. Here on the shores of the Mediterranean in the 9th century B. C., we suddenly find, with no evident progenitor, a perfected alphabet, in form, order and letter names nearly identical with our alphabet of to-day.[1]

Another inscription in the early Tyrian style of Phœnician writing, the oldest Phœnician inscription as yet discovered, is one engraved on some small fragments of a bronze bowl found on the island of Cyprus (Fig. 96). The bowl was given by a " citizen of Carthage " (Newtown), in Phœnicia — not the later Tyrian colony in Africa — and doubtless was deposited in the Temple

Fig. 96. Phœnician inscription on a bronze bowl from the Temple of Baal Lebanon

[1] It may not at once be easy for the reader to detect the rather close similarity between the Phœnician alphabet and our own capital letters. This is partly because the reading is from right-to-left, while ours is from left-to-right. Besides, in transmission through the Greek the Phœnician letters were reversed as the reading was changed. Below will be found the Phœnician alphabet, in parallel with the letters of our own alphabet, but *reversed* in reading and in form, to indicate more clearly the historical metamorphosis:

A B C D E F Z H Th I K L M N S O P Ts Q R Sh T of Baal Lebanon, from which it probably was pillaged and carried to Cyprus.

The longest inscription, as translated by Isaac Taylor, reads:

. . . V S(O)K(E)N Q(A)RT(A)Ch(A)D(A)Sh(A)T 'AB(E)D
Ch(I)R(A)M M(E)L(E)K Ts(I)D(O)N(I)M 'AZ YT(E)N L(E)
B(A)'AL L(E)B(A)N(O)N 'AD(O)N(A)I BR'ASh(E)T N(E)Ch(U)-
Sh(A)T Ch. . . .

". . . v, a citizen of Newtown, servant of Hiram, king of the Sidonians, gave this to Baal Lebanon his Lord, of good brass."

The left hand fragment reads:

. . . T(O)B S(O)K(E)N Q(A)RT(A)Ch(A)D(A)Sh(A)T. . . .

". . . tob, a citizen of Newtown."

The right hand fragment reads:

. . . 'AL L(E)B(A)N(O)N 'AD(O)N(A)I. . . .

"(To Ba)al Lebanon his lord."

If the Hiram mentioned in this inscription is the Hiram of King Solomon's time, the inscription may date from the beginning of the 10th century B. C. The Tyrian alphabet probably was in use from the 10th century to the 7th century B. C.

Two remarkable inscribed monuments in the second or Sidonian style of Phœnician writing have been discovered in Saïda, Syria, in the neighborhood of ancient Sidon; both of them sarcophagi, and both massive and extraordinary in their proportions. One of them is the great sarcophagus of King Tabnith, who ruled in Sidon during the short renaissance of her last national period, after the city had been sacked by the Persian hordes under Artaxerxes Ochus (352 B. C.), when 40,000 Sidonians burned themselves alive in their houses rather than to face nameless horrors to themselves and their families at the hands of the victorious enemy. The sarcophagus which now is in the Museum of Constantinople probably was stolen from Egypt, as it has every evidence of Egyptian workmanship, and bears the epitaph of an Egyptian general, one Perptah. The Phœnician inscription consists of eight lines of writing in beautifully formed letters, uniform and even throughout, bearing every evidence of the technical skill of the Sidonian engraver (Fig. 97). Tabnith's curse against desecrators is so vehement, and his expressions are so quaint, that we add an English translation of the inscription.[1]

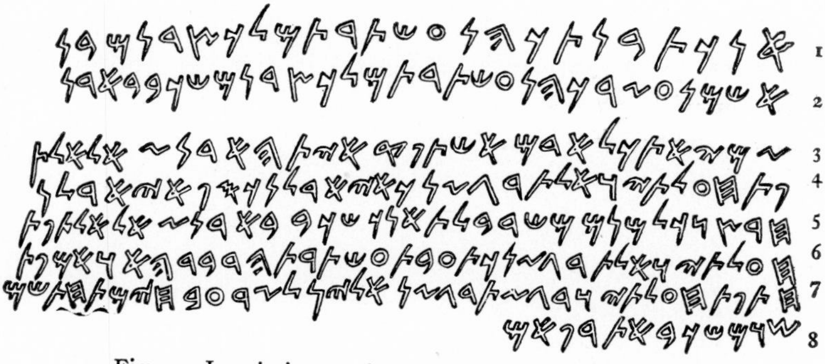

Fig. 97. Inscription on the sarcophagus of King Tabnith.

(1) I, Tabnith, priest of Ashtart, king of the Sidonians, son

(2) of Eshmun-azar, priest of Ashtart, king of the Sidonians, lie in this coffin.

(3) My curse be with whatever man thou art that bringest forth this coffin! Do not, do not

[1] From "A Text Book of North Semitic Inscriptions." Rev. G. A. Cooke.

(4) open me, nor disquiet me, for I have not indeed silver, I have not indeed

(5) gold, nor any jewels of . . . only I am lying in this coffin. Do not, do not open

(6) me nor disquiet me, for that thing is an abomination to Ashtart. And if thou do at all

(7) open me, and at all disquiet me, mayest thou have no seed among the living under the sun

(8) nor resting place among the shades!

The inscription on the second one of these Sidonian sarcophagi is one of the very finest examples of Phœnician paleography. It is from the immense monolithic sarcophagus of Eshmunazar II, king of Sidon, found in 1855 in a rock-cut tomb in the necropolis of ancient Sidon and now in the Louvre. This king, Eshmunazar, was the son of the Tabnith whose sarcophagus we have just examined. There are twenty-two long lines in the inscription, full of repetitious threats and curses against the violators of his last resting place. The first five lines are reproduced in Fig. 98, extending across pages 298 and 299.

Fig. 98(B). First five lines of the inscription on the sarcophagus of King Eshmunazar.

The reading begins on the right on page 299, and reads leftward across page 298. A translation of these few lines will suffice to indicate the general character and literary content of the inscription. The style as compared with his father's inscription is very ordinary, prolix and lacking in originality. The translation follows: —

(1) In the month of Bul, in the fourteenth year of the reign of king Eshmunazar, king of the Sidonians,

(2) son of king Tabnith, king of the Sidonians, saying: I have been seized

(3) before my time, the son of a short number of days, . . . an orphan, the son of a widow; and I lie in this coffin and in this grave,

(4) in the place which I built. I adjure every prince and every man that they open not this resting place,

(5) nor seek with me jewels, for there are no jewels with me here, nor take away the coffin of my resting place.

Fig. 98(A). First five lines of the inscription on the sarcophagus of King Eshmunazar.

Here is the king's name as it occurs at the end — the left — of the first line of the inscription: —

'AShM(U)N'AZ(A)R   M(E)L(E)K   Ts(I)D(O)N(I)M

Eshmunazar, King of the Sidonians.

The fifth line, which is a complete phrase, we will give in its phonetic equivalents, with the vowel sounds omitted, just as Eshmunazar prepared the inscription for the carver. It will enable the reader who is desirous of tracing the individual letters of our alphabet back to their original sources to observe the very marked similarity of most of our letters to the Phœnician characters, more particularly, however, to the Moabite than the Sidonian in which this inscription is written:

'L YBQSh BNMNM K'Y ShM BNMNM W'L
Y'Sh' 'YT HLT MShKBY W'L Y'M

The complete Sidonian alphabet taken from these two inscriptions is shown in the fifth column of characters in Fig. 101. The principal divergences from the primitive Phœnician alphabet (the Moabite) are most marked in the following letters: gimel, zayin, yod, lamed, mem, shin and tau.

There is another inscription in Phœnician characters to which we desire to refer, both on account of its paleographical value and for its wonderful historical interest in connection with passages in the Hebrew Scriptures. In 1880 there was discovered in a very ancient tunnel that conducted water from the Virgin's Pool to the Pool of Siloam an inscription that must have been carved shortly after the completion of the tunnel. The inscription although in the pure Hebrew language was inscribed in Phœnician characters, somewhat cursive in form as the reader will see by referring to Fig. 99. The date of the inscription must be centuries prior to

Fig. 99. Inscription of Siloam.

the development of the square Hebrew; and its close similarity to the Moabite inscription would place it before the Captivity, probably about the 7th century B. C., at the close of the Jewish monarchy.

Prof. A. H. Sayce has translated the inscription as follows:

1. (Behold the) excavation! Now this is the history of the tunnel. While the excavators (were lifting up)
2. the pick each to his neighbor, and while there was yet three cubits (to be broken through) — the voice of one call-
3. ed to his neighbor, for there was (an excess?) in the rock on the right. They rose up — they struck on the west of the
4. excavation, the excavators struck each to meet his neighbor pick to pick, and there flowed

5. the waters from the outlet to the Pool for the distance of 1000 cubits, and (three-fourths?)

6. of a cubit was the height of the rock at the head of the excavation here.

Now what does this quaint statement mean? Simply that these primitive workmen endeavored to do what engineering skill enables us of this age to do with consummate accuracy: to begin the excavation at both ends. The Hebrews failed to meet on line. They overlapped, as the physical condition of the tunnel shows to-day, and had to cut through on the west wall " each to meet his neighbor pick to pick." The Siloam alphabet is shown in the third column of characters in Fig. 101.

We give in Fig. 100 a final example of Phœnician

Fig. 100. Trilingual inscription in Latin, Greek and Phœnician.

writing. It occurs in a trilingual inscription, now in the Royal Academy of Science, Turin. The inscription is incised on the base of a bronze altar, and records its dedication to 'Eshmūn Mērrēh (Æsculapius), by one Cleon, a slave, who was superintendent of certain salt works in Sardinia, where the inscription was found. It dates from the middle of the 2d century B. C. It is among the very few bi-lingual and tri-lingual inscriptions that have helped to reconstruct the ancient Phœnician language.

It thus appears that the ancient alphabet of Israel was almost identical with that of Phœnicia, having been borrowed by the Jews probably at a very early period in their national development. This fact has been amply confirmed by the discovery of other inscriptions and by the many Hebrew coins in pure Phœnician characters that have come to light.

During the Captivity, modifications of the Phœnician alphabet known as Aramean were used alike by the Jews and their civilian captors in Assyria and Babylonia as well as throughout the countries north of Israel and Phœnicia. They were used in Nineveh and Babylon side by side with the cuneiform. The old cuneiform syllabary with its many cumbersome signs, indigenous in Mesopotamia and in use for almost forty centuries, gradually had been giving way to the more flexible alphabet of the west, disseminated by the enterprising Phœnician traders, but modified by the people of Aram and Syria. The Aramean alphabet began to appear some time in the 7th century B. C. in the highlands of Aram, on the caravan routes from Egypt and Phœnicia through Cilicia and Syria to Mesopotamia. Its rise was contemporaneous with the decline of Phœnicia following the sacking and destruction of Tyre by Nebuchadrezzar, and the consequent rise in importance of the highland races of Aram and Syria.

The Jews upon their return to Judea after the Captivity probably brought with them this Aramean corruption of the Phœnician letters then used throughout Western Asia as the alphabet of commerce. There were a number of local varieties of this alphabet, all of them being corruptions of the Phœnician letters, their common archetype. The one used in Nineveh in the 7th century B. C. is shown in the fourth column in Fig. 101. As the centuries advanced the degradation of the Phœnician characters in these Aramean alphabets became more and more marked, and the divergence from the original forms became so great as almost wholly to disguise any family relationship. It is only by tracing back period by period the successive changes in each letter that we can detect the common ancestor. The Jews in Palestine probably employed the Aramean alphabet down to the 2d century B. C. From this time on there was a rapid differentiation in the Aramean scripts. The southern Aramean in Palestine, about the 1st century B. C., began to be transformed into the square Hebrew. The modern square Hebrew of to-day is a comparatively late alphabet. It was not until the 10th century A. D. that it was fully developed into its present form, so entirely unlike its Phœnician prototype and so lacking in that diversity of form that ensures legibility and precludes ambiguity. It is illustrated in the eighth column in Fig. 101.

One of the purest types of the Aramean alphabets used by the Jews was the Samaritan, conserved to this day and employed in the sacred scrolls still in use in the little Samaritan community at Nabulus. This alphabet is shown in the sixth column in Fig. 101. Although dating from the 6th century A. D., the letters on the whole seem more closely to resemble their Phœnician prototype than the Aramean alphabet used in Nineveh in the 7th century B. C. Can it be possible that the Jewish rabbis at Nabulus had preserved for so many centuries manuscripts in the older script? In comparing this alphabet letter for letter with the Phœnician, there are only one or two letters that do not bear a noticeable resemblance to the parent alphabet; while it resembles in hardly any particular the square Hebrew, which at that time had been developing several centuries. The alphabet used in Jerusalem about the 1st century B. C., shown in the seventh column of the chart, is decidedly

Letter name	Phonetic value	Moab. IX.C., B.C.	Nineveh IX.C., B.C.	Siloam VIII.C., B.C.	Nineveh VII.C., B.C.	Sidon VI.C., B.C.	Samaritan	Jerusalem I.C., B.C.	Modern Hebrew	Modern Arabic
Aleph	'a									
Beth	b									
Gimel	g									
Daleth	d									
He	h									
Vau	v									
Zayin	z									
Cheth	ch									
Teth	t									
Yod	y									
Kaph	k									
Lamed	l									
Mem	m									
Nun	n									
Samekh	s									
'Ayin	'a									
Pe	p									
Tsade	ts									
Q'oph	q									
Resh	r									
Shin	sh									
Tau	t									
		I	II	III	IV	V	VI	VII	VIII	IX

Fig. 101. The Phœnician alphabet, showing the transformation of the Moabite and Sidonian letters into the Modern Hebrew and Arabic.

more like the modern square Hebrew than this Samaritan alphabet.

In the north the Aramean alphabet after passing through certain local modifications — as the alphabet used in Palmyra in the last three centuries before Christ and the Syriac alphabet which developed in the early Christian centuries — eventually developed through the dark ages into the modern Arabic. The gradual degeneration from the none-too-well differentiated forms of the Aramean alphabet into the curious " short-hand " of the Arabic, with its many ambiguous abbreviations of the historic letters, is one of the most remarkable transformations known in the history of calligraphy. The Arabic alphabet is shown in the last column in Fig. 101. As will be seen, a considerable proportion of the characters have deteriorated into mere punctuation marks; while many duplicate characters are distinguished from each other only by diacritical marks above or below the open line or curve. There is an almost total absence of looped or closed curves which give variety to the Phœnician letters. Almost every stroke is open and cursive.

It is a strange conclusion after two millenniums of transformations that we now should have remaining as the descendants of the primitive Phœnician alphabet: the square Hebrew, used by the Jews who follow the prophets of the Old Testament; the Arabic alphabet, used by the non-Christian people of Islam; and the Roman alphabet, employed by the Christian nations of Europe. The two former alphabets, during the early Christian centuries, lost almost every vestige of the primitive forms; while the European alphabets, after their transformation into the Gothic black letters of the Middle Ages, so dissimilar to the Roman alphabet, in the Renaissance restored the old Roman letters for initials and titles, while the minuscule was used for the body of the text. Thus was reëstablished in permanent use letters which have descended directly from the old Phœnician letters, and which closely resemble them in nearly every case. They are, like the parent alphabet, distinctive, varied, unambiguous and well differentiated.

It may be of interest to note that the names of the letters in all these alphabets,— the Aramean, Syriac, Arabic, or in nearly every alphabet in Europe and Asia,— the Slavonic, Armenian or Indian, are almost identical with those of the original Phœnician letters as preserved in the Hebrew language. All the local modifications in the names of the letters are similar to the following. The Syriac letters proceed: *ôlaf, bêth, gômal, dôlath,* etc.; the Arabic: *alif, be, jim, dal,* etc.; the Slavonic: *az, buki, glagol, dobro,* etc.; the Indian, *alf, bet, gemel, dent,* etc. It is hardly necessary to remind the reader that the Greek alphabet, borrowed from the Phœnician, runs: *alpha, beta, gamma, delta,* and so on. What an honor it confers upon this little nationality of Phœnicia, nestling along the shore of the Mediterranean Sea twenty-five centuries ago, that her written and spoken alphabet, modified to the extent that we have indicated, is used to-day practically the world over, up to the wall of China and the land of the Rising Sun.

We may remark in closing this chapter that it is a strange fatality that the one Oriental system of writing that has had the most direct influence in the formation of the letters of our own alphabet, as they have come down to us from the Greek, unfortunately should be, with the exception of the Hittite writing, the one whose origin we know the least about. Both of these systems of writing though they developed many centuries after the linear Babylonian, Assyrian and Egyptian systems of writing, still have their antecedents shrouded in mystery. The Hittite writing cannot even be read, while the origin of the Phœnician is to-day a matter of doubt and dispute. It seems that in the comparison of the earlier forms of writing with the Phœnician — the parent system of all the present European and mid-Asian alphabets — the knowledge of the historic development were inversely as the age of the system. The sources of the written characters of the Egyptians and Babylonians alike have been fully revealed to us in the primitive, graphic ideograms that represented and expressed the ideas of their early scribes, and which were continued through successive modifications, not at all extensive in the case of the Egyptians, into their ultimate, simplified signary. But whence the Phœnicians obtained their letters, through what channels of historic association or literary influence their letters received their distinctive forms, still is a mooted and unsettled question. Possibly this is not an altogether unmixed evil. If we were able at this time definitely to clear up all the mystery brooding over the origin and development of our alphabetic characters, the book would be finished in our generation. There would be nothing left for posterity, and coming generations of scholars would be denied wide fields of scholarship and research.

CHAPTER XI

In the last chapter we stated that the origin of the Phœnician alphabet is a mooted question. Leading authorities on archæology and paleography are not in accord in their theories concerning the probable source of these unique letters. That they were descended from an ancient lineage, and had passed through many centuries of transformation before the Phœnicians adopted them for their phonetic writing, seems almost certain. They do not appear to be an indigenous system that had developed *in situ* from the internal evolution of national ideals, like the Egyptian and Babylonian writing. They have the earmarks of an adopted art, composite in character, and possibly derived from more than one source. It seems highly improbable that this small nation with no certain history prior to the middle of the second millennium, B. C., perched upon the Mediterranean sea coast between powerful monarchies that for centuries had been developing their systems of writing around them, should have evolved an entirely independent system of writing. No one advocates such a theory. The Phoenicians were the traders of antiquity. They were veritable nomads of the sea. They came in touch with every nation around the Mediterranean basin, and very early must have become familiar with their culture and their arts. If the Phœnician alphabet were not an indigenous system, it must have developed under the influence of the Assyro-

Babylonian, the Hittite or the Egyptian system of writing, or have received its elements from the West. That it never could have been an outgrowth of or been influenced by the cuneiform writing is too apparent to need any argument. There are no visible points of similarity between one of the many hundreds of cuneiform, syllabic symbols and the twenty-two letters of the Phœnician alphabet. More than one eminent authority believes that the majority of the Phœnician letter names came from the East, but even a casual glance at the cuneiform characters must convince any one that the Phœnician alphabet never could have originated from this source. That it could have developed out of the Sumerian ideographs and syllabary, or the later linear Babylonian characters which formed the basis of the cuneiform text, is not at all improbable. There is, however, no tangible evidence that there was any direct connection between the two cultures, unless it existed before the western branch of the Semites emigrated from the Euphrates valley.

The linear Babylonian script, at least in Mesopotamia, had fallen into complete disuse before the time of Hammurabi (*circa* 2200 B. C.) and had been supplanted by the cuneiform syllabary. The linear forms from this time on were completely abandoned and probably forgotten, except by native lexicographers whose glossaries of linear and cuneiform signs on clay tablets occasionally have been discovered. It is possible, however, as we already have suggested, that the early Hittites in developing their primitive hieroglyphs may have borrowed more or less from their early eastern neighbors, the Akkadians and Sumerians. It appears as though this were an established fact; but as we yet do not know the syllabic value of but a very few of the Hittite signs, it

is impossible to trace specific parallels between the two
syllabaries.

The inquiry therefore becomes narrowed down to the
writing of the Hittites, the Egyptians or that of the
West, as yet unexplored by us. With both of the former
countries the Phœnicians traded. The Hittites were their
close neighbors on the north, and were on more or less
friendly terms with them as both were with the neighboring Israelites. We read in Genesis XXIII that Abraham
purchased the cave of Machpelah from Ephron, the
Hittite, in which to bury his wife Sarah. We know that
the great Hittite empire about the time of the Trojan
war and long prior thereto extended through Asia Minor
from Mesopotamia almost to the Mediterranean Sea.
Hittite inscriptions have been found in ancient Lydia,
Caria, Phrygia and Cilicia, countries north of Phœnicia.
So, beyond question the Phœnicians from the earliest
times were familiar with the system of hieroglyphic writing employed by their Hittite neighbors. They likewise
were fully acquainted with the Egyptian system of
hieroglyphic and alphabetic writing. It is known that
foreigners were permitted to settle in Egypt. As early
as the time of Usertesen (2681–2660 B. C.) there were
foreign settlements around the delta of the Nile. Dr.
W. M. Flinders Petrie has identified vases found at
Abydos among the remains of the first Egyptian dynasty,
at a depth corresponding to the strata of the Bronze Age,
with those found in the Palace of Knossos, Crete.
Phœnician wares have been found in many places in the
Delta in the débris and accumulations of very early Egyptian dynasties. It is known that the Phœnicians traded
with Pelusium, Bubastis, Zoan and other places in lower
Egypt, and that they settled in Memphis, having a temple of Astarte there in which they worshiped. He-

rodotus (II, 112) describing this temple says: " Phœnicians from the city of Tyre dwell all around this precinct,
and the whole place is known by the name of the camp
of the Tyrians. Within the enclosure stands a temple
which is called that of Venus the Stranger." Aahmes, first
king of the 18th dynasty, who expelled the Hyksos, speaks
of the " foreign people of the Fenekh." Certainly a very
significant name. It is therefore conclusively evident that
the Phœnicians, centuries before the date of the first
known inscriptions in their alphabet, had come in contact
with the Egyptian hieroglyphic and hieratic writing.

Attempts have been made, notably by a learned French
scholar, M. Emmanuel deRougé, to trace the origin of
the Phœnician characters to the hieratic characters of
the Egyptians. M. deRougé has made an exhaustive
study of the two systems of writing and has elaborated a
theory whereby he traces each one of the Phœnician characters back to an original hieratic sign.[1] It is true that
in a few cases the hieratic sign for a given alphabetic
sound, if somewhat modified, will rather closely resemble
the Phœnician character for this same sound, if it also
is somewhat modified. But on the whole, there are so
few real correspondences, and most of them seem so far
fetched, that we believe the present state of knowledge
of the subject does not warrant an acceptance of de-
Rougé's theory. It must be admitted that the temptation
is very strong to accept a theory so consonant with the
historic development of written characters from primitive pictures as this theory of the descent of the Phœnician alphabet from the hieratic modifications of the Egyp-

[1] " Mémoire sur l'origine Égyptienne de l'alphabet Phénicien." Paris,
1874. Edited by Jacques de Rougé. Also " The Alphabet. An Account
of the Origin and Development of Letters." Dr. Isaac Taylor. London,
1883.

tian hieroglyphs. But we are not yet in command of
sufficient historic facts to say that some of the Phœnician
characters may not have come from Egyptian sources.
Some reliable authorities believe this to be true. But the
general consensus of scholarly judgment to-day, in the
light of recent excavations and discoveries, is opposed
to deRougé's elaborate theory, or any theory looking
to the Egyptian writing as the source of the Phœnician
alphabet or any considerable number of its letters.

The first authentic Phœnician inscription to which a
definite date can be assigned, as we have shown, dates
from the latter part of the 9th century B. C.; but it is
highly probable that this was preceded by several hundred
years of transformation in which the alphabet developed
out of preëxisting forms derived from foreign sources.
Flinders Petrie in his " Tombs of Abydos " publishes a
very elaborate signary of several hundred characters in
use in countries around the Mediterranean Sea from a
period, according to his estimate, as early as 6000 B. C.
He has collected his data from potsherds, vases, engraved
stones and other objects found chiefly in Egyptian tombs
and the débris of ruined cities. His dates are estimated by
the known dates in Egyptian history, and by the vast accumulations of deposits. Prehistoric shards have been un-
earthed in neolithic strata with lines of continuous signs,
evidently writing, painted long — who can say how long
— before the hieroglyphs were invented. The great majority of the signs in this ancient syllabary are quite similar in general appearance to our present alphabetic characters, and familiar Phœnician and proto-Phœnician letters run through the entire series. This seems to open up
to us a new field of inquiry. Can the West after all have
had any influence in the molding of the Phœnician letter
forms, and are we to give credence to the thought that

the spread of the Phœnician alphabet throughout Asia is a return tide of Occidental culture following the recedence of the successive waves of culture from the Orient? These signs, fully three hundred in number, with scores of variants, were in use from Spain to Asia Minor from the very earliest Egyptian dynasties to the 18th dynasty of the Rameses. The characters used in far-away Spain and in Asia Minor were identical. Sixty-eight of these characters are found in the very ancient syllabary of Caria, a country on the Mediterranean sea coast of Asia Minor between Lydia and Lycia.

It is quite a notable fact that in the entire Odyssey there is no mention of the art of writing; but in the Iliad, the older epic, occurs this one reference: When the wife of Proetus wished to have Bellerophon put to death, " she sent him to Lycia as bearer of closed writing to her father-in-law, the king, that he should make him perish." What was this writing that the Lycians used at this period, the mythological age of Greek history, and whence did it come? Let us enter upon the general quest. Among the hundreds of objects found by Dr. Schlieman in ancient Mycenæ in his excavations in 1876 not one bore an inscription. One fragment of a vase handle found at Mycenæ in 1892 had a few strange characters which are not believed to be writing. The classical authors themselves did not agree upon the origin of the letters which they used. While the majority believed that they were invented by the Phœnicians, others entertained a different opinion. Diodorus Siculus, the Greek historian, wrote: " Some pretend that the Syrians were the inventors of letters, and that the Phœnicians learnt from the Syrians and brought the art of writing to Greece, whence the name of Phœnician alphabet. But the Cretans say that the first discovery came not from Phœnicia but from

Crete, and that the Phœnicians only changed the type of the letters, and made the knowledge of them more general among the peoples."

In the island of Crete there appears to have been from an exceedingly early age, long antedating advanced civilization in Greece proper, a highly civilized state in which the art of writing, apparently indigenous in its primitive stages, seems to have been practiced many centuries before its appearance on the mainland. Crete, it will be remembered before the Dorian invasion in the 12th century B. C. scattered its population over the Ægean islands, was the center of a very early Mycenæan civilization. Minos, king of Crete, was the first law giver of Greece. He is noted as the builder of the famous Labyrinth, one of the seven wonders of the world. Arthur J. Evans lately has discovered in the ruins of the Palace of Knossos, Crete, a large number of remarkable inscriptions belonging to this early Minoan period of civilization. This civilization extended over a period of 1200 years or more, beginning about 2500 B. C. and ending with the complete destruction of the Minoan civilization about 1300 B. C. It was thus contemporaneous with the most powerful dynasties in Egypt. Egyptian sculptures of the 12th and 13th dynasties (*circa* 2778 to 2098 B. C.) have been found in the lowest strata of deposits at Knossos. As we would expect, the oldest of these inscriptions are pictographic; while the later are in a linear script which has every appearance of being a phonetic syllabary. The pictographic inscriptions belong to an extremely archaic period, estimated by Mr. Evans to be in the third millennium, B. C. They contain quite a number of elements which are so surprisingly like the Hittite hieroglyphs as to point to a common use if not a common origin of quite a few conventional types of symbols.

Among the many symbols employed in these remarkable inscriptions are the following:[1]

Human body and its parts	11
Arms, implements and instruments	24
Culture objects and symbols	5
Houses and enclosures	6
Utensils, stores and treasures	10
Ships and marine objects	4
Animals and their parts	24
Insects	2
Plants and trees	20
Sky and earth	8
Uncertain objects and simple geometric signs..	21
Total number of signs	135

Many of these pictographic inscriptions are found on engraved gems and on three- and four-sided prismatic seals in carnelian, jasper, steatite and other stones, quantities of which have been found in ancient ossuaries, cemeteries and elsewhere throughout Crete. The belief that the symbols engraved on these seal stones are ideographic, perhaps syllabic, characters, and constitute a written record, becomes a conviction from which there

Fig. 102. Face of four-sided seal found in Crete, engraved with pictographs.

[1] "Scripta Minoa. The Written Documents of Minoan Crete with special Reference to the Archives of Knossos." Arthur J. Evans, 1909.

can be no escape when they once are seriously examined.

Fig. 102 is a characteristic example of these engraved seals. It illustrates one face of a four-sided seal. We see a wolf's head, an arm with a weapon, probably a star and what appears to be two leaves. Many of the signs representing the human body or its parts are in such striking positions, postures and attitudes as to lead to the conviction that they are gesture signs that have been carried over from the primitive sign language into the ideographic and syllabic stage of writing.

Fig. 103 is a four-sided seal in red carnelian, each

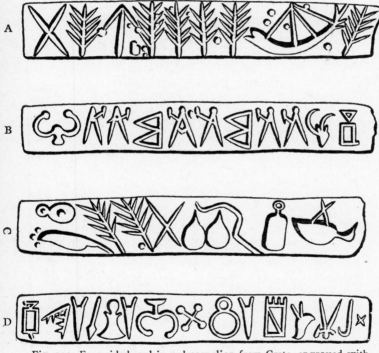

Fig. 103. Four-sided seal in red carnelian from Crete, engraved with pictographs and hieroglyphs.

face bearing an inscription, as shown in the illustration. One sees depicted plants, a boat, human beings, animals' heads, utensils and geometric forms. Some of the latter symbols are almost perfect counterparts of the linear Babylonian signs.

We give in Fig. 104 one more of these Cretan seals. It is one face of a three-sided seal in carnelian. The en-

Fig. 104. Three-sided carnelian seal engraved with various Cretan pictographs and symbols.

graved pictographs and symbols are decidedly reminiscent of the Hittite symbols. The double-headed battle ax on the left is an oft-recurring symbol in these Cretan pictographs. The reader who is desirous of learning more about this earliest phase of Cretan writing may consult " Cretan Pictographs and Pre-Phœnician Script," in which Mr. Evans has analyzed over a hundred of these pictographic symbols and shown the connection of many of them with the ancient Ægean signary and with the Phœnician alphabet.

There was discovered in 1908 by Dr. Luigini Pernier at Phaestos, at the other end of the island from Knossos, one of the most remarkable tablets yet found in the pre-historic débris of Crete. It is a circular disk of clay covered on both sides with hieroglyphics, chiefly picto-graphs (Fig. 105). The hieroglyphs were most cleverly impressed on the clay with stamps, the same stamp being used for each similar hieroglyph. The characters follow

Fig. 105. Disc of clay with hieroglyphs impressed from stamps. Found at Phaestos, Crete. Face A.

each other in a spiral band divided into sections or registers. If what appears to be the general rule in the reading of hieroglyphs holds good in this case, the reading should be from the periphery, where the four little circles are drawn on the register line, leftward into the facing heads and figures and winding around spirally until the center is reached. The tablet is believed to be purely exotic; as it seems to have no connection with the Cretan pictographs. But it is a significant phase of this epoch of evolution in writing, and throws an interesting side light upon the Cretan hieroglyphs. The figures and symbols

are non-Cretan, although some of the signs remotely resemble those used by the Minoans in Crete. The characters throughout decidedly resemble Hittite art. In
many ways the various figures and signs show a close relationship with the work of the ancient inhabitants of
Asia Minor. It is believed that the tablet may have come
from Lycia. The inscription like the Hittite and Cretan
hieroglyphics has not yet been translated.

The tablets in linear script, of which many hundreds

Fig. 106. Examples of Cretan linear script of A. J. Evans' Class A, found
    in the villa Hagia Triada, near Phaestos, Crete. Probable date, 1800
    B. C.

have been found, are of two kinds; the older, which Mr.
Evans calls Class A, consisting of highly conventionalized
forms, and Class B, a later geometric script. Two examples of the old script selected from 150 inscribed clay
tablets found in the villa of Hagia Triada, near Phaestos,
are illustrated in Fig. 106. The probable date of these
older tablet inscriptions is given by Dr. Evans as covering
the period 1800–1600 B. C.; a period from 700 to 900
years earlier than the oldest known Phœnician writing.

The later form of tablet inscriptions, which date from

about 1600 to 1300 B. C., while containing many elements of the earlier style is decidedly alphabetic in character and has, as Dr. Evans says, "a European aspect."
Many of the forms in the older script which were pictographic in character have been abandoned, leaving the
later signary almost devoid of any complex signs reminis-

Fig. 107. Geometric linear script from Knossos, illustration of A. J. Evans'
Class B inscriptions from Crete. Probable date, 1600 to 1300 B. C.

cent of the earlier pictographic or hieroglyphic stage.
Fig. 107 is a typical example of this perfected type of
the Cretan linear script. We detect in this tablet inscription from Knossos not a few forms quite similar
to our own alphabetic characters: **M H F S W** and a suspicion of others. Many engraved whorls, belonging to
this early Minoan period of civilization, used in weaving
or possibly for adornment, also have been found in
Knossos and elsewhere in Crete. One of them is illustrated in Fig. 108. It is most obvious that the markings

are not mere decoration. They are too irregular. There is no rhythm nor decorative sequence. When these Greek Minoans attempted the art of decoration, they were eminently successful. The engraving on this whorl evidently is writing. Of the six characters, five correspond with our own Roman letters. Yet this whorl was found among the débris of a primitive Greek civilization some seven centuries earlier than the earliest known historic, Phœnician inscription. It has been found that out of twenty-one signs appearing on different objects discovered at Knossos, ten are almost identical with the shapes of the later Greek letters.

Fig. 108. Inscribed whorl from Crete, with pre-Phœnician alphabetic characters.

This can hardly be accidental and undoubtedly shows a common source of influence.

These tablet inscriptions from the Palace of Knossos reveal to us the fact that 1000 years before any written record appeared in Greece, the Cretans had developed a syllabary which had progressed through every stage of evolution from the early pictographs to a highly conventionalized script. There may be much significance in the fact that this writing is from left to right in the European method, as distinguished from the reverse method of the Phœnicians. This can be verified by noting in Fig. 107 that every line of writing ends on the right with a vertical separating line, which throughout seems to be used to separate the words. However, where there are two or more lines of consecutive writing, the reading is boustrophedon as in the earliest Greek inscriptions. In the matter of the separation of words it will be remembered that in the Moabite inscription (Fig. 95) the words are separated by dots and the sentences by vertical lines.

When we come to compare the twenty-two letters of

the Phœnician alphabet, as found on the Moabite Stone, with the more numerous characters of the later form of Cretan linear script, there is a close resemblance in three-fourths of the letters of the former alphabet. This is a fact of the highest importance, sufficient to show a very close historic relationship the one with the other. Whether the respective characters between which these many resemblances may be noted in these two systems of writing had corresponding phonetic values, it is impossible to say. No Cretan inscription has yet been translated. We now seem to be face to face with an important problem. Were these independent systems of writing, or was one developed out of or influenced by the other, and if so which? The questions cannot be answered at once, and possibly the complete unraveling of the mystery may ever elude us, and the problem remain unsolved. At least much more knowledge must be forthcoming of the Cretan syllabary and language and that of the kindred syllabaries of the Mediterranean and of Asia-Minor before a definite answer can be expected. But encouraging progress in archæological research constantly is being made, and the excavation of ancient sites, of late prosecuted with such scholarly enterprise, daily is bringing to us more light on the subject, and heartens us in the hope of ultimate success in our quest.

Crete is not the only island in the Ægean where evidences of this early form of Mycenæan culture have been discovered. In the island of Cyprus a local variant of the ancient Mediterranean syllabary was in use and lingered late into the Greek period. It became very much transformed, losing much of the archaic form of the Cretan script and taking on a local phase somewhat different from the alphabets on the mainland of Asia Minor. Louis P. Di Cesnola, who spent a number of years in the island of Cyprus exploring and excavating the sites of ancient cities, brought to light an extraordinary amount of art objects. Among them are many inscriptions in the Cypriote signary, a syllabic script based on this very ancient Ægean signary, elsewhere abandoned but here retained until the middle of the 6th century B. C. It is significant that the reading of all these inscriptions, for they have been translated chiefly through the scholarship of George Smith, is from right to left, according to the Oriental method. Perhaps we should expect this from the geographical location of Cyprus; yet the language is a dialect of the Greek, very closely resembling the parent tongue.

The following is the reproduction of an inscription on a stone implement in the immense Cesnola collection of objects from Cyprus in the Metropolitan Art Museum in New York City:

Reading from right to left the syllables run: *e-ro-se-te-ke-to-a-po-lo-ni.* In Greek this would read:

'Ήρως ''ἔθηκε 'Από(λ)λωνι

" Heros offered it to Apollo."

Fig. 109 is an inscription somewhat rudely carved on

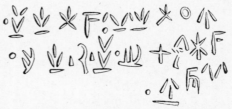

Fig. 109. Cypriote inscription from Golgoi. From the Cesnola collection, Metropolitan Museum of Art, New York City.

calcareous stone with figures in relief, found at Golgoi.

Reading these lines from right to left the syllabic values of the signs are as follows:—

> *Ti-ia-i-te-mi-to-i-te-o*
> *To-a-po-lo-no-o-ne-te-ke*
> *u-tu-ka*

The translation of this into the Greek that these Cyprians probably spoke shows the evident inadequacy of this syllabary for their language:

> Διαίθεμι[s] τῶι θεῶ
> το ᾿Από[λ]λωνι ὀνέθηκέ
> ὐ ι[ν]ι[ν] τυχα

> " Diyaithemis offered me to the god Apollo
>   in good fortune."

Fig. 110 is an inscription found by Cesnola at Paphos

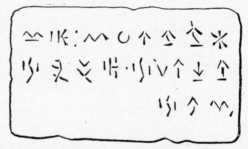

Fig. 110. Cypriote inscription found at Paphos, Cyprus. From the Cesnola collection, Metropolitan Museum of Art, New York City.

in Cyprus. It reads from right to left, like the former inscriptions, as indicated by the ending of the final line. Prof. Sayce interprets this inscription as follows:—

> *Mi-e-u-ya-ti-ka-si-a*
> *ne-ke-pi-e-ne-sa-ti-te-ka*
>   *ne-vo-u*

In Greek this would be:

Ἀσικαθίγαυ ἠμι κατέθισαν ἐρὶ κενευρόν.

"I am Asikathiyas. They set (me) up
over (this) Cenotaph."

We give in the following example one of the bilingual
inscriptions that have helped in the translation of the
Cypriote syllabary. It is from Golgoi.

In English this reads: " Karux am I."

The four inscriptions which we have shown are characteristic examples of Cypriote writing, and give us a
very good idea of the general character of the signs employed. There are some fifty-two or more characters in
this syllabary,[1] all linear like those shown, most of which
stand for phonetic syllables; — as *ta-te-ti-to-tu* — all
shown in our inscriptions — *pa, pe, pi, po, pu*, and so on.
It will thus be seen that the system had not evolved to
the final stage of an alphabet. The majority of the signs
represented compound syllabic sounds, which had not advanced to the full development of alphabetic analysis.
This achievement remained for other nations to work
out. There is not a vestige of pictography in any of these
Cypriote characters. The individual signs are reduced to

[1] Dr. Hermann Collitz in "Sammlung der griechischen Dialekt-In-
schriften" gives a chart of several hundred variants of this syllabary
taken from inscribed fragments found at Golgoi, Salamis, Idalion, Arsinœ
and other localities. Prof. Dr. Wilhelm Larfield in "Handbuch der
griechischen Epigraphik" also illustrates this signary, giving scores of
variants of the fifty-two phonetic syllables constituting the syllabary.

a few geometric lines, generally upright and symmetrical in arrangement, and, with very few exceptions, without outline or closed lines.

The question forces itself upon us: Whence comes this Cypriote syllabary? Authorities disagree in their theories regarding its origin. Practically all archæologists believe that the characters are the survivors of the very ancient and much more extensive syllabary disseminated by the spread of Mycenæan culture around the Mediterranean basin. It appears that throughout Asia Minor in the closing years of the second millennium B. C., an Ægean syllabary very similar to the Cypriote was in extensive use over a very wide territory. Inscriptions in this signary, very fragmentary in their nature, have been found in Troy and Hissarlick, the latter city being known to have been under Mycenæan culture. A very similar syllabary also was in use in Cilicia, Caria, Pamphylia, Lycia, and probably in Lydia. This area constitutes the fringe of countries on the Mediterranean littoral in Asia Minor settled by the Greeks and kindred peoples contemporaneous with the closing period of the Hittite civilization, which flourished in the immediate hinterland eastward from Cappadocia and Phrygia. Inscriptions in this syllabary also have been found as far east as Cappadocia. The coast lands mentioned were under Ægean influence for untold centuries before the Trojan war, the culture undoubtedly extending as far south as southern Canaan. Of late considerable credence has been given to the belief that the Philistines, living along the shore of the Mediterranean immediately south of Phœnicia about the close of the 13th century B. C., were Cretans, who after the destruction of the Mycenæan civilization incident to the Dorian invasion of the

Peloponnesus, were driven across the Ægean and took refuge in the coast lands of Palestine.

Some authorities trace the source of the signs in the Cypriote syllabary to the later, more cursive and simpler, variety of the Hittite hieroglyphs, as found in the bowl from Babylon. There are undoubted resemblances; but they are very few in number, and most archæologists seem inclined to treat as negligible any Hittite influence upon the Mediterranean syllabary. If there were transitional syllabaries through which the Hittite symbols were transformed and transmitted to the Phœnicians and other Mediterranean and Ægean peoples, traces of them have not yet come to light. While we must admit the wide influence of the great Hittite nation upon its neighbors, we must remember that the Ægean civilization had practical supremacy around the Mediterranean shores of Asia Minor for many centuries. Only in the neighborhood of Smyrna do the Hittites appear to have penetrated to the coast lands.

Now, on the other hand, we find in the island of Crete an indigenous system of writing developing through ages of national growth from a purely pictographic method of writing to a highly developed geometric script, which doubtless will prove to be a phonetic syllabary when some day the inevitable bilingual inscription will be discovered, which ancient scholars always have considerately prepared for us. In Cyprus, only fifty or sixty miles opposite the coast of Phœnicia, was employed for many centuries — as we have learned — a linear script of fifty-two characters, thirty-three of which closely resemble the characters in the much more ancient Minoan linear script of Crete. Now it is known that the Minoan Cretans had colonies in Syria and Asia Minor,— at

Miletus, Erythræ and in Lycia. Cyprus is but a stepping stone from the West to the East, and could have had its share in the early spread of Ægean culture to the neighboring mainland. It also could have assisted in any return tide of Phœnician culture bringing in later years an improved script to the mainland of Greece.

Flinders Petrie makes short work of the " Phœnician Theory." But it is unnecessary. The Phœnicians were a link in the chain, and an important one. Petrie has opened up to us by his wonderful discoveries in prehistoric Egypt a new chapter in European epigraphy; as Evans has done in a similar way in Crete. There is this difference, however: the Cretan linear script appears to be the outgrowth of an early, indigenous hieroglyphic system of writing; while the signary discovered by Petrie in Egypt, which he connects with that used in Spain, Caria and other places around the Mediterranean basin, preceded ideography or hieroglyphics. It arose in the use of property marks, numerical signs and manufacturers' memoranda on pottery and other wares exported in trade. In his book published in 1912, " The Formation of the Alphabet," Petrie gives several charts in which he shows in parallel the many hundreds of different signs in the " Mediterranean Signary "— which he classifies as one — from Egypt, Crete, Cyprus, Caria, Lydia, Lycia, Spain and other countries, and compares them with the alphabetic signs in use in Phœnicia, Thera, Melos, Athens, Etruria and Rome. Summing up the situation he concludes that " a wide body of signs had been gradually brought into use in primitive times for various purposes. These were interchanged by trade, and spread from land to land . . . until a couple of dozen signs triumphed and became common property to a group of trading communities, while the local survivals of other

forms were gradually extinguished in isolated seclusion."
He believes that the Phœnicians, trading with the Carians, not very distant neighbors, selected from the common syllabary used by the Carians and the Lycians, still
nearer neighbors on the north, the twenty-two characters
which they used for their alphabetic writing. In a letter
to Edward Clodd, reproduced in this author's admirable
book " The Story of the Alphabet," Prof. Petrie writes:
" A great signary (not hieroglyphic, but geometric, in
appearance, if not in origin) was in use all over the
Mediterranean 5000 B. C. It is actually found in Egypt
at that period, and was split in two, Western and Eastern, by the cross flux of hieroglyphic systems in Egypt
and among the Hittites. This linear signary was developed variously, but retained much in common in different
countries. It was first systematized by the numerical
values assigned to it by Phœnician traders, who carried
it into Greece, whereby the Greek signary was delimited
into an alphabet. But the fuller form of the signary
survived in Karia with thirty-six signs, and seven more
in Iberia, thus giving values to forty-three. This connection of the Iberian with the Karian is striking; so is that
of the Egyptian with the West rather than with the East.
Signs found in Egypt have thirteen in common with
the early Arabian, fifteen in common with Phœnician,
and thirty-three in common with Karian and Kelt-
Iberian. This stamps the Egyptian signary of the twelfth
and eighteenth dynasties as closely linked with the other
Mediterranean systems." Again Prof. Petrie says:—
" We stand therefore now in an entirely new position as
to the sources of the alphabet, and we see them to be
about thrice as old as had been supposed. That the
signs were used for written communications of spelled-
out words in the early stages, or as an alphabet, is far

from probable. It was a body of signs, with more or less generally understood meanings; and the change of attributing a single letter value to each, and only using signs for sounds to build into words, is apparently a relatively late outcome of the systematizing due to Phœnician commerce." (*Journal,* Anthropological Institute, Aug.–Nov., 1899, p. 205.)

It is a remarkable fact that in Greece proper hardly a trace of the Cretan or of the Ægean syllabary has been found. In three or four localities have been discovered very short inscriptions of a few characters each somewhat resembling the old Minoan script; but they are very fragmentary and inconclusive. Would not this fact alone seem to prove that the Greeks did not themselves develop their alphabet out of the Minoan or any other syllabary? In point of fact it is believed that the Minoan civilization was destroyed some time before the Greeks began to evolve their alphabet. Is there then any historical or archæological fact that seriously challenges the old Greek legend in regard to the dissemination in Greece of the Phœnician alphabet? We believe there is not. Prof. William N. Bates, of the University of Pennsylvania, in a lecture on the " Origin of the Greek Alphabet," reproduced in *Old Penn,* March, 1916, concludes his scholarly treatment of the subject by saying: " So much, I think, we may regard as sure, that the Greek alphabet originated in Crete. Furthermore, in the light of our present evidence, it seems likely, though it is not yet proved, that the Phœnicians simplified the characters which they got from Crete, and made the alphabet better known."

While there are only the scantiest remains of the old Ægean and Mediterranean syllabary in Greece, there are survivals in the local alphabets of certain Greek states of some of the old signs. Nearly every one of the five supplemental Greek letters, Υ Φ Χ Ψ Ω, can be found in the ancient syllabary, as well as several strange signs in the alphabets of Corinth, Delos, Argos, Melos and other Greek cities.

In Asia Minor, prior to the development of the Greek Ionian alphabet, the writing in the coast lands by every

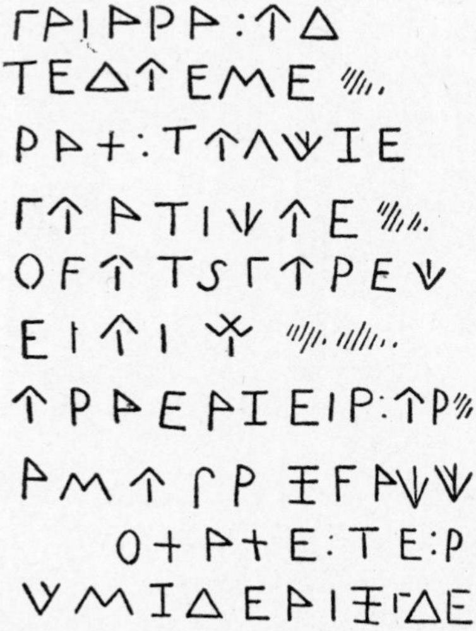

Fig. 111. Lycian inscription on a sarcophagus found at Xanthus.

historical evidence was with the characters of this ancient syllabary; but later as the Phœnician letters extended their boundaries of use they were in part adopted into the alphabets of these countries. Gradually the newer characters won supremacy and the ancient forms became obsolescent or were retained — a few of them — as the supplementary Greek letters, not borrowed from the Phœnicians but developed by the Greeks themselves, being enchoric in their early writing. Let us examine an inscription in the Lycian characters and see what the "closed writing" resembled that Bellerophon bore to Iobates, king of Lycia, that was fraught with so much fatefulness to the unhappy bearer. The inscription shown in Fig. 111, taken from "An Account of Discoveries in Lycia," by Charles Fellows, was found carved on a beautiful sarcophagus at Xanthus. It is a mixture of Greek and non-Greek characters, the latter being the last survivors of the old Mediterranean or Ægean syl-

Fig. 112. Lydian inscription from a fragment of marble found at Sardis.

labary, which, as we have said, were retained so much longer and more completely in the somewhat nearby island of Cyprus. Fourteen of the characters are similar to the Greek letters while eight are non-Grecian, being of the old syllabary.

In the neighboring country of Lydia in very early historic times an alphabet somewhat similar to that used by the Lycians was in vogue. There was the same general mixture of Greek letters and the characters of the ancient syllabary surviving in the written language, but eventually destined to become obsolete. Fig. 112 is a fragment of an inscription in Lydian writing which was found at Sardis carved on a slab of marble. The non-Grecian character of the letters seems slightly more marked than in the former, Lycian, example. The height of the letters and the strange stem to the W-like character are unusual features, but are characteristic of both Lycian and Lydian writing. On the whole the latter alphabet seems to belong to a somewhat later date than the former. Fig. 113 is an extensive inscription carved on the entrance door to a tomb in a ravine opposite the recently excavated Acropolis of Sardis. It is from

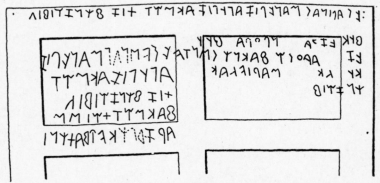

Fig. 113. Lydian inscription carved on the door to a tomb near the Acropolis in Sardis.

"Lydian Inscriptions from Sardis," by Albert Thumb (*Am. Journal of Archæology,* Vol. XV, 1911). The inscription was copied by Wm. H. Buckler and sent to Prof. Thumb, who has transliterated it. The inscription is cut on a block of limestone shaped like a paneled door, which seals the entrance to the tomb. The Greek letters in this alphabet so much resemble the corresponding letters of the Etruscan alphabet, shown in Fig. 140, that the belief is strong that the Etruscans either came from Lydia or that the two alphabets had a common origin. It may have been brought with them at the time of their migration into Italy late in the second millennium before Christ.

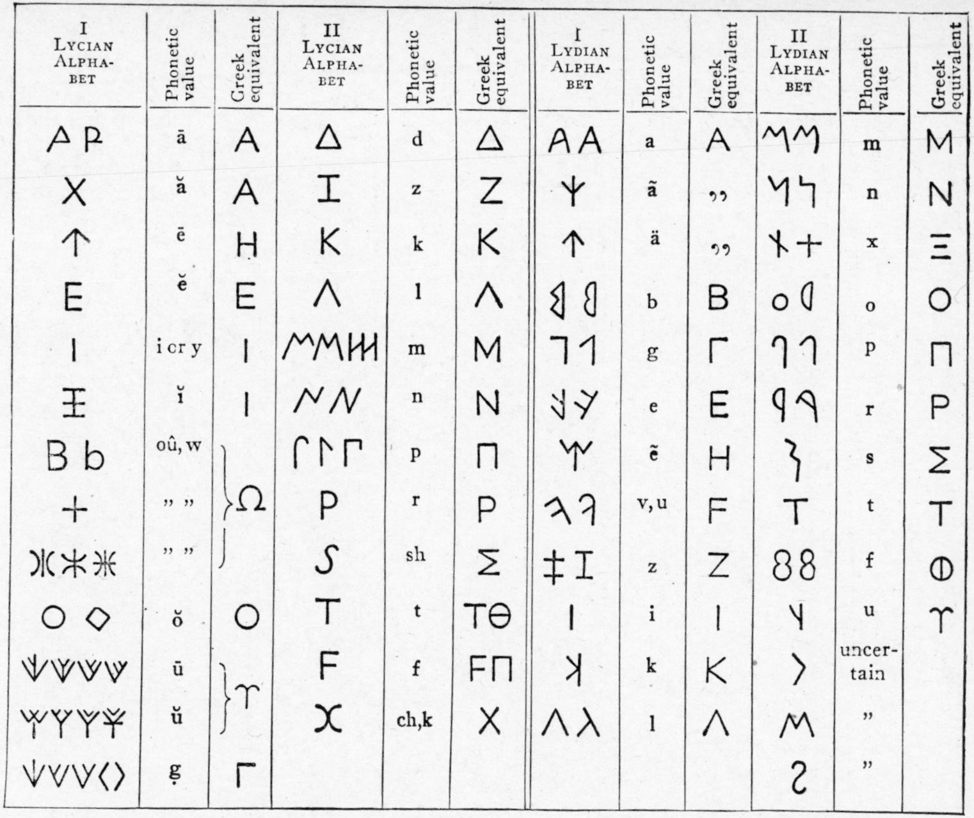

Fig. 114. Lycian and Lydian alphabets with phonetic values and Greek equivalents.

In Fig. 114 will be found the Lycian and Lydian alphabets, with their Greek equivalents. The former has
been completely reëstablished for some time past, but the
latter alphabet only lately has been restored, chiefly
through the labors of Prof. Thumb. The reader easily
will recognize the less simplified and more elaborate characters of the ancient syllabary, and note the large number of variants for the same phonetic value which were
in use even in one country. Space did not permit us to
show more of these variants, their number is so large.

CHAPTER XII

THE GREEK ALPHABET

EASTERN civilization and culture, about the closing centuries of the second pre-Christian millennium, began to spread into Europe by the maritime trade routes from the eastern shores of the Mediterranean Sea to the Ægean islands, and later to the mainland of Greece. The hardy Phœnician navigators not only traded at ports along the entire shores of the Mediterranean, but had established colonies in Melos, Rhodes and other Ægean islands as early as the 13th century before Christ. They carried with them their wonderful alphabet as a necessary part of their civilization, using it in conjunction with their trading enterprises and imparting it to the Hellenic people among whom they sojourned. No tradition seems ever more thoroughly substantiated, both by internal evidence and external fact, than that recorded by the Greek authors that the alphabet used in Hellas came from the Phœnicians. The classic authors differed in their opinions as to the origin of the Phœnician letters. Herodotus, the Greek, and Pliny, the Roman, believed that the Phœnicians invented the letters; while Brosius attributed them to the Babylonians and Tacitus to the Egyptians. But practically all the world now believes that it was the Phœnicians who introduced the letters into Greece proper. The Greeks themselves in their language called their letters: φοινικια γραμματα, " Phœnician letters."

If then the facts stated by Herodotus in his history be true, that " the Phœnicians introduced writing into

Greece, and that at first the Greeks shaped their letters exactly like the Phœnician letters," we naturally would expect to find in those localities where it is known that Phœnician colonists first settled evidences of the oldest form of the Greek alphabet and of types more closely resembling the Phœnician than elsewhere. The facts fully corroborate this assumption and abundantly confirm the opinion prevailing among classic writers in regard to the introduction of the alphabet into Greece. Herodotus, who speaks of " Cadmus, the Trojan, and the followers whom he brought from Phœnicia into the country which is now called Bœotia," says: " for Cadmus when he was sailing in search of Europé made a landing in this island (Thera); and . . . left there a number of Phœnicians " (Herodotus III, 147). So we have it on the authority of this most famous Greek historian that the Phœnicians first settled in Thera and Bœotia. There also were settlements of these enterprising colonists at Corinth, Thasos, Melos, Samothrace and other places along the Grecian littoral. Greek tradition refers to this colonization as having taken place some time in the 12th century B. C., or about two hundred years before the Trojan war. We will not consume time in discussing the authenticity of the Cadmean legend. It undoubtedly was a semimythological treatment of a race movement; the immemorial quest of the West on the part of the people of the East. That Cadmus means " Man of the East," and that the romance of the conquest of Europa — for romance it partly is though founded on historical fact — symbolizes the spirit of western emigration, does no violence to but rather confirms the early tradition in regard to the westward spread of eastern culture and particularly the introduction of the Phœnician letters into Greece.

In the ancient cemeteries of Thera — Santorin as it
is now called — have been discovered a number of inscriptions in the most archaic form of Greek epigraphy.
The alphabet employed in these early inscriptions is almost pure Phœnician, the letters differing but little from
their eastern prototypes. The oldest inscriptions were
written in the ordinary Semitic manner from right to left.
Later they were written boustrophedon, back and forth
like the Hittite writing, and finally, concurrent with the
progressive Hellenizing of the letters, they assumed the
left-to-right reading universally maintained thereafter
in European writing. Four of these extremely archaic
inscriptions from the buried cemeteries of Thera are
shown in Fig. 115.

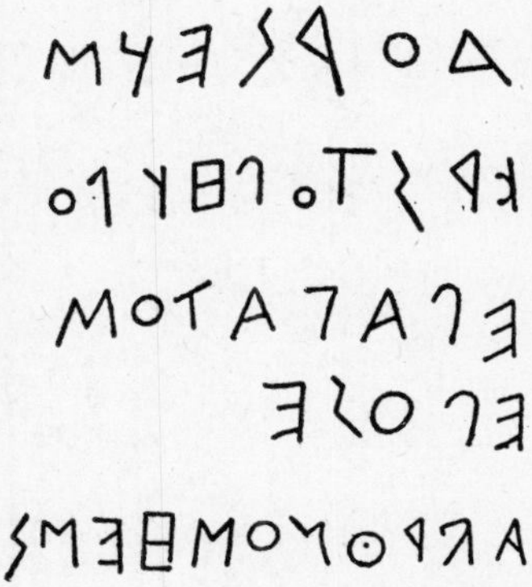

1. ΔΟΡΙΕΥΣ (Δυριεύς).

2. ΚΡΙΤΟΠΗΥΛΟ (Κριτοθύλου).

3. ΕΠΑΓΑΤΟΣ ΕΠΟΙΕ ('Επάγ-
ατος 'εποίει).

4. ΑΠΡΩΝΟΣΗΕΜΙ ("Απρωνός
'ημι).

Fig. 115. Earliest Greek writing from Thera.

The Phœnician parentage of these letters is stamped
in every lineage. They are distinctly more Phœnician
than Greek; yet they are the characters employed by a
purely Greek people that ultimately developed into the
Greek alphabet of the classic age. The proper transliteration into classic (Attic) Greek is given on the right that
the reader readily may compare the two alphabets. The

use of ΠΗ instead of the character ⊙ indicates the extremely early age of these inscriptions, which is believed to be for the oldest Greek inscriptions, reading from right to left like those reproduced, some time about the 9th or 8th century B. C. The strange character employed for **P** in the fourth example will be noted. It was distinctly local and did not appear again in any Greek alphabet. The closed **H** before **E** also is to be noted as indicating that *eta* had not yet been evolved.

Strange as it may seem to us to-day many queer experiments were tried by the early Greek scribes before they finally adopted the consecutive left-to-right writing of each succeeding line. A strong predilection was manifest for continuous and uninterrupted writing. This was carried out in a variety of ways before the writing became standardized. Sometimes the reading was boustrophedon with the letters reversed in the alternate lines, sometimes the boustrophedon lines were written in inverted characters, and sometimes the writing proceeded spirally from the middle, at times rightward, again leftward.

Fig. 116 is an extremely archaic inscription from Thera, reading from left to right throughout, but arranged spirally; the reading beginning on the left at the middle and proceeding outward, the letters constantly being kept upright to the bottom line as one reads, through a revolution and a half. The letters, therefore, always are in the same relative position to the reader if he faces inward as he reads. Again the unmistakable Phœnician characteristics of the letters are manifest, though some are beginning to change their form. We will simply comment in passing on the two very similar **M**-like characters. One — the third and ninth in the inscription — closely resembles the Phœnician and has the value of **M**, the other — the fifth and eighth in the inscription — has the value of **S**. Later on we will again refer to these two letters and trace their descent.

Fig. 116. Early Greek boustrophedon writing from Thera.

The first inscription shown in Fig. 117 also is from Thera and belongs to the middle transitional period, possibly the 8th or 7th century B. C. The fragment is written boustrophedon in the first and second lines; but the growing tendency toward left-to-right writing has caused the scribe to repeat the third line in this mode, returning to boustrophedon in the fourth line; but ending the line by turning the letters about to agree with those in the even lines. This position of the letters was finally adopted when left-to-right writing became the custom. The letters still quite closely resemble the Phœnician, more especially in the lines reading from right to left, in which the letters are reversed, as was customary. The Greek transliteration given on the right will assist the reader, if he will consult Fig. 131 in making comparisons.

Below the boustrophedon example are shown two other inscriptions from Thera in left-to-right reading, though

1.

ΠΕΚΜΑΝΩΡ
ΑΡΚΗΑΓΕΤΑΣ
ΠΡΟΚΛΕΣ
ΚΛΕΑΓΟΡΑΣ ΠΕΡΑΙΕΥΣ

2.

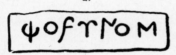

(Q)Ω(F)ΥΝΟΣ

3.

OPΘOKΛΕM   ΟΡΘΟΚΛΗΣ

Fig. 117. Inscriptions from Thera. 1. Early boustrophedon writing.
2 and 3. Later examples.

they may be the even lines of some boustrophedon writing. In the first we find *koppa* (**Q**) and *vau* (**F**) which
were adopted by the Greeks from the Phœnician, but
which early disappeared from the Greek alphabets. The
similarity of the *digamma*, as the character **F** subsequently was called, to our Italic f (*f*) is remarkable.
Doubtless the same carelessness in writing that produced
the present form of the minuscule out of the Roman **F**
existed in the ancient days. An entirely new character, **Y**,
occurs in this inscription, appearing also in the second
character in Fig. 116 in a rudimentary form. This vocal-
ization developed out of *vau;* the consonant constituent
being represented by **F**, while the vowel sound was expressed by the true vowel **U** or **Y**. This was the one con-
crete contribution that these early Greeks made to the

primitive alphabet. The new character took its place as the twentieth letter in the alphabet.

The early Greeks also may be credited with other substantial contributions to the alphabet. At the time when the earliest known Thera inscriptions were written there already had been evolved out of the Phœnician characters five true vowels: *alpha, epsilon, iota, omicron* and *upsilon* — as just explained,— respectively from *aleph, he, yod, ayin* and *vau.* The first four were not additions to the borrowed alphabet, but a development of obscure breaths into definite vowel sounds represented by a slight modification of the primitive characters. During the entire period of the Thera inscriptions other changes and additions were effected. In the earlier inscriptions the closed **H** was simply an aspirate as in the Phœnician (*cheth*). Later it developed into the long e (*eta*). Somewhat subsequent to this the character lost the upper and lower bars and thenceforth became the **H** of the Greek and Roman alphabets. *Theta* was developed out of *teth.* *Beta* appears in one instance in Thera inscriptions differing from the parent *beth* in this earliest example in having two lobes instead of one, thus establishing its European form.

Up to the end of the 5th century B. C., almost every Hellenic state had its own alphabet. There were at least ten different local alphabets varying somewhat in the characters used or in the shape or proportion of the characters. Among these alphabets were those of the Ægean Islands, Argos, Attica, Corinth, Corcyra, Ionia, Bœotia, Chalcis, Eubœa and Elis. There are to be distinguished among these alphabets two rather distinct types: the Eastern and the Western. The first, the older type, already has been referred to as having been introduced by the Phœnicians — probably Tyrian merchants — into the islands of the Ægean Sea, Ionia, and later into the mainland of Greece itself. The second type of alphabet, probably of a somewhat later period, is thought to have entered Greece by overland routes possibly from Lydian or Aramean sources. To the first class belong the alphabets of the Ægean Islands, Attica, Argos, Ægina, Corinth and her colonies, Syracuse and the Ionic alphabets including those of Miletus and Halicarnassus. To the second class belong the alphabets of Northern Greece and the Peloponnesus,— Eubœa, Chalcis and its colonies, Bœotia, Elis, Locris and other states.

There is on the whole a marked correspondence of form in the majority of cases in the respective letters in all these early Greek alphabets. The earlier types, as we have pointed out, more closely resemble the Phœnician; the later types show modifications tending in the Eastern alphabets toward the later classic Greek and in the Western alphabets toward the Roman letters. *Gamma* and *lambda* are used somewhat interchangeably throughout these early Greek alphabets, and it is not always easy to distinguish between them, as will be noted by referring to the inscriptions thus far examined. However, in the Eastern alphabets the shorter bar of *gamma* tended to favor a horizontal line at the top of the vertical bar, while the two bars of *lambda* progressively became more nearly equal. The Eastern alphabets, with the single exception of those of Attica, employed the Ionic form of *lambda,* Λ, or slight variations of it; while the Western alphabets as a general rule employed the form Ʋ, or variations of it. This became the precursor of our Roman L.

Many examples of the earliest age of Greek writing have been found in Attica. What is considered to be the oldest Attic inscription extant is shown in Fig. 118, taken from a Dipylon vase. The writing is so early and ar-

chaic that the A's, with a single exception, are lying on
their sides, as in the Phœnician. *Omega* is quite small, as
in the parent alphabet, and most of the letters strongly
resemble their ancient prototypes. Another proof of the
antiquity of this inscription is the fact that the direction
of the writing is from right to left, as in the Phœnician
writing. The translation which we append would seem to
indicate that the vase on which this inscription was etched
was a trophy presented to a prize dancer.

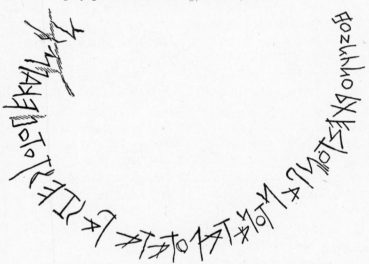

ΌΣ ΝΥΝ ΟΡΧΕΣΤΟΝ ΠΑΝΤΟΝ ΑΤΑΛΟΤΑΤΑ
ΠΑΙΞΕΙ ΤΟΤΟ ΔΕΚΑΝ ΜΙΝ.

"Who now of all dancers most delicately performs.
May he accept this."

Fig. 118. Inscription from a Dipylon vase. Believed to be the oldest known
Greek inscription. Boustrophedon reading. 8th century B.C.

The example given below is from a Panathenaic vase
found among the countless fragments of potsherds that
excavations are continually turning up in that region, so
rich in archæological remains. It dates from a very early

age, as is evidenced by its right-to-left reading; but it probably is not so remote as the Thera inscriptions. It has unmistakable Greek characteristics. There is evidence of the progressive improvement in the shape and uniform size of the letters and a suggestion of the conformity and standardization of form to which the Greek artistic taste ultimately attained. *Omicron,* which always was made very small in the Phœnician and early Greek alphabets, here is made almost uniform in size with its companions. **M** and **N** both have the high-stilted form of the Phœnician, but the first bar is shorter and the angle comes down somewhat nearer the bottom alignment of the letters than in their prototypes. One of the bars of the **M** has been eliminated. The vertical bar of the **E** is less prolonged downward, but the three short bars are practically horizontal as in subsequent alphabets. The **L**, as we already have remarked concerning the early alphabet of Attica, turns up at the bottom as in the Western alphabets. **I** has completed its full transition.

/ΜƎ:ΨΟVΟᎪΨΟƷΨƷΟᎪΨΟΤ

Τῶν Ἀθηνέων ἆθλον εἰμι.

" Of the Athenians a gift am I."

The following inscription, an epitaph from a marble stele, also is from Athens. It is in modified boustrophe-

don, and may be somewhat later than the former inscription, though **E** resembles the Phœnician more closely, and other letters as *gamma, rho* and *pi* depart but little from their archetypes. **D** has lost its Phœnician tail, but has not yet settled down into the horizontal position of the later *delta*. The possible date of these two inscriptions may be some time about the end of the 6th century B. C.

In Fig. 119 will be found the reproduction of an exceedingly archaic example of boustrophedon writing from Attica, in letters of marked Phœnician lineaments. It is written in the more regular form of boustrophedon writing such as that maintained so uniformly throughout the Cretan inscription, to be described. The remoteness of the age of this inscription is attested by the use of the closed **H** before the vowels. The character was still only a breath like its Oriental prototype, *eta* not yet having been evolved. Other Phœnician characteristics are noticeable in **E K M** and **N**.

Fig. 119. Early Greek boustrophedon writing from Attica.

One of the most interesting and remarkable of all the early Greek inscriptions is the very extensive inscription first brought to light by the excavations of Dr. Halbherr at Hagios Deka, Crete, in 1881. Gortyna, as the place was called in ancient times, was one of the three important cities in Crete and was referred to by Homer as " the well-walled." The famous Labyrinth of King Minos was in the immediate vicinity. It was a tradition of classic times, referred to by Homer and mentioned in Plato and

Strabo, that the best laws emanated from Krete, and that Lykurgus, Solon and other Greek savants obtained their laws from this island. Here at Gortyna was discovered a large curving corridor, part of the ruins of a theatre, on the wall of which was carved a series of laws relating to the status of slaves, the rights of widows, heirs at law, children born after divorce, the adoption of children, property rights and many other laws relating to domestic and family relations. The inscription consists of twelve vertical columns, some eight feet in height, eleven of them containing from 50 to 55 lines of writing. The twelfth column contains 30 lines. The reading is boustrophedon, starting on the right at the top and reading leftward in the odd lines, and rightward in the even lines. The letters are carefully reversed in the alternate lines, the same as in the Hittite hieroglyphics. Comparisons with the Phœnician letters, therefore, should be made with the letters in the odd lines. According to Augustus C. Meriam (*American Journal of Archæology,* Vol. I, 1885), the alphabet is the oldest Greek alphabet known, and contains no characters that were not transmitted by the Phœnicians, except *upsilon,* Y. The remoteness of the age of this inscription may therefore be judged when it is known that it had none of the supplemental letters, Φ X Ψ Ω. Mr. Meriam believes this remarkable inscription to be contemporaneous with Solon, who was born in the year 638 B. C.

Fig. 120 is a copy of the first, the right-hand, column of the inscription down to the injured lines near the bottom of the wall, sketched from a cast of the entire inscription in the Metropolitan Art Museum, New York City. There are 55 lines in this first column. Forty-seven of these are here shown, the others being more or less mutilated. Following we give Mr. Meriam's transliteration

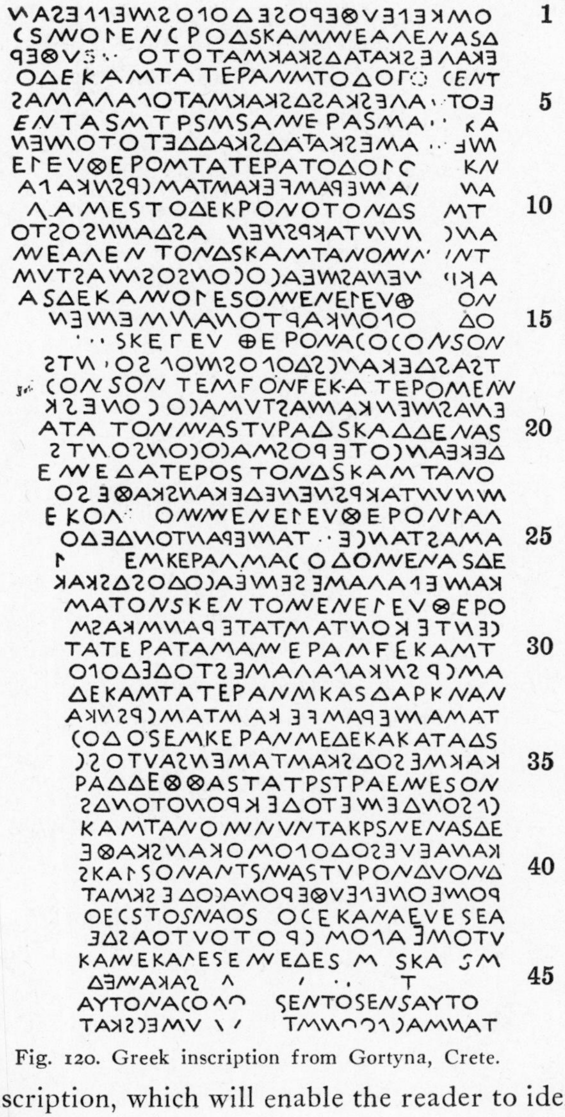

Fig. 120. Greek inscription from Gortyna, Crete.

of the inscription, which will enable the reader to identify the characters:

1. Ὅς κ' ἐλευθέρῳ ἢ δώλῳ μέλλη ἀν
φιμολῆν, πρὸ δίκας μὴ ἄγεν · αἰδ-
έ κ' ἄγῃ, καταδικαξάτω τῶ ἐλευθέρ
ω δέκα στατήρανς, τῶ δώλω πέντ-

5. ε ὅτι ἄγει, καὶ δικαξάτω λαγάσαι
ἐν ταῖς τρισὶ ἀμέραις, αἰ (δέ) κα
μὴ (λαγ)ασῃ, καταδικαδδέτο τῶ μὲν
ἐλευθέρω στατῆρα, τῶ δώλω(δα)ρχν
ἀν τ(ᾶς) ἀμέρας ϝεκαστας, πρίν κα λα

10. γάσῃ · τῶ δὲ χρόνω τὸν δι(κα) στ-
ὰν ὀ(μ)νύντα κρίνεν. αἰ δ'ἀννίοιτο
μὲ ἄγεν, τὸν δικαστὰν ὀμνύντ-
α κρ(ί)νεν, αἰ μὴ ἀποφωνίοι μαῖτυς.
αἰ δέ κα μολῇ ὁ μὲν ἐλεύθ(ερ)ον

15. ὁ δ(ὲ δ)ῶλον, καρτόνανς ἤμεν
(ὅτερο)ί κ' ἐλεύθερον ἀποφωνίωντι. αἰ δέ κ' ανφι δώλῳ μολίωντι
φωνίοντες ϝὸν ϝεκάτερος ἤμεν, αἰ μέν κα μαῖτυς ἀποφωνῇ, κ

20. ατὰ τον μαίτυρα δικάδδεν, αι
δέ κ' ἤ ἀνφοτέροις ἀποφωνίωντι
ἢ μηδ' ἀ τέρῳ, τὸν δικαστὰν ὀ-
μνύντα χρίνεν. ἠ δέ κα νικαθῇ ὁ
ἔχων, (τ)ὸμ μὲν ἐλεύθερον λαγ-

25. άσαι τᾶν πέ(ν)τ' ἀμερᾶν τὸν δέ δῶ
λ(ον) ἐς χέρανς ἀποδόμεν · αἰ δέ
κα μὴ λαγάσῃ ἢ μή ἀποδῶ δικακ
σάτω νικῆν τῶ μὲν ἐλευθέρω
πεντήκοντα στατήρανς καὶ σ

30. τατῆρα τᾶς ἀμέρας ϝεκάστας πρίν κα λαγάσῃ, τῶ δὲ δώλω
δέκα στατήρανς καὶ δαρχνάν
τᾶς ἀμέρας ϝεκάστας πριν κ' ἀ
ποδῶ ἐς χέρανς. ἠ δέ κα καταδι

35. κάξῃ ὁ διχαστάς, ενιαυτῶ π
ράδδεθθαι τὰ τριτρὰ ἢ μεῖον,
πλῖον δὲ μή · τῶ δὲ χρόνω τὸν δι

κασταν ὀμνύντα χρίνεν. αἰ δέ
κα ναεύῃ ὁ δῶλος ὡ κα νικαθῇ

40. ι, καλίων ἀντὶ μαιτύρων δυῶν δ-
ρομέων ελευθέρων ἀποδειξάτ
ω ἐπί τῷ ναῷ ὅπη κα ναεύῃ ἤ α-
ὑτὸς ἤ ἄλος προ τούτω · αἰ δέ
κα μή καλῇ ἤ μή δείξῃ, κατισ

45. (τάτ)ω τὰ ἐ(γραμ)ένα αἰ δέ κα μεδ
αὐτὸν ἀποδῷ εν τῷ ενιαυτῷ
τὰνς ἁπλὸονς τ(ι)μανς ἐπικατ

The transliteration of course is written throughout in classic Greek, in left-to-right reading, and offers some slight difficulty of comparison in the odd lines. As will be observed, the inscription, which was cut in marble, is of most excellent workmanship, the letters being well shaped and regular; the spacing, alignment and every other phase of the lapidary's art being carried out with taste and mechanical accuracy. Archaic as this inscription certainly is in the forms of certain of the letters, hardly at any time in the entire history of Greek sculpture have letters been carved more artistically than by this clever Cretan workman. It is little wonder that the Greeks of Hellas turned to Crete for inspiration not only in civic organization but in art as well.

Let us briefly analyze this early Greek alphabet and see how far in the comparatively short time that the Greeks had been using the Phœnician characters they had departed from the original types. *Alpha* is fully developed and is constant in shape. It is the old Phœnician *aleph* righted and made trim looking. *Beta* does not appear. It is absent in many Greek alphabets. *Gamma* in almost every instance has its two bars equal, resembling the Eastern form of *lambda;* while *lambda* in almost every case follows the Phœnician form of *gimel*. Where it departs from it, it takes the shape of the classic Greek form of *gamma*. *Delta* lacks the elongation of the right hand line of its prototype and has a horizontal instead of a slanting base. *Epsilon* drops the elongation of the side line which becomes vertical, while the three short slanting lines become horizontal. *Vau* seems to have begun in Crete as a modified form of the Phœnician *vau,* but apparently soon developed into the constant form F, which, however, was dropped from the Greek alphabets early in the 7th century B. C. Neither *zeta* nor *eta* appears in the inscription. As to the latter omission it is very unusual, almost all Greek alphabets having this letter. It is only a further evidence of the extremely early age of this inscription; being before *eta* (H) was evolved. Other inscriptions found in Crete have both the closed and the open form of *eta;* the latter being almost identical with the Phœnician *cheth,* from which the character was taken. *Theta* is true to its prototype. *Iota* is represented by a letter almost precisely like our modern S. It is a modification of the very earliest Z-shaped form of *iota* such as we find in the Thera inscriptions, which clearly are simplifications of the Phœnician *yod*. *Kappa* is simply a neater version of its prototype, resembling it in many cases by the long vertical bar and shorter slanting lines. *Lambda* bears little resemblance to the Phœnician. *Mu* and *nu* obviously are simplified variations of their originals. If the reader will make a careful inspection of these two letters wherever they occur in this inscription, he will note a tendency in both occasionally to revert to the ancient types with the long bar for the first stroke of the letter and the four angular lines well up at the top of the bar. *Xi* is missing, *kappa* taking its place. *Omicron* has increased in size, becoming equal to the other letters. *Pi* is strangely corrupted, taking the shape of our letter C. In

almost all other Greek alphabets it is but a slight modification of the Phœnician *pe*. *Koppa* is absent as it is in
many Greek alphabets. Wherever it appears, however,
it closely follows the Semitic original. *Rho* is rounded
as its prototype frequently is in many Phœnician inscriptions. *Sigma* has the shape of a sprawling **M**, so constant
in most early Greek alphabets; though it generally is
placed on its side, when it easily is convertible into our **S**.
Of course it descends directly from *shin*. *Tau,* present in
this and in every other Greek alphabet, has never changed
its primitive shape. It bears little resemblance, however,
to the Phœnician *tau*.

Fig. 121 is an example of the ordinary form of boustrophedon writing in the characters of the Corinthian
alphabet. The writing begins on the right as in most
boustrophedon writing and is read alternately leftward
and rightward in the odd and even lines respectively, the
letters being reversed in the alternate lines. The *digamma,* **F**, still lingers in this alphabet, and attests to the
early age of the inscription. *Iota* is again represented by
the zigzag line, which descends directly from the Phœnician *yod*. Attica very early changed the shape of **I**, and
somewhat later the older form disappeared from the Corinthian alphabet. Both *sigma* and *pi* in the middle line
of our inscription are inverted, as though the scribe were
accustomed to this method. We have found that this custom somewhat prevailed in very early times in Greece, in
letters in the even lines.

The three inscriptions given in Fig. 122 also are in the
Corinthian style of writing. The first one is from a bronze
votive tablet found in Corfu. Its possible date may be
about the end of the 6th century B. C. Being written from
right to left, the letters are reversed like their Phœnician
prototypes. It has the rudiments of the Eastern *lambda;*

the **Z**-shaped *iota;* while for *epsilon* appears an anomaly
in the Corinthian alphabets not met with in any other
Greek alphabet, the use of an angular form of **B**, employed for *beta* in several alphabets of the Western type.
The rounded form of beta employed for **E** will be noted
in the previous inscription. The purely Greek Φ again

Fig. 121. Boustrophedon writing from Corinth.

appears. No discrimination is made in the Corinthian
alphabet between *mu* (M) and *sigma* (Σ), except that in
the first two inscriptions here shown the former letter
still follows, in a modified degree, the high-stepped form
of the Phœnician. *Nu* also has the same characteristic in
both inscriptions. This apparent indiscriminate use of the
characters for M and Σ, almost uniform in the early alphabets of the Eastern type and disappearing only in those of
the Western type, is easily accounted for in the somewhat
similar forms of *mem* and *shin* in the Phœnician alphabet;
the latter character differing from the former only in the
elimination of the long bar. The Ægean Greeks borrowed both characters. Those in Melos and Crete made
little change in the form of M, while those of Thera
dropped one of the five lines. The character *shin* seems
to have been inverted from its earliest use in Greece.

This caused the two characters to look alike. In most cases where these two characters were used, the first bar of M was made long as in the Phœnician to distinguish it from *sigma*. Identification must have been difficult then as it is for us to-day; but the difficulty eventually was solved by turning the latter character over on its side, as was done uniformly in the succeeding alphabets of the Eastern group after the Ægean period.

The second inscription is also from Corinth and appears to be of an age contemporary with the first. In both alphabets **A** still seems experimental, **K** has the long Phœnician bar and the general irregularity and seeming archaism of the writing suggests a date much earlier than actual. When we compare much of the specimens of Greek writing before the 5th century with that of the masterpiece of Gortyna we become convinced that real artistic talent knows no age nor place. The tyro and the genius ever have been contemporary.

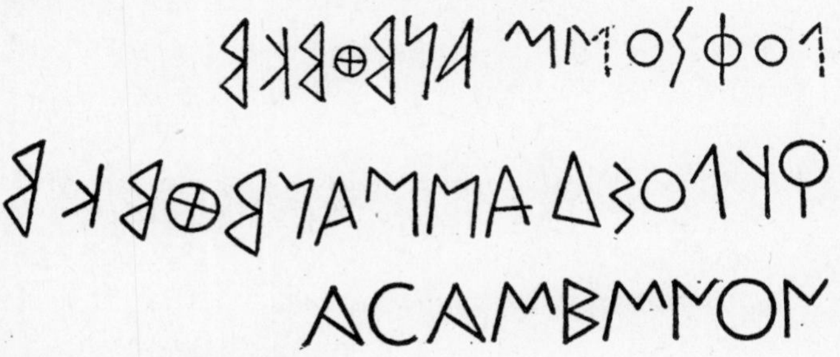

1. ΛΟΦΙΟΣ Μ'ΑΝΕΘΕΚΕ
    " Lophius set me up."

2. Ϙ ΥΛΟΙΔΑΣ Μ'ΑΝΕΘΕΚΕ
    " Cylodias set me up."

3. ΑΓΑΜΕΜΝΟΝ
    " Agamemnon."

Fig. 122. Inscriptions in Corinthian Greek letters.

The third inscription shown in Fig. 122 also is from Corinth. It belongs to the latest pre-Ionic period and may be assigned to the 5th century B. C. It is written from left to right, but in characteristic Corinthian letters in a style so elegant as to stamp the artist as a master. We give beneath these inscriptions their value in classic Greek.

In Fig. 123 will be found a beautiful example of early Greek writing just prior to the classic period when the alphabet had received under the skilled craftmanship of the Ionian Greeks its highest form of graphic development. It is an inscription on a bronze helmet of Hiero I, son of Deinomenes, king of Syracuse, dedicated to the Olympian Zeus, after his victory over the Etruscans at Cumæ, 474 B. C. The inscription is written in a modified form of the old Corinthian alphabet. The earlier form of *epsilon,* illustrated in Fig. 122, so foreign to all the Greek alphabets — doubtless a survival of the old Ægean signary — has been abandoned and the prevailing form, decidedly Phœnician in this example, has been adopted. The closed form of *eta,* peculiar to the earliest Greek alphabets, still is retained, though soon to be replaced by the open **H** used in the Attic and Ionian alphabets. *Iota* appears in its final transformation. *Kappa* retains its Phœnician characteristics in the long vertical bar and short slanting lines. On the other hand, tendencies toward the Western form of alphabets, which eventually developed into the Roman letters, appear in the V-shaped *upsilon* and the tailed *rho,* which seems first to have made its appearance in Greece proper about the middle of the 5th century B. C. The fifth letter in the inscription is not *koppa,* but *omicron;* accented to indicate *omega,* before the Eastern form of *omega* had been adopted.

We now have to speak of the most important branch of the Eastern division of the Greek alphabet: the Ionian

alphabet. This alphabet was developed by the Ionian
Greeks who had settled in western Asia Minor along the
Mediterranean littoral of Lydia, between the rivers Her-
mus and Mæander, about a century before the Trojan
war. Their principal cities were Ephesus and Miletus.
Closely associated with this Ionic civilization was the

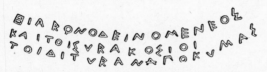

Fig. 123. Inscription on a bronze helmet of Hiero, King of Syracuse,
about 474 B. C. Late Corinthian Greek writing.

Greek city of Halicarnassus somewhat to the south in
Caria, founded by Dorian colonists from the parent country. It is interesting to know that the greatest Greek historian, Herodotus, was born in the latter city. Here
along the coast of Asia Minor, about where Smyrna now
is situated, these highly advanced Greeks developed their
language and literature to a point of commanding superiority, recognized by their kinsman in Greece divided as
they were into so many petty states, each with its own
local alphabet, to be sure not so widely different from
that of their eastern cousins.

In the year 403 B. C., after the close of the Pelopon-
nesian war, the Ionic alphabet was adopted at Athens and
later throughout all Greece; displacing from that time on
all the prevailing local alphabets. This alphabet had been
fully perfected before the 8oth Olympiad (460 B. C.).
An early inscription in this style exists under rather unusual and romantic circumstances. At Abu-Simbel (Ipsambul) in Upper Egypt, on the edge of the Nubian
desert, is the magnificent rock-cut temple of Rameses II,
with its four gigantic statues of this proud king support-

ing the roof. It was constructed while the " Children of Israel " were still under Egyptian bondage. A few years ago while excavations were being made there were discovered on the leg of one of these colossal statues six Phœnician and nineteen Greek inscriptions, nine of them of an early epoch, and three Carian inscriptions. One of the Greek inscriptions, the earliest Greek inscription to which a definite date positively can be assigned, was written by a Greek mercenary in the service of Psammetichus, a king of the 26th Egyptian dynasty. There were two kings by the name of Psammetichus, Psammetichus I, who reigned about 654–617 B. C., and Psammetichus II, whose date is placed at 594–589 B. C. In either case it places the inscription toward the beginning of the 7th century or the close of the 6th century B. C., 800 years after these stupendous monuments had been carved and yet before Athens had risen to power and before the alphabet had been fully perfected in Greece. Incidentally it is a praiseworthy commentary on the state of civilization of the day that mercenaries in a foreign country were able to write at all and so well. The writing of all these Greek inscriptions is so good and uniform as to convince any one that it was no experiment but must have been a wide-spread accomplishment, resulting in a fixed habit through generations of usage. The characters are practically identical in all, showing wide currency of culture, as the signers inform us that they came from widely separated places. They all are written from left to right.

A reproduction of this inscription, taken from the great work of Lepsius: " Denkmaler aus Aegypten," will be found in Fig. 124. The letters in the original were cut two inches high; so there can be little doubt about their shape. Even a casual inspection of the inscription cannot fail to show how closely the letters resemble the Greek

letters of the classic period; so far had the writing of the
Ionian Greeks progressed in the comparatively short time
since they received their letters from the Phœnician traders. In this alphabet the Phœnician vowels or breaths:
aleph, he, vau, cheth, yod and *ayin* (see Fig. 101), have
been amplified into the Greek vowels: A E Y H I O. Besides this development, three new letters were added:
Φ X Ψ. *Omega,* the last of the supplementary letters, is
not present in any of these Greek inscriptions at Abu-
Simbel.

Let us for a moment indulge in a bit of human history
and give the translation of our soldier's inscription. He

Fig. 124. Inscription at Abu-Simbel. Ionic Greek writing of the late 6th
century B. C.

says: "When King Psamatichos came to Elephantina,
those who were with Psamatichos the son of Theokles,
wrote this. They sailed and came above Kerkis as far as
the river permitted. Potasimto led the foreigners and
Amasis the Egyptians. The writer was Archon the son
of Amoibichos and Pelegnos son of Eudamos." There
were two then involved in the writing of this inscription.
If we needed the confirmation of these distinctly Greek
and Egyptian proper names, or the conclusive reference to
the obstruction in the river made by the second or Great
Cataract of the Nile, how invaluable would be the subject
matter of this inscription. But most valuable is it from an
archæological point of view as an authentic example of
early Greek writing of the 7th century; about interme-

diate between the earliest beginnings of writing in the Ægean Islands and the perfected Ionic of the 5th century B. C.

We give in the fragment shown below another example of writing in the Ionic style of epigraphy. The inscription was discovered incised on the chair of a seated statue of Chares, a petty ruler of a fortress near Miletus. It undoubtedly was written prior to the Ionic revolt of 500 B. C., when Miletus was destroyed by the Persians. Its possible date may be between the 58th and the 69th Olympiad (550 to 500 B. C.). Although probably a century later than the Abu-Simbel inscription, it is written boustrophedon. The letters are well shaped, for the most part upright and generally quite uniform in height, though *omicron* still shows a tendency to remain small. A, E and N still retain their slanting lines, being much more pronounced than in the earlier inscription. *Gamma* and *lambda* are quite indistinguishable, as in so many of the early Greek alphabets of the Eastern variety. *Eta* has made its full development from the closed Phœnician form to the open form of **H**. We meet for the first time with the new letter *omega*.

$$\{OX9A\}H\}OIXI\}T\}OI\}\}1\}OI\sim I\}H9AX$$

$$|A\Gamma AI^{''''''''''}\cdots\cdots H\cdots TOA\Gamma O\Gamma\Gamma\Omega NO\{$$

Χάρης εἰμι ὁ κλέσιος τειχιούσης ἀρχὸς
˒αγα(λμ)α τοῦ ᾿Απολλωνος.

"Chares I am, the Clesian; of Teichousa the ruler. A statue of Apollo."

Now let us examine some inscriptions of the Western division of the Greek alphabets. Fig. 125 is a very rare and early example which comes from ancient Eubœa. It is a quaint form of boustrophedon writing somewhat similar to the boustrophedon inscription from Thera, except that the reading proceeds spirally outward, beginning at the right instead of the left end of the middle line, the letters being reversed in the retrograde lines and changed about as soon as the reading becomes left to right. The reading continues rightward along the bottom line, around the opening line, with letters both reversed and inverted, unless one turns as he reads, when the letters become normal. The letters have pronounced Phœnician characteristics, especially **E K N**. On the other hand, the period when the inscription was cut was sufficiently advanced to

βύβων τῆτερῃ χἑιρὶ ὑπὲρ κεφαλὰς ὑπερέβαλε τὸ οὔθορα.

Fig. 125. Greek inscription from Eubœa, in boustrophedon writing.

include in the alphabet the purely Greek supplemental letters: Υ Φ Χ. The latter has an unusually lengthened vertical bar below the angle made by the side lines, which gives it a strange appearance; but it was by no means a peculiarity of Eubœan writing, being found in several other Greek alphabets, but rarely so exaggerated in form. Below the cut is given the classic Greek transliteration of the inscription, both being taken from " An Introduction to Greek Epigraphy," by E. S. Roberts. It is difficult to assign a date for this archaic looking writing. Its somewhat poor craftsmanship might lead us to place it earlier even than the elegant Cretan inscription from Gortyna, which also is boustrophedon, or the scholarly and skillful

Ionian writing from Abu-Simbel in the settled European mode of writing, respectively of the middle and beginning of the 7th century B. C. The probable date, however, of this Eubœan inscription is not earlier than the middle of the 6th century B. C.

We will give three examples of writing from Bœotia, that part of the mainland of Greece which the Cadmean legend relates was first settled by the Phœnicians. The examples that we give, however, are rather late specimens of the art. The following line of writing comes from old

ΑΜΘΑΛΚΕΣ ΣΤΑΣΕΡΙΚΙΤΥΛΟΙΕ ΔΕΡΙΔΕΡΜΥΙ

Tanagra. **E** and **K** still follow very closely the old Phœnician forms. In other respects the letters are quite " modern " and are respectably even and regular.

Fig. 126 is an inscription in the now settled European

Fig. 126. Greek inscription from Bœotia. An example of the Western division of Greek writing.

mode of writing, each line reading from left to right. Again *kappa* retains its Phœnician characteristics while the bars of *epsilon* are only slightly slanted. *Delta* has the upright position assumed by this letter in nearly all of the Western alphabets. *Rho* is tailed, as it was in the majority of these alphabets, while *lambda* and *upsilon* have the Roman form, as in most of the Western alphabets. Although slightly irregular in alignment, the inscription possesses considerable artistic merit, and is an example of the sculptor's art not to be passed over without a measure of praise.

The following inscription, also from Bœotia, is a notable example of advanced writing, and is perhaps one of the very earliest examples of ending the strokes of the letters with serifs, a style of finish so highly perfected in the classic period of sculptured writing. Although the alignment is surprisingly irregular, the shape of the letters is not lacking in elegance and refinement.

KRITONKAI⊗EIOSDOTOSTOI
DITOᴦOREI

One of the most perfectly preserved as it is one of the most beautiful inscriptions in the early form of Greek writing is the so-called Treaty of E'le'ens, a bronze tablet commemorating a treaty between the people of Elis and Heræan, of Arcadia; written about the time of the 50th Olympiad (580 B. C.). It is a defensive and offensive alliance between the people of these two cities, and goes on to say: " If there is need of help, in words or acts, they must be allies the one with the other, for peace as well as for war. If they break the alliance they are to pay a talent of silver to serve Jupiter Olympus whom they have violated," etc. The alphabet in which this inscription (Fig. 127) is written is a variant of the Bœotian style of Greek writing. It retains the oblique forms of **A E F** and **N**; the **E** having the vertical bar projecting below as in the Phœnician. *Omicron* (o) is considerably smaller than the other letters, as in the latter alphabet. Again we find the upright *delta,* as in most of the Western alphabets, and we should particularly note that *gamma* has the angular **C**-form peculiar to many of these alphabets;

both letters being in the transitional stage to our **D** and our **C** and **G** respectively. On the other hand, *lambda* retains the old Eastern form in common with the former Eubœan inscription, in contrast to the **L**-shaped form that distinguishes the Western alphabets in general, though more particularly of the Greek colonies in Italy.

Two remarkable bronze tablets have been found in

Fig. 127. The Treaty of E'le'ens. *Circa* 580 B. C.

Locris, Greece, each inscribed on both sides and each written in letters very similar in form, being one of the variants of the Western division of Greek alphabets. One of the tablets comes from Œantheia, in Ozolian Locris, the other comes from Opuntia in Locris. The alphabets differ only as to *gamma* and *lambda*. The former tablet follows the Eastern variety of these letters, while the latter follows the Western type that eventually influenced the Roman alphabet in its formative stages. The following alphabet has been assembled from the letters of the tablet of the Ozolian Locrians. Although distinctly Phœ-nician in many of the letters, on the whole it more closely resembles the Roman alphabet than it does the Ionian

Greek alphabet so soon to replace the many local variations in use throughout Greece:

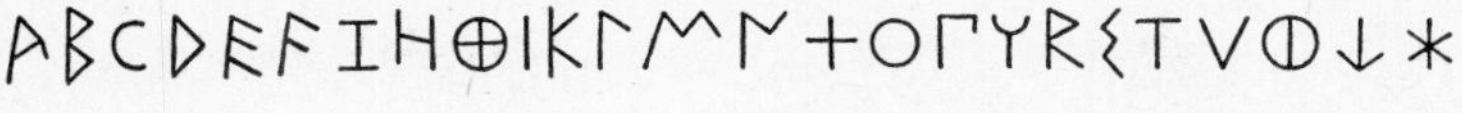

ΑΒΓΔΕFΙΗΘΙΚΓΜΥ+ΟΓΥΡϚΤΥΟ↓✳

The first six letters follow our Roman alphabet true to
order, and, barring angularity of outline, to form also;
and throughout the alphabet the general resemblance to
our letters is astonishingly close for a Greek alphabet.
The letters still are somewhat irregular as to height and
uprightness, so many generations has it taken to confine
the straggling Phœnician letters into regular unit forms of
recognized standard size. The Cretan craftsmen, generations earlier, impelled by the inspiration of genius, easily

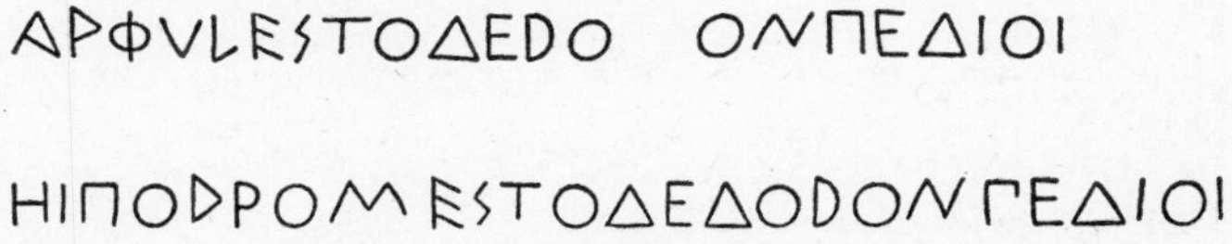

ΑΡΦΥΛΕϚΤΟΔΕΔΟ   ΟΛΠΕΔΙΟΙ

ΗΙΠΟΔΡΟΜ ΕϚΤΟΔΕΔΟΔΟΛ ΓΕΔΙΟΙ

Fig. 128. Inscriptions in the Chalcidian variant of the Greek alphabet.
Middle of the 5th century B. C.

broke away from the shackles of ancient traditions and
employed a system organized and orderly, corresponding
in all essential particulars to our own methods of to-day.
The date of these two tablets is some time immediately
prior to 455 B. C.

We will now give a closing example of writing in letters of the Western alphabets. Fig. 128 shows two inscriptions in the Chalcidian alphabet. They are not from
Chalcis itself, but from one of its extensive colonies. Like
the Locrian alphabet it has both Eastern and Western
characteristics. Both the Eastern and the Western D are
employed in the same line and word. L has the Western
form of this letter while R is without the tail as in the
Eastern alphabets. This is a recession in development,

On the other hand S has but three lines, like the majority of the Western alphabets. Taking the Chalcidian alphabets as a whole, more particularly those of the colonies in Italy and elsewhere, they possess so large a proportion of letters of the Roman type that they have come to be considered the progenitors of the Latin alphabet. This correspondence of type may be noted by consulting the chart, Fig. 131.

In the year 403 B. C., as we already have remarked, the alphabet of the Ionian Greeks was adopted at Athens as the state mode of writing. This was soon succeeded by the

ΒΑΣΙΛΕΥΣΑΛΕΞΑΝΔΡΟΣ
ΑΝΕΘΗΚΕΤΟΝΝΑΟΝ
ΑΘΗΝΑΙΗΙΓΟΛΙΑΔΙ

Fig. 129. Inscription from the Temple of Minerva, Prienne, in Ionia. An example of Ionic Greek writing. 3d century B. C.

formal adoption of this alphabet by the several states throughout Greece. This is the alphabet now known as classic Greek and is the style in which were carved some of the finest monumental inscriptions of classic times. We give two examples of this style, both from Prienne in Ionia. The first one (Fig. 129) is from the Temple of Minerva. It is a most dignified inscription in beautifully carved letters with serifs, the shape and proportion of the letters being most elegant and refined. The second example (Fig. 130) is from the Temple of Athene Polias at Prienne. The inscription concerns a long-standing dispute between the people of Prienne and those of Samos as to the ownership of Karion; the people of Samos contending that the occupation of Karion by the people of Prienne was an encroachment. The inscription dates from

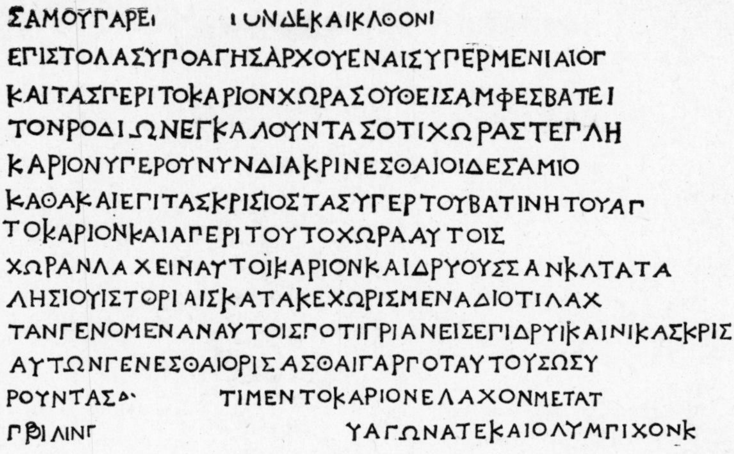

ΣΑΜΟΥΓΑΡΕι   ιΟΝΔΕΚΑΙΚΛΘΟΝΙ
ΕΓΙΣΤΟΛΑΣΥΓΟΑΓΗΣΑΡΧΟΥΕΝΑΙΣΥΓΕΡΜΕΝΙΑΙΟΓ
ΚΑΙΤΑΣΓΕΡΙΤΟΚΑΡΙΟΝΧΩΡΑΣΟΥΘΕΙΣΑΜΦΕΣΒΑΤΕΙ
ΤΟΝΡΟΔΙΩΝΕΓΚΑΛΟΥΝΤΑΣΟΤΙΧΩΡΑΣΤΕΓΛΗ
ΚΑΡΙΟΝΥΓΕΡΟΥΝΥΝΔΙΑΚΡΙΝΕΣΘΑΙΟΙΔΕΣΑΜΙΟ
ΚΑΘΑΚΑΙΕΓΙΤΑΣΚΡΙΣΙΟΣΤΑΣΥΓΕΡΤΟΥΒΑΤΙΝΗΤΟΥΑΓ
ΤΟΚΑΡΙΟΝΚΑΙΑΓΕΡΙΤΟΥΤΟΧΩΡΑΑΥΤΟΙΣ
ΧΩΡΑΝΛΑΧΕΙΝΑΥΤΟΙΚΑΡΙΟΝΚΑΙΔΡΥΟΥΣΣΑΝΚΛΤΑΤΑ
ΛΗΣΙΟΥΙΣΤΟΡΙΑΙΣΚΑΤΑΚΕΧΩΡΙΣΜΕΝΑΔΙΟΤΙΛΑΧ
ΤΑΝΓΕΝΟΜΕΝΑΝΑΥΤΟΙΣΓΟΤΙΓΡΙΑΝΕΙΣΕΓΙΔΡΥΙΚΑΙΝΙΚΑΣΚΡΙΣ
ΑΥΤΩΝΓΕΝΕΣΘΑΙΟΡΙΣΑΣΘΑΙΓΑΡΓΟΤΑΥΤΟΥΣΩΣΥ
ΡΟΥΝΤΑΣΑˑ   ΤΙΜΕΝΤΟΚΑΡΙΟΝΕΛΑΧΟΝΜΕΤΑΤ
ΓΡΙΛΙΝΓ   ΥΑΓΩΝΑΤΕΚΑΙΟΛΥΜΓΙΧΟΝΚ

Fig. 130. Inscription from the Temple of Athene Polias, at Prienne. Late Greek writing. 3rd century B. C.

the 3d century B. C. The writing in these two inscriptions is in the classic style of Greek writing, when every letter had been perfected in shape and size to conform to the Greek sense of artistic elegance and general uniformity of size and alignment, calculated to satisfy the eye and a cultivated taste. Whatever departures from the classic Greek type are noticeable in the second inscription are due to the faults of the local scribe who carved the inscription. We shall later on refer to the excessive height of the letters **K P Y** as influencing the formation of the minuscule at a much later date.

In Fig. 131 is illustrated in tabular form the development of the Greek alphabet from the parent Phœnician to the Attic Greek of the 5th century B. C. The different local alphabets are arranged in approximately historical order under the two principal divisions, Eastern and Western. No dates are certain prior to the Abu-Simbel inscription (*circa* 654–589 B. C.). The Thera inscrip-

Phœnician	Phonetic value	EASTERN						WESTERN					Athens 403 B.C.
		Thera	Crete	Attica	Corinth	Abu-Simbel	Miletus	Eubœa	Chalcis and Colonies	Bœotia	Elis	Locris	
𐤀	a	ΑΑΑ	ΑΑΑ	⋟ΑΑ	ΑΑΑ	ΑΑΡΑ	ΑΑΑ	ΑΑΑ	ΑΑΑΑ	ΑΡΑ	ΑΑΑ	ΑΡΑ	Α
𐤁	b	𐌁Β	𐌁Β	𐌁Β	⊓⊔⊓	ΒΒ	Β	ϷΒ	Β	ϷΒ	Ϸ	Ϸ	Β
𐤂	g,c	⌐ΓΓ	⌐ΓΛ	ΛΛ	⟨⟩C	ΓΛ	ΓΛ	Γ	ΓC	ΓΛΛ	⟨ΓC	ΛΓ⟨C	Γ
𐤃	d	ΔΔ	Δ	Δ	Δ	ΔΔD	Δ	DΔD	ΔD	DΔD	DΔ	D	Δ
𐤄	e̅	ЯΕΕ	ЯƎΕ	ΕΕ	ϷΒΒΕ	ΕΕΕ	ЯƎΕ	ЯΕΕΕ	ЯΕΕΕ	ЯΕΕΕ	ЯΕΕΕ	ΕΕΕ	Ε
𐤅	f,v	Ϝ	ΛⅎϜ		ЛⅎϜ				Ϲ	ϜϜC	ϜϜ	ϜϜ	
𐤆	z		Ⅰ	Ⅰ	Ⅰ			‡Ⅰ	Ⅰ·	Ⅰ	Ⅰ	Ⅰ	Ζ
𐤇	e̅,h	𐌇	𐌇𐌇	𐌇Η	𐌇	𐌇	𐌇Η	Η	𐌇Η	𐌇Η		·Η	Η
𐤈	th	⊗⊕	⊗⊕	⊗⊕⊙	⊗⊕	⊗	⊗⊕	⊗⊕	⊗⊕⊙	⊗⊕⊙	⊗⊙	⊕⊙	Θ
𐤉	i	⟨Ϟ	⟨Ϟ2Ϟ	ϟⅠ	ϟϞ	Ⅰ	Ⅰ	Ⅰ	Ⅰ	Ⅰ	Ⅰ	Ⅰ	Ⅰ
𐤊	k	ϞϞΚ	ϞϞΚ	ϞϞΚ	ϞΚΚ	ΚΚ	ϞΚϞ	Κ	ϞΚΚ	ϞϞΚ	ϞΚΚ	ΚΚΚ	Κ
𐤋	l	⌐Γ	⌐ΓΛ	⌐ЛↃ	ΛⅡΓ	ΛΛ	⌐ΓΛ	Λ	ЛↃↃ	Лↄ	ΛΛ	ΛΛL	Λ
𐤌	m	⋔Μ	⋔ΛΛⵍ	⋔ΛⵍΛ	ΜΜⵍΜ	ΜΜ	ⵍ	Μ	ⵍΜⵍ	⋔Μ	⋔Μ	⋔ΜⵍΜ	Μ
𐤍	n	⋔Γ	⋔ⵍ⋔	⋔ⵍⵍ	⋔ⵍⵍ	⋔ Ν	⋔ⵍⵍΝ	ⵍⵍ	ⵍⵍⵍ	⋔ⵍⵍ	⋔ⵍⵍ	ⵍⵍⵍ	Ν
𐤎	x	(ΚΜ)			ⲎⲎ		ⲎⲎ	+	+	+	+Χ	+	Ξ
𐤏	o	ΟΟ	Οⵙ	Ο	Οⵙ	Ο	Ο·	Ο	Ο	⋄ΟΟ	⋄⋄Ο	Ο	Ο
𐤐	p	⌐ΓΓ	⌐⟩C	⌐Γ	⌐ΓΓ	⌐ΓΓ	⌐Γ	Γ	ΓΓ	ΓΓϷ	ΓΓ	Γ	Π
𐤑	q	ϘϞ	Ϙ	Ϙ	Ϙ	Ϙ	Ϙ	Ϙ	ϘϘ	Ϙ	Ϙ	
𐤒	r	ΔϷϞ	ϞϞϷD	ϘϷΡΡ	ϞϷDϷ	ΡΡD	ϞϷD	ΡΡ	ϞΡΡ	ΡΡΡ	ϷDΡϷ	ΡΡΡ	Ρ
𐤓	s	⋔Μ	⋔	ϟϞϵ	⋔Μ	ϟϞϟ	ϟϞ	ϟϞS	ϟϞϟ	ϟϞS	ϟϞS	ϟϞϵ	Σ
𐤔	t	Τ	Τ	Τ	Τ·	·Τ	Τ	Τ	ΤΤ	Τ	Τ	Τ	Τ
	u	ϞϒϒΥ	ΥΥ·	ΥΥΤ	ϞϒϒΥ	ΥΥ	Υ·Χ	Υ	ϒΥ	ΥϒΥ	Υϒ	Υ	Υ
	ph	(ΓⰂ)	ⴲϕ	ⴲϕ	ⴲϕϕ	ϕ		ⴲ	ⴲ	ⴲϕ	ⴲ⊡	ϕⴲ	Φ
	ch			+Χ	+Χ	·Χ	Χ	⋁	⋁	⋁⋎		⋁	Χ
	ps			Ψ	⋁Ψ	⋁Ψ	⋁Ψ					✳	Ψ
	o					℧Ο							Ω

Fig. 131. Development of the Greek alphabet.

tions may date from the 9th, possibly even from the 10th
century B. C. The Cretan inscriptions are somewhat later
and the early alphabets of Attica and Corinth may date
from the middle of the 8th century. The dates of the Eubœan, Chalcidian and Bœotian alphabets also are some-

what conjectural; but those assigned are according to the best authorities and consequently probably are reliable.

It will be noticed in examining the chart that the letters **A K M N O T**, and in a less degree a few others, have been remarkably constant throughout the entire period. This is especially true of the letter **T**, which has never deviated from the original Greek modification of the Phœnician character. *Alpha* has had few modifications and these have been of unimportant details. In Attica alone it is found lying on its side, as in the Phœnician. *Beta,* where it occurs, has either rounding or angular lobes except in the case of the local use in Corinth of a strange symbol taken from the old Mediterranean syllabary; the angular *beta* having been appropriated for the letter **E**, an anomaly in Greek epigraphy. *Gamma,* as we already have explained, was from the first, in all the Eastern alphabets, poorly differentiated from *lambda* except in the early Attic alphabet, in which **L** seemed to follow the Sidonian variety of the Phœnician alphabet, which we have used in the first line of the chart instead of the Moabite. The upright angular form of *gamma* was the immediate precursor of the curving form, both more frequent in the Western alphabets, and was the parent of our **C** and **G**. The angular *delta* with one line horizontal is more constant in the Eastern alphabets, while the upright form or the curving form, like the Roman **D**, is characteristic of the Western alphabets. *Epsilon,* except in minor particulars, has been constant throughout, while *eta* has the closed form in the older alphabets and the **H**-form in the more recent ones. In Crete alone the old Phœnician form seems to have been employed. **F** early was dropped from the Eastern alphabets, but was retained in the Western alphabets to be passed on to Italy. It hardly changed its form from the earliest period. *Zeta* throughout the entire period followed the early Moabite prototype until the variant of the Sidonian form of this letter was introduced, when the Ionian alphabet was adopted at Athens. *Zeta,* however, rarely was used by the Ionian Greeks. We have used the Sidonian form of *zayin* in the first column in the chart. *Theta* remained remarkably constant except for the markings within the circle.

In the earlier alphabets *iota* had a zigzag form; obviously a modification of the Moabite character for *yod;* but in the Ionic and Western alphabets it had the familiar form which has descended to us through the Roman alphabet. *Kappa,* after the earliest period in Thera and Crete, remained constant; except for the reversing undergone by all the letters in the change from right-to-left writing to the later European method. *Mu* and *nu* in the earliest alphabets were high-stepped on the first bar, like the Phœnician. This peculiarity of the parent alphabet manifested itself for some centuries in many of the Greek alphabets until it was gradually superseded by the symmetrical shaped M. *Omicron,* small in the earlier alphabets, like the Phœnician, afterward became of uniform height with the other letters. *Pi,* which was only a slight variant of the Phœnician, for many centuries fluctuated between the older form which resembles an unfinished P and the form eventually adopted at Athens. The Western alphabets clung more steadily to the older form, which ultimately was transformed into the Roman P. The letter Q remained fairly constant, but became entirely obsolescent in the late Greek alphabets, but reappeared in the Italian alphabets. *Rho,* after starting out as a fairly true copy of the Phœnician, early began to develop a tail; which, however, did not become a constant appendage except in the latest varieties of the Western alphabets, from which it passed to the Romans. The development of *sigma* we already have fully described. The evolution is well shown in the examples given in the chart. The evolution of *upsilon* contains that of its derivatives the Roman **V** and **Y**. It begins in the earliest alphabets with both the latter forms which periodically reappear throughout the long cycle. The classic form of *upsilon*, Υ, seems to be a purely Attic invention, probably taken from the old Mediterranean syllabary, as before remarked.

CHAPTER XIII

THE ROMAN ALPHABET

THE Roman alphabet, from which the capital letters of our English alphabet have descended with hardly the change of a single stroke for an interval of over 2000 years, was, according to the best historical evidence, developed from one of the early Greek alphabets, the Chalcidian, a variant of the Eubœan mode of writing. It was introduced into Italy at a very early date contemporaneous with the wide-spread Hellenic emigrations over the entire north Mediterranean shores, from the Ægean Islands to Spain, by Grecian colonists from Chalcis, who established themselves in Cumæ, Sicily. It would appear that some time in the 10th century B. C., probably in the latter part and not so long after they had transmitted their precious alphabet to the inhabitants of Hellas, the Phœnicians retired from Greece and the Ægean. There then followed a rivalry for colonial supremacy among the Greeks. Miletus in Ionia contended with Chalcis in Eubœa, in Greece proper, for primacy in colonization. They eventually divided the territory of the Mediterranean between them, the Miletians being supreme in the east and throughout the Euxine, while the Chalcidians dominated Thrace and Italy. Thus it came about that the Western variant of the Greek alphabet was introduced into Italy.

Roman civilization owed everything to the earlier culture existing in the Peninsula before the arrival of the Latins. Several centuries prior to the Roman settlement, that is prior to the 11th or 10th century B. C., the Etruscans, a non-Aryan race, probably Turanian, invaded the land, emigrating — as most classic writers agree — from Lydia in Asia Minor. The Greeks called them Turrhenoi, while the Romans called them Etrusci. The Pelasgians, a primitive Greek race, preceded them in the occupancy of the land, being forced out or absorbed by the stronger race. But they imparted to the Etruscans their heritage of Greek culture, which became the basis of all subsequent Italian progress in civilization. It was the Spartan-like qualities of the Etruscans,— hardy, aggressive and war-like, combined with the softer virtues of the earlier race in the varied arts of peace, that made the Italian people for so many centuries the dominating force in European civilization; resulting in the wide dissemination, through the continental marches of the conquering Roman legions, of the arts of civilization to the benighted barbarians of Germany, Gaul and Britain.

Almost all record concerning the Pelasgians and Etrus-cans has been lost, as they left no literature, and what has been written about them by the classic writers largely has suffered a similar fate. Some massive walls of Pelasgian masonry remain and a very few specimens of their writing have been discovered. The Etruscans built no temples, but their tombs are scattered over all the territory of ancient Etruria. What is known of them has been recon-structed from the " disjecta membra " in the form of in-scriptions on bronze utensils, sarcophagi, burial stele, cinerary urns and vases found in the anicent tombs.

It is not known whether the Etruscans acquired the art of writing in the Greek characters prior to their invasion of Italy, but it is highly improbable. As we have noted, the earliest known Phœnician writing does not antedate the 9th century B. C. So it is reasonable to assume that the Etruscans did not bring the Greek alphabet with them when they left their ancestral home in Lydia. If they brought any written characters with them they probably were those of the ancient Ægean syllabary. Nor is it known that the Pelasgians whom they found first in Italy, were in possession of the Greek alphabet or any alphabet at that time. This too seems highly improbable. It would assign to this alphabet an age more remote than any paleologist is ready to ascribe to it. The alphabet probably was introduced by later Chalcidian colonists emigrating into Italy; being largely disseminated throughout Etruria by the Pelasgians.

It is probable that the Pelasgian and Etruscan civilizations, like the later Etruscan and Roman civilizations, were contemporaneous over extended periods of time before the final supremacy of the Etruscans was effected. On the other hand it was not until 600 years after the founding of Rome that the Latins finally overthrew the virtual supremacy of the Etruscans in the great battle of Cumæ, 281 B. C. Through these centuries of national growth, then, the Roman alphabet developed from the basic type introduced by the Chalcidian colonists; being influenced in its development by the Pelasgian Greek variant on the one hand and the Etruscan mode of writing on the other. The Pelasgian alphabet, called by some authorities the Greek-Etruscan and recognized as the primitive Italian alphabet and the prototype of the later Etruscan and Latin alphabets, is distinguished among the Greek alphabets for the use of the letters **C D L P** instead of Γ Δ Λ Π, used in most Greek alphabets. The Etruscans speaking a wholly different language from the Latins found no need of certain letters. They rejected **B D O Q X**. The Latins for similar reasons rejected Θ Φ Ψ. The Etruscans, at least prior to Roman influence, wrote from right to left. This is an indication of the very early date when they acquired their alphabet. Yet the Pelasgians wrote from left to right, and practically the entire body of Latin inscriptions after the very earliest examples is in this direction.

We give below two examples of the Pelasgian alphabet. No. 1 probably is the oldest proto-Roman alphabet in existence. It was found scratched on a vase in a tomb near Cervetri in Italy.

No. 2 was scratched on a black amphora found in a tomb at Formello. Both alphabets are rather crude specimens of writing, especially the first. In No. 1 **B** is reversed, probably through ignorance rather than habit, as the scribe does not seem to be one who would know that the letters were reversed in the earlier Greek retrograde writing. The letters **L** and **M** are injured by a fracture, and *koppa* (**Q**) is left out. The **M**-shaped letter in the 18th station in No. 2, whose value is given in the curious Greek character *san,* is derived directly from the old Phœnician *tsade.* It appears as if the scribe of No. 1 had transposed this character and the character he has used for the letter N. These alphabets contain the twenty-two original Phœnician characters and the supplemental Greek letters Υ Φ Χ Ψ, but not Ω. It consequently cannot be claimed that they date from an especially early period of Greek writing, though they doubtless do confer antiquity upon the art of writing in Italy. The Greek letters beneath these alphabets will assist the reader in identifying these earliest of Italian letters.

1. 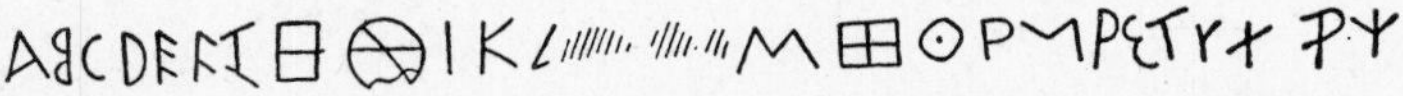

ΑΒΓ ΔΕFΖ Η Θ Ι Κ Λ Μ Ν Ξ Ο Π ϡ ΡΣΤ Υ Χ Φ Ψ

2. 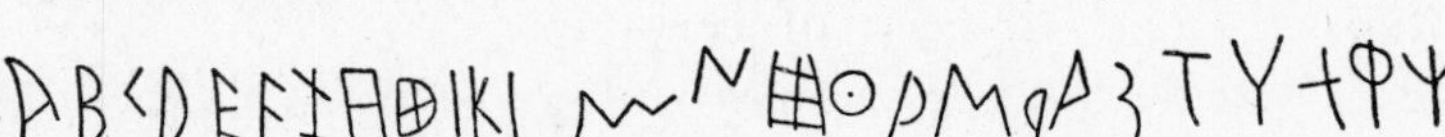

Α ΒΓΔΕFΖΗΘΙΚΛ Μ Ν Ξ Ο Π ϡ ϙ Ρ Σ Τ Υ Χ Φ Ψ

Quite a few abecedaria of Etruscan letters have been found, chiefly inscribed on vases discovered in ancient tombs. They all are very similar in the order and shape of the letters. It is difficult to say which are older or to assign any positive date to any of them. We give below reproductions of two of these alphabets which appear to be of the earliest type.

No. 1 was inscribed on the base of a little cap found in the necropolis of an Etruscan town near Bombarzo, Italy. The form of *zeta* is very rare. It is usually shaped as shown in No. 2. It seems to presage the later form of the minuscle of *zeta* and our present script character. No. 2 is a rudely scratched alphabet etched on a black bowl now in the museum at Grosseto, Italy. It contains **Q** which did not properly belong to the Etruscan alphabet. **B** and **D** are omitted in both alphabets, as are also O and Ω. The **R** is reversed, the curve bending in the direction that it does in the left to right writing.

Φ Χ Θ Υ Τ Σ Ρ Ϡ Π Ν Μ Λ Ι Θ Η Ζ Ε Ε Γ Α   1.

Φ Χ Θ Υ Τ Σ Ρ Q Ϡ Π Ν Μ   Λ Κ Ι Θ   Η Ζ   Ε Ε Γ Α   2.

In both alphabets there are two S's,— M and Σ. There is a bit of history connected with this that we have adverted to before. There were four sibilants in the Phœnician,— *samekh, zayin, tsade* and *shin.* (See Fig. 101.) The Greeks used but three,— *zeta* (dentil), *sigma* (hard), and *xi* (see Fig. 131). There was a fourth in use in early times, chiefly by the Dorians,— *san* (Ϡ).

This was lost before classic times. It will be interesting but perhaps a little confusing on account of the inter-changeability of the signs, to follow these sibilants through the different alphabets in Fig. 131, and compare them with the corresponding signs in the Phœnician alphabet, Fig. 101. At least the comparison will enable the reader to understand how our letter **S** has developed and been handed down to us in the heritage of the alphabet. It descended from the Greek *sigma*, Σ, which in turn came from the Phœnician *shin*, **W**, which is practically the same form turned about.

We fortunately are able through inscriptions on ancient Italian coins, a fairly large number of which have been discovered, chronologically to trace the development of the proto-Roman alphabet over quite an extended period. We give below a short list of names of gods and cities selected from these coins, arranged in approximately chronologically order beginning with the 6th century B. C. and ending with the 3rd century B. C. It appears from these Etruscan coins that the Pelasgian Greek influence toward left-to-right writing was exerted at least as early as the 5th century B. C. It doubtless was much earlier. The inscriptions on these coins are interesting as showing the evolution of certain letters through progressive changes in form during successive periods. The letter **R** has developed as follows:

The letter **S** has been evolved through the following forms:

DPꟼRR

ϟΣMƧS

It will be noticed that the **I** in Poseidan resembles the early forms of this letter in the Eastern alphabets.

There have been found from time to time in Italy in-numerable bronze hand mirrors, beautiful in outline and design, which were deposited by the Etruscans in the many tombs which have been discovered throughout an-

OPQ   ΓΟΞΕΙΔΑΝ

ΣΑЯΑΤ   ϽΠΛΚ

ΤΑΡΑΣ   8ΙΣΤLVΙΣ

ΙϽƎЯ   ROMΛ

ΛΑϽƎΜΟꓶ   ROMΛ

cient Etruria. They are adorned with etched drawings almost invariably of the Etruscan gods and goddesses. In most cases beside each figure is inscribed the name

Fig. 132. Bronze mirror from an Etruscan tomb.

of the god, as in the Etruscan mirror illustrated. in Fig. 132.

Following will be found a series of proper names taken from these mirrors. In all the older examples the writing is from right to left.

The English equivalents of these names are as follows:

Atunis, Adonis	Thalna, Juno
Herakle, Herakles	Nethuns, Neptune
Echtur, Hector	Apulu, Apollo
Menrfa, Minerva	Artumes, Artemis
Maris, Mars	Aiax, Ajax
Thesan, Aurora	Elaksantre, Alexander
Turan, Venus	Alksentre, Alexander

The Greek influence so manifest in the great body of coins is absent in most of the inscriptions on Etruscan mirrors. All the examples in the foregoing list are in the Etruscan mode of writing and show a distinct departure from the Greek alphabetic forms. Phœnician characteristics persist, however, and we still find the slanting E, the closed H with slanting bars, the high-stepped M and other peculiarities of the parent alphabet. The letters manifest a tendency to sprawl, much more marked than examples of Greek writing of the same period.

The history of the progressive development of Latin writing, culminating in the beautiful classic Roman inscriptions of the monumental structures of the Cæsars, is written in the fragmentary inscriptions discovered throughout Italy and to be seen in the many museums in that country. In these inscriptions, beginning with the earliest specimens in which the letters are almost purely Greek of the early Phœnician type, one may trace the gradual elimination of many Greek letters ultimately rejected by the Italians and the gradual development of purely Italian features. One also may note a progressive improvement in the shape and proportion of the letters, as well as a gain in uniformity of size and alignment, as in the later examples of Greek writing. At first the letters were written continuously without interruption, no attempt being made to separate words. Subsequently, yet very early, dots were employed for this purpose, there being at first little appreciable space left between words, the dots being crowded in between them. Later, provision was made for this new feature of writing, and the planning and spacing of words in the line were made with regard to these separating dots. This method of writing continued over a very extended period before the separating dots between words were relegated to the end of the sentence or paragraph, and the space which they occupied alone sufficing, as at the present day, to separate the words.

We give below a very early example of Italian writing, found in Etruria and classified in " Corpus Inscriptionum Italicum " as Etruscan. It reads from left to right, however; a very infrequent method with the Etruscans. It was not employed by them until a comparatively late epoch. The inscription, which seems to be of an extremely early date, may be designated as Pelasgian. The design of the inscription is decorative, as there is an engraved line immediately below the letters, and beneath this is another line of inscription, symmetrical with the first, but upside down. The reading of this line also is from left to right. We note in these letters the characteristic Phœnician **M** and **N**, and the **E** with the slanting bars. Apart from this the remaining letters resemble the Chalcidian alphabet. By the retention of the high-stepped Phœnician **M** the mix-up over **M** and **S** has been avoided and there is no ambiguity or confusion. The *digamma* (**F**), very early dropped from most Greek alphabets, is present in this inscription. It was reinstated as a permanent letter in the Italian alphabets:

Fig. 133 is a very early example of Etruscan writing, in retrograde reading. Though cruder in workmanship

Fig. 133. Early Etruscan inscription.

than the former inscription and careless in alignment, the general Phœnician characteristics of the letters, in common with those of the former, would indicate about the same early age of calligraphic art. The inscription contains a number of letters of marked archaism and is without any means of separating the individual words making up the sentence.

Fig. 134 is a characteristic example of Etruscan writing. The reading is from right to left as customary with the Etruscans. The five-barred M used in Crete, which is simply the old Phœnician M equalized in height, is here employed. We find it in other Etruscan inscriptions. It was also in somewhat common use in Lydia. In common with the other alphabets of Italy, *lambda* in this inscription has the Western form of L, always in the early stages of development upturned at the bottom instead of horizontal as in later times. Many of the letters are still Greek in form, not having advanced far in their ultimate transformation into the typical Roman alphabet

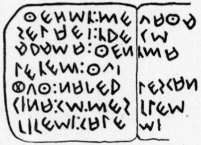

Fig. 134. Typical example of Etruscan writing.

A significant advance is evidenced in this inscription in the matter of separating words in the sentence. Dots in pairs are used for this purpose. In early inscriptions from both Umbria and Etruria words were separated by dots, sometimes singly, sometimes in pairs, as in this example. In the former province small triangular dots occasionally were employed for this purpose. In Roman writing of the classic period this device was very popular and was used to separate words as well as to indicate abbreviations, so extensively employed by the Romans in their monumental inscriptions, and imitated to this day.

As time progressed, gradually the letters improved in proportion, uniformity of size and alignment, and the spacing and general appearance of the letters in the line became more regular and pleasing to the eye; as in the two final examples of Etruscan writing shown below. The inscription shown in No. 2 will serve as an introduction to the well recognized mode of abbreviation later employed by the Romans. The example is from the Tomb of the Volumnii (family) at Perugia, and reads: Pup. Velimna Au. Caphatial. This would be expressed by the Latins: P. Volumnius. A. F. Violens Cafatia. Natus,— "Publius Volumnius, son of Aulus, by a mother named Cafatia." It is somewhat surprising to meet with the old Phœnician aspirate (*cheth*) persisting so late in the development of the alphabet. The character is here used for the sound *ph*. The local Etruscan forms of **M** and **N** resemble so strikingly the modern minuscules of these letters as to suggest a possible source of their origin.

1.

2.

One of the very earliest Latin inscriptions, possibly the oldest Latin inscription extant, is reproduced in Fig. 135. It was engraved on a gold fibula found at Præneste, and is written in exceedingly archaic letters, in retrograde. The diminution in the size of the letters toward the left is due to the tapering point of the fibula. Each word in the inscription is pointed off by separating dots, as will be noted by referring to the transliteration below the cut. The early Romans employed for these separating dots circles, semicircles and later small triangles. The latter were largely used in monumental sculpture in classic times, and frequently are used to-day with abbreviations in tablet and architectural inscriptions. The early date of the writing may be judged by the use of the closed *eta* as an aspirate, and the strange form of the Latin word fecit,— fhefhaked.

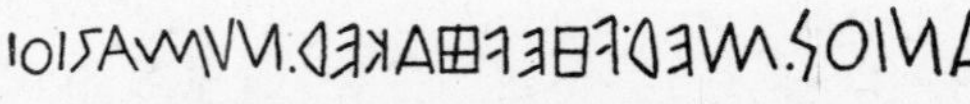

MANIOS MED FHEFHAKED NUMASIOI

Fig. 135. Oldest Latin inscription. Engraved on a gold fibula.

Our next illustration, Fig. 136, is an inscription from the City of Antinum. Although the Greek form of **P** persists, the other letters denote a progressive approximation to the Roman alphabet of the classic period. The letters are fairly upright, generally well proportioned, and the horizontal bars, save in the letter **A**, seem definitely to have abandoned their old-time Phœnician slant. The **M** and **N** follow the familiar archaic Greek types, with slanting

Fig. 136. Latin inscription from Antinum.

lines throughout, giving to the letters a sprawling appearance, dissonant with the general uprightness of the other letters. This was corrected in classic times by making in each case the outside lines vertical. It was contributions of this character, improvements in the proportion and shape of the letters, and corrections in form to harmonize letters with each other in their general relationship, for which we are so much indebted to the later Greeks and Romans, more especially the latter; for they have bequeathed to us an alphabet incomparable in its legibility and chaste beauty.

Fig. 137 is a Latin inscription on the Temple of Bona Dea at Lavernæ, now Prezza, Italy. It shows the Roman alphabet practically in its completely developed form. The letters are mainly upright and are fairly even in height with the exception of an occasional I that runs high above the line. Two or three of the N's still ex-

L·STATIVS·CN·F CHI LO
L·PETTIVS·C·F PANSA
C·PETTIVS·V·F·GEMELLV
L·TATTIVS·T·F COXSA
⊃·MAGISTRI·LAVERNEIS
MVRVM·CAEMENTICIVN
PORTAM·PORTICVM
TEMPLVM·BONAE·DEAF
PAGI·DECRETO·FACIENDN
⟨·RARVNT·PROBARVNTO

Fig. 137. Latin inscription from the Temple of Bona Dea, at Lavernæ, now Prezza, Italy.

hibit the historic tendency to slant, but the remaining ones are upright like the rest of the letters. The S also shows a slight tendency to slant; the A is somewhat overwide, and the M maintains the slanting side lines of the parent Phœnician, soon to be rectified in the later age of Roman writing, as it was in the classic age of Greek writing.

The beautiful inscribed marble tablet shown in Fig. 138 is from a Roman bath, and illustrates the letters of the Roman alphabet in their highest state of development in the classic age. For ·beauty and elegance, for refined proportions and subtle spacing, the lettering is almost unexcelled. While maintaining in the highest degree the formal exactness of the standard type of the letters, the sculptor has permitted himself sufficient freedom to introduce into the structure of the individual letters enough variety to counteract the severity of a too mechanical treatment. In a very definite degree the desirableness of variety in an alphabet is answered in the very nature of the Roman letters. The quality is inherent in this alphabet, and arises from the fact that only a little over one-half of the Roman letters are straight-lined, the remaining letters being curved. In the Greek alphabet two-thirds of the letters are straight-lined. This gives a severity to Greek writing, hardly offset by the paucity of the curving letters. Happily the severity of the straight-lined letters is turned into a stabilizing force in Roman writing, while the curving letters serving as a complement supply the grace and variety demanded of any inscription as a pattern in decorative arrangement. The reader may compare this example of the golden age of Roman epigraphy with the inscription shown in Fig. 129, of the corresponding age of Greek writing. The Greek inscription certainly is dignified, as we have said before, but it is incontestably severe and, we feel, formal and mechanical. Our Roman sculptor, on the other hand, has given to almost every letter individuality — almost personality — by the clever treatment of the serifs and spurs, and the tails to the **R**'s and **Q**'s. His inscription speaks to us as with a living tongue. The other impresses us only as a dead language.

Moreover, in addition to the vital touches that give action and emphasis to the Roman inscription, our sculptor has exhibited a breadth of vision concerning the function of a tablet inscription quite modern in its range. He has taken into account the idea of principality in the subject matter of the inscription. His lines of letters are not uniform throughout. They are of varying heights, with some words larger and more prominent than others. The tablet is a sign, an advertisement of a bath. The artist seems imbued with the spirit of the modern poster designer — he was perhaps the first past-master of the craft — and has made prominent the most significant words of the advertisement to catch the eye. Altogether the display, spacing and general style of the inscription is admirable.

THERMAE
M·CRASSIFRVGI
AQVA·MARINAET·BALN
AQVA·DVLCI IANVARIVS·

Fig. 138. Latin inscription on a Roman bath.

We give in Fig. 139 the Roman classic alphabet in letters selected from inscriptions in the Roman Forum. The shapes and proportions are according to the most elegant examples of these inscriptions. It will be noticed that our Roman capitals in the current book types differ somewhat from these classic capitals in the proportionate width of some of the letters and in the presence of serifs, wanting in certain letters in the classic alphabet. Our present Roman capitals, as we shall show in the next chapter, have descended to us from the modified

version of the classic examples evolved by the calligraphic
artists at the time of the Renaissance.

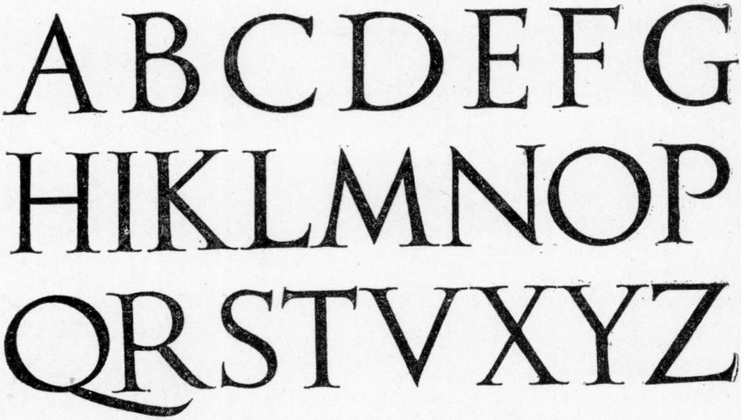

ABCDEFG
HIKLMNOP
QRSTVXYZ

Fig. 139. Classic Roman capitals. From inscriptions in the Forum.

The reader will find in Fig. 140 the historical development of the Roman alphabet from the original Phœnician
letters through the modification of these parent forms
as effected by the Greeks, principally those of Western
Greece and particularly of the Chalcidian colonists in
Italy. The reader will also be able to trace in the chart
the line of development of each letter through the
Pelasgian and Etruscan variants of the Greek alphabet
down to the completely developed Roman capital of the
classic monuments. The Latin alphabet differs in many
essential particulars from the classic Greek. There is
one new letter, some restorations, slight changes in the
order and phonetic value of the characters, and modifications in the shapes of most of the letters. It resembles
the old Phœnician alphabet more closely than the Ionian
Greek does, retaining twenty out of the original twenty-
two letters, while the Ionian retains only nineteen.

The letter C which stands in the place of the Greek *gamma* is not altogether a new character, as we already have met with it in certain Greek alphabets: the Corinthian and the Western variants,— Chalcis, Elis and Locris. In the Chalcidian alphabet C was used to express the sound G (hard). In the Etruscan language C and K were homophones, with the result that K ultimately became obsolescent. In Latin inscriptions throughout the classical period C was used as the representative of the unvoiced guttural stop (K). It would seem that up to about the middle of the 3rd century no discrimination in writing was made by the Romans between this sound and the voiced guttural stop (G hard). About this time, however, a distinction was made between these sounds, and a new letter G was evolved with this latter value, which was very much the same as the old *gamma*. C continued to express the sound of K. The new letter was placed in the seventh station, in the place of the Greek *zeta,* there not being up to this time any Latin word requiring this sound. However, about the 1st century B. C. the discarded Z was restored to the alphabet and placed at the end of the list. But it was the new Attic form of Z, the analogue of the old Phœnician character that was adopted and not the I-form character that had so long persisted throughout the various Greek alphabets. The letter K, which had descended without interruption and almost without change of form from the parent Phœnician through all the local Greek alphabets, was adopted by the early Latins and is found in their earliest inscriptions; but it was quite early replaced by C and survived only in two or three words. The *digamma* (F), which early became obsolete in certain Greek alphabets, as well as Q, which was generally obsolescent if not altogether missing — except in the ear-

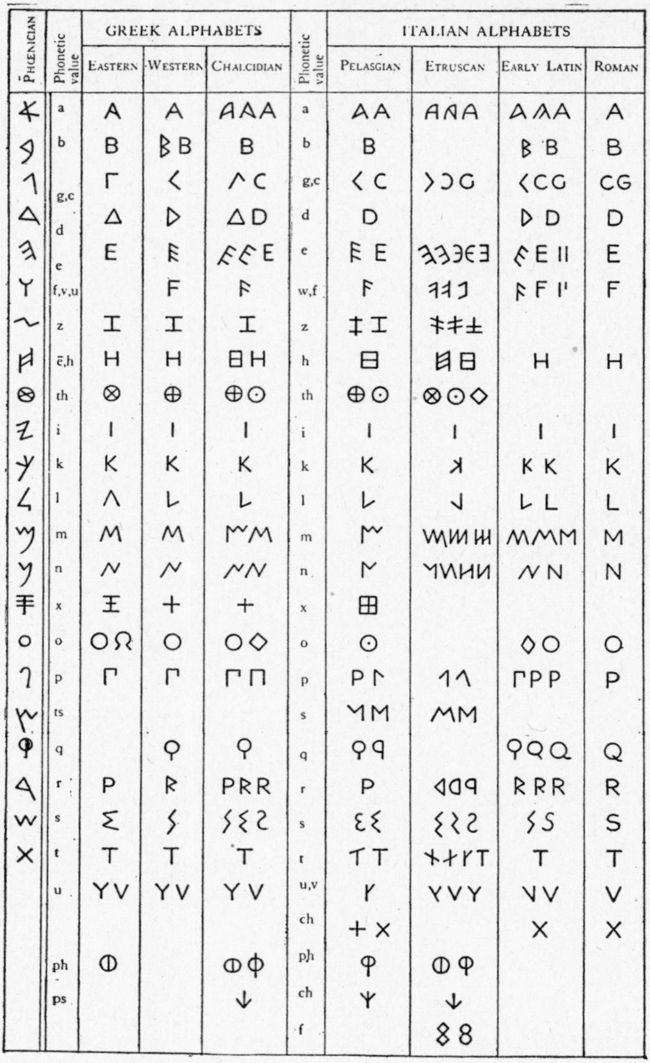

Phoenician	Phonetic value	GREEK ALPHABETS			Phonetic value	ITALIAN ALPHABETS			
		Eastern	Western	Chalcidian		Pelasgian	Etruscan	Early Latin	Roman
𐤀	a	A	A	AΛA	a	AA	ΑΛΑ	ΑΛΑ	A
𐤁	b	B	ℬB	B	b	B		ℬ B	B
𐤂	g,c	Γ	ᐸ	ΛC	g,c	ᐸC	ꓘϽG	ᐸCG	CG
𐤃	d	Δ	▷	ΔD	d	D		▷D	D
𐤄	e	E	ℰ	ℰℰE	e	ℰE	ƷƷƷℰƷ	ℰE Il	E
𐤅	f,v,u		F	ℱ	w,f	ℱ	ꓤꓤꓩ	ℱF Iˈ	F
𐤆	z	I	I	I	z	‡I	ꓮꓭꓮ		
𐤇	ē,h	H	H	⊟H	h	⊟	⊟⊟	H	H
𐤈	th	⊗	⊕	⊕⊙	th	⊕⊙	⊗⊙◇		
𐤉	i	I	I	I	i	I	I	I	I
𐤊	k	K	K	K	k	K	ꓘ	K K	K
𐤋	l	Λ	L	L	l	L	ꓯ	L L	L
𐤌	m	M	M	ꟼꟼM	m	ꟼ	WꟿⱲ	ΛMΛ	M
𐤍	n	Ν	Ν	ꟼꟼΝ	n	ꟼ	ꟿꟼℍꟼ	ΛΝ	N
𐤎	x	⊞	+	+	x	⊞			
𐤏	o	OΩ	O	O◇	o	⊙		◇O	O
𐤐	p	Γ	Γ	ΓΠ	p	PΓ	ꓥꓥ	ΓPP	P
𐤑	ts				s	ꟿM	ΛΛM		
𐤒	q		ϙ	ϙ	q	ϙϙ		ϙϙϘ	Q
𐤓	r	Ρ	ℛ	PℛR	r	P	ꓒꓒꟼ	RRR	R
𐤔	s	Σ	ꟊ	ꟊℰꟊ	s	ℰℰ	ꟊℰꟊ	ꟊS	S
𐤕	t	T	T	˙T	t	TT	�***T	T	T
	u	YV	YV	YV	u,v	ꓬ	YVY	VV	V
					ch		+X		X
	ph	Φ		Φϕ	ph	ϙ	ΦΦ		
	ps			⬇	ch	ꟙ	⬇		
					f		88		

Fig. 140. Development of the Roman alphabet from the Phœnician and Greek alphabets.

liest Greek alphabets — was restored by the Romans; both occupying their former relative positions. Y was borrowed from the Greek alphabet some time in the 1st century about the time that Z was restored.

We now have reached, in the classic days of the Roman civilization — a time about contemporaneous with the close of the Pagan period and the dawning of the Christian era — the complete development of the Roman alphabet. Its foundations were laid in the earliest Greek alphabets borrowed from the Phœnicians; its structure was framed by the Chalcidian, Pelasgian and Etruscan colonists in Italy; but the monumental perfection of these wonderful letters that the ages were so long preparing for us was the work of the Romans. The Roman letters in their extreme simplicity and remarkable mutual differentiation contain within themselves the elements of their popularity and widespread adoption. It is the most widely diffused alphabet in the world; being exclusively used in England, America, Australasia and South Africa; and is practically in use throughout Europe, except where the Gothic black-letter is employed in Germany and the Slavonic alphabet in Russia. It is also in official use in Egypt and India, and wherever the European nations, except Germany, hold sway. The Arabic alphabet alone competes with it in universality, being used throughout Central Asia.

CHAPTER XIV

WRITING IN THE MIDDLE AGES

THE beautiful, clear-cut and legible script of the Roman monuments, so simple and elegant in its chaste forms, was employed for several centuries, both in monumental inscriptions and in written manuscripts, with but very little change in the shape of the letters. This may be confirmed in the case of the monumental script by a comparison of the inscriptions on the Arch of Titus, erected about 70 A. D., and those on the Arch of Constantine, dating from 315 A. D., both now standing in the Roman Forum. Though nearly three centuries separated the construction of these two monuments, the lapidary script in use throughout this period of time underwent no important changes.

The Roman letters had been progressively improved through many centuries in their long development from their Phœnician and Greek archetypes, deteriorating to any considerable extent only when the Roman Empire began to crumble under the repeated assaults of the northern barbarians. When culture began to revive after the ravages of the Dark Ages, it was a very different type of alphabet that came into use from that employed in the classic age. But the changes were effected rather slowly, and in point of fact the origin of some of the modifications from the historic type date from the earliest years of the Christian era and even prior thereto.

From a very early age both in Greece and in Rome writing on wax tablets and on parchment was very extensively practiced. Examples of the former, owing to the temporary nature of the material, very largely have disappeared; but many precious specimens of manuscripts in parchment have been preserved. The use of this material for writing purposes came into general vogue some time prior to the Christian era, being extensively employed in Asia Minor. The name parchment comes from Pergamus, a city in Asia Minor, where skins were prepared for writing purposes. It is said that Eumenes II, king of Pergamus, being unable through the jealousy of one of the Ptolemies to secure papyrus from Egypt, introduced the use of parchment, which subsequently was called "pergamena." We may take occasion at this time to mention another material used for writing — surely an odd custom — that has resulted in its name being incorporated into our language. Many commercial transactions in Rome: tax collectors' receipts and business memoranda, have been found recorded on potsherds or *ostraca,* oyster shells; whence our word " ostracize," the posting of the name of an obnoxious person.

The writing in these early manuscripts, in both Greek and Latin, was in capitals, quite the same letters as those used in the sculptured Greek and Roman monuments. The small letters that to-day are used in the text of printed books, which we call " Roman " to distinguish them from " Italic," and which historically are known as " minuscules "— though the unromantic printer applies to them the term " lower case "— had not yet been evolved. Neither had the Italic. This form of letter did not appear until after the invention of printing in the time of the Renaissance. The minuscule, both Greek and Roman, was long in developing, and its complete history, far too long for the scope of this treatise, is a most interesting one. The earliest Roman manuscripts dating from the beginning of the Christian era were written in letters known as " square capitals." These at first were almost identical with the monumental script, but differed from it mainly through variations arising from the medium of their execution. These manuscripts were written on parchment, vellum or on papyrus from Egypt, with a flexible quill or reed, *penna;* and as the scribes became more expert in their art, acquiring speed in its execution, certain tendencies toward ligatures and cursiveness crept in, resulting in departures more or less marked from the historic capitals. Fig. 141 is a fragment of a manuscript written on papyrus in Roman capitals which

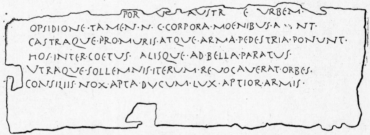

Fig. 141. Manuscript written on papyrus. From Herculaneum.

was discovered in Herculaneum. Something like 1800 such manuscripts, more or less charred, were found in one box in a recess in the wall of a house. The owner, one Lucius Piso Cæsonius, was a medical specialist, and nearly all his manuscripts were of the Epicurean philosophy. Most of the inscriptions in the manuscripts from Herculaneum are in Greek. Greek influence at both Herculaneum and Pompeii was very pronounced. The scribes largely were educated Greek slaves, known as *librarii,* and were equally learned in the Greek and Latin languages and skillful in the writing of both. There were thousands of these educated slaves in Rome who spent their entire lives in copying books. Some editions, it is known, ran as high as 2,000 copies. It was due to these educated scribes in Rome and its neighboring cities that in their hands during the first century of our era the old Greek and Roman capitals first began to degenerate and to assume forms that later led to an entirely different form of writing.

Very few Latin manuscripts have been found earlier than the 4th century A. D., after which time they became more common. It would appear that the changes in the forms of the letters at first more largely involved the Greek than the Latin writing, and that in some cases the former changes reacted upon the latter, causing similar modifications in the old Roman letters.

The date of the Herculaneum manuscript which we reproduce, cannot be later than 79 A. D., when the city was destroyed and buried. It may have been some little time prior, but probably not long. Already certain changes in the shapes of the capitals may be detected. A is beginning to lose its upright position and to slant to the left, while the right hand line projects slightly at the top; but further than this — except in the word " paratus "— it gives no promise of the strange transformation soon to be effected. E and H already have made half of their transformation into the minuscules e and h. T is beginning to be cursive. The remaining letters in this particular manuscript do not depart far from the Roman capital type. Additional changes undergone in the form of the letters at this period, and somewhat later, will be noted from a study of other of these early manuscripts. Fig. 142 illustrates some of the more significant of these transformations. A has progressed still further toward the ultimate minuscule. The upper lobe of B is approaching the vanishing point. D has acquired a form very similar to the Greek minuscule *delta,* a shape that it maintained for several centuries. E has almost reached its goal. F is in its last stage of transformation and the progress is as evident as an open book. The various forms of G developed through several centuries. But the whole process of evolution — or rather devolution — of a capital into its minuscule is best illustrated in the series of successive shapes through which the letter H has progressed. The final variant is our modern minuscule. I K T and other letters in these manuscripts have entered upon the cursive stage, which with most of the letters was the intermediate stage leading to the " uncial " and, later, to the minuscule letters. N rather early acquired its minuscule form, almost attained in our list; yet the capital persisted in many incunabula into the Middle Ages. The transformation of V into u is most interesting. The slipping by of the right hand stroke is suggestive of the origin of *y.*

Fig. 142. Progressive transformation of certain letters in manuscripts of the early Christian centuries.

In Pompeii during the progress of excavations there were found 132 wax tablets in a box hidden over the portico of the house of a wealthy Roman, L. Cæcilius Jucundus. The tablets were for the most part business documents,— notes of payment, tax receipts, etc. They reveal the existence as early as the middle of the 1st century A. D. of a cursive form of Latin writing employed chiefly for secular manuscripts, business documents and letters, inscribed on rolls, codices and wax tablets. This cursive writing was somewhat similar in general appearance to our modern handwriting, except that it consisted of capital letters, Greek or Latin as the case may be, more or less connected by ligatures. This style of writing in secular manuscripts was in vogue for several centuries, undergoing during an extended period progressive changes, slow to be sure, which eventually affected the more conservative type of the classic letters employed in scientific and religious manuscripts.

That so little is left of the enormous quantity of manuscripts that existed in the classic period is a painful and distressing fact. It is known that some Roman scholars acquired as high as 60,000 volumes (rolls) of manuscripts. The destruction of manuscripts and libraries has been appalling. At Alexandria under the Ptolemies an era of high culture and refinement existed for a long period. The culture was essentially Greek in learning and language, as it was politically. Under Ptolemy Philadelphus (200 B. C.) a great library was founded which eventually grew to a total of 700,000 volumes. Every volume of this immense library perished when Cæsar burned his ships in the harbor of Alexandria. Subsequently, Mark Antony transported to Alexandria the library of King Eumenes from Pergamus, to found a new library in the Serapeum or Temple of Serapis.

It was added to for three centuries and then scattered
(390 A. D.) by the fanatic Theophilus, patriarch of
Alexandria under Theodosius the Great. The library
was in a measure restored and added to during the ensuing three centuries only to be utterly destroyed by the
Arab conquerors of Egypt when Alexandria was pillaged in the year 642. It is said that it took six months
to burn the last of the 500,000 volumes in the 4,000 baths
in the city.

The square capital was used in manuscript writing over
an extended period, falling into more or less complete
disuse sometime in the 6th century. In its purity it departed but little from the monumental script, as will be
noted by reference to the example given in the second
alphabet in Fig. 159, taken from the pages of a copy
of "Virgil's Æneid," now in the Vatican Library at
Rome; being a manuscript of the 4th century. It contains two forms of A, characteristic of the manuscripts
of the period; the typical form and a transitional one
merging into the minuscule. F L Y run above the line.
This is another peculiarity of manuscripts of this age. A
beautiful example of the square capital is illustrated in
Fig. 143, the reproduction of a fragment of the first page
of a manuscript copy, also of Virgil, in the Vatican Library. The entire work consists of nine verses, from 41
to 49, of the first book of the Georgics beginning: —

Ignarosq(ue) viae mecum miseratus agrestis
Ingredere et votis jam nunc adsuesce vocari
Vere novo gelidus canis cum montib.(us) umor

The manuscript is a beautiful specimen of the Roman
capital or "majuscule," as it is technically called, lingering into the 6th century. The letters follow very closely
the classic models, with slight but significant changes in

IGNAROSQVIAEMECVMMISERATVSAGRESTIS
INGREDERIETVOTISIAMNVNCADSVISCEVOCARI
VIRENOVOGELIDVSCANISCVMMONTIB·VMOR
LIQVITVREEZEPHYROPVTRISSEGLAEBARESOLVIT
DEPRESSOINCIPIATIAMTVMMIHITAVRVSARATRO
INGEMEREETSVLCOADTRITVSSPLENDESCEREVOMER
ILLASEGESDEMVMVOTISRESPONDEREIAVARI
AGRICOLAEBISQVAESOLEMBISFRIGORASENSIT
ILLIVSIMMENSAERVPERVNTHORREAMESSES

Fig. 143. Page from a manuscript copy of Virgil's Æneid, written in
" Square Capitals." 6th century.

a few cases. The A has lost its horizontal bar, while
the serif at the bottom of the left slanting line is beginning to curl up to form the body of the incipient
minuscule. E and F are considerably condensed, presag-
ing the " rustic " capitals; while F and L go above the
line, as in the previous manuscript, forecasting the
characteristics of these letters in our present minuscules.

The shading of the letters is unusually strong and bold,
adding greatly to their effectiveness. This was produced
by the shape of the quill or reed pen used by the scribes
of manuscripts throughout the Early and Middle Ages.
It was cut with a broad nib, sometimes square, sometimes
slightly oblique, and was held at such an angle that,
even without pressure, the right hand slanting lines, as
in the letter A, were drawn heavy with the broad side
of the pen, while the left hand slanting lines were drawn
light with the pen held edgewise. Z is the only letter in
which a left-hand stroke was made heavy. One easily
can judge in examining the shading of the round letters,

especially O, how the hand and pen were held, enabling the scribe to draw and shade the letters in two strokes of the pen, left and right.

A variety of the square capital known as the " rustic capital " early was evolved out of the classic letters. It became a very popular form of letter and was extensively employed. A beautiful example of these capitals is given in Fig. 144, a manuscript of the 5th century, now in the Vatican Library. It is a free treatment of the classic letters and evidences the tendency of the pen to break down the conventional type of the monuments. The serifs and horizontal bars made by the varying pressure and position of the pliable quill or reed pen and the strong shading of the letters — so much heavier than in the classic letters — give us the first hint of the " black-letter " so extensively used throughout the Middle Ages. Certain significant tendencies should be noted in this inscription, as they subsequently became fixed characteristics of the minuscule letters for all time. B F L in every case run well above the horizontal level of the other letters. This peculiarity of running above or below the line in a number of the capital letters very early manifested itself, and in every case has been handed down to this day and is retained in the modern minuscules. This type of letter, the rustic capital, so frequently met with in manuscripts of this period, will be found illustrated in the third line of Fig. 159. It illustrates an important stage in the historic development of the minuscule letter, as shown in this figure.

Although the rustic capitals fell into complete disuse as a book-hand, and were superseded along with the square capitals first by the uncial and then by the minuscule, as we shall proceed to show, they were not altogether lost sight of, but were retained for several centuries by the talented monks of the Christian church who followed the profession of scribes. They continued occasionally to use them in their manuscripts, along with the new book-hand in which the bulk of the text was

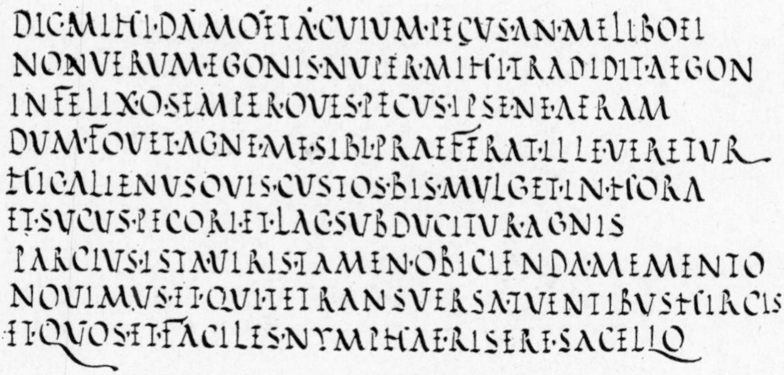

Fig. 144. Manuscript written in "Rustic Capitals." 5th century.

written, for titles, sub-titles, initials and rubrics. Three lines written in rustic capitals will be found in the second column of text in the Speculum of St. Augustine (Fig. 147). The sub-title "TERRA REGIS," and most of the capital letters throughout the page from the Domesday Book of Berkshire (Fig. 156) are rustic capitals only slightly modified. The paragraph initials in this manuscript, however, are the ordinary medieval black-letter uncials.

The progressive changes undergone by the Roman capital letters in the early centuries of our era were affected and accelerated by, if not wholly due to, the writing of manuscripts in the cursive style, both in Latin and in Greek; for there were concurrent changes in the Greek capitals, which were passing through a transformation very similar to that of the Latin. The greater speed with which secular manuscripts were written as

compared with scientific treatises, works on philosophy
and the precious copies of the gospels, and the increasing
temptation to carelessness on the part of the scribes,
in time reacted upon the more careful writing of the
latter class of manuscripts and progressively modified
the shapes of the square capitals in which they were written.

We will give a typical example of one of the many

Fig. 145. Letter written on papyrus in cursive Greek writing. 15 A.D.

fragments of cursive Greek manuscripts of the classic period, many of which have been recovered. Fig. 145 is a small and rather mutilated fragment of a papyrus of the year 15 A. D. The original is in the British Museum. It is written in capitals which with a few exceptions closely follow the Greek originals. The letters are for the most part written separately, there being few ligatures. As in nearly all Greek and Roman manuscripts, there is little or no separation of individual words, though there does appear to be a partial division of the inscription into sentences. This itself is an innovation; and in this particular manuscript also may be noted the beginnings of the new style, some centuries in fully asserting itself, of commencing sentences with a large letter. The first noticeable division of a page into paragraphs, in incunabula of this period, was made by a slight break in the text and a mark. Later, the initial letter of the first line of the paragraph was written out in the margin and made larger. These initial letters came into use about the 6th or 7th century.

Fig. 146 is the reproduction of an exceedingly rare Latin manuscript of the 3rd century, now in the Bibliothéque Nationale in Paris. It is written on papyrus, for the most part in debased Roman capitals, in a beautifully free, cursive style, with many ligatures and flourishes, executed in the finest style of professional penmanship. The letters really are part capitals and part uncials — the new style of letters then being developed — some of them being written separately, while others are connected by curves and flourishes.

By the 4th century the change in the shape of the capitals, through the corrupting influence of the cursive writing of secular documents, became so marked as to constitute the beginnings of a new style of letter, the

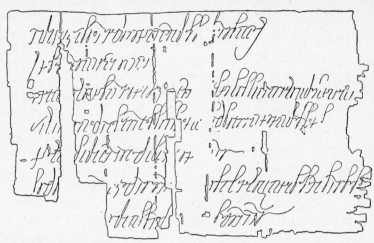

Fig. 146. Manuscript on papyrus in Latin cursive writing. 3d century A. D.

"uncial." The capital letters, however, were not altogether abandoned; but continued over a long period occasionally to be used in the body of the text, later, only as initial letters at the beginning of paragraphs. In some localities, in Italy, they were used throughout the text of the manuscript as late as the 6th or 7th centuries, or even later. The uncial was a large letter, one inch in height, as its name implies, resembling the capitals, but with strong tendencies toward rounding. Fig. 147 is a typical example of this new style of letter. It is a portion of the Speculum of St. Augustine, a palimpsest, now in the library of the Earl of Ashburnham. Thirteen leaves of the original manuscript, which is written on vellum in double columns, are extant. It dates from the end of the 7th century. It is written in full-size uncials without separation of words, but with large capitals at the beginning of paragraphs, according to the new style slowly establishing itself. At the first casual glance the writing seems to be in the old capitals, but a moment's

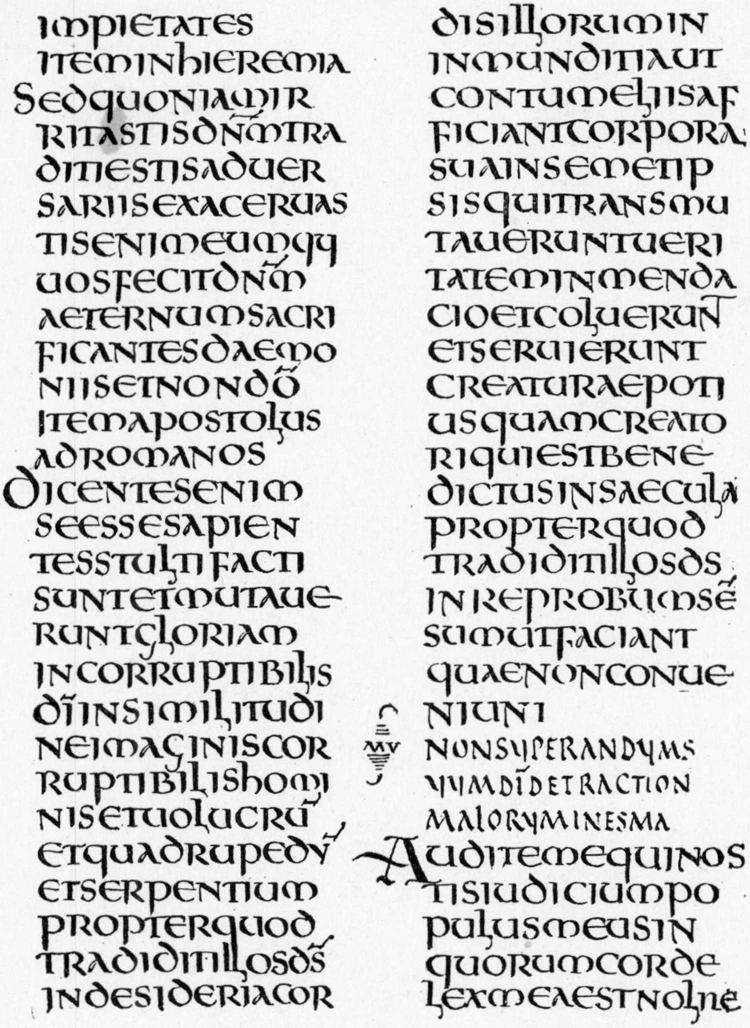

IMPIETATES
ITEMINHIEREMIA
SEDQUONIAMIR
RITASTISONMTRA
OMESTISADUER
SARIISEXACERUAS
TISENIMEUMQY
UOSFECITDNM
AETERNUMSACRI
FICANTESDAEMO
NIISETNONDO
ITEMAPOSTOLUS
ADROMANOS
DICENTESENIM
SEESSESAPIEN
TESSTULTIFACTI
SUNTETMUTAUE-
RUNTCLORIAM
INCORRUPTIBILIS
DIINSIMILITUDI
NEIMAGINISCOR
RUPTIBILISHOMI
NISETUOLUCRU
ETQUADRUPEDY
ETSERPENTIUM
PROPTERQUOD
TRADIDITILLOSOS
INDESIDERIACOR

DISILLORUMIN
INMUNDITIAUT
CONTUMELIISAF
FICIANTCORPORA
SUAINSEMETIP
SISQUITRANSMU
TAUERUNTUERI
TATEMINMENDA
CIOETCOLUERUN
ETSERUIERUNT
CREATURAEPOTI
USQUAMCREATO
RIQUIESTBENE
DICTUSINSAECULA
PROPTERQUOD
TRADIDITILLOSOS
INREPROBUMSE
SUMUTFACIANT
QUAENONCONUE
NIUNT
NONSUPERANDYMS
YVMDIDETRACTION
MALORYMINESMA
AUDITEMEQUINOS
TISIUDICIUMPO
PULUSMEUSIN
QUORUMCORDE
LEXMEAESTNOLNE

Fig. 147. Speculum of St. Augustine, written in "uncial letters." End
of the 7th century.

study reveals the changes that already had been effected
toward the ultimate minuscule. Six letters in particular,

a d e h m u, are noticeable for their rounding tendencies. The strange looking A, first met with in the Herculaneum manuscript, at once strikes the eye. D and E
either have been borrowed from the Greek *delta,* δ, and
epsilon, ε, respectively, or have been modified under the
same common influences that operated to produce these
letters. H and M have departed very far from their
straight line prototypes. D H L F G P Q go above
or below the line and presage even at this early age this
peculiarity of just one-half of the minuscules in our
alphabet to-day. Of the remaining number of these
minuscules in our modern alphabet, b j k t y z (cursive),
the tendency to go above or below the line in manuscripts
of this period may be detected in B K Y.

Fig. 148 taken from a manuscript in the Bibliothéque
Nationale in Paris, beginning with the Latin title:
" VENIAMUS AD ILLUM Locum," etc., is a very
fine example of the French uncial. Certain letters still

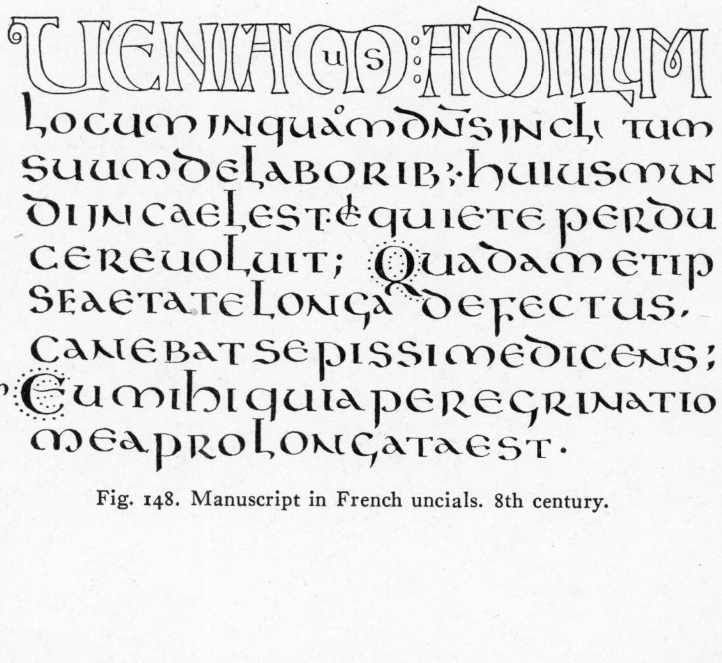

Fig. 148. Manuscript in French uncials. 8th century.

remain practically unaffected; — as B O I O S. A has almost entirely effected its transformation, while G is advancing. E shows two varieties,— the classic E and a form very similar to the Greek minuscule, *epsilon,* ε. F consistently remains considerably below the line, while L keeps well above it. Tendencies toward the Gothic minuscule, the black-letter of the Middle Ages, may be detected only in the letter S.

The uncial continued to be the prevailing book-hand for all clerical and literary productions down to the 8th or 9th centuries, or even later on the continent. But even as early as the 6th century, its degeneracy, owing to the influence of secular documents in the cursive style of writing, became marked. In time this constituted an epoch in writing, dominated by the "half-uncial" style of letter which obtained for a century or more. The innovations were most noticeable in the letters a b d e l m n r s, which were rapidly progressing toward the minuscule. Two examples of the uncial letter will be found in Fig. 159, an early and a later variety, separated by about four centuries. The alphabet in the fourth line is from a palimpsest of "Cicero's Republic," in Latin, and dates from the 3rd century. The alphabet in the fifth line is from the Speculum of St. Augustine (Fig. 147), also in Latin, and of the 7th century.

Contemporaneous with the decline and ultimate extinction of the uncial letters, the cursive style itself gradually passed out of use, to be revived in the late Middle Ages. Both of these styles of writing which had been practiced in Italy and the Roman provinces for several hundred years, during the Dark Ages merged into the new book-hand, the minuscule, which rose to its perfection in the 11th and 12th centuries. We will give one final example of the cursive writing of this period (Fig.

149), further to illustrate the contemporary hand that shared in the transformation of the old Roman capitals and uncials into the minuscule letters. It is a fragment of a manuscript in Lombardic cursive writing of the 9th century. The original is in the Monastere de la Cava in Naples. The letters are for the most part separate, not many being connected by glides or ligatures. The exaggerated strokes of the letters b d l are strongly characteristic. The Cursive alphabet will be found illustrated in the sixth line in Fig. 159.

It was in the provinces that the changes in the type of

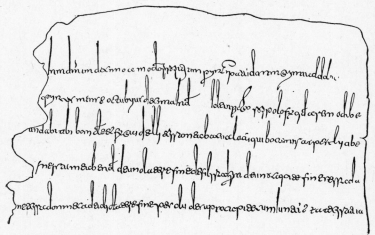

Fig. 149. Fragment of a manuscript in Latin, written in Lombardic cursive writing. 9th century.

the letters became most rapid and marked. The minuscule had firmly established itself in Irish and Anglo-Saxon manuscript writing before it had become at all marked in Roman or Italian manuscripts. Roman missionaries had introduced the art of writing into Ireland and England in the early centuries of the Christian era.

The Irish monks, being apart from the warring turmoil of the continent, became free to develop at their leisure their own local style of calligraphy. Under the pens of these cloistered monks, removed from the conventional forms that might hold them fast to traditional types, the old capitals underwent a more rapid transformation than on the continent. The Irish uncial was not only a distinctive script, but it was perhaps the most beautiful of all the book-hands. There is a tradition that St. Patrick (432–458 A. D.) carried the uncial style of writing — it probably was the half-uncial — into Ireland from Gaul, where he is believed to have acquired the art.

There are extant to-day two books, classics in the history of Irish epigraphy, which contain numerous examples of extraordinary beauty of the wonderful art of the Celtic monks. The more famous is the " Book of Kells." Kells is in County Meath, Ireland. Here in the 6th century St. Columba, or Columbkille, founded a monastery that became a renowned center of learning. Nothing now remains of the monastery; but the wonderful Book of Kells, an illuminated copy of the Gospels in Latin, containing also local records dating from the 6th century, has survived all the ravages of the Saxon and Danish invasions and the wars of the English conquest. It is now preserved in the library of Trinity College, Dublin. The other book is known as the Book of Armagh, a manuscript containing books of the New Testament, written by Ferdomnach, a scribe who died in 844. The writing in both of these books, more particularly the former, is of extreme beauty and delicacy, being embellished with illuminations in color that are among the rarest examples of Celtic tracery and interlacing, for which the Irish monks were famous. The following alphabet of Irish

uncials — really " half uncials " as they are called, for
they have almost completed even at this early age their
full transformation into the minuscule — has been taken
from the pages of the " Book of Kells " :

abcɔdefᵹhilmnꞃopqrꞃsꞇuxᵹƶ

The Irish uncial was fully developed in the 6th century, and traveling monks carried their art into England where it markedly affected the Anglo-Saxon book-
hand. In the Saxon invasion of England the continuity
of the Roman civilization had been largely destroyed,
and the art of writing languished with other elements of
Roman culture. As early as the days of King Alfred the
Great, the Danes had destroyed the greater part of all
the books in England. King Alfred pathetically exclaims:
" I saw, before all were spoiled and burnt, how the
churches throughout Britain were filled with treasures
and books." When learning revived, the influence of the
Irish book-hand was strongly manifest in ecclesiastical
writing in England. The Irish missionary Aidan founded
the see of Lindisfarne in the north of England in the
year 635, where he established a school of writing. The
Lindisfarne Gospels or " Durham Book," written by
Eadfrith, bishop of Lindisfarne, about 700, is the best
example of the Anglo-Saxon round-hand of this period.

Fig. 150 is a fragment of the New Testament from
the Bodleian Library, Oxford. It is a beautiful example
of the Anglo-Saxon half-uncial letter of the 7th century.
It is, however, even at this early period well advanced
toward the minuscule, the latter being far more in evidence than the former. The only letters that have not
completely effected their transformation into the minuscule are F R T, and these are more advanced than any

yet shown. The tendency, however, toward the medieval Gothic or "black-letter," is little more marked. The general form of the letter is still Roman, and the perfected minuscule as shown in e h m n u are almost precisely like our modern minuscules or small Roman letters with which this book is printed. Many other letters almost as strongly resemble them. Tendencies toward Gothic or Old English, soon to be the prevailing style of letter for centuries, are seen only in O S T. The division of the writing of the manuscript into separate words and sentences with partial use of punctuation marks shows the distinct contribution of these scholarly monks to the progress of the art of writing in Europe.

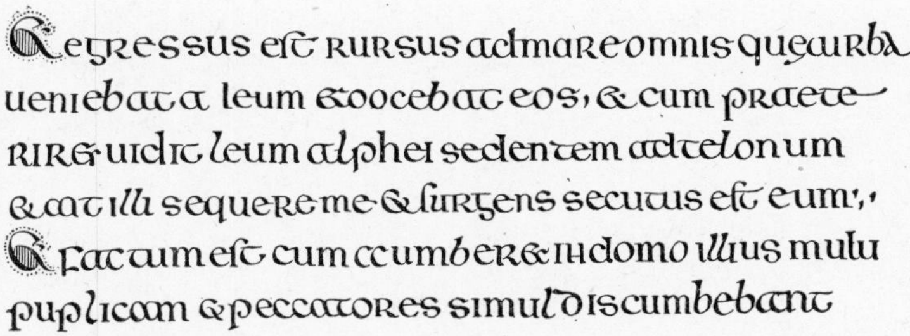

Fig. 150. Manuscript copy of the New Testament, written in Anglo-Saxon half-uncials of the 7th century.

The inherent difficulties and disadvantages of the uncial hand as the basis of a practical book-hand arose from the fact that they could not be made rapidly. Being founded on the Roman capital letters, of which they were the direct descendants, they retained to a considerable extent their straight-line characteristics; although many of the letters, more particularly in the Irish and Anglo-Saxon scripts, early had developed rounding characteristics. Gradually, through the continued debasing tendencies of the cursive writing, the forms of the letters from

decade to decade underwent further changes, and the
gradual development of the new minuscule hand was the
result. This development was under way on the continent
about the 8th or 9th century and reached its highest
perfection in the 11th or 12th century, when it degenerated until the invention of printing. The northern type
of the Anglo-Saxon script, the elements of which had been
introduced into England by Irish monks, was among the
most beautiful of the semi-uncial scripts and was destined
to have a marked influence upon the future development
of writing in Europe. It prevailed up to about the 9th
century. It was the immediate precursor of the Caroline
minuscule, which soon spread throughout Europe, displacing the old monastic uncial and the cursive writing.

Another beautiful example of the round Anglo-Saxon
minuscule, written in England in the 8th century, is reproduced in Fig. 151. It is one of 41 leaves of vellum,
being the " Account of the Passion from the Gospels,"
followed by a series of Prayers on the " Life and Passions of Our Lord." The page begins:

Gratias tibi reffero et per hoc exoro sol
ue a me misero uelamen uitiorum uirtu
tibusque indue pro uitiis, Ut in illo nuptiali
conuiuio non nudus sed indutus ueste nupti
ali intrare merear, Domine iesu christe amen.

We detect at once a change in the general appearance
of the letters. They are less rounding and more angular
than in the earlier manuscripts. The serifs are no longer
horizontal but are slanting, and the curves of the letters
are giving way to angular strokes. It is in fact a transitional letter between the minuscule and the black-letter.
One will notice a further change in the letter A. The
curve of the body reaches fully to the top of the right

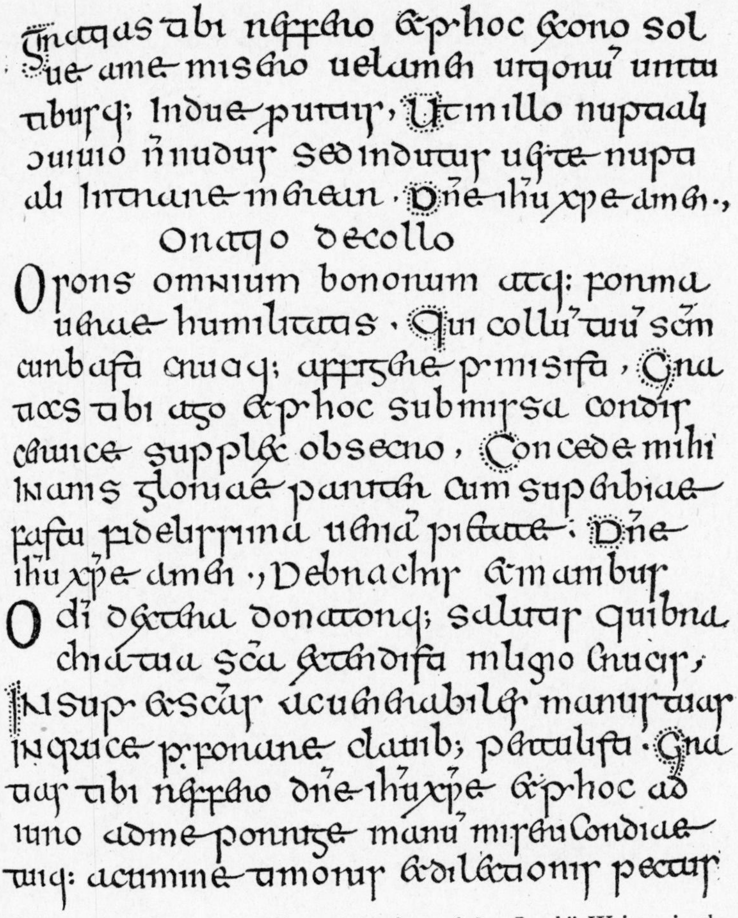

[Facsimile of Anglo-Saxon minuscule manuscript text]

Fig. 151. Leaf from the " Life and Passions of Our Lord." Written in the Anglo-Saxon minuscule of the 8th century.

hand bar, as it does in our modern handwriting and in certain varieties of the black-letter. Two varieties of N are employed: the old uncial capital and the new minuscule. Two varieties of R also are employed: the old uncial capital, the bar of which runs below the line,

and the far more frequent one that much resembles the
minuscule n. Likewise two S's are used: the one that resembles the capital letter and one that runs far below
the line and explains the old-fashioned $\int$, only recently
obsolete in the last century. In this manuscript, now for
the first time, we note a consistent purpose, consciously
and systematically carried out, of dividing the writing
into paragraphs, with headings; the paragraphs into sentences, with initial letters; the sentences into separate
words, with punctuation marks to indicate clauses. It was
not until the 11th century, on the continent, that the
custom of spacing the words throughout the manuscript
became general, and then only in manuscripts in Latin.
Greek manuscripts were not separated into words with
punctuation marks until the Age of Printing. The first
punctuation mark was the stop at the end of the sentence. At first it was made the same as our colon. Later,
one of the dots was dropped, and the remaining one
served as a period, a colon or a comma, according as
it was placed even with the top, the middle or the bottom of the small letters. The Anglo-Saxon half-uncial
alphabet is illustrated in the seventh line in Fig. 159.

One of the most unique of medieval manuscripts is
the one represented in Fig. 152. It is one of 171 leaves
in vellum of the " Lex Salica," or " Laws of the Salian
Franks together with the Laws of the Visigoths and
Allamanni." It was written in the year 794 by Van-
dalgarius who signs his name at the end of the volume.
The writing is in Lombardic minuscules. The first four
lines read:

IN NOMINE D(OMI)NI N(OST)RI
(I)esu Christi incipiunt titulus legis salice
I : de mannire
Si quis ad mallu(m) legib(u)s dominicis

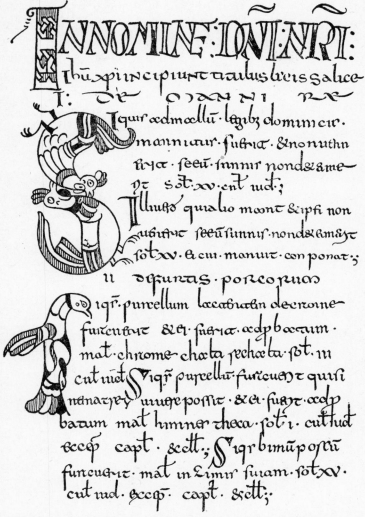

Fig. 152. Leaf from the Lex Salica. Written in Lombardic minuscules.
794 A. D.

The Salic Law originated with the Salian Franks, who, in the 5th century, founded the Frankish kingdom.

According to this law women are precluded from succession to the throne. Again we detect in these letters the angular serifs and the angular strokes in place of curves in the body of the letter. They now have become the permanent characteristics of medieval writing employed in all incunabula, to be still more emphasized and developed in the Gothic black-letter in use throughout the Middle Ages and abandoned only after the invention of printing in the renaissance of learning, when there was a return to the Caroline minuscule. We find in the letters in this manuscript two types of A: the one that resembles our modern minuscule (a) and the one similar to our script (*a*). The uncial capitals: N R and their respective minuscules both are employed, as in the former manuscript.

In the development of the minuscule letter, which preceded the black-letter of the Middle Ages, the English monks played no small part by their splendid contribution to the art of writing. Alcuin of York, England, who had been invited to France by the Emperor Charlemagne, to become instructor in the school of the palace, established a school of calligraphy at the Abbey of St. Martin at Tours, in 796, maintaining it until the year 809. Alcuin became Abbot of the convent of St. Martin, making Tours famous by attracting to it monks from all parts of Europe who came to acquire the new style of book-hand. It was chiefly the Benedictine monks who wrote the manuscript copies of the scriptures, the incunabula and other literary productions through the Dark and Middle Ages. It is to them that we are indebted for the conservation of literature in these many years of struggle and warfare. A room in the monastery, known as the " scriptorium," was set apart for this work. The outfit consisted of parchment from calves, goats or sheep; vellum from unborn lambs or kids; pumice stone for smoothing the skins; quills, reed pens; black ink, and red ink from red earth (rubrica) for the rubrics.

The new book-hand was based on the beautiful set minuscule of the English manuscripts of this period; which, as we have learned, had developed in the Irish monasteries. It was a half-uncial hand, part uncial and, part minuscule — largely the latter — influenced by the best features of the French and Italian — Lombardic — models. It eventually developed, early in the 9th century, into the Caroline minuscule, which continued until the black-letter was fully established in the 12th and 13th centuries. The perfected Caroline minuscule was a small, somewhat rounded, set letter, legible and rapid of execution, and unexcelled as a book-hand. The Caroline minuscule is illustrated in the eighth line of letters in Fig. 159. The alphabet has been taken from "Tropes and Sequences for the Mass," a manuscript written at Winchester, in the reign of Ethelred (979–1016).

It is the minuscule of the 10th and 11th centuries that served as a model for our modern book-type. In incunabula written in this style of writing we find spaces between words, capitals for sentences, division of the pages into paragraphs and the use of punctuation and diacritical marks, somewhat the same as in our modern printing. It was Alcuin who first systematized the punctuation of manuscripts. He insisted that copyists should pay attention to the pauses,—"*per cola et commata.*" The semicolon at first was used in manuscripts to denote the Latin *bus* and *que*. Later, commas, colons, periods and hyphens were used; but the full system of punctuation as followed to-day was not fully developed until after the invention of printing.

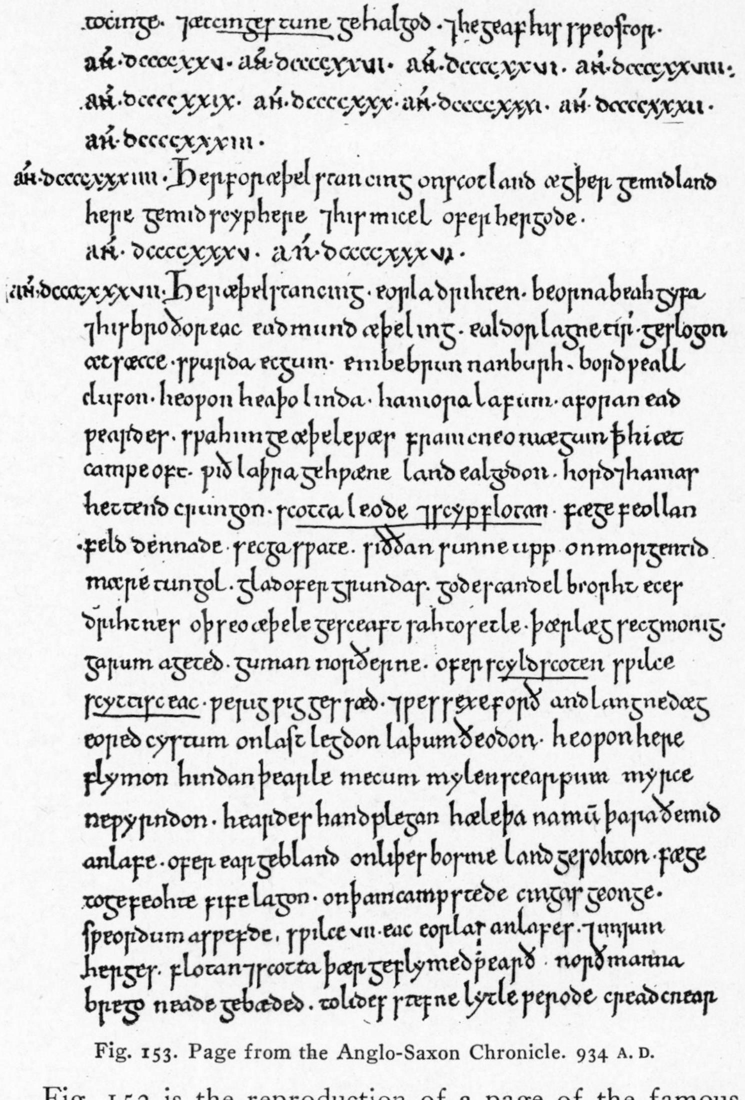
tacinge. 7 æt cingestune gehalgod. 7 he geaf his sweostor.
an. dccccxxv. an. dccccxxvi. an. dccccxxvii. an. dccccxxviii.
an. dccccxxix. an. dccccxxx. an. dccccxxxi. an. dccccxxxii.
an. dccccxxxiii.
an. dccccxxxiiii. Her for æþelstan cining on scotland ægþer ge mid land
here ge mid scyphere 7 his micel ofer hergode.
an. dccccxxxv. an. dccccxxxvi.
an. dccccxxxvii. Her æþelstan cining eorla dryhten beorna beahgyfa
7 his broþor eac eadmund æþeling ealdorlangne tir geslogon
æt sæcce sweorda ecgum embe brunnanburh. bordweall
clufon heowon heaþolinda hamora lafum afaran ead
weardes swa him geæþele wæs fram cneomægum þ hi æt
campe oft wiþ laþra gehwæne land ealgodon hord 7 hamas
hettend crungun sceotta leode 7 scipflotan fæge feollan
feld dennade secga swate siððan sunne upp on morgentid
mære tungol glad ofer grundas godes candel beorht eces
drihtnes oþ sio æþele gesceaft sah to setle þær læg secg monig
garum ageted guman norþerne ofer scild scoten swilce
scyttisc eac werig wiggessæd wesseaxe forð andlangne dæg
eorod cystum onlast legdon laþum ðeodum heowon here
flymon hindan þearle mecum mylenscearpum myrce
ne wyrndon heardes handplegan hæleþa nanum þara ðe mid
anlafe ofer ear gebland on liþes bosme land gesohton fæge
to gefeohte fife lagon on þam campstede cyninges geonge
sweordum aswefede swilce vii eac eorlas anlafes 7 unrim
heriges flotan 7 sceotta þær geflymed wearð norðmanna
bregu neade gebæded to lides stefne lytle weorode cread cnear

Fig. 153. Page from the Anglo-Saxon Chronicle. 934 A. D.

Fig. 153 is the reproduction of a page of the famous "Anglo-Saxon Chronicle" which was kept continuously in England from the coming of the Saxons to the time of the Conquest in 1066. There are but fifty pages of the Chronicle extant: The first complete record in the page here illustrated is for the year 934 and reads:

> Anno dccccxxxiiii. Her for æthelstan cinq on scot-land æther ge midland here g:: mid scyphere and his micel oferhergode. " This year went King Athelstan into Scotland both with a land force and a sea force and laid waste much of it."

The type of letter in which this precious record of the early history of England is written is a late form of the Anglo-Saxon minuscule verging into the black-letter. In the body of the text the cursive form of A (*a*) is used throughout, but in the dates the earlier form (a) consistently is used; as is also the old uncial capital N.

Gradually through the early Middle Ages the Anglo-Saxon minuscule developed from the round, set minuscule of the 7th and 8th centuries, illustrated in Fig. 150 and Fig. 151, through the more angular type of the 10th century, as shown in the Anglo-Saxon Chronicle, until finally it developed into the black-letter or Old English letter in the 12th and 13th centuries. With the coming of the Normans and the general introduction of Norman-French culture, the purity of the Anglo-Saxon language began to suffer from the admixture of foreign elements, and for several centuries the language passed through the formative stages that eventually gave us our fully developed English speech of the Elizabethan period. Writing developed along quite the same lines of historical culture, passing through a period quite similar to that of the spoken language and to the somewhat parallel development on the continent, which gave rise to the Gothic black-letter used until the invention of printing, but soon thereafter abandoned, except in Germany.

Fig. 154. Charter of the City of London. Granted by William the Conqueror (*circa* 1066).

Fig. 154, a facsimile of the Charter of the City of London, granted by William the Conqueror in 1066, is written in the beautiful Saxon minuscule of the 11th century. The transformation into the black-letter or Old English is almost complete, as far as the small letters are concerned. The English in which the charter is written is so early and quaint that it actually needs translation to be understood to-day. It reads:

" William, king, greets William, bishop, and Geoffrey, Portreeve, and all the Burghers within London, French and English, friendly. And I make known unto you that I will that ye be worthy all those laws the which ye were in King Edward's day, and I will that each child be his father's heir after his father's day, and I will not suffer that any man do you any wrong. God give you health."

The reader will detect a few strange characters in this Anglo-Saxon writing. The character for " and " is an innovation. Two other characters have been taken from the ancient runes and incorporated into the written script. They both resemble the letter p. The one that occurs in the word " will " (wylle) is the rune " wen " (w). The other one that occurs several times in the words " the " and " that " is the rune " thorn " (th).

The latter character continued in use for several centuries, finally changing into y and persisting into very recent times in the word "ye" (the). A noted example of this usage is to be found in the inscription on Shakespeare's tomb in the old church at Stratford-upon-Avon (Fig. 155).

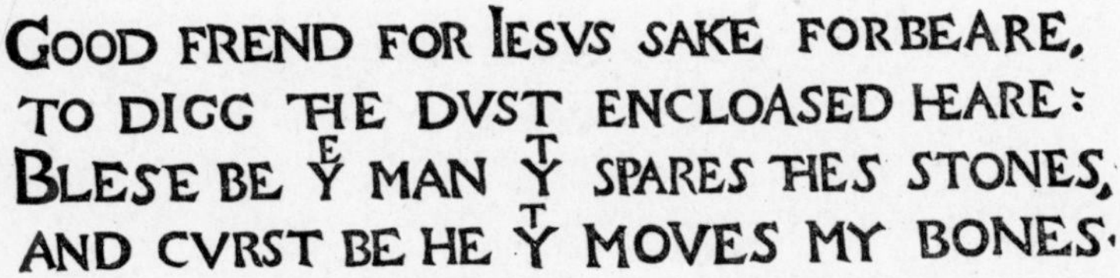

GOOD FREND FOR IESVS SAKE FORBEARE,
TO DIGG THE DVST ENCLOASED HEARE:
BLESE BE Yͤ MAN Yͭ SPARES THES STONES,
AND CVRST BE HE Yͭ MOVES MY BONES.

Fig. 155. Inscription on Shakespeare's tomb. Stratford-upon-Avon.

Another very precious relic written in the Anglo-Saxon minuscule of the period is the famous "Domesday Book," a survey of the counties in England, executed in 1086 under the orders of William the Conqueror. There were several of these Domesday Books, all of them written in Latin, but executed by many different hands, as is attested by the individuality of the handwriting. There is one in the Public Record Office in London, in two volumes. The first volume consists of 382 double columns, nine and one-half inches by fourteen and five-eighths inches, written in double columns. The second volume consists of 450 double pages of single columns. It is a survey of the counties of Essex, Suffolk and Norfolk. Another large section is in the Exeter Chapter Library. It is the survey of the counties of Dorset, Wilts, Somerset, Cornwall and Devon. There are in all 532 pages of this survey, written in Latin by several different hands, the scribe who completed the final page writing at the bottom: "Consummatum est."

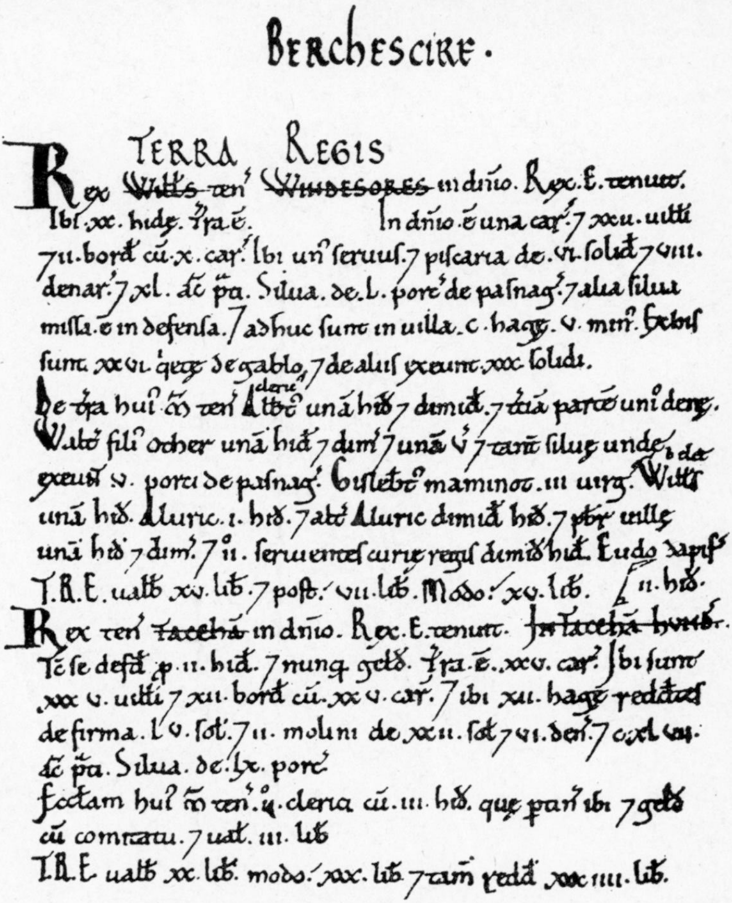

BERCHESCIRE·

TERRA REGIS

[facsimile of handwritten Domesday Book text]

Fig. 156. Page from the " Domesday " of Berkshire.

We reproduce in Fig. 156 one of the pages of the Domesday Book containing the survey of Berkshire. The language is so quaint that we will give the transcription of the first paragraph:

THE KING'S LAND

King William holds Windsor in demesne. King Edward held it. There are twenty hides. There is land for . . . In demesne is one plough and twenty-two villeins and two bordars with ten ploughs. There is one serf, a fishery with six shillings and eight pence and forty acres of meadow. A wood for pannage of fifty hogs, and another wood enclosed, and there are yet a hundred hagae, less five in the vill. Out of these twenty-six are quit of gabel, and the issue of the others is thirty shillings."

The lines drawn through some of the proper names — William, Windsor, Thatcham, Hundred — are not erasures, but red ink lines to indicate importance, that have taken black on the photograph.

As a whole the writing in all these books is quite uniform in style, all being in the Anglo-Saxon minuscule current in the 11th century. The letters are in a pointed, set hand, transitional between the round Saxon minuscule and the black-letter. The capitals in the superscription, and elsewhere, are almost pure uncials, with hardly a trace of Old English. Up to the end of the 12th century the old square capitals, and the uncials that developed out of them, were used for initial letters with the angular minuscules for the text; but in the 13th century arose the new series out of the Caroline, and the Gothic capitals rapidly displaced the old forms and continued in use until the original Roman capitals were restored in the time of the Renaissance.

The reader will perhaps recognize in the last two manuscripts a perfected type of letter markedly different from the earlier Anglo-Saxon letter, which was full and rounding. This new type of letter is the medieval black-

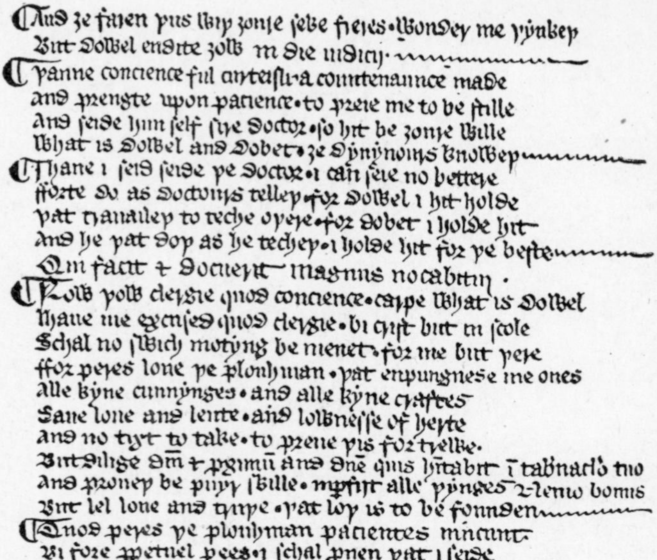

And ȝe faren þus wiþ ȝonȝe sibe freres·Wonder me þynkeþ
But Dowel ende ȝow in die indici·
Þanne conience ful curteisli a comtenaunce made
and prengte vpon patience·to prene me to be stille
and seide hym self siye Doctor·so hit be ȝonȝe wille
What is Dowel and Dobet·ȝe Dyuynouns knoweþ
Þanne i seid seide þe Doctor·i can seie no bettere
fforte Do as Doctours telleþ·for Dowel i hit holde
þat þanaueþ to reche oþere·for Dobet i holde hit
and he þat Doþ as he techeþ·i holde hit for þe beste
Qui facit & Docuerit magnus nocabitur·
Now Pow clepeþ qnod conience·carpe What is Dowel
haue me excused qnod clergie·bi crist but in scole
Schal no swich motyng be menet·for me but þere
ffor peres loue þe plowhman·þat enpungnese me ones
Alle kyne cunnynges·and alle kyne craftes
Saue loue and lente·and lowenesse of herte
and no tyt to take·to prene þis for treuþe·
But dilige Dm & pgximu and One qnis hitabit I tabnaclo tuo
and þronei be puiy stille·myfiȝt alle þynges r lenio bonus
But lel loue and truþe·þat loy is to be fonnden
Qnod peres þe plowhman pacientes vincunt
Bi fore þpetuel pees·i schal prnen þat i seide
And a wolbe bi fore Dod·and for saue hit neneþe
þat Dilige Doce Dilige Dm·and þyn enmy·
þereuch pow him helpe·enene forþ þi miȝt
Laiȝ hote coles on his hed·of alle kynde speche
ffond wiþ þi Wrth and Wiþ þi Word·his loue forte Wynne
and ȝef him eft and eft·oneþe at his nede
Comforte hym wiþ þi catel·and wiþ þi kynde speche
and lanþe on him þus wiþ loue·til he lanþe on þe
and but he wolbe for þis beþyng·blynd mote i worþe
And When he hadde i wordes þus·Wiste no man aft
Whey peres þe plowhman bi can·so prenenli he Wente
and reson þan aftey·and jrlj wiþ him ȝede
Saue conience and cleysie·i wonde no mo aspie
And patience prenenli spak·þo peres was þus passed
þat loney lelli qnod he·but litel þing conetteþ
Wolde and i wil hadde·Wynne al frannce
wiþ oute brennyng of beynes·or eny blod scheþyng
I taȝe Wrthnesse qnod he·at holibyrth a prize pacientes vincunt

Fig. 157. Page from the poem of "Piers Plowman." Anglo-Saxon book-
hand of the 14th century.

letter. It is condensed and angular, the curves of the Caroline letters giving way to points. It is an economical letter, taking up comparatively little room, but hard to read on account of its uniformity. This letter with little modification remained the popular book-hand in England until the invention of printing.

We will give two final examples of English manuscript writing in the black-letter. Fig. 157 is a reproduction of a page of " Piers Plowman," a poem composed by William Langland, who lived 1362–1393. The full title of the work is: " The Vision of William concerning Piers Plowman together with Vita de Dowel, Dobet and Dobest." The writing is in the English minuscule or Old English of the latter half of the 14th century. That the reader may identify the letters and at the same time obtain a hint of the historic growth of the language and especially of the orthography of this age, we will give a transcript of a part of this quaint old English poem, beginning at the third line:

Thanne concience ful curteisliche a countenaunce made
And prengte upon pacience. to preie me to be stille
And seide him self sire doctor. so hit be youre wille
What is dowel and dobet. ye dyuynours knoweth
I haue I seid seide the doctor. I can seie no bettere
Forte do as doctours telleth. for dowel I hit holde
That trauaileth to teche othere. for dobet I holde hit
And he that doth as he techeth. I holde hit for the
 beste.
Qui facit et docuerit magnus uocabitur.
Now thou clergie quod concience. carpe what is dowel
Hauve me excused quod clergie. bi crist but in scole
Schal no swich motyng be meuet. for me but there

For peres loue the ploughman. that enpungnese me
  ones
Alle kýne cunnýnges. and alle kýne craftes
Saue loue and leute. and lownesse of herte
And no tixt to take. to preue this for trewe.
But dilige deum et proximum and dominie quis. habi-
  tabit in tabernaculo tuo
And proueth be puyr skille. inparfit alle thýnges Nemo
  bonus
But lel loue and truthe. that loth is to be founden.

Our final example of the English black-letter or Old
English, is a manuscript copy of the " Poem de Regimine
Principum," by Thomas Occleve, dedicated to Henry,
Prince of Wales (Fig. 158). It is written in the English
minuscule of the court hand type, in a set angular form,
arranged in poetic stanzas, with illuminated initials. It
is a beautiful example of early 15th century writing, just
prior to the invention of printing.

In the last two manuscripts we notice a peculiar form
of capital letter used for initials at the beginning of each
line of the poem, according to our modern custom. The
letters are widely different from the capitals used in the
earlier centuries,— the square, rustic and uncial letters.
They are the medieval capitals, the Gothic uncials, of
which there was a large variety. The devolution and
evolution of the classic capitals is a strange story of degradation, elimination and complete ultimate restoration.
For a few centuries the square capitals illustrated in the
second line in Fig. 159 were exclusively used in written
manuscripts, as illustrated in Fig. 143. All the letters in
every word were capitals, only very slightly changed
from the classic letters. There being no small letters em-

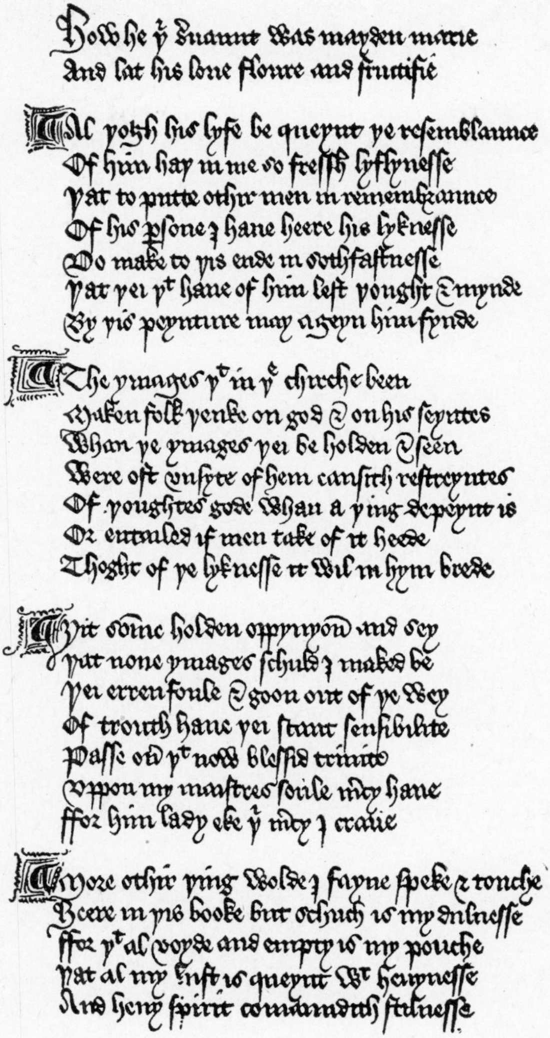

Hou he y^i seruaunt was mayden marie
And lat his loue floure and fructifie

Al yogh his lyfe be queynt ye resemblaunce
Of him hay in me so fressh lyflynesse
yat to putte othir men in remembraunce
Of his psone I haue heere his lyknesse
Do make to yis ende in sothfastnesse
yat yei y^t haue of him lest yought & mynde
By yis peynture may ageyn him fynde

The ymages y^t in ye chirche been
Maken folk yenke on god & on his seyntes
Whan ye ymages yei be holden & seen
Were oft unsyte of hem causith restreyntes
Of youghtes gode whan a ying depeynt is
Or entailed if men take of it heede
Thoght of ye lyknesse it wil in hym brede

Yit somme holden oppynyon and sey
yat none ymages schuld I maked be
yei erren foule & goon out of ye wey
Of trouth haue yei scant sensibilite
Passe on y^t now blessid trinite
Uppon my maistres soule mercy haue
ffor him lady eke y^i mercy I craue

More othir ying wolde I fayne speke & touche
Heere in yis booke but such is my dulnesse
ffor y^t al voyde and empty is my pouche
yat al my lust is queynt w^t heuynesse
And heuy spirit comaundith stilnesse

Fig. 158. Page from the "Poem de Regimine Principum," by Thomas Occleve. Written in English minuscules of the "court-hand type." Early 15th century.

ployed, such as we now use throughout the text of a printed book, initial letters, when used — which was rarely — were simply enlarged capitals. During a part of this early period, and later, the free variety of the square capital known as the rustic capital was used for manuscripts, as has been shown in Fig. 144. This form of letter was a more marked departure from the classic capital than the square capital; but it possessed undoubted elements of grace and beauty. Again the entire manuscript was written in these capitals. There were no small letters and no initial letters employed except the rare use of enlarged capitals of the style of letter used throughout the text of the manuscript.

In the 5th and 6th centuries the classic capitals became degraded into the uncial letters, which contained a strange mixture of the old capitals and the incipient forms of the approaching minuscule letters. Still, only the one alphabet was used throughout the manuscript. Words, as a rule, were not separated, and the use of large letters for initials still had not come into vogue. When, however, in the 7th and 8th centuries, the semi-uncial and in the next century the minuscule letters became fully developed in Ireland and England and later on the continent, and it became the settled practice to divide the pages into paragraphs, sentences and clauses, the use of initial letters for the opening words of the literary divisions of the manuscript began to be the custom. The choice of letter for these initials varied with the preference of the scribe. Sometimes the type of letter chosen was an enlarged form of the minuscle with which the body of the manuscript was written; sometimes it was the old uncial, the old rustic or the early square capital that was used for the initial letter. These various usages will be observed in the manuscripts illustrated in this book.

Fig. 159. Evolution of the minuscule letters from the Roman capitals.

I. Roman monumental capitals. II. Square capitals. Manuscript copy of Virgil's Æneid in the Vatican Library. 4th century. III. Rustic capitals. Manuscript in the Vatican. 5th century. IV. Early uncial letters. Palimpsest of Cicero's Republic. 3rd century. V. Late uncial letters Speculum of St Augustine. 7th century. VI. Cursive letters. VII. Anglo-Saxon uncial letters. Life and Passions of Our Lord. 8th century. VIII. Caroline letters. Tropes and Sequences of the Masses. 10th century. IX. Early black letters. Charter of the City of London. 1066.

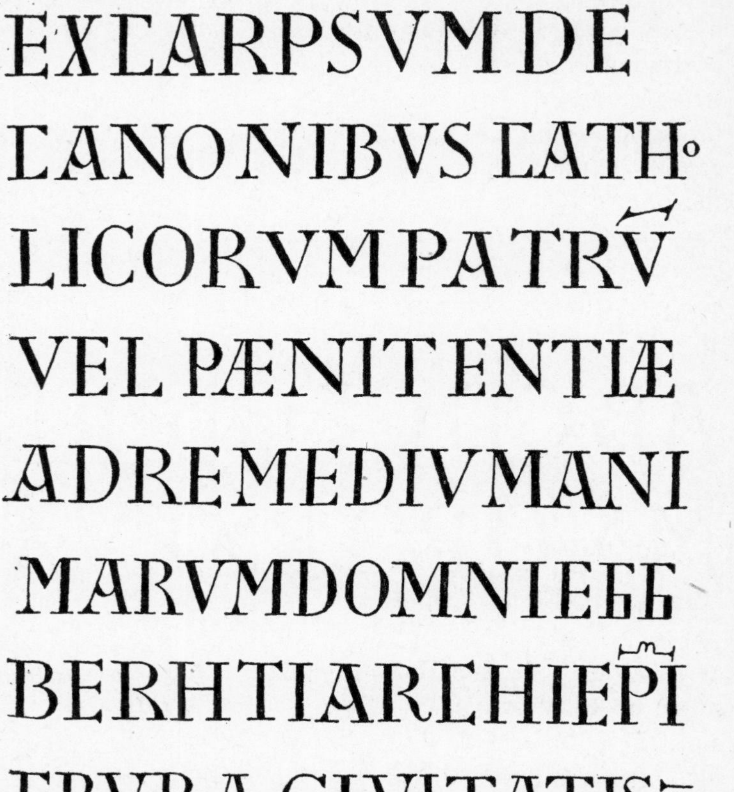

EXCARPSVM DE CANONIBVS CATHᵒ LICORVM PATRV̂ VEL PÆNITENTIÆ ADREMEDIVMANI MARVMDOMNIEGG BERHTIARCHIEPI EBVRA CIVITATIS⸝⸝

Fig. 160. Title page in Roman capitals of a manuscript written in the Anglo-Saxon minuscule of the 10th century.

That the old classic capitals were never lost sight of, even by scribes in farthest Britain, is confirmed by the beautiful title page (Fig. 160) to a manuscript written in the Anglo-Saxon minuscule of the 10th century. The manuscript is a copy of the different prayers, liturgical readings, services for ordination and confirmation, etc., prepared by Egbert, Archbishop of York, brother of Egbert, King of England (827). The only letter that at all has changed its form from the classic Roman type of the early empire — save a certain severity of treatment entirely defensible in a title page — is the letter G. An interesting example of capital letters used in the following century is the alphabet shown in Fig. 161, selected from the inscription on the tomb of Gundreda, sister of William the Conqueror (1085). The Roman spirit predominates, only four uncial forms being employed. The letters are beautiful in shape and proportion, and with hardly an exception would dignify any modern poster design.

ABCDEFGhIkL
MNOPQRSTVX

Fig. 161. Capital letters selected from an inscription on the tomb of William the Conqueror. 1085.

When the Caroline minuscule finally had become superseded by the black-letter in the 12th and 13th centuries and the full spirit of Gothic medievalism prevailed throughout Europe, the old capitals began to be obsolescent and finally became a very rare occurrence. A new series of capital letters arose, based largely on the uncial modification of the old capitals, especially evidenced in the letters D E G H K M N T V. These new Gothic capitals were marked by an increasing degree of floridity in their treatment. At first this feature was only a moderate characteristic, as shown in the following alphabet selected from a manuscript of the 12th century. Two forms of D were used,— at first the old capital, then later the uncial variation. Both were given scrolls.

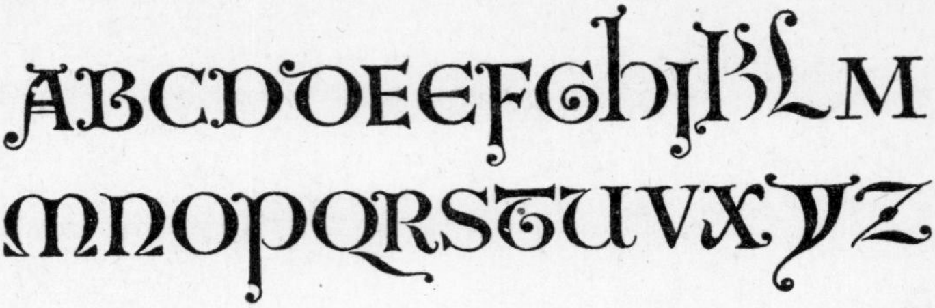

ABCDOEFGHJKLM
MNOPQRSTUVXYZ

Two forms of E and M were used,— the old capital, actually looking out of place with its rounding and florid companions, and the more cursive, uncial form. The alphabet is very ornamental, and manuscripts illuminated with initials and rubrics in these beautiful letters are a positive delight to the artistic eye.

The alphabet illustrated in Fig. 162 is one of the finest examples of the medieval Gothic capital letters employed in stately inscriptions and monumental brasses in the cathedrals and abbeys of England and the continent. The letters are selected from the inscription on a tomb in the Cathedral at Lübeck, which bears the date 1341. Letters similar in shape and ornamentation are to be seen in St. Margaret's Church at Lynn Regis, Norfolk, England, bearing the date 1349. These letters are so precisely

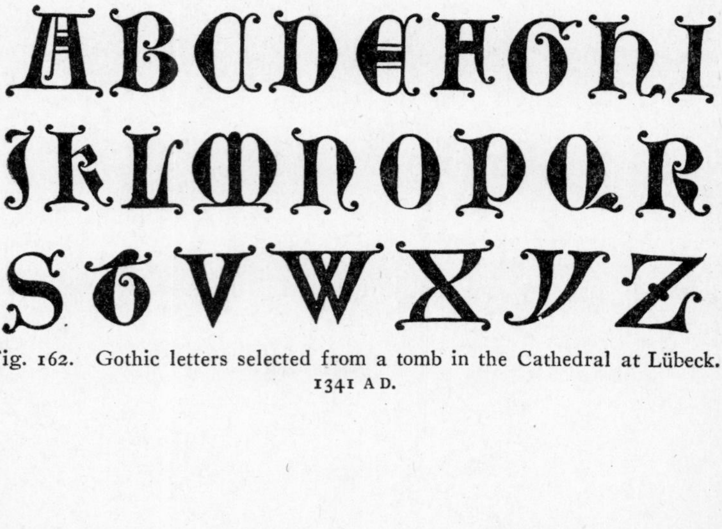

ABCDEFGHI
JKLMNOPQR
STVWXYZ

Fig. 162. Gothic letters selected from a tomb in the Cathedral at Lübeck. 1341 A D.

similar to those at Lübeck that one decides at once that the same talented artist designed both monuments.

In the 14th and 15th centuries, as we know, manuscripts were written in the pointed black-letter, the medieval Gothic minuscule prevailing at this period. The style of capital letters used for initials and rubrics with this type of letter varied considerably with the individual scribes, some being exceedingly ornate with scrolls and elaborate foliations in color and shading. The general type, however, through the late Middle Ages conforms rather closely to the Gothic uncials illustrated in Fig. 163. This is the style of capital that we associate most intimately with the medieval black-letter of the monasteries. It frequently is called the " monastic script."

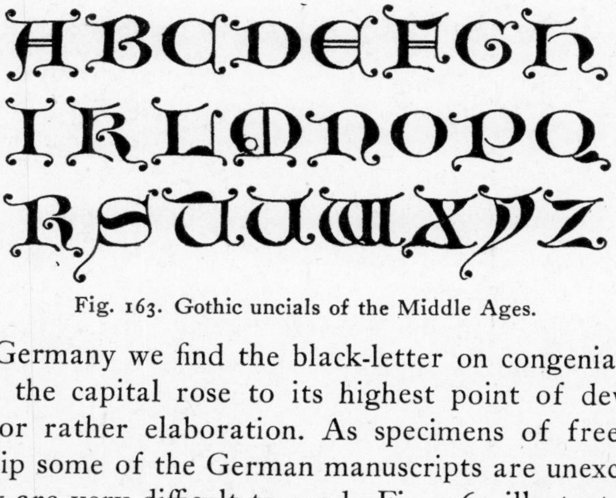

Fig. 163. Gothic uncials of the Middle Ages.

In Germany we find the black-letter on congenial soil. There the capital rose to its highest point of development or rather elaboration. As specimens of free penmanship some of the German manuscripts are unexcelled, if they are very difficult to read. Fig. 164 illustrates the German Gothic capitals drawn by a most clever penman in a free, facile manner, executed with a broad quill pen, and decorated with sparkling embellishments that do not too much disguise the character and shape of the letters. This alphabet, of the 13th or 14th century, seems to take us to the very summit of digression from the classic capital from which it developed step by step through the intervening centuries. Let the reader turn back now to the Roman capitals shown in the first line in Fig. 159 and compare the two alphabets letter for letter. Is it not an extraordinary transformation? If we were not long familiar with Gothic capitals and the sequence of the letters in the alphabet, it would be difficult at once to identify them, they have so widely departed from their Roman prototypes.

Fig. 164. German Gothic or Black Letter.

Contemporaneous with the book-hand in England there existed throughout the Middle Ages a somewhat cursive form of writing employed in state and legal documents known as the " Court " or " Charter " hand. It grew out of the book-hand, being based like it on the Caroline minuscule of the 9th and 10th centuries. It did not begin to be distinctive until about the 12th century, deteriorating after the middle of the 13th century. It was employed in making grants, charters and legal documents. It was a smaller letter than that used in religious manuscripts, and not so black, being a much lighter letter. At first the letters were separated, as in the book-hand; but later they became linked up with ligatures and connecting strokes. Up to about 1350 the letters were comparatively round;

but about this time they became increasingly more pointed or angular, until late in the 15th century, when there was a return to the round letter, resulting in greater freedom in penmanship. The reader probably is familiar with one example of the Court hand, the famous Magna Charta, signed by King John in 1215, granting rights and privileges to the barons and people of England. Facsimile copies of this manuscript printed in colors are quite common. The letters in this manuscript are small and neat, neither pointed nor cursive, and show the type of letter which with successive modifications ultimately developed into our modern script used in handwriting.

The style of writing known as the " Chancery " hand, used in the law courts of England, a variety of the Court hand and very similar to it, was a neat, set, decidedly beautiful letter when well written, as may be judged by the alphabet shown below:

This hand remained in vogue in the writing of all records which passed the Great Seal until the 16th century. So long as these court hands remained pointed, the writing continued to be cramped. There was little freedom. In the more cursive examples of the court hand, as seen in the letters of the more intelligent classes, the handwriting in many cases was a sad degeneration of the current hand. This is illustrated by the writing shown in Fig. 165, a letter written by the Prince of Wales in the reign of Henry IV (1399–1413). It is among the earliest specimens of English written script. With the invention of printing and the return to the round Caroline letters, there was a marked reaction upon the penmanship of court scriveners and educated people who read and wrote. Writing became much freer and more regular. Also a new type of script capitals was evolved. After 1500 letter-writing became common, as the average of intelligence increased under the inspiration of the Renaissance which was then fully under way in Europe.

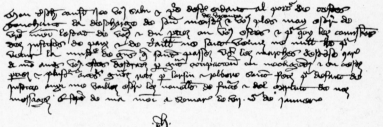

Fig. 165. Handwriting in the reign of Henry IV (1399–1413). Extract from a letter of the Prince of Wales.

At the close of the 15th century the formal book-hand disappeared, being superseded by the printing press. Coincident with this the cursive hands increased in importance; the northern, pointed type giving way to the southern, rounded forms, more especially to the Italic script, a new form of letter invented by Aldus Manutius in Venice, in 1495. It is said that this Italic script was a close imitation of the handwriting of Petrarch. It produced a profound effect upon the handwriting of the day in Italy and in other European countries and in England. This period may be said to mark the birth of modern handwriting. Gradually the cursive hand lost its angular character and became rounder and more regularly linked-up in the line. It was the Chancery hand, that was so much used in the courts and in domestic correspondence in England, improved by the adoption of Italic features, from which our modern English handwriting has developed. We should also mention as another formative factor in our present script letters the somewhat angular " Secretary " hand, used by lawyers and scriveners.

In the 16th century letter-writing began to be quite an ordinary accomplishment among intelligent people. But the " hand " in which correspondence was written varied as much as the individuals who penned it. Some wrote every letter separately, the page looking like printing; some wrote a round Italic hand; while others wrote with an angular, pointed letter. Letters to Queen Mary of England from potentates in Europe, about 1550, nearly all are in fine, rounded letters, slanted and generally separated. Such is a letter from Cosmo de' Medici, September 1, 1553, to Queen Mary. The queen herself wrote a perfect Italic hand, unexcelled by any of her correspondents; though the general average of the handwriting of the English nobility of the period was decidedly poorer than that of the European courtiers and literary men. Da Vinci, who was left-handed, printed his letters in his voluminous notes on art, mathematics, astronomy, geometry, science and mechanics. Michael Angelo and Tasso wrote remarkably fine hands, conspicuous for their well-formed letters. Lady Jane Grey, the talented and tragic victim of her cousin Mary's jealousy and bigotry, wrote a beautiful hand in round letters, sometimes printing each letter separately, again writing cursively with the letters regularly linked-up. Her writing shows her to be the prodigy which she really was among her sex. Queen Elizabeth also at times printed her letters — generally in her younger years — and again wrote cursively, always with well-shaped letters, extremely legible, as we would well

If any euer did try this olde saynge that a kinges worde was more tha
a nother mas othe I most humbly beseche your . M . to verefie it in
me and to remeber your last promis and my last demaunde that I
be not codemned without answer wiche it semes that now I am for
that without cause proud if am by your counsel frome you comanded
to go vnto the tower a place more wonted for a false traitor, tha a tru
subiect wiche thogh I knowe I deserue it not, yet in the face of
al this realme aperes that it is proued wiche I pray god I may the
shamefullist dethe that euer any died afore I may mene any suche
thinge, and to this present hower I protest afor God (who shal iuge
my trueth) whatsoeuer malice shal denis) that I neuer practised
conciled nor cosented to any thinge that mioth be preiudicial
to your parson any way or daungerous to the state by any
mene, and therfor I hubly beseche your maiestie to let
me answer afore your selfe and not suffer me to trust your
counselors, yea and that afore I go to the tower (if it
be possible) if not afor I be further codemned; howbeit I
trust assuredly your hichnes wyl giue me leue to do it afor
I be thus shamfully I may not be cried out on as now I shal
be yea and without cause let cosciens moue your hithnes to
take some bettar way with me tha to make me be codened
in al mes sicht afor my desert knowen Also I most hubly
beseche your hichnes to pardon this my boldnes wiche my
innocety procures me to do togither with hope of your natiyal
kindnis wiche I trust wyl not se me cast away without desert
wiche what it is I wold desier no more of God but that you
truly knewe . Withe thinge I thinke and beleue you shal
neuer by report knowe vnles by your selfe you hire I haue
harde in my time of many cast away for want of cominge
to the presence of ther prince and in late days I harde my
lorde of Somerset say that if his brother had bine suffered
to speke with him he had neuer sufferd but the
perswasions wer made to him so gret that he was brogth
in belefe that he coulde not liue safely if the admral liued
and that made him giue his consent to his dethe thogh
thes parsons ar not to be copared to your maiestie yet I
pray god as iuel perswatios perswade not one sistar agai
the other and al for that the haue harde false report and
not harkene to the trueth
knowen

Fig. 166. Part I. Letter of the Princess Elizabeth to Queen Mary.

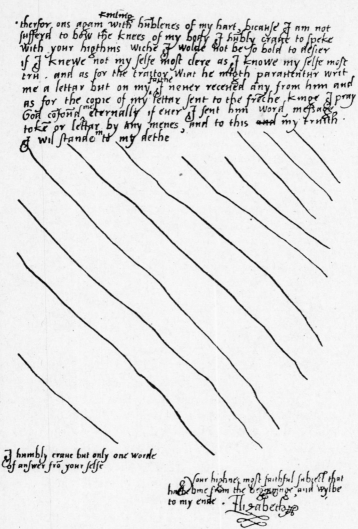

therfor ons agam with hublenes of my hart, bicause J am not
suffera to bow the knees of my body J hubly crane to speke
with your highnis wiche J wolde not be so bold to desier
if J knewe not my selfe most clere as J knowe my selfe most
trh. and as for the traitor, Wiat he migth paraututur writ
me a lettar but on my faythe never receued any from him and
as for the copie of my lettar sent to the freche kinge J pray
God cofound me eternally if euer J sent him word message
toke or lettar by any menes, and to this my trutih
J wil stande to my dethe

J humbly crane but only one worde
of answer fro your selfe

Your highnes most faithful subiect that
hathe bme from the beginynge, and wylbe
to my ende. Elizabeth

Fig. 166. Part II. Letter of the Princess Elizabeth to Queen Mary.

imagine. In Fig. 166 we reproduce a remarkable letter of hers to Queen Mary, written March 16th, 1553–4, when as Princess Elizabeth she was undergoing imprisonment in the Tower, at the hands of her half-sister Mary, the queen. Pathetic though this letter is, we are the more impressed with the unusual sagacity and maturity of mind of the young princess, then but twenty years of age. Mary, Queen of Scots, the unfortunate and ill-fated queen of France and Scotland, printed her words in very large and bold letters, entirely separated from each other. Her letters from the Tower during her nineteen years of imprisonment are very pathetic, especially the one dated June 1, 1569, and addressed " To the Queen of England, madame, my good Sister and Cousin."

The handwriting of the men of Elizabeth's court seems very much more cursive and more sophisticated than that of the women. Essex, Buckingham, Leicester, Bacon and Raleigh, all wrote hands quite similar to those of to-day; though the latter sometimes resorted to printing, as in the postscript to a letter to his rival, Dudley, which we reproduce above. It reads: " The Queen is in very good tearms with you and thank be to god well pacified and you ar agayne her sweet Robyn."

We will give a final example, Fig. 167, of the handwriting of the Elizabethan period, which is perhaps a fair average of the penmanship of the day, though it may be a trifle less legible than many of the letters of well-known men of that period. The letter is one of John Knox's broadsides. But the subject of his attack, Queen Mary, the Catholic monarch of Protestant Scotland, and one who was brought up amid the gayeties and frivolities of the French court, is most adroitly concealed, leaving no incriminating evidence. It is impersonal, but Cecil must have read the meaning between the lines.

Knox writes as follows:

" Benifittes of Goddes handes receaved, crave that menne be thankfull, and daunger knowen wolde be awoided. Yf ye strik not att the roote, the branches that appear to be brocken will budd agane (and that mor quicklye then menne can beleve) with greattar forse then we wolde wishe. Turn your eie unto God. Forgett yourself and yours, when consultation is to be had in matters of such weight as presently lye upon you. Albeit I have been full medly handilled, yet was I never enemey to the quietnes of England. God grant you wisdome. In haist of Edinburgh the 2 of Janner 1569.

> Yours to command in
> God,
> John Knox with his
> one foote in the
> grave

More daies then one
wolde not suffice to expres
what I think.

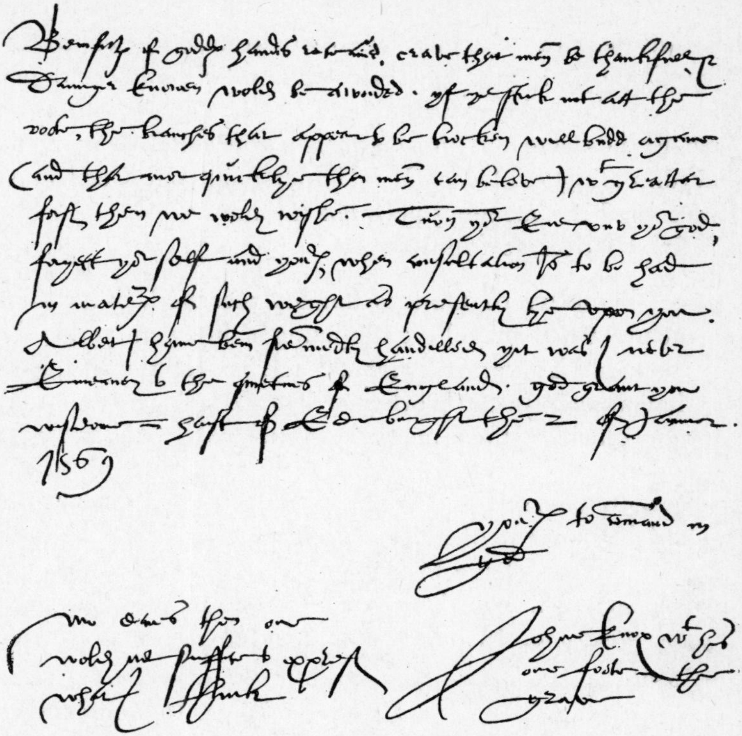
Benefitz of goddis handis ressavid, crave that thei may be thankfullie
Danger knawin wold be avoided. If ye strik not at the
rote, the branches that appear to be brokin will budd agane
(and that more quicklie than men can beleve) with greater
force than we wold wishe. Turn ye to the Lord your God,
forgett your self and yours, when consultation is to be had
in matteris of such weght as presentlie lie upon you.
Albeit I have bene fremmedlie handelled, yet was I never
enemey to the quyetnes of England. God grant you
wisdome. Hast of Edinburgh the 2 of Januar.
1569

Yours to command in
God

Mo wordis than on
wold not suffer to expres
what I think

John Knox with the
one foote in the
grave

Fig. 167. Letter of John Knox to Sir William Cecil. January 2, 1569–70.

CHAPTER XV

EUROPEAN ALPHABETS DERIVED FROM THE GREEK

BEFORE the culture of Rome carrying with it the Latin alphabet spread over Europe after Cæsar's conquest of Gaul and Britain, there was in use in northern Europe, particularly in Scandinavia — Norway, Sweden and Denmark — a system of writing with alphabetic characters known as " Runes." In the Scandinavian countries mentioned have been found thousands of inscriptions in this ancient alphabet. Runic inscriptions also have been found in the valley of the Danube, but not in Germany; in certain parts of England, but not in Ireland; and in general they have been found only in those places where the Scandinavian races were known to have lived or colonized. The transmission of alphabetic writing to the Baltic tribes must have taken place in very early times, as it is known that the northern Goths traded with the Greeks in the countries north and northwest of the Black Sea in classic times. Dr. Isaac Taylor (" The Alphabet ") believes that this transmission must have occurred some centuries prior to the Christian era.

The old name of the Runic alphabet, " Futhorc," in which these inscriptions were written, was applied to it on the same principle of acrology that gave the Greek name to our own alphabet, being derived from the initials of the ancient names of the first six runes: *fe* (*f*), *ur* (*u*), *thorn* (*th*), *os* (*o*), *rad* (*r*), and *cen* (*c*). There were several variants of this alphabet, all very much alike but differing according to the locality in which the alphabet was

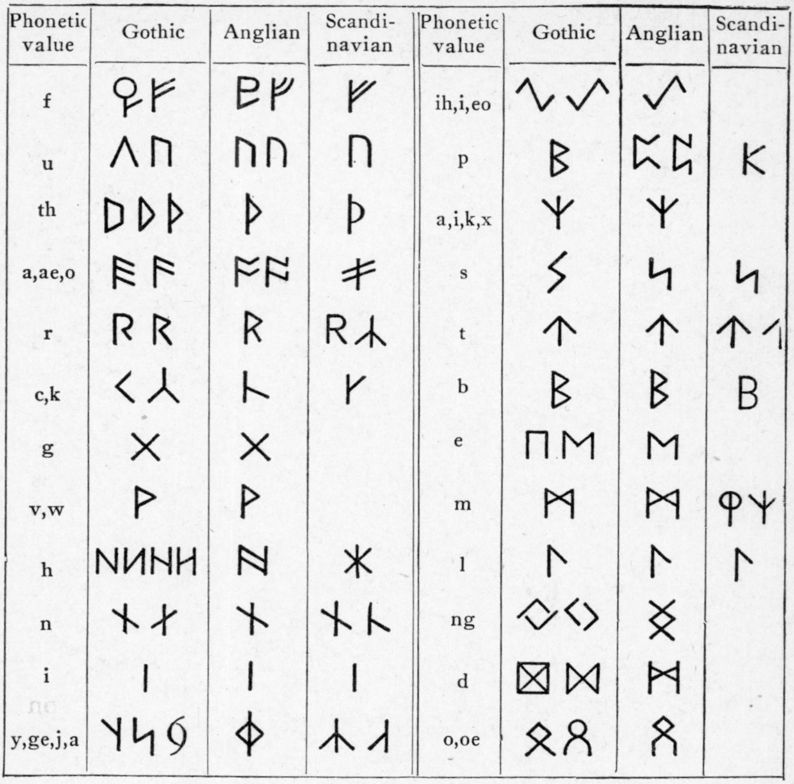

Phonetic value	Gothic	Anglian	Scandinavian	Phonetic value	Gothic	Anglian	Scandinavian
f	�genF F	ᛒᚹ	ᚡ	ih,i,eo	ᚥ ᚤ	ᚤ	
u	ᚱᚤ	ᚤᚤ	ᚤ	p	ᛒ	ᚤᚤ	ᚴ
th	ᛝᛝᚦ	ᚦ	ᚦ	a,i,k,x	ᚤ	ᚤ	
a,ae,o	ᛖᚠ	ᚢᚤ	ᚡ	s	ᛋ	ᛋ	ᛋ
r	ᚱ ᚱ	ᚱ	ᚱᛏ	t	ᚧ	ᚧ	ᚧᛁ
c,k	ᚷᚤ	ᚴ	ᚤ	b	ᛒ	ᛒ	ᛒ
g	ᚷ	ᚷ		e	ᚤᛗ	ᛗ	
v,w	ᚹ	ᚹ		m	ᛗ	ᛗ	ᚥᚤ
h	ᚺᚺᚺᚺ	ᚺ	ᚼ	l	ᚱ	ᚱ	ᚱ
n	ᚤᚤ	ᚤ	ᚤᛏ	ng	ᚦᚦ	ᚤ	
i	ᛁ	ᛁ	ᛁ	d	ᚤᚤ	ᚤ	
y,ge,j,a	ᚤᚤᚷ	ᚤ	ᛏᚤ	o,oe	ᚤᚤ	ᚤ	

Fig. 168. The Runic alphabet

used. We are indebted to Dr. Taylor for the following
brief summary: The oldest runes are the Gothic. They
were in use throughout northern Europe prior to the 6th
century A. D. It is the primitive type from which the
others were developed. Dr. Taylor in a very scholarly
analysis, which there will be no occasion to quote at length
here, convincingly traces back most of the Gothic runes
to Greek alphabetic prototypes, and concludes: " It appears therefore that a Greek source remains as the only

possible hypothesis for the origin of the Runes." Two other distinctive types of runes were in use through the Dark Ages: the Anglian, used in Northumbria from the 7th to the 9th centuries, and the Scandinavian Futhorc of sixteen runes, used in Norway, Sweden, Denmark, Cumberland and the Isle of Man, from the 10th century onward.

The three types of the Runic alphabet will be found in Fig. 168, as given by Dr. Taylor. Greek origins for a number of the runes easily will be recognized by the reader, as the resemblance is quite obvious. The order of the letters, however, is strangely perverted from the original Greek alphabet. There appears to be almost no sequential relationship between the two. P S T follow each other; but this seems to be the only parallel, unless we identify *th* with *d,* when we find *ae* following it. The angular nature of the runes, the absence of curves and horizontal lines indicate that they originally were carved on wood rather than written on skins or paper of any sort. Being cut in the direction of the grain, as shown in the " clog almanacs " with runic characters still extant, serifs or horizontal lines would be a disadvantage.

A most precious and unique specimen of Runic writing combined with quaint carvings is the so-called " Frank's Casket," a small box of whale's bone, nine inches long by seven and one-eighth inches wide and five and one-eighth inches in height, found at Auzon, Department of Haute-Soire, France. It is now in the British Museum. Three sides and the top are preserved, but the remaining side is wanting. The left side and the back are reproduced in Figs. 169 and 170 respectively. The carving on the left face of the box illustrates the finding of Romulus and Remus. The inscription begins on the left at the lower corner and proceeds over the top and right-hand side, reading from left to right. The reading continues on the lower line, but with inverted letters, still reading from left to right. The dialect is the Anglo-Saxon of the 8th or 9th century, and is as follows:

(Left) Othlæun neg (top) romwalus and reum-walus twœgen (right) gibrothær (bottom) a fœddæ hiæ wülif in romæcæstri.

Translated: "Outlay (were exposed), nigh, Rom-walus and Reumwalus, twain brothers: fed them a (she) wolf in Rome city."

Fig. 169. Left face of the Frank's Casket, showing the finding of Romulus and Remus, with the Runic inscription.

The back face illustrates the storming of Jerusalem by Titus (the left half) and the flight of the Jews (the right half). Beneath on the left is a tribunal, as explained by the word *dom,* "judgment." On the right a prisoner is being carried away and beneath the word *gisl,* "host-age." The writing begins on the left, as in the left face, and reads in Anglo-Saxon up to the middle, where the throne is, as follows:

(Left) " her fegtath (top) titus end giutheasu."

Beyond the figures on the arch the inscription is taken up in Latin, and proceeds:

"hic fugiant hierusalim (right) afitatores " (or habibatores).

Translated the two inscriptions read:

" Here fight Titus and the Jews."
" Here fly from Jerusalem the inhabitants."

Fig. 170. Back face of the Frank's Casket, showing the capture of Jerusalem, with the Runic inscription.

The front of the box — not shown by us — carries an inscription in Runic which quaintly describes the history of the box itself. The characters run around the carvings the same as in the two side inscriptions, except that the bottom line is not inverted and reads from right to left. It is known that many of the older Runic inscriptions were either retrograde or boustrophedon in their reading. This is one of the arguments advanced to prove that alphabetic characters were introduced into northern Europe at a very early age, when in Greece and Italy the direction of writing followed the Oriental method.

The entire inscription on the front face of the box reads as follows:

" hronæs ban fisc flodu ahof on fergen berig warth gastric grorn thær on greut giswom."

In modern English: " The whale's bone from the fish flood I lifted on Fergen Hill. He was gamboling (?) crushed, where he on the grit (shingle) swam."

As the reader may discover, the inscription is written in the Anglian type of runes, shown in the second column of runes in Fig. 168. As the language is the old Anglo-Saxon, he may find some pleasure and perhaps some profit in translating the runes; characters that have descended from the old heathen Northmen, who in the earlier centuries of the Dark Ages invaded the fair south lands of Thrace, Greece, Italy and France, laid waste their cities and despoiled them of their priceless inheritances of art. This precious Runic casket from France, which the Northmen invaded, plundered and finally claimed as their own — in Normandy — is a rare bit of historical legendary. It links the Christianity of its day with the dawning Christianity as well as the paganism of ancient Rome, and is eloquent to us of the then recent conversion of Rolf — or Rollo — Duke of the Northmen, who in 912 was baptized in France, taking the baptismal name of Robert, and offering at the same time the allegiance of Normandy to Charles, King of the Merovingians.

A strange alphabet known as the " Ogham " alphabet was in use in Ireland, Wales and in limited localities in Scotland and southwestern England, before the Christian missionaries disseminated the knowledge of the Roman alphabet through the manuscript copies of the Scriptures.

It is known that Scandinavians settled in these parts, but no trace of Runic inscriptions have been found here. Most of the earliest records of Ireland and Wales were written in these strange characters, known as " Oghams." The word may have come from the old Celtic *ogma,* signifying letters written in cipher; or from the Welch *ogan,* meaning an augury or a divination. Dr. Taylor believes that " Ogham writing was simply an adaptation of the runes to xylographic conveniences, notches cut with a knife in the edge of a squared staff being substituted for

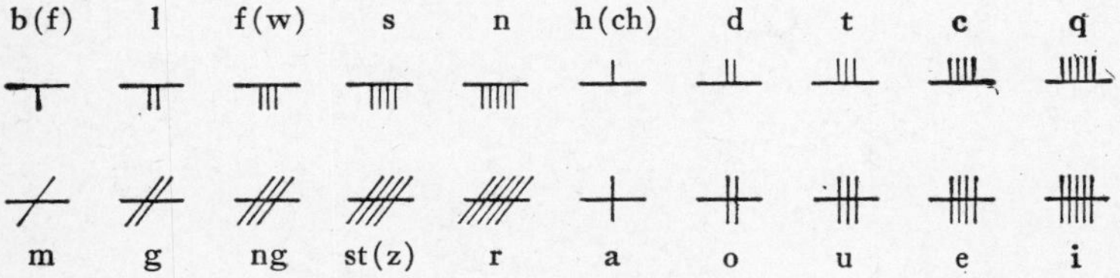

Fig. 171. The Oghams. The ancient Celtic alphabet.

the ordinary runes. That the Oghams were derived from the runes is indicated by the fact that they are found exclusively in regions where Scandinavian settlements were established, and also by the fact that the names of the Oghams agree curiously with the names of the runes of corresponding value " (" The Alphabet ").

We give in Fig. 171 the Oghams arranged according to their groupings, with their phonetic values. The most ancient values are enclosed in brackets. Dr. Taylor further writes: " An explanation of the mode in which this alphabet was obtained from the runes is suggested by the somewhat similar Scandinavian ' tree runes,' which were a sort of cryptograms, constructed on the plan of indicating, by the number of branches on the tree, the place occupied in the Futhorc by the corresponding ordinary rune." The runes were divided into families; branches to

the left of the stem indicating the family, and branches
to the right the place of the rune in the family. No exact
date can be ascribed to this peculiar system of writing,
but it is believed they were in use in the 5th century A. D.
Their use did not extend outside of the British Isles.

The Slavonic alphabets of northern and southeastern
Europe — the Russian, Bulgarian, Servian and Ruthe-
nian — have descended from the Cyrillic of the time of
the Greek Emperor Michael III (842–867) and of
Boris, Prince of Bulgaria (855–863). Tradition relates
that " formerly the Slavonians had no books, but they
read and made divinations by means of pictures and figures cut on wood, being pagans. After they had received
baptism, they were compelled, without any proper rules,
to write their Slavonic tongue by means of Greek and
Latin letters. But how could they write well in Greek
such words as: *bog, zhivot, zelo,* or *tserkov* . . . and
others like them? And so many years passed by. But then
God, loving the human race, had pity upon the Slavonians,
and sent them St. Constantine the Philosopher, called
Cyril, a just and true man, who made for them an alphabet of thirty-eight letters, of which some were of the
Greek style, and some after the Slavonic language."
(From memoirs of Khrabre, a Bulgarian monk, recorded
in the works of John, Exarch of Bulgaria (890–922).)

Cyril's original alphabet consisted of thirty-eight letters, which later was increased to forty-eight. Additional
characters were needed to represent the peculiar vowels,
sibilants and nasals of the Slavonic tongue. Many of the
letters of this amplified alphabet — over twenty — were
identical with the Greek uncials of the 8th and 9th centuries; others were taken from an older Slavonic alphabet
and syllabary known as the Glagolitic, which was used by
the Croatians as early as the 7th century, or even much

А	a	Л	l	Ч	ch
Б	b	М	m	Ш	sh
В	v	Н	n	Щ	shch
Г	g	О	o	Ъ	(e)
Д	d	П	p	Ы	y
Е	ye	Р	r	Ь	(i)
Ж	zh	С	s	Ѣ	ye
З	z	Т	t	Э	e
И	ê, i	У	u	Ю	yu
І	i, y	Ф	f	Я	ya
Й	ê	Х	kh	Ѳ	ph
К	k	Ц	ts	Ѵ	i, ü

Fig. 172. The Russian alphabet.

earlier. The remaining characters were invented, as the legend runs.

In the reign of Peter the Great (1672–1725) the old Russian alphabet was revised, many characters being discarded and one new letter added. Fig. 172 shows the Russian alphabet of to-day. The reader will recognize it as being more than an alphabet, as it contains several syllabic characters, besides modified vowels and consonants. Nineteen of the characters either are identical with the Greek letters or are only slight modifications of them.

This can easily be explained. It probably was not until about the 6th century that the state of culture of the Slavs brought them to the point where they began to use the Greek letters to any considerable extent in their written records. At this late period, as we already have learned, the classic Greek capitals had undergone many centuries of modification. The cursive writing of secular documents and letters, with their modifying tendencies, had produced by this time a series of uncials, intermediate between the classic Greek capitals and the later minuscules. It was from these uncial letters that the Greek letters in the Slavonic alphabets of Europe were taken. The departures from the classic capitals, however, are very slight, and their Greek parentage is most obvious. The reader who wishes to see the strange-looking Glagolitic characters and the Cyrillic alphabet from which the modern Slavonic alphabets have descended, will find them — along with almost every other alphabet — in Dr. Taylor's monumental book: " The Alphabet."

CHAPTER XVI

THE AGE OF PRINTING

AT the close of the Middle Ages, scholarly inclined men outside of the Church monasteries — up to this time the only institutions in which literature of any character had been conserved — began to desire a more liberal education. The catechism and the church services and rituals alone failed any longer to satisfy the more intelligent among the masses, and there arose a wide-spread demand for more general information than the Church up to this time had provided. This period marks the emergence of the intelligent classes from the narrow bigotry and despotism of the priests, and the emancipation of the minds of thinking men from the ecclesiastical fetters with which medieval orthodoxy had bound them. It was the era of the revival of classic learning, of literature, philosophy and art. Dante (1265–1321) already had written his immortal poem, the "Divina Commedia," and Petrarch (1304–1374), the great Italian poet and scholar, had opened the doors to the realm of the Latin and Greek classics, and disclosed their incomparable beauties. With Boccaccio (1313–1375) writing in a lighter vein, the foundations of modern literature were at this time established in Italy. A renaissance of learning had set in which soon spread from Italy throughout all parts of Europe. By the middle of the 15th century many men of learning had appeared. These great scholars and writers revived the learning and revised the philosophy of the ancient world, and even dared to discuss the principles of the

Christian religion. New universities of learning were established throughout Europe, and libraries for the preservation of books were founded. The University of Leipsic was established in 1409, Louvain in 1426 and the Vatican Library was founded in 1447.

Prior to this period practically all books were laboriously written or copied by the hands of consecrated monks, *scriptores,* as they were called, working in their quiet cloisters in the church monasteries. The production of a single Bible was the effort of many months — perhaps years — of assiduous and painstaking labor. This copy was kept for the exclusive use of the clergy, the great body of worshipers being kept in ignorance and illiteracy. Most of the nobles, even kings, were unable to read or write. This condition of civil illiteracy was not deplored by the Church, but rather encouraged by it. A council of the Church as late as 1229 forbade the translation of the Bible into the vernacular, and decreed that none but the clergy could have copies of it — the Latin version — in their possession. As late as 1536, William Tyndale was burned alive in the public square along with his English translations of the Latin Bible.

At this period of comparative respite from the devastating wars of the Middle Ages, when men turned from militaristic affairs to embrace the arts of peace, literature again came into its own. The 100 years' war between England and France, which had paralyzed the energies of both countries, had ended. In Italy the various Italian states had long since rallied from the invasions of the northern races, and were further advanced in progressive civilization than any other country in Europe. The forgotten — or tabooed — classics became resurrected and were read by scholars who had access to them; while widening fields of thought and inquiry in the realms of literature and science were opened up by the recent excavations among Greek and Roman ruins. By degrees there sprung up an increasing demand for books, that could not easily be met. They were produced slowly and only with great labor and rare skill, and were entirely beyond the means of every one but those of the wealthiest families. Some more expeditious means of production by duplication than the slow copying of manuscripts by hand began to be the great desideratum, and occupied the thoughts of thinking men.

The art of duplication by engraved wooden blocks was by no means unknown at this period. So early as the time of William the Conqueror engraved stamps and seals were used in authorizing legal documents, charters and other state papers. Many impressions of such seals may be seen affixed to documents preserved in England and on the continent. As for this, we know by the quantities of seals and signets preserved in almost every archæological museum that they have been employed from the earliest Babylonian period. While this can hardly be classed as printing, the engraved seal or plate must have suggested the first idea of the means of duplicating in the production of books. Some rubrics in medieval incunabula are so uniform throughout the pages of the book as to lead to the conclusion that they were printed in by hand from wooden blocks after the manuscripts were written. We are compelled to admit the priority of the East in the matter of printing. Printing from wooden blocks is known to have been practiced in China and Japan from a very early period — it is said as early as the 2nd century in China — while the printing of books from engraved wooden blocks was quite common in the 10th century in that country. Printing from movable types cut in wood is reputed to date from the middle of the 11th century in China. A book printed in Korea from movable type, in 1337, is in the British Museum.

Prior to the invention of printing in Europe there were in common use playing cards, image prints or picture books, which originally had been drawn and colored by hand, and the inscriptions — whenever they occurred — written in with the pen. But the increasing desire for knowledge and the demand for cheaper books outran the resources of the monastic scribes, and in the course of time was met by the invention of xylographic printing, in which each entire page was printed from an engraved block of wood. In the early stages of the new art only single sheets were printed from the engraved blocks, being printed on one side only by rubbing on the back of the sheet. Sometimes the sheets were bound together back to back; sometimes they were pasted together to form one sheet. Again, impressions from two wooden blocks were printed on one sheet, which was folded up back to back. When made up in book form several of these folded sheets were bound together. This gave to this kind of book the name " Block-Book." These books at first were largely religious picture-books, which the clergy employed in educating the lower classes as well as the illiterate monks, and instructing them in the truths of the scriptures. They were originally printed on cloth or vellum, but later on paper. They became very popular throughout Germany, Flanders and Holland, in the 14th and 15th centuries. The earliest block-books contained only pictures; then pictures with inscriptions and brief reading matter engraved on the same block. Later, they consisted chiefly of engraved text with artistic illuminations and woodcut illustrations. The development of the art of wood engraving in pictorial illustration and the art of printing from movable types were almost concurrent;

the beginnings of the former art antedating the latter by only a few years. The earliest dated woodcut was 1418, the next, 1423; but others doubtless were earlier. At first the drawing was very crude; but improvements in the artistry of the engravers were so rapid that when printing was invented in the middle of the century we find the art in a highly advanced stage of development.

One of the most popular block-books was the " Biblia Pauperum," a book of forty pages consisting of illustrations of important events in the scriptures. The first page of the Biblia Pauperum is shown in Fig. 173. The central picture is the Annunciation. Eve's temptation is illustrated on the left, and Gideon's fleece saturated with the morning's dew is pictured on the right. The letter " a " indicates that it is the first page of the book. The book is believed to have been first printed early in the 13th century. When one realizes that the artist in producing the text, as well as the illustrations shown on the page, had to cut away the wood of the block wherever it shows white in the print, leaving the fine lines of the letters raised, the difficulty of the task and the importance of the revolution effected by the invention of printing from movable types may well be conceived.

Another popular block-book was the " Speculum Humanæ Salvationes " or " Mirror of Human Salvation." One of the copies of this book is a transition book from the block-book to the type-printed book. It consists of sixty-three pages, twenty of which were printed from wood-blocks and forty-three from movable types. Large numbers of these block-books were printed, and not a few of them are preserved to-day in national and civic museums and in private collections.

As in the case of many great inventions, there are several claimants to the honor of being the inventor of the

Fig. 173. First page of the Biblia Pauperum. One of the earliest Block-Books.

art of printing from movable types. Although the pre-ponderance of popular belief undoubtedly confers this honor upon Johann Gutenberg (1398–1468), it probably

will surprise most readers, who have from youth read
that Gutenberg invented the art, to know that there is no
written evidence in existence that can stand the test of
legality that Gutenberg ever printed a book. The evidence is wholly inferential, but nevertheless convincing
from the reliable nature of collateral, historical facts concerning his life and associates. It is known that in 1450,
possibly from 1450 to 1455, a partnership of some
kind existed between Gutenberg and Johann Fust,[1] in
Mainz (Mayence), Germany. It is not positively known
whether any books were printed by them during their
partnership, if partnership it was. It appears that Gutenberg was impecunious; indeed an inveterate bankrupt,
and borrowed large sums of money from Fust, which were
not returned even after judgment was secured in a suit
brought against him by the latter. In defending himself
in this suit and explaining how he had spent the money,
Gutenberg refers to: " tools, paper, vellum and ink . . .
used in the work of the books." This is the only contemporary evidence we have that Gutenberg was engaged in
printing books from movable types between 1450 and
1455, unless we except a most important record of the
French court which relates that Charles VII, hearing of
Gutenberg's experiments, dispatched in 1458 Nicolas Jenson, who had been Master of the Mint at Tours, to
Mainz to obtain Gutenberg's secret. The record says:
" On the 3rd of October 1458, the king having found
that Sieur Gutenberg, Knight, living at Mayence, Germany, a man dexterous in engraving and in making letter
punches, had brought to light an invention for printing

[1] The family name was originally Fust; but in 1506 Johann Schöffer,
the son of Peter Schöffer who married Fust's daughter, in a dedication
to the Emperor Maximilian of a translation of "Livy," calls his grandfather: Faust. Ever since this the family has used this spelling.

with metal characters," etc. The Royal instructions to Jenson were: " to secretly inform himself of the ' forme et invention.' " This is pretty strong collateral evidence that Gutenberg was engaged in developing the art of printing books.

Within two years of the termination of the partnership between Gutenberg and Fust appeared an edition of the " Psalterium," a sumptuous folio of 350 pages, in large missal type, printed in Mainz by Fust and Schöffer, and dated August 14, 1457; being the first printed book with a date. Beyond question the five years of experimental work conducted by Gutenberg, even if he never refers in the suit to anything but the " tools " he had made or was going to make, must have been productive of some tangible results, if his financial backer was able within two years to print in conjunction with his adopted son, Peter Schöffer, so important a book as this Psalter. The book to this day is remarkable for its typography and for the beauty of its illuminated initials, which were printed in two colors, red and blue, from two-piece types. It is generally believed that Gutenberg was the brains of the firm, in this short partnership, engraving the types and conducting the experiments in printing from the movable types — the " tools " to which he refers — and that Fust was the one to profit by these experiments.

Before continuing further with the account of printing in Mainz, we feel obliged in the interest of historical facts to say that even if Gutenberg did print books in Mainz between 1450 and 1455, there is very strong evidence that Lourens Janszoon Coster of Haärlem, Holland, printed books from movable types between 1440 and 1446. Coster was at first a block printer, but subsequently printed books from movable types. The first word of challenge of Mainz being the cradle of the art of printing comes from a very near contemporary of Gutenberg, one Koelhoff, himself a printer in Cologne, who writes in the Cologne *Gazette,* in 1499, that the art of printing was found first of all in Germany, at Mainz. " In 1450," he writes, " they began to print, and the first book that they printed was the Bible in Latin, in a large letter, resembling that with which at present missals are printed. Although the art was found at Mainz, as aforesaid, in the manner in which it is generally employed now, yet the first prefiguration was found in Holland from out the Donatuses [1] which were printed there before that time, and from out of them was taken the beginning of the aforesaid art, and it was found much more masterly and exact than that other manner was, and has become more and more artistic." This is a pretty candid statement for a contemporary German printer to make, and is worthy of credence, unless it is too much colored by professional rivalry that may have existed between the two cities, Cologne and Mainz, both centers of the new art.

Many of Coster's printed books are preserved in museums in Holland. There are numerous fragments in Haärlem, or its neighborhood, of as many as forty-seven different editions, all very much resembling each other in type and in workmanship. Some of these are entire books, some but single pages. The majority were printed on vellum, which was in use before paper became popular for printing purposes. Some of these books, or fragments of them, are printed only on one side of the sheet like block-books; while others are partly printed from blocks and partly from type. The types vary considerably, there

[1] The Donatus was a Latin grammar, the work of Ælius Donatus, a Roman grammarian of the 4th century. It was one of the earliest books printed from movable type. A 27-line Donatus was printed from the same types used in printing the 31-line Letter of Indulgence (1454) generally ascribed to Gutenberg.

being as many as eight or nine different fonts, with much variation in each font; appearing — as is suspected — that Coster did not cast his type, but cut each individual letter by hand and frequently renewed them. Besides, he probably did not use a durable metal. In any event Coster's work seemed to have failed in its outcome in Holland; while Gutenberg's art by the perfection of his mechanical processes, and by reason of its excellence, even in the earliest stage of its development, created an epoch in European affairs as his art spread from one great center of intellectual life to another.[1]

The first printed documents with a date, 1454, were two different editions of the same " Letter of Indulgence " of Pope Nicholas V. Authorities differ as to the printer of these two letters; but Gutenberg is generally believed to be the printer of the 31-line " Letter of Indulgence." Gutenberg also is generally credited with being the printer of the so-called " Mazarin Bible," a copy of which was found in the library of Cardinal Mazarin. It is commonly called " Gutenberg's Bible," although many assert that it probably was printed by Peter Schöffer. It is also described as the Latin Bible of 42 lines. It is entirely probable that Gutenberg cut the types, but that Fust — probably Fust and Schöffer — performed the presswork. It is considered to be the first Bible printed in Europe, or elsewhere. The sumptuous work is a folio of 1282 pages, printed in double columns, with spaces left for illuminated initials and rubrics. The few copies that have been preserved are magnificent specimens of typography and would be a credit to any

[1] A most complete historical sketch and critical commentary on the Coster-Gutenberg controversy will be found in " A History of tne Art of Printing." N. Noel Humphreys, London, 1868. Also in the Encyclopædia Britannica.

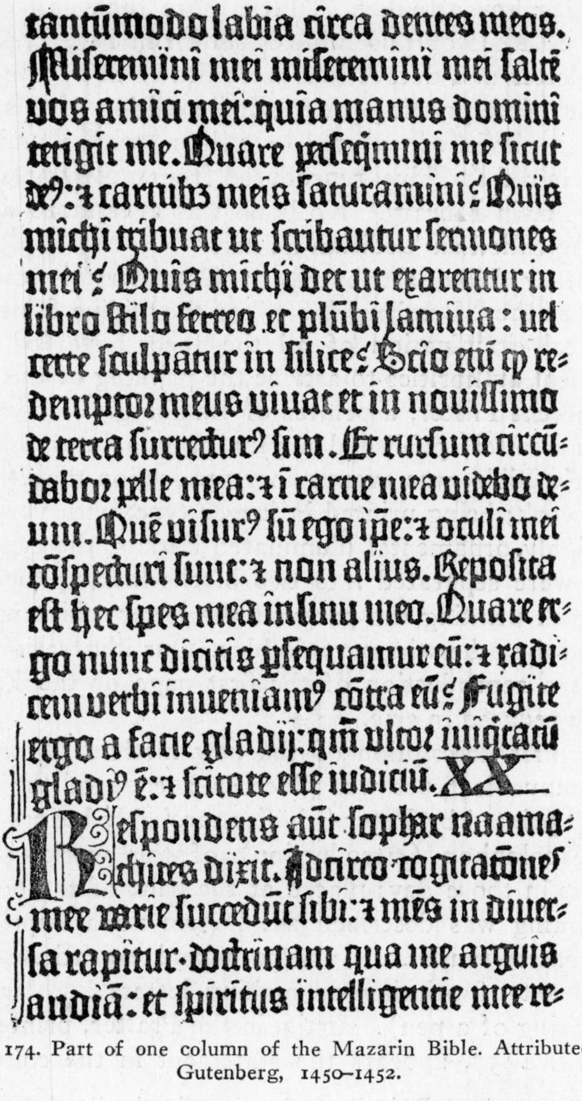

tantumodo labia circa dentes meos.
Miseremini mei miseremini mei salte
vos amici mei:quia manus domini
tetigit me.Quare psequmini me sicut
de9:z cartubz meis saturamini? Quis
michi tribuat ut scribautur sernones
mei ? Quis michi det ut exarentur in
libro stilo ferreo .et plubi lamina : uel
certe sculpatur in silice? Scio em cp re
demptoz meus uiuat et in nouissimo
de terra surrectur9 sum .Et rursum circu
dabor pelle mea:z i carne mea uidebo de
um .Que uisur9 su ego ipe:z oculi mei
cospecturi sunt:z non alius.Reposita
est hec spes mea in sinu meo.Quare er
go nunc dicitis psequamur eu:z radi
cem uerbi inueniam9 cotra eu? Fugite
ergo a facie gladij:qm ultoz iniqtatu
gladi9 e:z scitote esse iudiciu. XX
Respondens aut sophar naama
chites dixit. Idcirco cogitacones
mee varie succedut sibi:z mes in diuer
sa rapitur·doctrinam qua me arguis
audia: et spiritus intelligentie mee re

Fig. 174. Part of one column of the Mazarin Bible. Attributed to
Gutenberg, 1450–1452.

publishing house to-day. A little more than half of one
of the columns of this Bible is shown in Fig. 174. The
initial letter and decorations were drawn in by hand subsequent to the printing. A fac-simile edition of this Bible
has been published, printed on vellum, with illuminated
initials in red and blue, reproduced from a copy preserved
in the Berlin Library.[1] No book was ever more worthy
of being called an " édition de luxe."

Another Bible attributed to Gutenberg is the one
known as the " Bamberg Bible " or the 36-line Bible. But
a critical examination of all the facts have led many
prominent authorities to ascribe the printing of this work
to Albrecht Pfister, a printer of Bamberg.

The Psalter, published a year or two later than the
Mazarin Bible, was even a finer production than this famous work; being printed in larger type, with very bold
and highly ornamental illuminated initials, the types for
which were separated into two blocks locking together;
one block printing the parts of the letter which were in
red and the other the parts in blue. Our illustration, Fig.
175, is a reproduction of the first page of the Psalter,
greatly reduced in size.

The first description of the new method of printing
from movable types was given in a copy of the " Donatus " printed by Peter Schöffer, probably before 1456.
In the colophon (introduction) of this work — which
printers in those days placed at the back of the book —
its printing was described as: " Arte nova imprimendi
seu caracterizandi . . . absque calami exaratione " (by
a new art of printing or making letters . . . without
the writing of a pen). Again, in the Psalter, printed August 14, 1457, appears the statement in the colophon:

---

[1] " The Gutenberg Bible. From the Copy in the Royal Library in
Berlin." Leipsic, 1914.

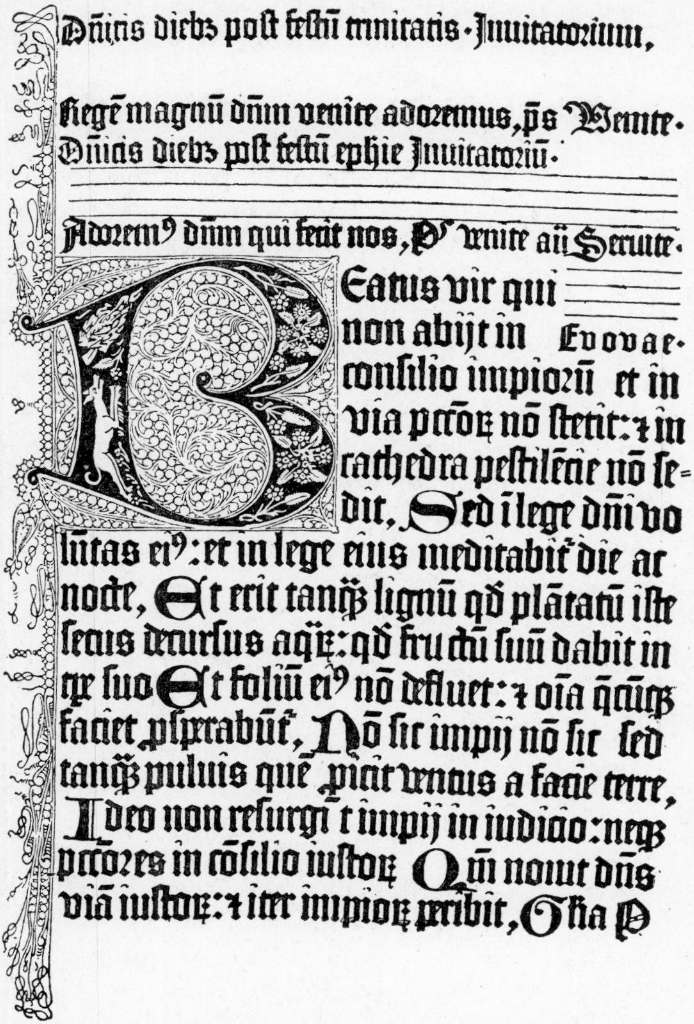

Dñicis diebȝ poſt feſtū trinitatis · Inuitatoriuu,

Regē magnū dñm venite adoremus, pſ Venite·
Dñicis diebȝ poſt feſtū epħie Inuitatoriū·

Adorem⁹ dñm qui feut nos, ꝓ venite aū Seruite·

Eatus vir qui
non abijt in Euovae
conſilio impiorū et in
via peccoȝ nō ſtetit: ⁊ in
cathedra peſtilētie nō ſe=
dit, Sed ī lege dñi vo
lūtas ei⁹: et in lege eius meditabit die ac
nocte, Et erit tanꝗ lignū qd plātatū iſt
ſecus decurſus aꝗē: qd fructū ſuū dabit in
tpr ſuo Et foliū ei⁹ nō defluet: ⁊ oīa ꝗcūꝗ
faciet pſperabūt, Nō ſic impij nō ſic ſed
tanꝗ puluis que picit ventus a facie terre,
Ideo non reſurgt t impij in iudicio: neꝗ
peccores in coſilio iuſtoȝ Qm nouit dñs
viā iuſtoȝ: ⁊ iter impioȝ peribit, Oria ꝓ

Fig. 175. First page of the Psalter. Printed by Fust and Schöffer, 1457.
The first book printed with a date.

that it was perfected at Mainz by " adinventio artificiosa imprimendi ac caracterizandi absque calami ull exaratione."

The experience of printers in printing block-books must have taught them how short-lived this material was, and prompted them to seek a more durable medium. It is believed by some authorities that the first movable types were cut from wooden blocks; but this belief is based largely upon the irregularity of the printing from some of the early types, more particularly Coster's. John Ph. de Lignamine, in 1474, refers to types as " metallicæ formæ." Types early were called " formæ," and before this, as early as 1468, they were spoken of as " caragma," and later " caracter." Hence our two modern words, " form " and " character," as applied to movable types. The word " typographus " seems first to have appeared in print in the preface to the first edition of the " Astronomicon " of Manilius, by P. Stephanus Dulcinius Scolæ, printed at Milan in 1488.

The types used by Gutenberg and by Fust and Schöffer in their printed books were letters copied after the prevailing book-hand of the day, the pointed black-hand or Gothic of the Middle Ages, locally used in Germany at that period. They selected as models for their letters well-written manuscripts of strong characteristics, and proceeded to copy the letters with the utmost fidelity, imitating as nearly as possible the actual pen or reed writing of the scribe. To carry out this object and to simulate as closely as they could the handwriting in the manuscript, they employed a number of " by-forms " of letters having serifs or spurs modified to suit certain combinations with other letters, as well as several combinations of two letters. The combinations: bo, da, de, do, ha, pe, va, and ve, will be found in our illustrations from the pages of the Mazarin Bible and the Psalter. Manuscripts had been used for so many centuries and the style and mannerisms of the scribes were so familiar to the clergy and the reading public, that they set the standard of form in the letters, from which the early type-cutters naturally hesitated to depart. These conditions prevailed for many years until the printer's art had built up its own technique, and established rules and principles recognized by literary men.

The first types were made substantially as they are to-day, being cut in relief by hand on a soft steel punch, which was hardened after the letter was finished. These punches were used only as dies to be driven into a block of soft metal, iron or copper, to form a matrix for the casting of the types. The original punches, being in hardened steel, outlasted many fonts of type and even the matrixes, which were renewed from time to time as they showed wear after many castings of the types. Some authorities believe that each one of the individual types used by Gutenberg were cut by hand, as they show so many slight differences. If this be true, it is no wonder that so much of his time and Fust's money were spent on his " tools," as the court evidence shows. However, a broad examination of the type used in the Mazarin Bible does not support this theory. It is certain, however, that Fust and Schöffer used cast types. We are indebted to De Vinne (" The Practice of Typography ") for the following information in regard to the sizes of types used in the earliest printed books. The Mazarin Bible was printed in 20-point type; the Bamberg Bible was printed in 24-point type, and the Psalter of Fust and Schöffer was printed in 36-point type. Even the smallest of these types is considerably larger — about twice — than the types in which modern books are printed.

The following alphabet, engraved by Albert Dürer, is a very good example of the Gothic black-letter in use in Germany at the time of the invention of printing.

abcdefghiklmno

pqrstuvwxyz.

Dürer was as clever with the engraver's tools as he was with his pen and brush. The inscription on his tomb describes him as: " The light of the arts — sun of artists,— painter, engraver, sculptor, without example." He was as practical and scientific-minded as he was artistic. The use of letters in engraving and printing occupied his mind equally with artistic engraving on wood and copper. He was a thorough artist in all forms of applied art, as is attested by the reproduction shown in Fig. 176 of the first page of the Gospel of John, containing a part of the first seven verses, engraved by this artist in a very beautiful rendering of the prevailing black-letter. Dürer was more progressive than the generality of his countrymen, who have tenaciously clung to the medieval black-letter; for when the reform immediately set in — outside of Germany — for the return to the Roman letters, he was among the first to design a beautiful set of Roman characters with rules and proportions for every line and curve, and complete diagrams for type cutting.

In 1462 Mainz was sacked and mainly destroyed by the conquering army of Adolphus of Nassau. Printing in consequence ceased in this city, and became more or less

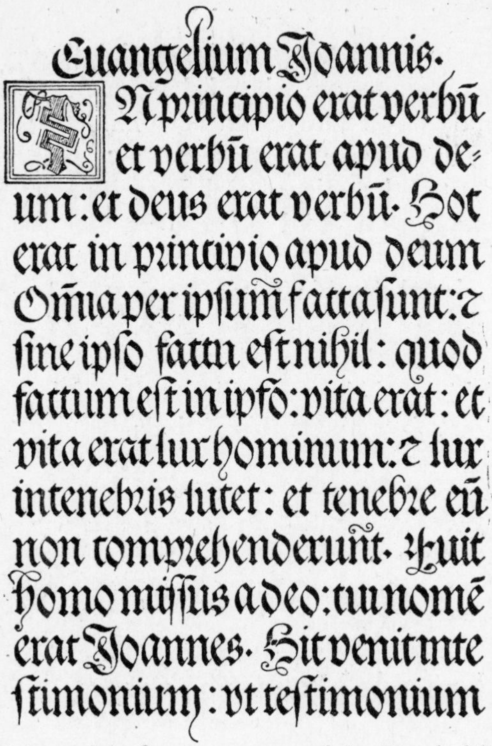

Euangelium Joannis.

In principio erat verbū et verbū erat apud deum: et deus erat verbū. Hoc erat in principio apud deum Omnia per ipsum facta sunt: z sine ipso factū est nihil: quod factum est in ipso: vita erat: et vita erat lux hominum: z lux in tenebris lutet: et tenebre eū non comprehenderunt. Fuit homo missus a deo: cui nomē erat Joannes. Sic venit inte stimonium: vt testimonium

Fig. 176. Part of the first seven verses of the Gospel of St. John.
Engraved by Albert Dürer. 1515.

stagnant throughout Germany. The tide of printing and printers turned toward Italy, where the Renaissance had become well established and where wealthy nobles patronized the arts and liberal-minded ecclesiasts encouraged the wider dissemination of learning. Printers from Germany carried their art, with their fonts and matrices for founding the types, into Italy. Here they found manuscripts and incunabula in great abundance awaiting printers to convert them into books for the reading public. These Italian manuscripts were largely in the Carlovin-

gian and Lombardic hands; which, we have learned, were
the immediate outgrowth of the uncial letter before it
had reached its extreme pointed development in northern
Europe. Italy never had taken very kindly to the medieval Gothic; but always had favored a rounder hand. As
she had adopted the pointed arch in architecture only with
great reluctance, and had clung most tenaciously to the
round arch, so she adopted very late and quite half-heart-
edly the pointed Gothic letters, only to abandon them
about the time of the invention of printing for the round
Caroline letter. The small letters shown below give a
very good idea of the prevailing type of letter used in
Italian manuscripts about this period:

The crowns of the letters show a marked tendency to
be rounding rather than angular; and several of the letters come squarely down to the bottom without a break;
or, if there be one, it is a rounding one, rather than an
angle, as in the Gothic letters. The capitals show how
little Lombardic writing, at least in southern Italy, had
advanced beyond the old uncials of the 10th century.
These particular capitals were written at the bottom of a
page taken from a Commentary of St. Gregory upon the
Book of Job, written in the middle of the 15th century;
that is, just the period of time we are now talking about.
All of these letters, whether capital or minuscule, are but

slightly pointed. The four lines of writing illustrated in Fig. 177 are of an earlier age of Italian writing, being reproduced from a page of an incunabulum of the first half of the 12th century: " Homilies and Lessons for Sundays and Festivals from Advent to Easter Eve.," at present in the British Museum. The manuscript consists of 317 leaves of the most beautiful writing, so regular as to be discovered not to be printing only by the closest scrutiny. It suggests to us the kind of manuscripts that the printers who first went to Italy selected for their types.

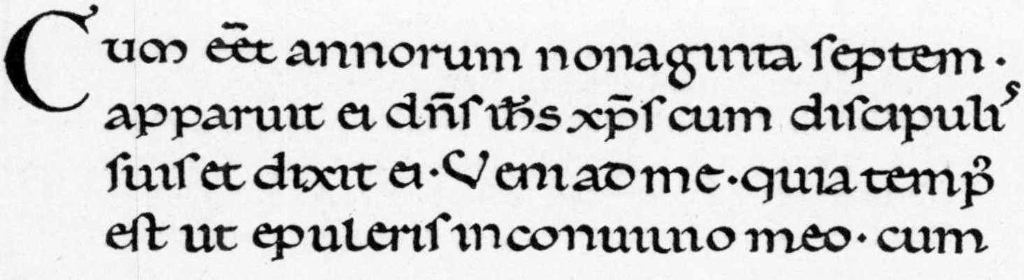

Cum ēct annorum nonagīnta septem . apparuit ei dñs ihs xp̄s cum discipuli' suis et dixit ei · Veni ad me · quia temp̄ est ut epuleris in conuiuio meo · cum

Fig. 177. Part of a page from " Homilies and Lessons for Sundays and Festivals from Advent to Easter Eve." Italian manuscript of the 12th century, illustrating the writing from which types were made in the 15th century.

The first German printers who emigrated to Italy appear to have been Conrad Sweynheym and Nicholas Pannartz, who took their printing presses to Subiaco, near Rome, and worked in the Benedictine monastery. Cardinal Torquemada, who had been Inquisitor General in Spain under Queen Isabella, appeared to treat them with more consideration than he had shown the liberal-minded Catholics in Spain and the Low Countries; for he gave them every encouragement to advance their art in Rome. Sweynheym engraved the types and Pannartz did the printing. They first printed Donatuses; then in 1465 they printed the sumptuous " Lactantius," a large folio volume, a page of which is reproduced in Fig. 178. It was printed in an entirely new style of type, very sim-

Lattanÿ firmiam de diuÿs institutoibꝫ
aduersus gentes rubrice primi libri incipiunt
quanta sit et fuerit scriptꝫ cognito neutratis Et qp uer siuc eligi
sapientia uer siue sapientia sit profunda religio demonstratum

AGNO & excelleti ingenio uiri quom se doctrine pe-
nitus dedidissent: quicquid laboris poterat impendi:
contemtis omnibus publicis & priuatis actionibus:
ad inquirede ueritatis studiu se contulerut: existima-
tes multo esse preclarius humanaru diuinaruqꝫ reru
inuestigare ac scire ratione q struedis opibus aut cu-
mulandis honoribus inherere: Quibus rebus quoniam fragiles terreneqꝫ
sunt: & ad solius corporis prinent cultum nemo melior: nemo iustior effici
potest. Erat quidez illi ueritatis cognitione dignissimi quam scire tatopere
cupiuerut: atqꝫ ita ut eam rebus omnibus anteponeret: Nam & abiecisse
quosda res familiares suas et renutiasse uniuersis uoluptatibus constat: ut
sola nudamqꝫ uirtute: nudi expeditiqꝫ sequerent: tantu apud eos uirtutis
nomen et auctoritas ualuit: ut in ea omne summi boni premium pdicaret.
Sed neqꝫ adepti sut id quod uolebat: & opera simul atqꝫ industria pdide-
rut: quia ueritas idest archanu sumi dei qui fecit omnia ingenio ac ppriis
sensibus no potest compbedi: alioquin nihil inter deu homineqꝫ distaret si
cosilia & dispositiones illius maiestatis eterne cogitatio assequeret humana. Quod quia fieri no potuit ut homini pse ipsu ideo diuina noscere: non
est passus homine:n deus ltime sapientie requirentem diutius errare: ac sine
ullo laboris effectu uagari per tenebras inextricabiles: aperuit oculos eius
aliquando: & notionem ueritatis munus sui fecit: ut & humana sapientia
nulla esse monstraret: & errati ac uago uiam colloquende immortalitatis
ostederet. Veru quonia pauci utunt hoc celesti beneficio ac munere: quod
obuoluta in obscuro ueritas latet: eaqꝫ uel contemtui doctis est: quia ido-
neis assertoribus eget: uel odio idoctis ob insita sibi austeritate: qua natra
bominum procliuis in uicia pati non potest: Nam quia uirtutibus amari-
tudo pmixta e: uicia uero uoluptate condita sunt: illa offensi: hac delmiti
feruntur in pceps: ac bono specie falsi mala p bonis amplectunt. Succur-
redu esse bis erroribus credidi ut et docti ad uera sapientiam dirigant: et
indocti ad uera religione. Que professio multo melior: utilior: gloriosior:
putanda est q illa oratoria in qua diu uersati: non ad uirtute sed plane ad
arguta malicia iuuenes erudiebamus. Multo qppe nuc rectius de pceptis

Fig. 178. First page of the Lactantius, printed by Sweynheym and
Pannartz at Subiaco, 1465.

ilar to our present Roman minuscule, or lower-case letter of the books of to-day. The letters were copied from current Italian manuscripts written in rounded Caroline letters, to which the Italians had just returned after their short familiarity with the pointed Gothic black-letter. If the letters are examined under a reading-glass, however, it will be detected that they are without serifs; the heavy vertical strokes ending with an angle at the bottom, instead of resting squarely on horizontal serifs, and that the curves at the top are still inclined to be a little angular. The capitals also are partly Gothic and partly Roman. The Lactantius was the first book printed in Italy with a date, 1465. Sweynheym and Pannartz printed books in Subiaco from 1467 to 1472, averaging about eight works a year. Copies of their works are found in many libraries and museums in Europe.

Venice was the rival of Rome in the printing of books in the last quarter of the 15th century. John of Speyer, Germany, had settled there in 1469, and printed his "Letters of Cicero." He had cut a font of beautiful, round letters in the pure Roman style, with serifs, and with capitals to match; the first purely Roman letters cut by any printer. Sweynheym and Pannartz have generally been reputed to be the first to have used Roman type; but we have just pointed out that their letters were transitional between the Caroline letters and the later Roman minuscule. The types of John of Speyer are in the full Roman style. An example of his printing is given in Fig. 179, being the reproduction of a page of his "Tacitus," printed in Venice in 1469. The crowns of the letters are rounding, showing no angles. The straight limbs end squarely on the bottom horizontal line, with heavy horizontal serifs both below and above, instead of the angled or clubbed ending of former types. The reader will rec-

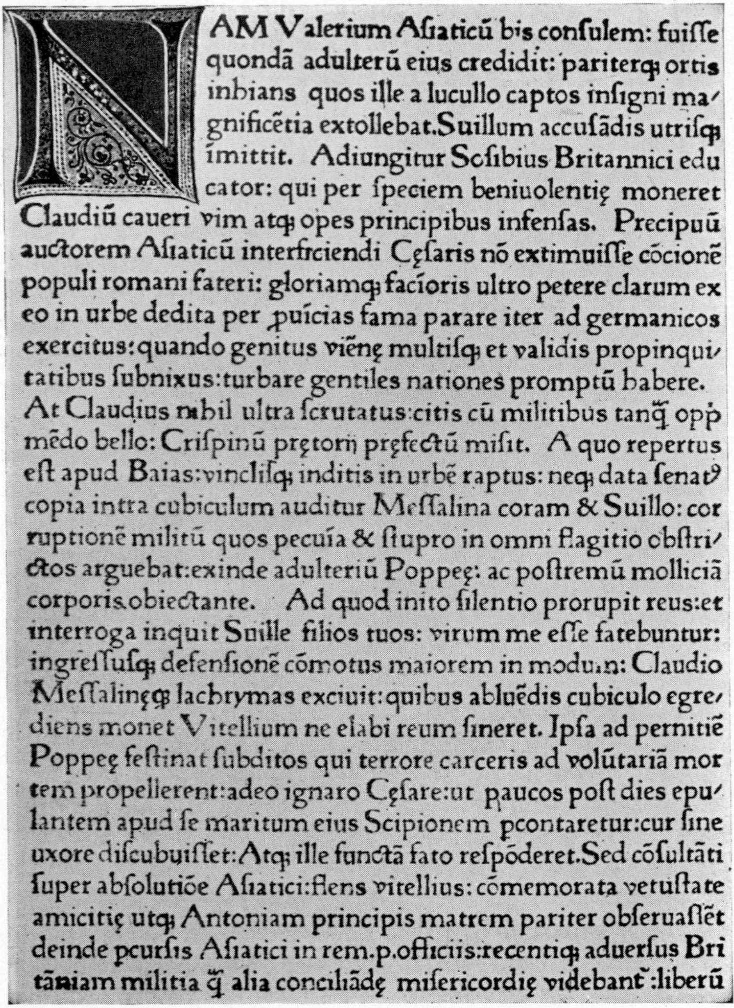

AM Valerium Aſiaticũ bis conſulem: fuiſſe quondā adulterũ eius credidit: pariterq̃ ortis inhians quos iſle a lucullo captos inſigni ma⸗ gnificẽtia extollebat.Suillum accuſãdis utriſq̃ imittit. Adiungitur Soſibius Britannici edu cator: qui per ſpeciem beniuolentiẽ moneret Claudiũ caueri vim atq̃ opes principibus infenſas. Precipuũ auctorem Aſiaticũ interficiendi Cẽſaris nõ extimuiſſe cõcione populi romani fateri: gloriamq̃ facioris ultro petere clarum ex eo in urbe dedita per ‿puicias fama parare iter ad germanicos exercitus:quando genitus viẽnẽ multiſq̃ et validis propinqui⸗ tatibus ſubnixus:turbare gentiles nationes promptũ habere. At Claudius nihil ultra ſcrutatus:citis cũ militibus tanq̃ opp medo bello: Criſpinũ pretorij prẽfectũ miſit. A quo repertus eſt apud Baias:vincliſq̃ inditis in urbẽ raptus: neq̃ data ſenat⸗ copia intra cubiculum auditur Meſſalina coram & Suillo: cor ruptione militũ quos pecuía & ſtupro in omni flagitio obſtri⸗ ctos arguebat:exinde adulteriũ Poppeẽ: ac poſtremũ molliciã corporis obiectante. Ad quod inito ſilentio prorupit reus:et interroga inquit Suille filios tuos: virum me eſſe fatebuntur: ingreſſuſq̃ defenſione cõmotus maiorem in modum: Claudio Meſſalineq̃ lachrymas exciuit:quibus abluẽdis cubiculo egre⸗ diens monet Vitellium ne elabi reum ſineret. Ipſa ad pernitiẽ Poppeẽ feſtinat ſubditos qui terrore carceris ad volũtariã mor tem propellerent:adeo ignaro Cẽſare:ut paucos poſt dies epu⸗ lantem apud ſe maritum eius Scipionem pcontaretur:cur ſine uxore diſcubuiſſet:Atq̃ ille functã fato reſpõderet.Sed cõſultãti ſuper abſolutiõe Aſiatici:flens vitellius: cõmemorata vetuſtate amicitiẽ utq̃ Antoniam principis matrem pariter obſeruaſſet deinde pcurſis Aſiatici in rem.p.officiis:recentiq̃ aduerſus Bri tãniam militia q̃ alia conciliãdẽ miſericordiẽ videbant:liberũ

Fig. 179. Part of a page from "Tacitus," printed by John Speyer, Venice, 1469.

ognize, now for the first time, a page of printing in true Roman minuscules, very similar to the kind of type which has come to be called " old-style," and which varied only in unessential and minor features during succeeding generations.

Nicolas Jenson (1420–1480), who went from France to Mainz in 1458 to learn the art of printing, later went to Venice. Here he first printed the famous " Decor Puellarium," a book of deportment for young girls, instructing them in matters of behavior and etiquette. The book was a small quarto volume intended for the pocket, and contained 118 leaves, twenty-two to twenty-three lines to the page. The colophon declares it was printed by Nicolas Jenson in 1461. It is the general belief, however, that the date is wrong, and should be 1471. The date is printed in Roman numerals — as was and has been the prevailing custom for some centuries — and probably one of the x's was omitted. This is judged to be the fact by known events in Jenson's life, and from the fact that none of his books bears any date between 1461 and 1471; whereas his books were fairly numerous every subsequent year, he having printed up to the time of his death in 1480 at least 155 different editions of books. He surely was not idle for ten years.

The style of type used by Jenson was a Roman type of his own engraving, for he was a skillful engraver. He perfected the Roman small letters to such a degree that they became the standard models for all subsequent printers. His fonts were renewed from time to time, but the types used throughout the eleven years of his business life in Venice appear largely to have been made from matrices struck from the original punches. The perfection of Jenson's types, the setting-up and general presswork hardly have been excelled.

Aldus Manutius succeeded to the Jenson press, in Venice, using Jenson's splendid outfit of fonts of Roman and other types; for Jenson cut a fine Gothic type, an improvement on the old black-letter. Aldus was the founder of the famous Aldine Press, of world-wide fame. He printed in 1501 an edition of Virgil in a new type, since called " Italic "; the model for which was the handwriting of the poet Petrarch. The letters were somewhat less inclined than they later became, and the capitals were — at first — plain, like our ordinary Italic capitals. In the hands of subsequent printers a more florid style of Italic letter (Fig. 180) was evolved, which has remained popular to this day.

ABCDEFGHI
JKLMNOPQ
RSTUVWXYZ

Fig. 180. Flourished Italic letters. Italian Renaissance.

Under the spirit of the Renaissance the Italian architects and sculptors modified and refined the old Roman letters used in monumental inscriptions, and developed an alphabet that for grace and refinement hardly can be equaled. It is the authority for sculptured inscriptions to this day. Fig. 181 illustrates this Roman alphabet. It has been selected from architectural and monumental inscriptions of the Renaissance period. The letters are as full and round as the classic letters, more delicately shaded, and much more uniform in appearance and treatment. Nearly all architectural inscriptions of the present day, that are in Roman letters, are in the style of the Italian Renaissance.

ABCDEF
GHIKLM
NOPQRS
TVWXYZ

Fig. 181. Roman capital letters. Italian Renaissance. 16th century

The first books printed in England were printed from black-letter types. William Caxton, the first English printer, had resided in Bruges for over thirty years; though as he says in the Prologue to his first printed book, his translation of the popular medieval romance, " The Recuyell of the Historyes of Troye," from the French of Raoul le Fèvre: " I was borne and lerned myn Englissh in Kente in the Weald." As ambassador in Bruges for many years in the court of the Dukes of Burgundy, Caxton had access to the rich library of the court. His Recuyell was printed in Bruges in 1474 or 1475. In the epilogue to this book Caxton quaintly undertakes to explain the advantages of a printed book. He says:

" Thus ende I this book, whyche I have translated after myn auctor as nyghe as God hath gyven me connyng, to whom be gyven the laud and preysing. And as for as moche as in the wryting of the same my penne is worn, myn hande wery and not stedfast, myn eyn dimed with over moche looking on whit paper, and my corage not so prone and redy to laboure as hit hath been, and that age crepeth on me dayly and feebleth all the bodye, and also because I have promised to dyverce gentilmen and to my frendes to addresse to them as hastely as I myght this sayd book; therefore I have practysed and lerned at my grete charge and dispense to ordeyne this said book in prynte after the manner and forme as ye may here see, and it is not wreton with penne and ynke as other bokes ben, to thende that every man may have them attones, ffor all the books of this story, named the Recule of the Historyes of Troyes, thus imprynted as ye here see, were begonne in oon day and also finished in oon day," etc., etc.

Of course Caxton means by this that all may have copies at once, for they were all struck at one time.

In September, 1476, Caxton returned to England, taking with him a new font of improved types, and established a printing press in Westminster. The first book printed by him in England with a date was Lord River's translation — revised by Caxton, who was very much of a scholar — of "The Dictes or sayengis of the Philosophres," dated 1477. From this time on Caxton was busy writing, translating and printing, until his death in 1491. He made voluminous translations and wrote much original matter of his own. In all Caxton printed ninety-six different works or editions of works. Among them may be mentioned: Chaucer's "Canterbury Tales," Mallory's "Morte d'Arthur," "Trolius and Creseide" and the "Golden Legend," which he translated in 1483, very late in life, despite his "wery hande" and "dimed

eyn " and " age that feebleth all the bodye." This book
was illustrated with seventy woodcuts. In the " Royal
Book," or book for a king, printed in 1484, we find the
Caxton type at its best. The initial letters and woodcuts also were well executed. Fig. 182 is reproduced
from a page of this book in the British Museum. It will
be of interest to know that a copy of this book sold in
1902 for $11,125.

Fig. 182. A page from the Royal Book. Printed by William Caxton
in 1484.

Caxton used eight different fonts of type in his press
work. One of them was an exact copy of the type used
by Fust and Schoeffer, and was the size known as double

long primer, or 20-point; a very large type, as will be noted in the illustration, which by the way is much reduced. The capitals of this font, however, were the Flemish " secretary " letters. The familiar Old English black-letter of to-day is very similar to the type used by the first English printers. It remained for several generations the prevailing type used in charters, acts of Parliament, legal documents and ecclesiastical literature, despite the wide use of the Roman letter on the continent. Gradually, however, the latter type, on account of its greater legibility, won its way in the printing of secular matter; but the Old English letter long continued in use for ecclesiastical purposes, and remains to this day a popular type for much church printing.

After Caxton, presses were set up at the Universities of Oxford, Cambridge, and a famous one was established at St. Alban's Abbey. The Roman Catholic party in England were powerful enough for many years to prevent the printing of the Bible in English, or even the reading or the possession of the Latin Bible by the laity. Pope Hildebrand in 1080 had decreed that " it is the will of God that his word should be hidden, lest it should be despised if read by every one." We already have stated that in 1229 a council of the church published a decree which not only forbade the translation of the Bible into any " vulgate tongue," but also forbade all but the clergy to have copies in their possession. Nevertheless, in 1535, Tyndale's translation of the Bible into English, copies of which had found their way into England, was revised by Miles Coverdale, printed abroad — without the name of the printer, for fear of meeting with Tyndale's fate — and allowed by the then reigning king, Henry VIII, to be circulated and read. Several editions were successively printed, to keep pace with King Henry's

The first boke of Moses, called Genesis.

The first dayes worke. The seconde dayes worke. The thirde dayes worke.

The fourth dayes worke. The fifth dayes worke. The sixte dayes worke.

The first Chapter.

IN ye begynnynge God created heauen & earth: and ye earth was voyde and emptie, and darcknes was vpon the depe, & ye spirite of God moued vpō the water.

And God sayde: let there be light, & there was light. And God sawe the light that it was good. Then God deuyded ye light from the darcknes, and called the light, Daye: and the darcknes, Night. Then of the euenynge and mornynge was made the first daye.

And God sayde: let there be a firmament betwene the waters, and let it deuyde ye waters a sunder. Then God made ye firmamēt, and parted the waters vnder the firmamēt, from the waters aboue the firmament: And so it came to passe. And God called ye firmament, Heauen. Then of the euenynge & mornynge was made the seconde daye.

And God sayde: let the waters vnder the heuen gather themselues vnto one place, that the drye londe maye appeare. And so it came to passe. And God called ye drye londe, Earth: and the gatheringe together of waters called he, ye See. And God sawe that it was good.

And God sayde: let ye earth bunge forth grene grasse and herbe, that beareth sede: & frutefull trees, that maye beare frute, euery one after his kynde, hauynge their owne sede in them selues vpon the earth. And so it came to passe. And the earth broughte forth grene grasse and herbe, that beareth sede euery one after his kynde, & trees bearinge frute,

Fig. 183. First page of the "Coverdale Bible." Printed in 1535.

marital changes. The first one referred in the dedication to the King to "your dearest, just wyfe and vertuous prencesse Queene Anne." In the next edition, issued the same year, 1535, " Queen Jane" had to be inserted! In Fig. 183 the first page of the " Coverdale Bible," printed out of England, is reproduced. The type is a variety of the black-letter, not very different from Caxton's font.

Richard Grafton, an author and scholar like Caxton, was one of the early printers whose scholarly attainments assisted in the early development of the printer's art in England. He was the founder of the Grafton Press. In 1540 he printed the fine folio Bible commonly called " Cranmer's " or the " Great Bible." From this time on no particularly important edition of the Bible was printed. In the short reign of Queen Mary no encouragement whatever was given to the printing of the Bible, and in Queen Elizabeth's reign the printing of general literature attained for the first time national importance and its use became greatly extended.

The change from the black-letter to the Roman letter in England was largely assisted by John Day, who was a celebrated printer under Queen Elizabeth. He cut a beautiful Roman font in 1572 in 24-point, for books for the church service. Archbishop Parker in a letter to Lord Burleigh dated December 13, 1572, writes:

" To the better accomplishment of this worke and other that shall followe, I have spoken to Daie the printer to cast a new Italian letter, which he is doinge, and it will cost him XL marks; and loth he and other printers be to printe any Lattin booke, because they will not heare be uttered, and for that Bookes printed in Englande be in suspition abroad."

Day's most important work was his " Acts and Monuments, &.," better known as " Fox's Book of Martyrs," a caustic arraignment of the acts of Romanism in England. On the title page, as in most of his books, was printed his trade device,— a sleeping man awakened by the rising sun, with the words: " Arise for it is Day." In his native parish of Bradly Parva this epitaph is engraved on his tomb: —

Here lyes the Daye that darkness could not blinde,
When Popish foggs had overcast the sunne;
This Daye the cruel nighte did leave behinde,
To view and shew what blodie actes were donne.

The ablest type founder of the 18th century in England was William Caslon (1692–1766). He was the founder of the Caslon Press conducted successively under four generations of the same family name, and still in active business. Caslon's Roman " old-style " types are the models to-day for this style of type. They have been closely copied by modern type founders and bear the name " Caslon." This book is printed in 11-point Caslon type.

Through the 17th and 18th centuries types held very closely to what modern printers call " old-style," or " old-face," which they had acquired from the *scrittura umanistica* of the Latin Renaissance. These letters had developed under the skillful hands of the master printers: Jenson, Aldus, the Estiennes of Paris and Caslon. Claude Garamond also should be mentioned, for he is known as the " father of letter-founders." He cut in 1515 a font of beautiful Roman letters, the model to-day of the French type cutters.

Later in the 17th century began a slow change from the old-face to the " modern-face " type. This new type was mainly due to Giambattista Bodoni, a noted scholar and printer of Parma, Italy. He cast a series of fonts in the new style. From the last half of the 18th century to the middle of the 19th century nearly all books were printed in this modern-face type. Later, however, there was a revival, and the old-face types, largely shaped on the lines of Caslon's type, were restored to favor and remain to this day the most popular Roman type. However, the modern-face type is still largely used in all lines of printing, to lend variety to the make-up of printed matter, in headings, titles, advertisements and the many uses that modern times demand of type. The modern-face types are narrower in the " set " or width of the type as compared with the old-face, and the shaded lines are proportionally heavier, while the fine lines are much finer, being described as " hair lines." The curves, or " crowns " of the minuscule letters (lower case), are vertically symmetrical instead of slanting as in the old-face, which is a close copy in every detail of broad pen lettering.

De Vinne [1] has this to say about modern-faced type: " As a bit of drawing each letter of a well-made modern-face is exact, and carefully finished in all its details; but when any letter is seen with its mates in a mass of composed types, its high finish does not seem to be a merit. A letter of modern-cut is really not so distinct as the same letter in the old style. The old punch-cutter and the modern punch-cutter worked to reach different ends. The old cutter put readability first; he would make his types graceful if he could, but he must first of all make them distinct and readable in a mass. His object was to aid the reader. The modern punch-cutter thinks it is his first duty to make every letter of graceful shape, but his notion of grace is largely mechanical; the hair-line must be sharp and tend to its invisibility; the curving stem

1 " The Practice of Typography." Theodore Low De Vinne, A.M.

must dwindle to its hair-line with a faultless taper; the slender serif must be neatly bracketed to the stem. Every curve and angle is painfully correct and precise, but the general effect of types so made, when put in a mass, is that of the extreme of delicacy, and of the corresponding weakness of an over-wrought delicacy. To use a painter's phrase, the work is niggled, or overdone."

Some of the most popular of old-face types employed to-day are: Caslon, Cheltenham, Jenson and De Vinne. The following line of printing illustrates this type of letter:

THIS LINE IS SET IN 14-POINT CASLON CAPITALS.

This line is set in 14-point Caslon lower case.

A good example of modern-face type is illustrated in the following style of letter:

THIS LINE IS SET IN 12-POINT MODERN CAPITALS.

This line is set in 12-point Modern lower case.

By far the greater proportion of all modern printing in English, whether in books, magazines, newspapers or other publications, or for advertisements in these publications, is in the Roman type, or modifications of it. This probably also holds true for advertisements of every kind,— posters, show bills, etc. The fundamental kinds of types are very few in number, though there are almost innumerable varieties of each. After the Roman, we may enumerate what the printers of to-day call

"Gothic." It is an inexcusable misnomer, that at some time in the past crept into the trade nomenclature. It is less Gothic than any other historical name that could be applied to it. It is in fact the basic letter of the original alphabet: Greek, Etruscan or early Roman; but is capable of endless variety in form, in condensation or extension, in light or heavy lines and bars. The pure Gothic letter is without serifs; but the addition of serifs converts it into a legion of types that occupy scores of pages in the trade catalogs of modern type founders. The following line illustrates the pure letters:

THIS LINE IS SET IN 8-POINT GOTHIC CAPS.

This line is set in 8-Point Gothic lower case.

The different varieties of "Italic" and "script" letters about complete the enumeration of the fundamental forms of our modern letters. There are, of course, hundreds — we may say thousands — of fonts of types of every conceivable modification of these fundamental types. They fill heavy trade books issued by the present-day type founders; and we see them displayed in the advertisements in current magazines and periodicals.

One of the many important activities that the exigencies of the great world-war unexpectedly brought to the front in the service of this country, as well as in England and France, was the very large number of pictorial posters issued by the several governments to give publicity to the national loans, war savings plans and other measures needing the financial aid of the people. These various enterprises were presented to the public in attractive and forceful war posters, with colorful drawings and striking lettering. A large variety of lettering was employed by the designers of these posters. As in almost every case the artist was no novice, and was experienced in this

Fig. 184. Reproduction of War Posters issued by the United States Government.

line of art expression, and as most of the designs were selected by competition or by the judgment of juries, we find illustrated in this series of posters the kind of letters that were sure to be generally acceptable and to meet with popular approval.

The actual range of type in these posters was not wide, the differences being those of proportion rather than of change in type; as will be seen by referring to our last illustration, Fig. 184, a selection of fourteen posters from those issued by the United States Government during the last two years. The Roman capitals and small letters — lower case — still predominate, as in all lines of printing. They are of the stronger, old-style variety with heavy serifs. The next popular type was the plain Gothic letter, condensed or extended, and with bars thick or narrow, to give — according as desired — importance or subordination to the reading matter; the widths being conditioned upon the color selected for these letters. Some of the Gothic letters have slight spurs instead of the customary square corners; but the general tendency was toward rugged strength in the letters, rather than for over refinement. Italic letters were rarely used, as their slant militates against the symmetry that seems to be called for in the lettering of a poster.

In the selection of types of letters the modern poster artist lays under contribution all the best work of the masters of the past, whose art has endured by reason of its beauty or grace, its strength or decorative quality, and which will lend itself by its appropriateness to the purposes of the poster. In the poster the art of writing seems to reach the acme of its possibilities of development in its service to man. Its purpose of conveying information is the same as in all ages, but the designer of to-day has the art of all the ages to draw upon; and never was his work more intelligently or artistically executed.

The ages of development that separate the effort of

the poor scribe of the Monuments Blau, who also combined pictorial and written appeal in his slate-stone message, and the brilliant posters of our war-time billboards, have been filled with the sincere labor and aspirations toward higher ideals of humble workers, striving to improve the transmitted forms of the Art Preservative, to pass them on to succeeding generations for still further improvement. These letters which have come down to us in this rich inheritance of the ages are as talents to be improved, to be put to interest, not to be laid away as received. It is for us, as with our forebears, to improve the shape of these letters in our books, our monuments or in use for public display, until we achieve the highest ideal attainable in the art of writing.

A BIBLIOGRAPHY OF THE ART OF WRITING

AMERICAN INDIANS

A. NORTH AMERICA

Archives of Aboriginal Knowledge. Henry R. Schoolcraft, LL.D. 1860.

Art in Shell of the Ancient Americans. William H. Holmes. Bureau of American Ethnology. 1880–'81. Also many other works by the same author.

Calendar History of the Kiowa Indians. James Mooney. Bu. Am. Ethn., Vol. XVII, 1895–'96.

Considerations of the Art of Picture Writing and the System of Mnemonic Symbols of the N. American Indians. Henry R. Schoolcraft, 1844.

Essays of an Americanist. Daniel G. Brinton. 1890.

The Graphic Art of the Eskimos. William J. Hoffman. Smithsonian Institution Report. 1895. Also other works by the same author.

Historical and Mythological Traditions of the Algonquins. E. G. Squire. Indian Miscellany. Edited by W. W. Beach.

The Indian Sign Language. Capt. W. P. Clark. 1885.

The Indian Tribes of the United States. Francis S. Drake.

The Lenape Stone. Henry C. Mercer.

Letters and Notes on the Manners, Customs and Conditions of the N. American Indians. Geo. Catlin, 2 Vols., 1841.

Library of Aboriginal American Literature. Daniel G. Brinton. 1885. Also other works by the same author.

The Menomini Indians. Walter J. Hoffman. Bu. of Am. Ethn. 1892–'93. Pt. I.

The Midéwiwin of the Ojibwa. W. J. Hoffman. Bu. of Am. Ethn., Vol. VII, 1885–'86.

Mythology of the N. American Indians. Major J. W. Powell. First Annual Report, Bu. of Am. Ethn. 1879–'80.

Origin and Traditional History of the Wyandotts. Peter Clarke.

Picture Writing of the N. American Indians. Garrick Mallery. Bu. of Am. Ethn. 1888–'89. Also by the same author: Report of the Smithsonian Institution. 1880–'81. Pictographs of the N. American Indians. Bu. of Am. Ethn. 1882–'83. (The Report of 1888–'89 is the most complete.)

Sign-Language among the N. American Indians. Garrick Mallery. First Annual Report. Bu. of Am. Ethn. 1879–'80.

Twenty Years among the Hostile Indians. J. Lee Humfreville. U. S. A.

The Walam Olum, Its Origin and Authenticity. Library of Aboriginal American Literature. Daniel G. Brinton. 1882–1890.

B. AZTEC AND MAYA

Aids to the Study of the Maya Codices. Cyrus Thomas. Bu. of Am. Ethn. Vol. VI. 1884–'85. Also by the same author in these publications: Central American Hieroglyphic Writing (1903); Day Symbols of the Maya Year (Vol. XVI, 1894–'95); Maya Calendar Systems (1900–'01).

Antiquities of Mexico. Edward K. Kingsborough. 9 vols. 1831–'48.

The Aztecs. A. Van Doren Honeyman. 1905.

Essays of An Americanist. Daniel G. Brinton. 1890.

An Introduction to the Study of the Maya Hieroglyphs. Sylvanus G. Morley. Bulletin 57, Smithsonian Institution. 1915.

Mexican Picture Writings. Alex. von Humboldt.

Nombres Geograficos de México. Antonio Penafiel. 1885.

A Primer of Mayan Hieroglyphics. Daniel G. Brinton.

BABYLONIA AND ASSYRIA

Archaic Forms of Babylonian Characters. Theophilus G. Pinches. Also other works by the same author.

Assyrian Discoveries. George Smith. 1873–'74.

Assyrische Lesestuecke, etc. Friedrich Delitzsch. Leipsic, 1900. Also other works by the same author.

The Code of Hammurabi. Robt. Francis Harper. 1904.

Cuneiform Texts from Babylonian Tablets in the British Museum.

Découvertes en Chaldée. Ernest De Sarzec.

Délégation en Perse. J. De Morgan, Délégue Général. 1902.

Die Entstehung des ältesten Schriftsystems. Friedrich Delitzsch.

Discoveries among the Ruins of Nineveh and Babylon. Austen H. Layard. 1883.

Early Babylonian History. Rev. Hugo Radau. 1900.

Easy Lessons in the Cuneiform Inscriptions. Leonard W. King.

Eléments D'Epigraphie Assyrienne. Les Écritures Cuneiformes. M. Joachim Ménan.

Exploration in Bible Lands. Herman V. Hilprecht. 1903.

Grammar of the Assyrian Language. A. H. Sayce.

A History of Sumer and Akkad. Leonard W. King. London. 1916.

Light on the Old Testament from Babel. Albert T. Clay. 1907.

The Monuments Blau. (A) The Monument Blau. Dr. William Hayes Ward. Jo. Am. Oriental Soc. Oct., 1885. (B) Some Notes on the Blau Monuments. Dr. George A. Barton. Jo. Am. Oriental Soc. 1901.

Les Deux plus anciennes Inscriptions proto-cunéiformes connues. (Description of the "Monuments Blau," with a translation and illustrations.) Thureau-Dangin. Révue Sémitique. 1896.

A New Boundary Stone of Nebuchadrezzar I. Wm. J. Hinke. The Babylonian Expedition of the University of Pennsylvania. Vol. IV. 1907.

Nineveh and Babylon. A. H. Layard. 1853.

Notes on an Archaic Inscription published by Father Schiel. Also on the Hoffman tablet. Dr. Geo. A. Barton.

Old Babylonian Inscriptions chiefly from Nippur. Herman V. Hilprecht. Babylonian Expedition of the Univ. of Pennsylvania. Vol. 1, Pt. 2.

On the Hieroglyphic or Picture Origin of the Characters of the Assyrian Syllabary. Rev. William Houghton. Soc. of Biblical Archaeology. Vol. VI. 1877-'79.

Origin and Importance of the Gunu Signs. Charles F. Kent. Am. Jo. of Semitic Language and Literature. Vol. XIII.

Récherches sur l'origine de l'écriture cunéiforme. Thureau-Dangin. 1898.

Recent Thoughts on the Origin of the Cuneiform Writing. Ira M. Price. Am. Jo. Semitic Lang. and Lit. Vol. XV.

The Sculptures and Inscriptions of Darius the Great at Behistun. L. W. King and R. C. Thompson.

Sur l'Origine des Inscriptions Cunéiformes. Jules Oppert. Athenaeum Française. Oct. 20, 1854.

Tableau Comparé des Écritures Babylonienne et Assyrienne Archaiques et Modernes. A. Armiand et L. Méchineau. 1887.

The Tell-el-Amarna Letters. Hugo Winkler.

CHINA

L'Antiquité de L'Histoire de la Civilisation Chinoises. M. G. Pauthier. Journal Asiatique. April-May, 1868.

Beginnings of Writing in and around Tibet. Terrien de Lacouperie. Jo. Royal Asiatic Soc. Vol. XVII. 1885.

The Development of Chinese Writing. L. C. Hopkins.

Dictionary of the Chinese Language. R. Morrison.

An Explanation of the Elementary Characters of the Chinese. Joseph Hager. London, 1801.

The Evolution of Chinese Writing. Prof. George Owen. Oxford, 1910.

Introduction to the Study of the Chinese Characters. Joseph Edkins. London, 1876.

The Middle Kingdom. S. Wells, Williams. 1851.

The Nichols Mo-so Manuscript. Berthold Laufer, Ph.D. Field Mus. of Natural History, Chicago, Ill.

Syllabic Dictionary of the Chinese Language. S. Wells Williams. 1874.

CRETE AND CYPRUS

Anthropology and the Classics. Arthur J. Evans.

Cretan Pictographs and Pre-Phoenician Script. A. J. Evans. 1895.

Cyprus. Its Ancient Cities, Tombs and Temples. George Louis Palma Di Cesnola. 1877.

The Cypriote Inscriptions of the Di Cesnola Collection. Jo. Am. Oriental Soc. Vol. X. 1875.

A Descriptive Atlas of the Cesnola Collection of Cypriote Antiquities in the Metropolitan Museum of Art, New York City. G. L. P. Di Cesnola, L.L.D.

Law Code of the Kretan Gortyna. Augustus C. Merriam. Am. Jo. of Archaeology. Vol I, 1885.

The Palaces of Crete and their Builders. Angelo Mosso. 1907.

The Palace of Knossos in Its Egyptian Relations. A. J. Evans. Egypt
    Exploration Fund. 1899–1900.
The Palace of Minos. A. J. Evans. Smithsonian Inst. Report, 1901.
Scripta Minoa. A. J. Evans. 1909.

EGYPT

Archaeological Survey of Egypt. The Hieroglyphics. F. Ll. Griffith.
    Egypt Expl. Fund. Vol. VI.
The Book of the Dead. E. A. Wallis Budge.
Cleopatra's Needle. The London Obelisk. Rev. James King, M.A.
Denkmäler aus Aegypten. Karl R. Lepsius. 1845.
A Dictionary of the Egyptian Language. Edward Y. McCauley. Trans.
    Am. Phil. Soc., Oct., 1882.
Dictionnaire Égyptien en Écriture Hiéroglyphique. J. F. Champollion,
    Le Jeune. Paris, 1841.
Egyptian Obelisks. Henry H. Gorringer.
First Steps in Egyptian. E. A. Wallis Budge.
Grammaire Égyptienne. Champollion, Le Jeune, Paris, 1836.
A History of Egypt. James H. Breasted. 1905.
History of Egypt under the Pharaohs. Brugseh-Bey.
Histoire de L'Art Égyptien. Prisse D'Avennes.
Inscriptions of the Nile Monuments. Garrett Chatfield Pier.
Life in Ancient Egypt. Adolf Erman.
Life in Ancient Egypt. Gaston Camille Maspero. 1892.
The Monuments of Egypt. Francis L. Hawks, L.L.D.
The Monumental History of Egypt. William Osbourn. 2 vols.
Pharaohs, Fellehs and Explorers. Amelia B. Edwards. 1892.
Ten Years Digging in Egypt. William M. Flinders Petrie.
A Thousand Miles up the Nile. Amelia B. Edwards.
The Tombs of Abydos. Wm. M. Flinders Petrie. Egypt Exploration
    Fund.

GENERAL

Alphabets. Edward F. Strange. 1907.
The Alphabet. An Account of the Origin and Development of Letters.
    Isaac Taylor, L.L.D. 2 vols. London, 1883.
Ancient Handwritings. William Saunders.
Anthropology. Edward B. Tylor. The International Scientific Series.
Aperçue de l'Origine des Diverse Écritures de Ancien Monde. Heinrich
    Julius von Kleproth.
Beginnings of Writing. William J. Hoffman.
The Calendar of the Prayer Book Illustrated. Joseph Parker & Co., Ox-
    ford, Eng.
Cavernes du Périgord. M. Edw. Lartet et H. Christz.
Dawn of Civilization. Gaston Camille Maspero.
The Dawn of History. C. F. Keary.
Early History of Mankind. Edward B. Tylor.
Early Man in Britain. Boyd Dawkins.
Écritures Figuratives. De Rosny. Paris, 1870.

The Engraved Pictures of the Grotto of La Mouthe, Dordogne, France. Smithsonian Institution Report, 1901.

The European Diffusion of Pictography in Its Bearings on the Origin of Script. A. J. Evans.

Evolution in Art. A. C. Haddon.

Excavations at the Kessleloch near Thayngen (Switzerland). Conrad Merk.

The Five Great Monarchies. George Rawlinson. (4 vols.)

The Formation of the Alphabet. Wm. M. Flinders Petrie. Geographical Journal, 1912.

Illustrirte Geschichte der Schrift. Karl Faulman. Leipsic, 1880. (Profusely illustrated.)

Herodotus. George Rawlinson. (4 vols.)

The Hieroglyphs of Easter Island. J. Park Harrison.

Hieroglyphic Inscriptions of Easter Island. Wm. J. Thompson. Smithsonian Inst. Report, 1889.

History of Antiquity. Maximilian W. Dunker. London, 1881.

History of Mankind. Friedrich Ratzel. London, 1896–'98.

Histoire Ancienne des Peuples de L'Orient Classique. G. C. Maspero.

Histoire de L'Écriture dans L'Antique. Philippe Berger. Paris, 1891.

L'Ile de Paques (Easter Island) et ses Monuments Graphiques. C. de Harlez. Louvain, 1896.

Man, Past and Present. Augustus H. Keane. 1899.

Manuscripts, Inscriptions and Muniments. Being the History of the Art of Writing. Henry Smith Williams. 4 vols.

Materials used to Write upon before the Invention of Printing. Albert Maire. Smithsonian Institution Report. 1904.

The Mediterranean Signary. Wm. M. F. Petrie. Illustrated in introduction to the Royal Tombs of Abydos. Egypt Exploration Fund. Pt. I. 1900.

Men of the Old Stone Age. Henry Fairfield Osborn. 1914.

The Native Races of S. Africa. George W. Stow.

A New Pacific Script. J. Macmillan Brown. (Article 43, Man, Vol. XIV, 1914.)

Origin and Progress of Writing. Thomas Astle.

The Origin and Progress of the Art of Writing. Henry Noel Humphreys.

Pantagraphia. Edmund Fry. London, 1799. (Illustrations of all alphabets.)

Peintures et Gravures Murales des Cavernes Paléolithiques. Emile Carthailhac et l'abbé Henri Breuil.

Prehistoric Art. Thomas Wilson. Smithsonian Inst. Report, 1900. Also Smithsonian Report, 1896.

Primitive Pictographs. A. J. Evans. Jo. of Hellenic Studies, 1894.

Recent Theories of the Origin of the Alphabet. Dr. John P. Peters. Jo. Am. Oriental Soc. Vol. XXII. 1902.

Science of Language. A. H. Sayce.

The Story of the Alphabet. Edward Clodd.

The Story of Primitive Man. Edward Clodd.

Universal Palaeography. J. B. Silvestre.

GREECE

Corpus Inscriptionum Graecarum.
Corpus Inscriptionum Atticarum.
Denkmäler des Klassischen Altertums. A. Baumeister. 1889.
Dictionnaire des Antiquities Grecques et Romaines.
Graeciae Septentrionalis.
Greek Coins and their Parent Cities. John Ward.
Griechsichke Epigraphik. Dr. William Larfeld.
Handbuch der griechischen Epigraphik. Dr. William Larfeld.
An Introduction to Greek Epigraphy. E. S. Roberts. 1905.
Journal of Helenic Studies.
Origin of the Greek Alphabet. Dr. William N. Bates. "Old Penn" (Univ. of Pennsylvania), March, 1916.
Sammlung der Griechischen Dialekt Inschriften. Dr. Hermann Collitz.

HITTITE HIEROGLYPHICS

Altaic Hieroglyphs and Hittite Inscriptions. Col. C. R. Conder.
The Ancient Hittites. Dr. Leopold Messerschmidt. Smithsonian Inst. Report, 1903.
The Empire of the Hittites. William Wright.
Explorations in Bible Lands. Herman V. Hilprecht.
The Hittites. The Story of a Forgotten Empire. A. H. Sayce, L.L.D. London, 1890.
The Hittites and their Language. Col. C. R. Conder, London, 1898.
The So-called Hittites and their Inscriptions. D. P. Jenson.

LYCIA, LYDIA AND ASIA MINOR

An Account of Discoveries in Lydia. Charles Fellows.
History of Art in Phrygia, Lydia, Caria and Lycia; and History of Art in Sardinia, Judea, Syria and Asia Minor. George Perrot and Charles Chipiez.
Lydian Inscriptions from Sardes. Albert Thumb. Am. Jo. of Archaeology. Vol. XV, 1911.

MIDDLE AGES

Art of Illuminating. Tymns and Watt. 1860.
Book of Kells. Sir Edward Sullivan.
Celtic Illuminative Art. In the Gospel Books of Durrow, Lindisfarne and Kells. Rev. Stanford F. H. Robinson, M.A.
Celtic Ornaments from the Book of Kells. T. K. Abbott.
The Court Hand. Illustrated. Hilary Jenkinson.
The Development of the Book Hand. Williams.
English Court Hand. 1066–1500. Charles Johnson and Hilary Jenkinson, Oxford, 1915.
Facsimiles of Autographs in the British Museum. George F. Warner.
Facsimiles of National Manuscripts. England. Sir Henry James. 4 vols. 1865–'68.
Facsimiles of National Manuscripts (Scotland). Sir Henry James. 3 vols.

Palæography and the Practical Study of the Court Hand. Hilary Jenkinson, F.S.A. Cambridge, England, 1915.
Palæographical Album of Facsimiles of Writings of all Nations and Periods. J. B. Silvestre. 4 vols. 1841.
The Palæographical Society, London. Facsimiles of Manuscripts and Inscriptions. Edited by E. A. Bond and E. M. Thompson. 5 vols.

PHŒNICIA

L'Alphabet Phénicien. François Lenormant.
Corpus Inscriptionum Semiticarum. 1881.
Handbuch der Nordsemitisch. Mark Lidzbarski.
Mémoire sur l'origine Égyptienne de l'alphabet Phénicien. M. Jacques de Rougé. Paris, 1874.
The Story of Phœnicia. George Rawlinson.
A Text Book of N. Semitic Inscriptions. Rev. G. A. Cooke.

PRINTING

The Art of the Book. Charles Holme, Editor. 1914.
Early Venetian Printing. Ferd. Ongania.
A History of the Art of Printing. H. Noel Humphreys. London, 1868.
The Invention of Printing. Theodore L. De Vinne, 1878.
The Invention of Typography and History of Printing. Nos. 49 to 54. Typographic Technical Series for Apprentices.
The Practice of Typography. Theodore L. De Vinne.
The Venetian Printing Press. Horatia F. Brown.

ROME AND ETRURIA

The Cities and Cemeteries of Etruria. George Dennis.
Corpus Inscriptionum Italicarum. Fabretti.
Denkmäler des Klassiken Altertums. A. Baumeister.
Etruscan Researches. Isaac Taylor. 1874.
The Italic Alphabets. Isaac Taylor.

THE RUNES

The Old Northern Runic Monuments of Scandinavia and England. Dr. George Stephens, F.S.A. 1884.

INDEX

Abecedaria, 375, 376
Abu-Simbel inscription, 359
Acrology or acrophony, 59, 129, 215
Adjedatigs, Indian grave posts, 89, 90
Akkad, 230
Alcuin of York, 416, 417
Alphabetic writing, 57
Anglo-Saxon Chronicle, 418, 419
Anglo-Saxon half uncial, 411
Anglo-Saxon minuscule, 412 to 424
Arabic alphabet, 305
Arabic numerals, 5
Aramean alphabets, 303, 304
Arbitrary signs used in writing and printing, 12, 13, 14
Astronomical signs, 10, 11, 12
Attic inscriptions, 345, 346, 347
Aztec writing, 124 to 130

Babylonian boundary stones, 9
Bamberg Bible, 464
Bards. Their rhythmical narration of traditions, 19, 20
Behistun inscription, 227, 228, 264, 265, 266
Birch bark used for writing, 70
Block-books, 456, 457, 458
Bœotian writing, 362
Book of Armagh, 409
Book of the Dead, Egypt, 200, 201
Book of Kells, 409, 410
Bushmen cave paintings, 44 to 48

Cadmus, 338
Capitalization in writing, 426, 427, 428
Cardandan, Yunnan, China, 31, 179
Caroline Islands script, 151, 152
Caroline minuscule, 417, 423
Caslon, William, 483, 484
Cave men, 41, 42, 43, 103, 104

Caxton, William, 477, 478, 479
Census roll of Indians at Mille Lac, 80
Census roll of Red Cloud, 78, 79, 81
Ceremonial songs of the Ojibwa and Dakota Indians, 84 to 88
Chalcidian writing, 365
Champollion. Translation of the Egyptian hieroglyphs, 188
Chancery hand, 435
Charter hand, 434
Cheyenne Indian's letter to his son, 83
Chinese radical or indicative signs, 165 to 171
Chippewa Indian's petition to the U. S. Government, 81, 82
Classic Greek writing, 366, 367
Clogg almanacs, 36, 37
Codices, Mexican, 131, 132, 133
Corinthian Greek alphabet, 353, 354, 355
Cortes, 112, 113
Coster, Lourens Janzoon, 460, 461
Court hand, 426, 427
Coverdale Bible, 480, 481
Cranmer's or the Great Bible, 482
Cretan writing, 315 to 323, 348, 349
Cursive writing, 402, 403, 404, 408
Cypriote Inscriptions, 325 to 328

Darius, 33, 263, 264, 265
Day, John, early English printer, 482, 483
Demotic writing of the Egyptians, 221
de Rougé, Emmanuel, 312
Determinative signs in Egyptian writing, 22, 53
Dighton Rock inscription, 63, 64
Domesday Book, 421, 422, 423
Donatus. One of the earliest printed books, 461

Dürer, Albert, 468, 469
Durham Book, 410

Easter Island hieroglyphic writing, 146 to 150
Egyptian alphabet, 207, 208, 209
Enshagkushanna's tablet inscription, 248
Entemena's tablet inscription, 252
Eshmunazar's inscription, 298, 299
Eskimo pictographic inscriptions, 101, 102, 103, 106, 107, 108
Etruscans, 373
Etruscan writing, 381, 382, 383
Eubœan Greek writing, 361
Evans, Arthur J., 104, 315

Father Schiel's tablet inscription, 238
Frank's Casket, 445, 446, 447, 448
Fust, Johann, 459, 460

German Gothic capitals, 434
Gesture signs and symbols, 159
Gortyna inscription, 349, 350, 351
Gothic uncials, 433
Grafton, Richard, 482
Greek alphabets, Eastern and Western, 368
Grotefend, Dr. Georg Friedrich, 227
Gudea, Priest-king of Lagash, 247
Gutenberg, Johann, 459, 460

Hamah inscriptions, 269
Hammurabi's great cylinder, 260, 261
Hand writing (script), 434 to 442
Hawaiian "Revenue Book," 35
Hebrew alphabet, 305
Herculaneum manuscripts, 394
Herodotus, 33, 277, 278, 337, 338
Hieratic wrting of the Egyptians, 218, 219
Hieroglyphic writing, 25
Hittite bowl from Babylon, 282, 283
Hittite inscriptions, 129, 269, 278, 279, 281

Hoffman, William J., 31, 32, 85, 88, 101, 106
Hoffman tablet, 242, 243
Homeric epics, 4, 21
Humboldt Mexican manuscripts, 127, 128, 129

Ideographic writing, 51, 52
Ikonomatic writing, 123
Index signs, 22
Indian autographs, 27
Inscription Rock, Lake Superior, Canada, 68
Ionian Greek alphabet, 357 to 360, 366, 367
Irish half-uncial, 410
Ipsambul inscription, 359

Japanese writing, 161
Jenson, Nicolas, 475

Kadesh, 273, 274
Karabel, Pass of, 278
Kheta Sira, 275
Kiowa calendar counts, 76
Knossos inscriptions, 315
Knotted cords, 4, 32, 33
Korea, Movable types used in 1337, 455

Lacouperie, Terrien de. Theory of a Babylonian origin for the Chinese written characters, 183
Lapp troll drums, 104, 105
Latin inscriptions, 384, 385
Lenape Stone, 95
Leni-Lenape Indians, 91
Letters of Indulgence. The earliest printed documents, 462
Libraries destroyed, 397, 398
Linear Babylonian script, 235, et seq.
Locrian inscription, 364, 365
Lo-lo writing, 183
Lombardic minuscule, 414, 415
Lone Dog's Winter Count, 73, 74
Lycian inscriptions and alphabet, 332, 335
Lydian inscriptions and alphabet, 333, 334, 335

Mallery, Garrick, 75, 81
Manutius, Aldus, 475, 476
Marco Polo, 31, 179
Materials used in writing, 14, 15
Mazarin Bible, 462, 463
Medas of the Ojibwa and Dakota
  Indians, 84 to 88
Mediterranean signary, 313, 329,
  330
Memory jogs and tallies, 28
Mesha, King of Moab, 290, 291
Metal types, 466
Metonymy, 160
Mexican codices, 131 to 135
Mexican picture writing, 114 to 121
Mimicry, 54, 55
Minnesingers of Germany, 20
Mnemonic devices, 30, 31, 32
Moabite Stone, 290, 291, 292, 293
Modern-face type, 484
Monastic script, 433
Monuments Blau, 240, 241
Mo-so hieroglyphic writing, 179 to
  182
Movable types, 459

Nebuchadrezzar, 231
Negation signs, Egyptian and Maya,
  22, 23
Nibelungen Lied, 20
Nichols Mo-so Manuscript, 179 to
  183
Notched sticks, 4, 31, 32

Obelisks in various cities, 187, 195
  to 199
Occleve, Thomas. Poem de Regi-
  mine Principium, 426, 427
Oghams, 449
Ojibwa medicine songs, 84 to 88
Old-face type, 483
Oral tradition, 18, 19, 20
Our-Nina tablet, 245
Ownership marks, 28

Palenque inscriptions, 142, 143
Paloni Indians, 32
Pannartz, Conrad, 471, 472
Papyrus of Hu-nefer, 201 to 205

Papyrus Prisse, 218, 219
Parchment, 393
Pelasgians, 373, 374
Pelasgian writing, 375, 376, 381
Penn Treaty belt, 98, 99
Petrie, William Flinders, 313, 329,
  330
Petroglyphs in N. America, 61 to 67
Phœnician alphabet, 305
Phonetic writing, 2, 54, 55
Pictographic symbols of the N.
  American Indians, 111
Pictographic writing, 51
Pictographic writing of the N.
  American Indians, 71, 72, 73
Piers Plowman, 424, 425
Pima Indians' calendar count, 76,
  77, 78
Poster lettering, 486, 487
Printing in China, Korea and
  Japan, 455
Psalter of Fust and Schöffer, 464,
  465
Punctuation marks, 417

Queen Elizabeth's handwriting, 438,
  439
Quipus, 34, 35

Rafinsque, Samuel R. Schmaltz, 91
Rameses II, 273 to 276
Rawlinson, Sir Henry, 227, 228
Rebus-writing, 124 to 130, 217
Red Cloud's census, 79
Reindeer Men, 41, 42, 43, 104
Renaissance alphabet, 477
Renaissance of learning, 453
Roman alphabet, 388, 389, 390
Roman inscriptions, 385, 386, 387
Roman numerals, 5
Rosetta Stone, 188, 193, 194, 195
Runes, 443 to 448
Russian alphabet, 451
Rustic Roman capital, 400, 401

Sanscrit Vedas, 19
Sargon I, inscription, 258
Schöffer, Peter, 459, 460
Sidonian inscriptions, 297, 298, 299

Sign-language of the North American Indians, 21, 22
Siloam inscription, 300, 301
Slavonic alphabets, 450
Speyer, John of, 473, 474
Square Roman capitals, 394, 398, 399
Stages in the evolution of writing, 50 to 53
Sumerians, 230
Sweynheim, Conrad, 471, 472

Tabnith's inscription, 297
Tally sticks, 38
Tarkondemos, Boss of, 283
Thera, inscriptions, 339 to 342
Thot. The inventor of writing in Egypt, 39
Tonga Islands. Awe shown by the savages for the art of writing, 29, 30
Totem poles, 23, 25
Totem signs, 23 to 26
Trope, 160

Tyndale, William, 454
Types used by the first printers, 466, 467

Uncial letters, 404 to 408

Vedas. The oral transmission of traditions, 19

Walam Olum of the Lenape Indians, 31, 91 to 94
Wampum belts, 96 to 100
Wax tablets, 397
Wingenund's inscription, 71, 72
Winter Counts of the Dakota Indians, 73 to 76

Xylographic printing, 456

Young's translation of the Egyptian hieroglyphics, 193

Zodiacal signs, 7, 8, 9, 10
Zuni Indians. Use of Knotted cords, 32

171 -